A LESSON FOR EVERY DAY

8–9 YEARS

MATHS

8–9 YEARS

A & C Black • London

Contents

Published 2010 by A & C Black Publishers Limited
36 Soho Square, London W1D 3QY
www.acblack.com
ISBN 978-1-4081-2544-1

Editors: Dodi Beardshaw, Jane Klima, Marie Lister, Clare Robertson, Lynne Williamson
Compiled by Mary Nathan and Fakenham Photosetting

The authors and publishers would like to thank Ray Barker, Fleur Lawrence and Rifat Siddiqui for their advice in producing this series of books.

A CIP catalogue record for this book is available from the British Library.

Printed and bound in Great Britain by Martins the Printers, Berwick-on-Tweed.

A & C Black uses paper produced with elemental chlorine-free pulp, harvested from managed sustainable forests.

Introduction

A Lesson for Every Day: Mathematics is a series of seven photocopiable activity books for the Foundation Stage and Key Stages 1 and 2, designed to be used during the daily maths lesson. The books focus on the skills and concepts outlined in the National Strategy's *Primary Framework for literacy and mathematics*. The activities are intended to be used in the time allocated to pupil activities; they aim to reinforce the knowledge and develop the facts, skills and understanding explored during the main part of the lesson and to provide practice and consolidation of the objectives contained in the Framework document.

A Lesson for Every Day: Mathematics Ages 8–9 supports the teaching of mathematics to children aged 8 to 9 by providing a series of activities to develop:

- processes for using and applying mathematics in real situations
- skills in talking about the mathematics in real situations
- essential skills in counting and recognising numbers
- the learning of simple number facts
- an understanding of ideas of addition, subtraction, multiplication and division
- spatial vocabulary in order to increase awareness of properties of shape and measurement concepts
- understanding of key concepts within the handling data cycle
- the skills of collecting, organising, presenting, analysing and interpreting data.

On the whole, the activities are designed for children to work on independently, although due to the young age of the children, the teacher may need to read the instructions with the children to ensure that they understand the activity before they begin working on it.

Extension

Many of the activity sheets end with a challenge (**Now try this!**), which reinforces and extend children's learning, and provides the teacher with an opportunity for assessment. These might include harder questions, with numbers from a higher range, than those in the main part of the activity sheet. Some extension activities are open-ended questions and provide opportunity for children to think mathematically for themselves. Occasionally the extension activity will require additional paper or that the children write on the reverse of the sheet itself. Many of the activities encourage children to generate their own questions or puzzles for a partner to solve.

Organisation

Very little equipment is needed, but it will be useful to have available: coloured pencils, counters, cubes, scissors, dice, glue, coins, squared paper, number lines, grids and tracks, 2D and 3D shapes, a variety of different classroom items.

Where possible, children's work should be supported by ICT equipment, such as data handling programmes on interactive whiteboards, or computer software for moving pictures or photographs to show similarities and differences between groups and also charting information. It is also vital that children's experiences are introduced in real-life contexts, such as those portrayed in home/role play areas and through practical activities and number or nursery rhymes that they know. The teachers' notes at the foot of each page and the more detailed notes on pages 5 to 23 suggest ways in which this can be done effectively.

To help teachers select appropriate learning experiences for the children, the activities are grouped into sections within the book. However, the activities are not expected to be used in this order unless stated otherwise. The sheets are intended to support, rather than direct, the teacher's planning.

Some activities can be made easier or more challenging by masking or substituting numbers. You may wish to re-use pages by copying them onto card and laminating them.

Teachers' notes

Brief notes are provided at the foot of each page, giving ideas and suggestions for maximising the effectiveness of the activity sheets. These can be masked before copying.

Solutions can be found on pages 214 to 216.

Assessment

Use the completed activities as part of your day-to-day assessment to help you to build a picture of children's learning in order to plan future teaching and learning. Activities can also be used as examples of significant evidence for your periodic assessment. In order to help you to make reliable judgements about your pupils' attainment, the assessment focuses for each activity are given in the grids on pages 5–23.

Some of the activities provide opportunities for children to carry out self assessment. Encourage children to reflect on their learning and discuss with them whether there are areas that they feel they need to practise further.

The CD-ROM

All activity sheets can be found as PDF and Word versions on the accompanying CD-ROM. These can be printed or displayed on an interactive whiteboard. The Word versions can be customised in Microsoft Word in order to assist personalised learning.

They can be accessed through an interface that makes it easy to select worksheets and display them. You can also search for lessons that will meet a particular Assessment Focus for Assessing Pupils' Progress. For more information on system requirements, please see the inside front cover.

If you have any questions regarding the *A Lesson For Every Day* CD-ROM, please email us at the address below. We will get back to you as soon as possible.
educationalsales@acblack.com

Whole class warm-up activities

The following activities provide some practical ideas that can be used to introduce or reinforce the main teaching part of the lesson, or provide an interesting basis for discussion.

Targets

Write several numbers on the board (such as 80, 50, 9, 6, 4), and a target number (for example 244). Set the children the challenge of hitting or getting as close as possible to the target number, using some or all of the numbers and operations of their choice (example: 9 — 6 = 3, 3 x 80 = 240, and 240 + 4 = 244).

Hit or miss?

The constant function facility on a calculator is a useful way to explore decimals. Write a sequence rule, for example: 'Start at 1 and count on in jumps of 0.2'. Ask the children to predict whether the sequence will 'hit' or 'miss' other numbers, for example: *Will it hit 3 or 4.5 or 11*? Provide the children with calculators and ask them to check their predictions by continuing the patterns using the constant function facility, for example pressing these keys (check with the calculator manual if necessary). 1 + + 0.2 = = = = = = etc.

Twenty questions

Hide a 3-D shape in a bag and ask the children to find out which shape it is by asking questions. You can only answer *yes* or *no* to their questions. Challenge the children to guess the shape in twenty questions.

Run-around rounding

Around the walls of the hall or classroom, pin pieces of paper showing zero and the multiples of one thousand from 1000 to 10 000. Ask the children to stand in the middle of the room and call out four-digit numbers. Ask them to round the number to the nearest thousand and run to the correct sign. This can be played as a game where children who are standing by incorrect signs are out. As a further activity, children could be asked to stand by a sign and give a number that would correctly round to this multiple.

Negative

Invite two children to the front of the class with some positive and negative cards. Give each child a positive or negative number to hold up. Invite a third child to come to the front and hold their hands appropriately to represent either the greater than or less than sign, for example –5 > –6 or –4 < 1. Ask the class to read the statement aloud in words, for example: *negative five is greater than negative six or negative four is less than one*.

Chains

Say a number, such as 'three thousand, five hundred and thirty-two', which the children write down. Now say a series of instructions, asking the children to write the outcome each time. For example, say, 'Add ten', 'Subtract one thousand', 'Add three hundred'. After several instructions ask, 'What's your number now?' If the children have kept a record, then it is easy to see where they went wrong if they make an error.

Fraction choices

Write a number on each of four pieces of paper, e.g. 4, 3, 6 and 8. Pin these around the room, one on each wall. Call out a question, e.g. 'What is one-fifth of twenty?' The children point to the piece of paper showing the number 4. Other questions could include: 'What is one-half of sixteen, one-third of nine, two-thirds of nine, one-fifth of forty, three-quarters of four?'

Twenty questions

Hide a 3-D shape in a bag and ask the children to find out which shape it is by asking questions. You can only answer 'yes' or 'no' to their questions. Challenge the children to guess the shape in twenty questions.

Count me in

Practise counting on and back in intervals of 2, 5, 10 and 100. These skills will help children to interpret pictograms where one symbol represents more than one unit.

Activity name	Strand and learning objectives	Notes on the activities	Assessment Focus	Page number
Number puzzles	**Using and applying mathematics** Report solutions to puzzles and problems, giving explanations and reasoning orally and in writing, using diagrams and symbols	**Number puzzles** *Processes: look for pattern, reason, explain* Provide the children with number squares to help them with this activity if necessary. SUGGESTED QUESTION: • Can you explain how you worked this out?	**Communicating**	24
Full stretch Metamorphosis Partition Penguins Rounding puzzle Hotel lift Caterpillar crawl Signs of a thaw	**Counting and understanding number** Partition, round and order four-digit whole numbers; use positive and negative numbers in context and position them on a number line; state inequalities using the symbols < and > (e.g. –3 > –5, –1 < +1)	**Full stretch** It is simple to make these expanding numbers using strips of paper or card. Write the number in either of the two expanded forms and fold up the paper, so that only the digits of the contracted form can be seen. This is a useful classroom resource. Templates of both expanded forms can be made without digits and then laminated. New digits can then be written onto the plastic and wiped off to create a more flexible resource. SUGGESTED QUESTIONS: • Which is the largest/smallest number? Write these in first. • How many tens/ones has this number? **Metamorphosis** At the start of the lesson, to practise changing one digit of a number, draw a string of instructions and write a four-digit number into the starting position, for example: 4726 +1000 +1 –100 +1000 –100 +10 –1 Ask the children to show each step, changing one digit at a time. Extend this activity to include multiples of 1000, 100, 10 and 1, for example: 4726 +5000 +4 –300 –2000 –100 +60 –3 SUGGESTED QUESTIONS: • What happens to the other digits when you add one thousand? • Have you checked your answers? **Partition penguins** This game encourages the children to find simple totals and to partition them into thousands, hundreds, tens and ones. Place value arrow cards can be used to introduce or revise partitioning. SUGGESTED QUESTION: • How could you partition this number? **Rounding puzzle** Children enjoy this kind of playground puzzle and it can lead them to practise rounding outside maths lessons, such as at home or in the playground. The children need a sheet each. HOW TO MAKE THE PUZZLE: • Cut out along the dotted line. • Fold the corners of the square into the centre so that the words are still visible and crease well. • Turn the puzzle over and again fold the corners into the centre, this time concealing the words 'Cool', 'You're amazing!' etc. • Crease the shape into four quarters and open again. • Slide fingers under the 'Rounding to the nearest 100' sections to form and squeeze the sections together so that only the 'Rounding to the nearest 100' questions are visible. HOW TO USE THE PUZZLE: • Player 1 holds the puzzle between both thumbs and forefingers. • Player 2 chooses a question from the top of the puzzle and answers it. Both players should agree on the answer. This should be crossed off the grid. • Player 1 moves the puzzle the number of times shown by moving thumbs and fingers together and apart revealing the sets of questions inside the puzzle. • Player 2 is shown the new questions and picks one to answer. Again, both players should agree on the answer. This should be crossed off the grid. • The puzzle is then moved the number of times shown. • This continues until Player 2 has crossed off four in a line. • As the last number is crossed off, this section should be lifted to reveal how well the player has done. **Hotel lift** Introduce this context for describing floors at a hotel using positive and negative numbers. Give children a sheet and call out different rooms in the hotel. Ask them to state the number that indicates how far the floor is above or below ground level, for example the kitchens are at negative two, the car park at negative six. SUGGESTED QUESTIONS: • Which floor is one below –3? • Which floor is two floors above –6? **Caterpillar crawl** Ask the children to write their own number line from –6 to 6 at the start of the lesson. As an oral activity, call out number trails starting at zero, similar to the ones in the extension activity. SUGGESTED QUESTION: • Go backwards 4, go forwards 7, go backwards 2. Ask the children to say where the caterpillar will end up after moving backwards and forwards. **Signs of a thaw** This sheet involves temperatures above and below freezing. Explain to the class that water freezes at 0°C (zero degrees Celsius) and ask them to draw their own thermometer with temperatures between –15 °C and 10 °C. Ensure that children understand the < and > signs before tackling this sheet. SUGGESTED QUESTION: • Which temperature is colder?	**Numbers and the number system**	25 26 27 28 29 30 31
Difference walls	**Knowing and using number facts** Use knowledge of addition and subtraction facts and place value to derive sums and differences of pairs of multiples of 10, 100 or 1000	**Difference walls** At the start of the lesson build up lists of numbers with given differences to encourage the children to spot patterns in the digits of the numbers, for example: Difference of 20 — Difference of 70 20 → 40 — 20 → 90 30 → 50 — 30 → 100 40 → 60 — 40 → 110 50 → 70 — 50 → 120 60 → 80 — 60 → 130 etc. Do this for other differences and encourage the children to describe patterns they notice in the numbers. SUGGESTED QUESTIONS: • What will the tens digit of the number be if it is 60 more than 130? • What is the difference between 170 and 230?	**Mental methods**	32

Activity name	Strand and learning objectives	Notes on the activities	Assessment Focus	Page number
Spot the dice Fingers of fun	**Knowing and using number facts** Derive and recall multiplication facts up to 10 × 10, the corresponding division facts and multiples of numbers to 10 up to the tenth multiple	**Spot the dice** At the start of the lesson, say the 8× table as a class. Discuss patterns in the answers in the table and ways to remember them. For the extension activity, the children can play the game in pairs. They will require two dice per pair. **Suggested questions:** • What times-table could you use to help you work out facts in the 8 times-table if you can't remember them? • Which 8 times-table facts do you find easiest or hardest to remember? **Fingers of fun** Learning the ×9 or 9× tables can be introduced quite early, as this method of finding the answers using their fingers provides lots of confidence for children who find memorising facts difficult. Gradually, over time, the children require less use of their fingers to find the answers. **Suggested questions:** • What is 6 × 9? • What will the tens digit be? • How do you know? • Does this work for all facts in the ×9 table?	**Mental methods**	33 34
Under the microscope	**Calculating** Multiply and divide numbers to 1000 by 10 and then 100 (whole-number answers), understanding the effect; relate to scaling up or down	**Under the microscope** At the start of the lesson, practise counting up in tens and ask the children to say the answer for any given one-digit number multiplied by 10. Then extend to any two-digit number multiplied by 10. **Suggested prompt/question:** • Describe what happens to a number when it is multiplied by 10. • What happens to the digits of the number?	**Operations and relations between them**	35
Double or halve	**Knowing and using number facts** Identify the doubles of two-digit numbers; use these to calculate doubles of multiples of 10 and 100 and derive the corresponding halves	**Double or halve** This sheet can be used for a range of doubling and halving purposes and could be available in the classroom for children to use as and when they feel necessary. Partitioning can be done in a variety of ways, including three-digit numbers, for example: 136 →120 + 16 60 + 8 →68 **Suggested questions:** • What is double 76? Half 132? • How could you partition the number to help you?	**Mental methods**	36
Calculator calamities: 1 and 2	**Calculating** Use a calculator to carry out one-step and two-step calculations involving all four operations; recognise negative numbers in the display, correct mistaken entries and interpret the display correctly in the context of money	**Calculator calamities: 1 and 2** *Processes: reason, explain, record* These problems involve understanding how mistakes can be corrected using inverses, or by adjusting calculations. **Suggested prompt/question:** • Describe in words what Meena's mistake is. • How could she correct it?	**Solving numerical problems**	37–38

Block A Unit 2

Activity name	Strand and learning objectives	Notes on the activities	Assessment Focus	Page number
3 for 2!	**Using and applying mathematics** Report solutions to puzzles and problems, giving explanations and reasoning orally and in writing, using diagrams and symbols	**3 for 2!** *Processes: reason, explain* The children could make up their own offers for others to investigate. They should be encouraged to report their findings to the class. **Suggested question:** • Can you explain how you worked this out?	**Communicating**	39
Animal walkabout Decimal snap	**Counting and understanding number** Recognise and continue number sequences formed by counting on or back in steps of constant size	**Animal walkabout** At the start of the lesson ask the children to say a simple sequence such as counting in twos from 11. Encourage them to talk about what happens at the tens' boundary, for example 19, 21… Provide the children with a 0–100 number line if they are experiencing difficulty. **Suggested questions:** • Which number comes next? • How do you know? **Decimal snap!** Once the class has completed the game, ask them a range of questions about their recorded numbers. **Suggested questions:** • How many tenths has this number? • Can you find a number with three hundredths/ tenths/ ones? • Does any number have the same 'hundredths' digit and the same 'tenths' digit, such as 5.22? What is the value of the 'ones' digit? • James has the numbers 2.36 and 5.36. How much smaller than 5.36 is 2.36?	**Numbers and the number system**	40 41

Activity name	Strand and learning objectives	Notes on the activities	Assessment Focus	Page number
Pocket money Exploding numbers	**Counting and understanding number** Use decimal notation for tenths and hundredths and partition decimals; relate the notation to money and measurement; position one-place and two-place decimals on a number line	**Pocket money** As a further extension, ask the children to say how much more one amount is than another on their worksheet, for example, 'How much more than 4.38 is 5.28?' **Suggested questions:** • How many tenths of a pound has this amount? • How many hundredths of a pound has this amount? • How much money in pence is seven tenths of a pound? • How much money in pence is three hundredths of a pound? **Exploding numbers** Ensure children write the value of each digit, not just the digit itself. **Suggested question:** • How many tenths/hundredths has this number?	**Fractions and decimals**	42 43
Sleepover dreamtime	**Calculating** Add or subtract mentally pairs of two-digit whole numbers (e.g. 47 + 58, 91 – 35)	**Sleepover dreamtime** This activity encourages the children to recall facts from the ×7 and 7× tables. Revise the multiples at the start of the lesson and encourage the children to describe patterns, for example odd × 7 = odd even × 7 = even etc. **Suggested question:** • What helps you to remember this fact?	**Mental methods**	44
Curious cube Supermarket stacks	**Calculating** Refine and use efficient written methods to add and subtract two-digit and three-digit whole numbers and £.p	**Curious cube** At the start of the lesson, discuss the strategy of looking at the units digits of the two numbers to be added and seeing which will add to make a multiple of 10, for example numbers ending with the units digits 3 and 7, 4 and 6, etc. **Suggested prompt:** • Explain how you worked out the answer. **Supermarket stacks** This activity encourages the children to add adjacent numbers and to write the total. **Suggested questions/prompt:** • How could you work out this answer on paper? • How could you set it out in columns? • Show me what you would do.	**Written methods**	45 46
Animal antics	**Knowing and using number facts** Derive and recall multiplication facts up to 10 × 10, the corresponding division facts and multiples of numbers to 10 up to the tenth multiple	**Animal antics** Ask the children to work in pairs, and provide each pair with timers or stopwatches to use to time each other tackling each block. **Suggested questions:** • Which times-tables facts do you find easiest or hardest to remember? What could you do to help you to remember them or work them out?	**Mental methods**	47
Tidying up	**Calculating** Multiply and divide numbers to 1000 by 10 and then 100 (whole-number answers), understanding the effect; relate to scaling up or down	**Tidying up** Ask the children to explain what happens when numbers are multiplied or divided by 10 or 100. Highlight explanations that involve digits moving rather than zeros being added to or removed from the ends of numbers. **Suggested prompt/questions:** • Describe what happens to a number when it is multiplied by 100/10/ divided by 10/100. • What happens to the digits of the number? • What has happened to change this number into this number?	**Operations and relations between them**	48
Dicing with dinosaurs	**Calculating** Develop and use written methods to record, support and explain multiplication and division of two-digit numbers by a one-digit number, including division with remainders (e.g. 15 × 9, 98 ÷ 6)	**Dicing with dinosaurs** Discuss with the children the commutative and associative laws of multiplication (without using these terms), i.e. that multiplication can be done in any order, grouping numbers in any way, and the answer will be the same, for example 3 × 5 × 4 can be worked out by multiplying the 5 and the 4 together first to make 3 × 20, which is perhaps an easier calculation than 15 × 4. More confident children could use a 1–10 dice. **Suggested questions:** • What method did you use to multiply those numbers together? • How do you decide what method to use to multiply a two-digit number by a one-digit number?	**Written methods**	49

Block A Unit 3

Activity name	Strand and learning objectives	Notes on the activities	Assessment Focus	Page number
Codebreaker Pebble positions	**Using and applying mathematics** Solve one-step and two-step problems involving numbers, money or measures, including time; choose and carry out appropriate calculations, using calculator methods where appropriate	**Codebreaker** *Processes: make decisions, record, reason, explain* These problems require the children to make their own decisions as to how to answer the questions. The children should be encouraged to describe these methods and strategies and demonstrate how different equipment, such as 100-squares and number lines, could be used to help them reach answers. **Suggested questions:** • How did you work out the answer to this question? • How did you know what to do? • Can you show me what method you used for this question? • How did you know to multiply? **Pebble positions** This activity can be introduced practically. Ask the children to bring in a selection of pebbles and to paint a four-digit number on each. The pebbles can be kept in a large bucket. The class can then use them to practise ordering numbers. **Suggested questions:** • Which of these numbers is the smallest? Which is the largest? Which numbers come in between them?	**Problem solving** **Solving numerical problems**	50 51

Activity name	Strand and learning objectives	Notes on the activities	Assessment Focus	Page number
Raffle tickets Join the dots		**Raffle tickets** Children who find this difficult could copy the numbers onto scraps of paper and arrange these below each other, physically moving them around as they compare the digits. **Suggested questions:** • Which is the smallest number in this list? How do you know? • How many thousands has it? • How many hundreds? **Join the dots** In this activity, children will quickly be able to see whether they have ordered a set of numbers correctly. As a further extension activity, the children could make up a puzzle like this that spells their name. **Suggested questions:** • Which is the smallest number? Which is the largest number? • Remember to compare the digits in each number working from the left.		52 53
Integer dominoes	**Counting and understanding number** Partition, round and order four-digit whole numbers; use positive and negative numbers in context and position them on a number line; state inequalities using the symbols < and > (e.g. $^{-}3 > {}^{-}5$, $^{-}1 < +1$)	**Integer dominoes** These domino cards could be copied onto A3 card and laminated for a more permanent place value resource. Revise the 'greater than' and 'less than' symbols at the start of the lesson. Write a number and a 'greater than' or 'less than' sign and ask the children to state a number that could go to its right, for example 0 > ? When a number has been suggested and written, such as 0 > –2, rub out the first number and the sign and write a new sign to the right of the second number, i.e. rub out 0 > and leave on the board –2 < ? Ask the children to suggest a new number. Repeat for other numbers. **Suggested questions:** • Which sign is this? • Tell me a number greater/less than –2, –6, 4…	**Numbers and the number system**	54
Little Miss Moneybags! Animal hospital Shooting stars	**Counting and understanding number** Recognise and continue number sequences formed by counting on or back in steps of constant size	**Little Miss Moneybags!** In this activity, the children count on and back in equal steps in the context of money. Before children start, discuss the notation used for money and the value of each digit in, for example, £1.23, £4.44. **Suggested questions:** • What would this sequence look like if you counted back in steps of 20p? • Do you think that £2.40 will be in this sequence? Why? **Animal hospital** In this activity the children count on and back in equal steps in the context of length. Before children start, discuss the metric notation used for length and the value of each digit in, for example, 3.45 m, 7.77 m. **Suggested questions:** • What would this sequence look like if you counted on in steps of 50 cm? • Do you think that 5 m will be in this sequence? Why? **Shooting stars** Provide number lines and calculators for this activity so that children can check their sequences using the constant function facility on a calculator. **Suggested questions/prompt:** • What did you key into the calculator to check this sequence? Show me what you did. • Were all the numbers in this sequence correct?	**Numbers and the number system**	55 56 57
Nature trails Super Squirrel	**Counting and understanding number** Use decimal notation for tenths and hundredths and partition decimals; relate the notation to money and measurement; position one-place and two-place decimals on a number line	**Nature trails** Counting on in steps of one tenth or one hundredth helps children to begin to move towards writing decimals on a number line. Create a decimal number track for display by sitting the children in a circle and giving each child a small piece of coloured paper (different shapes will make the finished display more attractive). Begin counting on in tenths or hundredths around the circle and ask each child to write their number onto their paper shape. These paper shapes can then be used to make a decimal number track display. **Suggested question:** • What will the next number in the pattern be? **Super Squirrel** This sheet can be used as an introduction to positioning decimals on a number line. **Suggested questions:** • How do you know that question 2 is 0.5? • What fractions do you know that are equivalent to $\frac{5}{10}$? How do we write them as decimals?	**Fractions and decimals**	58 59
Animal additions Captain Dynamic	**Calculating** Refine and use efficient written methods to add and subtract two-digit and three-digit whole numbers and £.p	**Animal additions** The children could be asked to find the totals of other three-letter words, for example: bed, row, toy, buy, old, toe, die, mix, hit, pen, cup, ice, ham, zoo. **Suggested prompt:** • Explain to me how you worked out the total of these three numbers. **Captain Dynamic** These questions involve subtracting a two-digit number from a three-digit number. The children could use a written column method of subtracting involving partitioning or they could use more informal methods, as appropriate. **Suggested questions/prompt:** • How could you work out this answer on paper? • How could you set it out in columns? • Show me what you would do.	**Written methods**	60 61
Movin' on	**Knowing and using number facts** Derive and recall multiplication facts up to 10 × 10, the corresponding division facts and multiples of numbers to 10 up to the tenth multiple	**Movin' on** This sheet encourages quick recall. As an extra extension activity, the children can make up their own tracks. **Suggested questions:** • Which multiplication fact did you use to help you work out that division? How could you check that your answer is correct?	**Mental methods**	62
Crazy calculations Detective dog	**Calculating** Develop and use written methods to record, support and explain multiplication and division of two-digit numbers by a one-digit number, including division with remainders (e.g. 15 × 9, 98 ÷ 6)	**Crazy calculations** At the start of the lesson, ask children to tell you different methods that they know for working out the answer to a calculation such as, 53 × 7. Write these on the board and discuss which children consider to be most efficient. **Suggested prompt:** • Explain to me how you worked out the product of these two numbers. **Detective Dog** These kinds of puzzle can be written onto large sheets of paper and displayed on the classroom wall as a puzzle board. The numbers themselves could be changed each day to provide a new challenge and the children could try to find the solutions in spare moments during the school day. **Suggested question:** • How did you work out this answer?	**Written methods**	63 64

Activity name	Strand and learning objectives	Notes on the activities	Assessment Focus	Page number
Sponsored spell Spend, spend, spend! Splish! Splash! Splosh!	**Calculating** Use a calculator to carry out one-step and two-step calculations involving all four operations; recognise negative numbers in the display, correct mistaken entries and interpret the display correctly in the context of money	**Sponsored spell** The children should work in pairs to discuss the situations and to decide upon the most appropriate calculation to enter into the calculator to find the answer. Check how the children enter amounts given as pence only – they should be keyed in as decimal numbers less than 1. Always encourage estimating and checking. During the plenary, discuss how the children solved the problems, and demonstrate different ways of finding the answers. SUGGESTED QUESTIONS: • How did you answer this question? • What did you key into the calculator? • Did anyone else try it a different way? • Do you think that is a sensible answer? **Spend, spend, spend!** During the plenary, discuss how the children solved the problems, and demonstrate different ways of finding the answers. SUGGESTED QUESTIONS: • How did you answer this question? • What did you key into the calculator? • Did anyone else try it a different way? • Do you think that is a sensible answer? **Splish! Splash! Splosh!** Revise inverses at the start of the lesson and discuss how calculations can be solved quickly by performing a different calculation. Missing number questions are often answered incorrectly in calculator tests as children see the operation shown and always want to press this key on their calculator. Often they use an ineffectual trial and error approach which can take an endless amount of time. SUGGESTED QUESTIONS: • How did you answer this question? • What did you key into the calculator?	**Solving numerical problems**	65 66 67

Block B Securing number facts, understanding shapes Unit 1

Activity name	Strand and learning objectives	Notes on the activities	Assessment Focus	Page number
Confetti colours The rules of the rows Hard cards	**Using and applying mathematics** Identify and use patterns, relationships and properties of numbers or shapes; investigate a statement involving numbers and test it with examples	**Confetti colours** *Processes: visualise, compare, reason* Explain to the children that when something is 'next to' another it can be horizontally or vertically next to it, but not diagonally. For example in question 3, the horseshoe shape is next to the two stars; it is not classed as being next to any of the other three shapes. SUGGESTED QUESTIONS: • How easy did you find this? • Did you work through the clues in order? • Would it have helped if you had worked through in a different order? **The rules of the rows** *Processes: trial and improvement, test ideas, record, explain, reason, be systematic, look for pattern* Encourage the children to work systematically. Some children will begin to notice that, to an extent, they can use one set of answers to help them find the next, for example by doubling the numbers. For the extension activity, compile a class list of the different possible rules for the hexagons. SUGGESTED QUESTIONS: • What patterns did you use to help you? • What patterns did you notice? **Hard cards** *Processes: reason, test ideas, explain* Encourage the children to try examples to help them to decide whether an answer will be odd or even, for example the answer to 3 add 4 is odd. As a further extension, the children could draw diagrams, for example of sets of counters in pairs and 'odd ones', to accompany each card to show why the answers are as given. SUGGESTED QUESTIONS: • What does the term 'product' mean? • How do you know it will always be even/odd?	**Reasoning**	68 69 70
Be a detective Market stall Sheila's shopping basket	**Using and applying mathematics** Solve one-step and two-step problems involving numbers, money or measures, including time; choose and carry out appropriate calculations, using calculator methods where appropriate	**Be a detective** *Processes: reason, record, make decisions* Allow the children to make their own decisions about what the number must be, based on the clues. Encourage them to write all the possible numbers for each clue and then to find which number appears in both lists. Revise the meaning of the word 'product' before beginning. SUGGESTED QUESTIONS: • How did you find this solution? • What does the word 'product' mean? • How could you write this as a number sentence? **Market stall** *Processes: reason, record, explain* Allow the children to make their own decisions about what to do and encourage them to use number sentences or pictorial methods on the back of the worksheet to record their working. As a further extension, the children could be asked to find out how much change each person would get from a £10 or a £20 note. SUGGESTED QUESTION: • How did you find this solution? **Sheila's shopping basket** *Processes: explain, reason, record* At the start of the lesson, ask the children to tell a partner all the units of measure that they know and the relationships between them. Check that they know that 1000 g = 1 kg, and 1000 ml = 1 l. SUGGESTED QUESTIONS: • How did you work out this answer? • Did you have to find the exact amount? • Was it always necessary to work out the exact answer to the multiplication?	**Problem solving**	71 72 73
In a flap	**Using and applying mathematics** Report solutions to puzzles and problems, giving explanations and reasoning orally and in writing, using diagrams and symbols	**In a flap** *Processes: explain, reason, ask own questions* At the start of the lesson, ask the children to give the inverse operations for addition, subtraction, multiplication and division. Write a missing number problem on the board, for example 53 – ☐ = 78, and ask the children how they would solve it. SUGGESTED QUESTIONS: • What would you do? • Which calculation did you do to help you find the missing number? • What other ways could it be done?	**Communicating**	74

Activity name	Strand and learning objectives	Notes on the activities	Assessment Focus	Page number
Cheese triangles Square dance	**Knowing and using number facts** Use knowledge of addition and subtraction facts and place value to derive sums and differences of pairs of multiples of 10, 100 or 1000	**Cheese triangles** Encourage the children to use their knowledge of additions of single-digit numbers to help them answer these multiples of 10 questions, for example 7 + 4 + [ ] = 18 is related to 70 + 40 + [ ] = 180. SUGGESTED QUESTIONS: • How quickly did you answer these? • How did you work this out? **Square dance** This activity encourages the children to develop using and applying strategies to solve these problems, including perseverance and trial and improvement strategies. A further tactic which could be recommended is for the children to find the total of all the cards (3600) and subtract this from the total number multiplied by 4 (for example 1200 × 4). The number that this produces (4800 – 3600 = 1200) tells you the total of the four corner numbers. In other words this can help you to find the four numbers at the corners of the square first. The children should also be encouraged to work with these numbers as single-digit numbers, such as 3 + 8 rather than 30 + 80, to enable them to work more quickly and then to adjust the answers at the end. SUGGESTED QUESTIONS: • What number facts did you use to help you work out that those numbers total 1400? • How could you arrange four of these numbers so that there is always a difference of 200 between them?	**Mental methods**	75 76
Proper properties game Shapes: 1 and 2	**Understanding shape** Draw polygons and classify them by identifying their properties, including their line symmetry	**Proper properties game and Shapes: 1 and 2** Discuss the properties on the property cards and ensure that the children are familiar with the terms 'vertical' and 'horizontal'. The cards on Shapes: 1 and 2 can be used for other activities, such as picking a card and writing a detailed description of it including, where appropriate, the coordinates of the vertices, or describing one of the shapes to a partner for them to guess which shape it is. SUGGESTED QUESTIONS: • How many sides/corners/angles does this shape have? • Does this shape have a line of symmetry? • Is it vertical or horizontal?	**Properties of shape**	77 78–79
Party presents Cube challenge	**Understanding shape** Visualise 3-D objects from 2-D drawings; make nets of common solids	**Party presents** Ensure that the children know the terms 'faces', 'vertices' and 'edges', and know that 'vertex' is the singular of 'vertices'. SUGGESTED QUESTIONS: • What shapes are the faces of a cube/cuboid/triangular prism? • Which shapes have one or more curved faces? **Cube challenge** The children can be asked to make a further range of shapes with the four models and to sketch the shapes made. Please note that there is more than one way to make the fourth shape (see Answers on page 214). SUGGESTED QUESTIONS: • How many cubes have you used to make this shape? • Can you colour the picture to match the colour of your cubes?	**Properties of shape**	80 81

Block B Unit 2

Activity name	Strand and learning objectives	Notes on the activities	Assessment Focus	Page number
Necklace numbers Sticks Dividing exactly	**Using and applying mathematics** Identify and use patterns, relationships and properties of numbers or shapes; investigate a statement involving numbers and test it with examples	**Necklace number** *Processes: visualise, compare, look for pattern, test ideas, trial and improvement* Encourage the children to look for patterns and to describe them to others. SUGGESTED QUESTION: • What is the rule for this sequence? **Sticks** *Processes: reason, visualise, explain* Encourage the children to describe their reasoning and invite them to explain their thinking to others. SUGGESTED QUESTIONS: • How did you work out the solutions? • What did this clue tell you? • Which was the most helpful clue? **Dividing exactly** *Processes: look for pattern, test ideas, predict, reason* At the start of the lesson, practise different times-tables and write these on the board. Ask the children to pick out numbers that appear as answers in different tables, and to explain what that means, for example 30 is in the 2 times-table, the 3 times-table, the 5 times-table and the 10 times-table. That means that it divides exactly by 2, 3, 5 and 10. SUGGESTED QUESTION: • What is special about multiples of 3/4/5/6/7/8/9/10?	**Reasoning**	82 83 84
Andy, Sandy and Mandy	**Knowing and using number facts** Use knowledge of rounding, number operations and inverses to estimate and check calculations	**Andy, Sandy and Mandy** At the start of the lesson revise rounding numbers to the nearest ten and making suitable estimates. SUGGESTED QUESTION: • What is 67 to the nearest ten?	**Mental methods** **Operations and relationships between them**	85
What a puzzle!	**Using and applying mathematics** Report solutions to puzzles and problems, giving explanations and reasoning orally and in writing, using diagrams and symbols	**What a puzzle!** *Processes: explain, compare, reason* At the start of the lesson, write a vertical addition on the board (for example for 286 + 347 =), and ask the children to describe the steps they take to work out the answer (633). Erase some of the digits, and ask the children how they could use the digits that are left to work out the missing digits. What calculations would they use? Would they use an inverse operation? SUGGESTED QUESTIONS: • How did you work this out? • What was your thinking? • How could you explain this on paper/in words?	**Communicating**	86

Activity name	Strand and learning objectives	Notes on the activities	Assessment Focus	Page number
Double trouble At the sales	**Knowing and using number facts** Identify the doubles of two-digit numbers; use these to calculate doubles of multiples of 10 and 100 and derive the corresponding halves	**Double trouble** This activity can help children to begin to appreciate that when doubling larger numbers, such as between 75 and 100, the number can be thought of as 50 + a number, for example 76 = 50 + 26 and therefore they can double the number quickly and effectively: double 50 = 100 and double 26 is 52, thus double 76 = 152. **Suggested question:** • Have you checked your answers? **At the sales** Discuss different ways in which each number could be partitioned to halve it, for example 134 could be partitioned into 130 + 4, 100 + 34, 120 + 14, 120 + 10 + 4 etc. Encourage the children to say which way they find easiest to halve the number. **Suggested questions:** • How did you halve this number? • Could you partition the number in a different way? • Which way do you find easier?	**Mental methods**	87 88
Brooches Decorations	**Understanding shape** Draw polygons and classify them by identifying their properties, including their line symmetry	**Brooches** Encourage the children to use small mirrors to test their answers. Perspex equipment (such as a MIRA) that allows not only the reflection to be seen but also the drawing on the other side of the line can be a useful resource for those children who struggle with mirrors. Discuss any lines drawn incorrectly. **Suggested questions:** • Is this brooch symmetrical? • How many lines of symmetry does this brooch have? **Decorations** This activity revises the shape names and encourages the children to realise that pentagons and hexagons can take many forms. At the start of the lesson, demonstrate how a two-criteria intersecting Venn diagram is used to sort data. Discuss the intersection and remind the children that numbers can be written outside the circle (inside the rectangle) to represent items that do not meet either of the criteria given. **Suggested questions:** • Do you know what a four-sided shape is called? • How many sides/vertices/angles has this shape?	**Properties of shape**	89 90
Crazy cubes	**Understanding shape** Visualise 3-D objects from 2-D drawings; make nets of common solids	**Crazy cubes** As the children begin to appreciate what a net is they can begin to explore patterns on different faces. Some children will find this visualisation very difficult, whereas other, more spatially aware, children may find this easier. Children who struggle need to be given situations where they can explore the nets practically by cutting out and folding the nets to see what happens to the shape. **Suggested prompt/questions:** • Look at the net. How many faces have squares on? • What does this tell you about this cube? • Are the 'L' shapes all in a straight line?	**Properties of shape**	91

Block B Unit 3

Activity name	Strand and learning objectives	Notes on the activities	Assessment Focus	Page number
Tell me True statements Halfway house	**Using and applying mathematics** Identify and use patterns, relationships and properties of numbers or shapes; investigate a statement involving numbers and test it with examples	**Tell me** *Processes: explain, co-operate, compare, record* Since each card shows a triangle and a rectangle, this activity focuses attention on describing accurately what each looks like and where they lie in relation to each other. Encourage the children to use specific language, such as those words in the box on the worksheet, making sure that their descriptions cannot also apply to other cards. For example, 'There is an equilateral triangle and a rectangle' applies to more than one card. Shapes and descriptions can be mounted on a wall as puzzles for the children to solve, and as a lively and stimulating display. **Suggested questions:** • In what way is this card different from this one? • How could you describe this card? • Which word could you use to describe where the triangle is? • What about the rectangle? • Does your description only fit that card, or could it describe one of the others ones too? **True statements** *Processes: look for pattern, compare, be systematic* At the start of the lesson, revise all the terms used on the worksheet. **Suggested questions:** • Have you found all the possible true statements? • How can you be sure? **Halfway house** *Processes: look for pattern, explain, reason, compare, record, justify, test ideas* Encourage the children to give different examples that show when a statement is true or false. **Suggested questions:** • How do you know that that statement is true? • Why isn't one example enough to show that that statement is true?	**Reasoning**	92 93 94
Badge sale Fair share: 1 and 2	**Using and applying mathematics** Solve one-step and two-step problems involving numbers, money or measures, including time; choose and carry out appropriate calculations, using calculator methods where appropriate	**Badge sale** *Processes: reason, make decisions, explain* Discuss strategies that the children chose to work out the answers, drawing attention to the use of equipment such as number lines, 100-squares, coins, counting materials, or other written or mental methods. **Suggested questions:** • How did you find the answer? • What method did you use to find the answer? • Did you use the same method for each question or did you do anything different on this question? Why was that? **Fair share: 1 and 2** *Processes: reason, make decisions, explain, be systematic* Observe the methods that the children use to find the answers, for example noting which children use the picture, their fingers, equipment, or a mental method. **Suggested questions/prompt:** • How easy did you find this? • Did you find the answer straight away? • Can you find other answers? How do you know that you have found them all? • Let's write a class list of all the possible answers we can find.	**Problem solving**	95 96–97

Activity name	Strand and learning objectives	Notes on the activities	Assessment Focus	Page number
Computer glitch	**Knowing and using number facts** Use knowledge of rounding, number operations and inverses to estimate and check calculations	**Computer glitch** Any written or informal methods of calculation are suitable for checking these calculations. Discuss inverses and ensure that the children appreciate that they should take the final answer and apply the inverse calculation to it in order to check the calculation. SUGGESTED QUESTIONS: • What is the inverse of subtraction? • How did you know that half of 184 is not 72?	**Mental methods** **Operations and relationships between them**	98
Grid reasoning	**Using and applying mathematics** Report solutions to puzzles and problems, giving explanations and reasoning orally and in writing, using diagrams and symbols	**Grid reasoning** *Processes: explain, reason, test ideas, trial and improvement, visualise* This challenging activity encourages the children to persevere in a problem-solving activity, and to describe the strategies they used. SUGGESTED QUESTIONS: • Did you manage to solve the problem? • What was your thinking? • What did you learn? • If you were going to do it again, what would you do differently?	**Communicating**	99
Water slide Sitting ducks	**Knowing and using number facts** Use knowledge of addition and subtraction facts and place value to derive sums and differences of pairs of multiples of 10, 100 or 1000	**Water slide** Remind the children to watch out for whether the question is an addition or a subtraction. Children could work with a partner and take it in turns to use a stopwatch to time each other to see how long they take and whether they can do it quicker on a second occasion. SUGGESTED QUESTIONS: • What is 400 + 700? How do you know? • Which fact did you use to help you? **Sitting ducks** The children should be encouraged to work with these numbers as single-digit numbers, for example 3 thousand + 8 thousand rather than 3000 + 8000, to enable them to work more quickly and then to adjust the answers at the end. In the extension activity, the children have to find ways to land on five multiples of 1000, for example 3000 + 8000 + 4000 + 5000 + 7000. Children could then find which have the largest and smallest totals. SUGGESTED QUESTION: • Can you make a puzzle like this where the route has different answers with the answer 13000?	**Mental methods**	100 101
Double bugs Half bugs	**Knowing and using number facts** Identify the doubles of two-digit numbers; use these to calculate doubles of multiples of 10 and 100 and derive the corresponding halves	**Double bugs** Double bugs make a useful classroom display and encourage the children to see the link between doubling multiples of 1, 10 and 100. SUGGESTED QUESTION: • Have you checked your answers? **Half bugs** Half bugs can be displayed in the classroom to encourage the children to see the link between halving multiples of 1, 10 and 100. SUGGESTED QUESTION: • How could you check your answers?	**Mental methods**	102 103
Stick 'em up	**Knowing and using number facts** Derive and recall multiplication facts up to 10 × 10, the corresponding division facts and multiples of numbers to 10 up to the tenth multiple	**Stick 'em up** For this activity the children need to derive quickly, or recall, division facts for the more difficult times-tables facts, for example 6 × 7 and 7 × 8. It might be useful for some children to have access to the 6, 7, 8 and 9 times-tables for them to refer to. SUGGESTED QUESTION: • How could you use facts in the 2 times-table or the 4 times-table to help you to divide by 8, if you can't remember facts in the 8 times-table?	**Mental methods**	104
The great shape game	**Understanding shape** Draw polygons and classify them by identifying their properties, including their line symmetry	**The great shape game** Playing the game outlined in the teachers' notes at the foot of the page encourages the children to visualise and make different 2-D shapes and explore the properties. It is possible to make many different grey shapes with the cards. Here is an example of the shapes that have been made from all the cards at the end of one game: The children could score bonus points for saying the number of right angles that a completed shape has. The children could also work individually to try to put different cards together to make three squares. As an alternative individual activity, the children could try to make as many different symmetrical shapes as they can. SUGGESTED QUESTIONS: • Do you know the name of this shape? • How many sides/right angles/lines of symmetry has this shape?	**Properties of shape**	105
Nets with pentagons Nets with triangles Nets with rectangles Nets with circles	**Understanding shape** Visualise 3-D objects from 2-D drawings; make nets of common solids	**Nets with pentagons/triangles/rectangles/circles** It is important that children have experience in making their own nets and joining them together to form 3-D shapes. These four worksheets provide templates for making different types of 3-D shapes, including pyramids, prisms, cuboids, a cone and a cylinder. Once the children have made the shapes they could go on to explore different nets that could be used to make the same shapes, for example where the faces are arranged in different positions to make the same shape. SUGGESTED QUESTIONS: • What shape do you think this one will make? • How many faces has this shape? • How do you think it will fit together?	**Properties of shape**	106 107 108 109

Block C Handling data and measures Unit 1

Activity name	Strand and learning objectives	Notes on the activities	Assessment Focus	Page number
Fruit segments Thinking thimbles	**Using and applying mathematics** Suggest a line of enquiry and the strategy needed to follow it; collect, organise and interpret selected information to find answers	**Fruit segments** *Processes: explain, ask own questions, reason* This activity can help the children to see how many different questions can be asked about a context, and encourages them to make up their own questions. SUGGESTED QUESTIONS: • How many different questions have we asked in our class? • How would you answer Jo's question? • How many different ways did you find? **Thinking thimbles** *Processes: be systematic, check, compare, visualise, look for pattern, record* Ensure the children realise that in this activity, there does not have to be a different number of thimbles on each shelf: it is possible to have the same number on each shelf. Discuss whether this means that there will be more or fewer answers than if there has to be a different number of thimbles on each shelf. (There are more possible answers.) SUGGESTED QUESTIONS: • What have you discovered? • How can you be sure that you have found all the ways? • Did you sort them in a particular way? • How could you check? • Were you systematic?	**Reasoning**	110 111
Rain recorder No shoes allowed! Rock, paper, scissors Sorting symmetry Monsters' tea party Odd one out: 1 and 2 Marble run	**Handling data** Answer a question by identifying what data to collect; organise, present, analyse and interpret the data in tables, diagrams, tally charts, pictograms and bar charts, using ICT where appropriate	**Rain recorder** At the start of the lesson, explain how rainfall is measured using a rain gauge and point out that the data in the table has been rounded to the nearest centimetre. Ask the children to think about what the data does and does not show, using the suggested questions below. Some children might suggest that there could have been concentrated rainfall during part of the month and the rest of the month could have been hot and sunny. Although the focus is on interpretation of the table, the children could represent the data on a vertical or horizontal bar chart. SUGGESTED QUESTIONS: • How much rain fell in September? • Does the data tell us whether it rained every day? • What might have happened in October? **No shoes allowed!** The data shows a tally of the number of pairs of different types of footwear taken off by children who had a go on a bouncy castle. Question 5b requires the children to contextualise the data and to draw conclusions about the weather on the day of the fête, supported by reasoning that flip-flops were a popular choice and that it was probably too hot to wear boots. In the extension activity, the total number of pairs will give the total number of children who went on the bouncy castle, with the exception of the two children who turned up with bare feet. The children should, therefore, include the bare-footed children in the data to give an accurate result. SUGGESTED QUESTIONS: • How many children wore flip-flops/school shoes/trainers? • What does a tally of IIII II show? **Rock, paper, scissors** Game rules The children should play the game in pairs. Both partners make a fist of one hand. Simultaneously, they gently punch the air in front of them three times and on the third punch they show a rock (keep as fist), paper (flat hand) or scissors (first two fingers open like a pair of scissors). The following shows who the winner of each pair is, including a rationale: – rock beats scissors – it blunts them; – scissors beat paper – they cut it; – paper beats rock – it covers/wraps around it. Emphasise that it is useful to keep a tally chart here because the data is collected over a period of time and needs to be counted at the end. This can be linked to the importance of keeping a correct score in any game situation. SUGGESTED QUESTIONS: • What sort of data is recorded using a tally chart? • When might it be important to keep a tally chart? **Sorting symmetry** Recap horizontal and vertical lines of reflective symmetry before the children begin this activity. Ensure they understand that the alphabet on the worksheet is made up of a mixture of capital and lowercase letters. The extension activity asks the children to complete the labels 'Symmetrical and capital' and 'Not symmetrical, not capital'. Some children might find the sorting easier if these labels are already filled in. SUGGESTED QUESTIONS: • What does 'symmetrical' mean? • How can a mirror help you to decide whether a letter is symmetrical or not? • How many of the letters are symmetrical and capital? **Monsters' tea party** Ensure that the children understand how the two criteria are represented on the Carroll diagram. Look at diagrams showing one criterion to consolidate the concept, if necessary. The focus here is on the interpretation of the data in the diagram. SUGGESTED QUESTIONS: • How could we record someone who had lemonade and fruitcake? • What did Wolfy have? How do you know? **Odd one out: 1 and 2** Ensure that the children are familiar with a range of representations, including tally charts, tables, pictograms and vertical and horizontal bar charts. This activity requires the children to compare three different representations of the same data in order to identify which one is incorrect and, therefore, the odd one out. You could use this as an assessment activity or as a way of checking whether the children find reading particular diagrams difficult. SUGGESTED QUESTIONS: • What information will help you to spot the odd one out? • In set B, how did you know that the pictogram was the odd one out? **Marble run** *Processes: visualise, trial and improvement, test ideas, explain* Encourage the children to focus on describing strategies they developed when looking for solutions. SUGGESTED QUESTION: • Can you explain how you worked this out?	**Processing and representing data** **Interpreting data**	112 113 114 115 116 117–118 119

Activity name	Strand and learning objectives	Notes on the activities	Assessment Focus	Page number
Measure for measure	**Measuring** Choose and use standard metric units and their abbreviations when estimating, measuring and recording length, weight and capacity; know the meaning of 'kilo', 'centi' and 'milli' and, where appropriate, use decimal notation to record measurements (e.g. 1.3 m or 0.6 kg)	**Measure for measure** This practical activity is best done in pairs or in small groups as it encourages discussion and requires fewer pieces of measuring equipment. If the children are not using electronic scales to measure the mass of the shoe and the trainer then the degree of accuracy will need to be changed before the worksheet is given to the children. Begin the lesson by discussing the meaning of the terms 'mass' and 'weight'. In the extension activity, the children should realise that length and width together give an idea of size. As a further extension, they could be asked to measure other aspects of the items in order to describe them fully, for example collar size. SUGGESTED QUESTIONS: • What piece of measuring equipment did you use to measure the mass of the shoe? • What unit of measurement did you use to describe the length of the sleeve of the jumper? Could you have used a different unit? • How accurately did you measure?	**Measures**	120

Block C Unit 2

Activity name	Strand and learning objectives	Notes on the activities	Assessment Focus	Page number
Book counting	**Using and applying mathematics** Suggest a line of enquiry and the strategy needed to follow it; collect, organise and interpret selected information to find answers	**Book counting** *Processes: make decisions, record, co-operate, predict, be systematic* This worksheet encourages the children to work together to make decisions and to plan how to go about collecting information about the number of books in a library area. SUGGESTED QUESTIONS: • How did you decide what to do? • How well did you work together as a group? • What do you think the outcome might be? • Were you systematic?	**Reasoning**	121
2s and 3s Sweet success Minibeasts Summer fête Mr Folly's lollies	**Handling data** Answer a question by identifying what data to collect; organise, present, analyse and interpret the data in tables, diagrams, tally charts, pictograms and bar charts, using ICT where appropriate	**2s and 3s** Before starting the activity, revise the 2 times- and 3 times-tables. Ensure that the children understand the layout of the Carroll diagram, reinforcing the two criteria (multiple of 2, multiple of 3) and the sections which include both multiples of 2 and 3, and neither multiples of 2 nor 3. SUGGESTED QUESTIONS: • Is this number a multiple of 2? Is it a multiple of 3? Where should it be placed in the diagram? • Which numbers should be placed in this section of the diagram? **Sweet success** Before starting the activity, ensure that the children have had an opportunity to sort objects and to discuss the criteria by which they have sorted them. This activity requires the children to decide how they want to sort the sweets and to record the data on the relevant diagrams. Further ideas for sorting can be recorded on a separate piece of paper. As an extension, the children could explain to a partner how they sorted the sweets. SUGGESTED QUESTIONS: • How many different ways can you sort the sweets? • Is there a way of sorting the sweets so that they are all included in one region of a Venn diagram? **Minibeasts** This activity revises pictograms where one symbol represents one unit of data. Children could discuss why there does not need to be a numbered scale along the bottom of the diagram. SUGGESTED QUESTIONS: • What does the symbol of the magnifying glass mean? • How many worms were found? **Summer fête** This activity looks at a pictogram where each symbol represents ten units of data, with half a symbol representing five units of data. To consolidate understanding of the value of the symbol, the extension activity requires the children to use the symbol to represent a given number. SUGGESTED QUESTIONS: • What does the symbol represent? • How many people would nine symbols represent? **Mr Folly's lollies** This activity requires the children to interpret a tally chart and then present a pictogram of the same data. The children choose how many units are represented by one symbol of the pictogram. SUGGESTED QUESTIONS: • How many lollies were sold on Saturday? • How did you work this out? • How many lollies are represented by one symbol?	**Processing and representing data** **Interpreting data**	122 123 124 125 126
Game, set and match: 1 and 2		**Game, set and match: 1 and 2** This activity is best done towards the end of the year to consolidate the children's handling data skills. The focus is on discussion, reasoning and interpretation of charts in order to match them to a simple scenario. SUGGESTED QUESTIONS: • If we drew a bar chart for B/D, how many bars would there have to be? • Tell me another situation that could fit the data in D.		127–8

Activity name	Strand and learning objectives	Notes on the activities	Assessment Focus	Page number
Measure together	**Measuring** Choose and use standard metric units and their abbreviations when estimating, measuring and recording length, weight and capacity; know the meaning of 'kilo', 'centi' and 'milli' and, where appropriate, use decimal notation to record measurements (e.g. 1.3 m or 0.6 kg)	**Measure together** This activity involves the children selecting the correct unit of measurement and then trying to estimate or find out the answers to each question, using appropriate instruments where possible. At the start of the lesson, ask the children to tell you all the units of measurement that they know and list these on the board. Ask the children to link the measures together and to order them by size, for example 10 mm = 1 cm, 100 cm = 1 m, 1000 m = 1 km; mm, cm, m, km. These cards could be enlarged and laminated to create a more permanent resource. SUGGESTED QUESTIONS: • How could you find the answer to this question? • Can you estimate the answer and then measure to check? • What piece of equipment will you use to find out the answer?	**Measures**	129
Mix and match: 1 and 2	**Handling data** Compare the impact of representations where scales have intervals of differing step size	**Mix and match: 1 and 2** The children should discuss their choice of pairs with a partner (or in a small group), giving explanations, and reasoning orally about their choices. SUGGESTED QUESTIONS: • What clues can you find to help you to work out which pairs match? • How do you know that these two bar charts show the same data?	**Interpreting data**	130–1

Block C Unit 3

Activity name	Strand and learning objectives	Notes on the activities	Assessment Focus	Page number
Planning enquiries: 1 and 2	**Using and applying mathematics** Suggest a line of enquiry and the strategy needed to follow it; collect, organise and interpret selected information to find answers	**Planning enquiries: 1 and 2** *Processes: make decisions, record, co-operate, predict* These worksheets encourage the children to make decisions and to plan how to follow lines of enquiry by collecting data. SUGGESTED QUESTIONS: • How did you decide what to do? • What do you think the outcome might be?	**Reasoning**	132–3
After-school sports Splish, splash What a smoothie! Bounce 4 charity Top of the mountain: 1 and 2	**Handling data** Answer a question by identifying what data to collect; organise, present, analyse and interpret the data in tables, diagrams, tally charts, pictograms and bar charts, using ICT where appropriate	**After-school sports** At the start of the lesson, ask the children to say what they know about bar charts. Ask them to list everything that a bar chart should have on it. SUGGESTED QUESTIONS: • How many people took part in the survey? • Looking at the bars on the bar chart, what can you say about the data? **Splish, splash** This activity gives the children an opportunity to draw a bar chart where the scale is labelled in ones. SUGGESTED QUESTIONS: • How many babies were in the small pool on Wednesday? • On which day were there 19 babies in the small pool? **What a smoothie!** This activity involves the children drawing a bar chart and using a scale where the intervals are in twos. At the start of the lesson, practise counting in twos. Then draw a scale on the board where the numbering goes up in steps of two. Ask the children to say where, for example, 13, 23, 17, 5 would be shown on the scale. SUGGESTED QUESTIONS: • How did you know to end that bar there? • Where is 9 shown on this scale? **Bounce 4 charity** This activity focuses on the interpretation of a horizontal bar chart where the scale shows intervals of five. It also gives an opportunity for the children to consider what the data means, or could mean, by asking why they think that more money was raised by one particular class (suggestions are included in the answers). SUGGESTED QUESTIONS: • Which class raised £85? • Which class raised £65? **Top of the Mountain: 1 and 2** This track game for two players (or more if preferred) is designed to consolidate concepts and skills linked to handling data. The answers can be discussed between players for an agreement to be reached, or a third child could act as adjudicator. SUGGESTED QUESTIONS: • Do you think that the answer is correct? • How could you check?	**Processing and representing data** **Interpreting data**	134 135 136 137 138–9

Activity name	Strand and learning objectives	Notes on the activities	Assessment Focus	Page number
Made to measure	**Measuring** Choose and use standard metric units and their abbreviations when estimating, measuring and recording length, weight and capacity; know the meaning of 'kilo', 'centi' and 'milli' and, where appropriate, use decimal notation to record measurements (e.g. 1.3 m or 0.6 kg)	**Made to measure** At the start of the lesson, remind the children that 100 cm is the same as 1 m and discuss how far this distance is in relation to a metre stick. **Suggested questions:** • How do you know that 3.2 m is equivalent to 320 cm? • Is a 3.5 m scarf longer or shorter than 35 cm?	**Measures**	140
Scaly fish: 1 and 2	**Handling data** Compare the impact of representations where scales have intervals of differing step size	**Scaly fish: 1 and 2** In this activity, the children plot the same data on four different vertical bar charts, each of which has a different scale. They should first plot the data, then evaluate the representations and discuss which one they would choose and why. (This will lay the foundation for children to understand, at a later date, how data representations can be manipulated to tell a particular story in, for example, the media.) **Suggested questions:** • What is the total number of fish counted? • Do you think that this is the total number of fish in Mika's aquarium? • What makes you think this?	**Interpreting data**	141–2

Block D Calculating, measuring and understanding shape Unit 1

Activity name	Strand and learning objectives	Notes on the activities	Assessment Focus	Page number
Time teaser Post office problems	**Using and applying mathematics** Solve one-step and two-step problems involving numbers, money or measures, including time; choose and carry out appropriate calculations, using calculator methods where appropriate	**Time teaser** *Processes: reason, make decisions, explain* As a quick way of checking the answers to this worksheet, the only clock left unmatched shows the time 9:18 pm. **Suggested questions:** • How would you say this time in words? • Can you show me this time on a clock face? • Is this in the morning, the afternoon, or the evening? **Post office problems** *Processes: reason, explain, record* The children could work together in pairs on this activity to promote discussion. Revise equivalent units of mass and decimals to one decimal place. Talk about strategies for answering each question and encourage the children to describe the methods they used. **Suggested questions:** • How did you find this solution? • What strategies did you use?	**Problem solving**	143 144
The banker's game Save and spend cards	**Calculating** Add or subtract mentally pairs of two-digit whole numbers (e.g. 47 + 58, 91 – 35)	**The banker's game and Save and spend cards** It is important that the children understand how a balance sheet works, where amounts earned are added to the existing balance or amounts spent are subtracted from the balance. Emphasise that each new transaction should be recorded on a new line of the balance sheet. **Suggested questions:** • What method did you use to add £37? Would you use a similar method to add £39? What other method could you use?	**Mental methods**	145 146
Fi's fruitcake	**Measuring** Interpret intervals and divisions on partially numbered scales and record readings accurately, where appropriate to the nearest tenth of a unit	**Fi's fruitcake** Ensure the children appreciate that the previous ingredients remain in the pan of the scales as the new ingredient is added. As a further extension, the children could write out a list of ingredients and the amounts for a new recipe and then draw arrows on scales to show these amounts. **Suggested question:** • What is each interval worth on these scales?	**Measures**	147
Time dominoes Time bingo	**Measuring** Read time to the nearest minute; use am, pm and 12-hour clock notation; choose units of time to measure time intervals; calculate time intervals from clocks and timetables	**Time dominoes** Encourage the children to check each other's clocks before beginning the bingo game. The times can be altered to make them easier or harder, as appropriate. **Suggested questions:** • What time does this clock show? • Can you find a matching clock? **Time bingo** Encourage the children to check each other's clocks before beginning the bingo game. The times can be altered to make them easier or harder, as appropriate. **Suggested questions:** • What time does this clock show? • Can we describe this time in a different way?	**Measures**	148 149

Activity name	Strand and learning objectives	Notes on the activities	Assessment Focus	Page number
Dan's day		**Dan's day** At the start of the lesson, ask children what they might be doing at six o'clock. Discuss how their answers vary according to whether they think it is six o'clock in the morning or six o'clock in the evening. Show how 'am' and 'pm' are used to differentiate between morning, afternoon, evening and night. Explain that noon is 12 pm and midnight is 12 am. **Suggested questions:** • If the time had been 7:30 pm instead, which of those activities might Dan have been doing? • What are the differences between what you might be doing at 9:00 am and at 9:00 pm?		150
Optical illusions Cinema seating Counter attack	**Understanding shape** Recognise horizontal and vertical lines; use the eight compass points to describe direction; describe and identify the position of a square on a grid of squares	**Optical illusions** These common optical illusions can be discussed and then the children encouraged to colour the horizontal lines blue ('think of the horizon over the sea') and the vertical lines red ('think of a tall red tower'). **Suggested question:** • Is the line vertical or horizontal? **Cinema seating** This activity provides practice in identifying squares on a grid using letters and numbers. The descriptions on the worksheet can be altered to provide further practice and variety. **Suggested question:** • Which seats are either side of D3? **Counter attack** This activity involves direction, using the eight compass points, and distance. It can help children to appreciate that there are opposite directions, for example one square NE followed by one square SW returns you to the same position. Encourage the children who complete the extension activity to use as many different directions as they can in their puzzles. **Suggested questions:** • Can you follow this set of instructions? • Where would you end up?	**Properties of position and movement**	151 152 153

Block D Unit 2

Activity name	Strand and learning objectives	Notes on the activities	Assessment Focus	Page number
Reading the signs	**Using and applying mathematics** Solve one-step and two-step problems involving numbers, money or measures, including time; choose and carry out appropriate calculations, using calculator methods where appropriate	**Reading the signs** *Processes: reason, make decisions, record* The children should work in pairs and decide upon the appropriate calculations for each problem to show what they think should be done. Encourage the children to draw diagrams to help them to visualise the problems. **Suggested questions:** • How did you find this solution? • Can you explain why these two road sign questions require a different calculation?	**Problem solving**	154
Tallest man ever	**Calculating** Refine and use efficient written methods to add and subtract two-digit and three-digit whole numbers and £.p	**Tallest man ever** As a further extension, the children could research and compare the heights of other famous people. **Suggested prompt:** • Explain to me how you worked out the difference between these two numbers.	**Written methods**	155
Magic ingredients Beautiful brooches	**Calculating** Develop and use written methods to record, support and explain multiplication and division of two-digit numbers by a one-digit number, including division with remainders (e.g. 15 × 9, 98 ÷ 6)	**Magic ingredients** For this activity, the children could use partitioning to help them multiply two-digit numbers by a one-digit number. Discuss early ideas of distributivity (without using this term); that is, that a number to be multiplied can be partitioned and each part multiplied separately before they are recombined. **Suggested questions:** • Why did you choose that method to multiply those numbers? • How could you check that you have completed that calculation correctly? **Now try this!** 1784 **Beautiful brooches** Encourage the children first to work out all the multiplications and then to use the key to find the related letters. If the children complete the extension activity suggested in the Teachers' note, they should find that 18cm of wire is wasted. **Suggested questions:** • What multiplication fact helped you to work out the answer? • How could you check your answers?	**Written methods**	156 157

Activity name	Strand and learning objectives	Notes on the activities	Assessment Focus	Page number
From 'metre' you	**Counting and understanding number** Use decimal notation for tenths and hundredths and partition decimals; relate the notation to money and measurement; position one-place and two-place decimals on a number line	**From 'metre' you** For the extension activity, encourage the children to realise that 0.8 m and 0.80 m are equivalent and are both 80 cm on the metre stick. **SUGGESTED QUESTIONS:** • How many hundredths of a metre is 0.41 m? What is this in centimetres?	**Fractions and decimals**	158
Guinea pig food	**Measuring** Choose and use standard metric units and their abbreviations when estimating, measuring and recording length, weight and capacity; know the meaning of 'kilo', 'centi' and 'milli' and, where appropriate, use decimal notation to record measurements (e.g. 1.3 m or 0.6 kg)	**Guinea pig food** At the start of the lesson, remind the children that 1000 g is the same as 1 kg and pass round weights so that the children can begin to develop a sense of how heavy 1 kg or 1000 g is. Explain that 1 g is the weight of water that would fit into a centimetre cube (if that were possible). **SUGGESTED QUESTIONS:** • How many grams is the same as 1 kilogram? • Can you suggest something that would weigh about 1.5 kg?	**Measures**	159
Scale shapes	**Measuring** Interpret intervals and divisions on partially numbered scales and record readings accurately, where appropriate to the nearest tenth of a unit	**Scale shapes** This activity involves a wide variety of scales. Encourage the children to count up in even-sized steps to check that the value of each interval matches the given numbers. As an extension, the children can write something that is being measured for each of the scales on the worksheet, for example 30 ml could be the amount of concentrated drink put in a mug before filling with water. **SUGGESTED QUESTION:** • What do you think might be being measured here?	**Measures**	160
Spot the rectangles Hickory, dickory, dock Magic spell	**Measuring** Draw rectangles and measure and calculate their perimeters; find the area of rectilinear shapes drawn on a square grid by counting squares	**Spot the rectangles** Ensure that the children know the terms 'horizontal' and 'vertical', and they appreciate that for this activity the rectangles must have horizontal and vertical sides. **SUGGESTED QUESTIONS:** • What is the length of this side? • What do you notice about the length of the opposite side? **Hickory, dickory, dock** This first angle activity encourages the children to see patterns in the sizes of angles on a clock. They should notice that the number of degrees goes up in thirties and that a right angle is 90°, a straight angle is 180° and a full turn is 360°. **SUGGESTED QUESTIONS:** • Which clock shows a right angle? • How many degrees in a full turn/a half turn? **Magic spell** Introduce this activity practically by drawing a large wheel on paper or in chalk on the playground. Explain that each section of the wheel is 30°. Choose a child to stand in the centre of the wheel and ask him/her to rotate as other children give instructions. **SUGGESTED QUESTIONS:** • Can you follow your partner's instructions? • What word do you spell?	**Measures**	161 162 163
That's an order!	**Understanding shape** Know that angles are measured in degrees and that one whole turn is 360°; compare and order angles less than 180°	**That's an order!** In the final activity in this series of worksheets, the children are given static angles to order. Again, make the link between the sizes of the angles and scissor blades to encourage the children to appreciate the amount of turn. Some children may need to trace the angles and place them on top of each other in order to compare the sizes. **SUGGESTED QUESTIONS:** • Is this angle larger than this angle? • If these were pictures of scissors, have these blades been opened further than the ones in this picture?	**Properties of position and movement**	164
Zap 'em: 1 and 2	**Understanding shape** Recognise horizontal and vertical lines; use the eight compass points to describe direction; describe and identify the position of a square on a grid of squares	**Zap 'em: 1 and 2** It is important that children remember which colour their own counters are and that they understand that they have to try to remove the other player's coloured counters from the game board. **SUGGESTED QUESTIONS:** • In which direction would you travel from here to here? • Which card do you need in order to win the game?	**Properties of position and movement**	165–6

Activity name	Strand and learning objectives	Notes on the activities	Assessment Focus	Page number
Loopy witches	**Using and applying mathematics** Solve one-step and two-step problems involving numbers, money or measures, including time; choose and carry out appropriate calculations, using calculator methods where appropriate	**Loopy witches** *Processes: reason, make decisions* At the start of the lesson, remind the children about the notation 'ml' and 'l', and that 1000 ml is the same as 1 l. As a quick way of checking the answers to this worksheet, the letters at the bottom right of each card will spell 'BROOMSTICK'. This activity could also be used as an oral and mental starter. **Suggested questions:** • How did you find this solution? • If you can't find the answer, is it because the answer is in millilitres rather than litres?	**Problem solving**	167
Crack the codes	**Calculating** Refine and use efficient written methods to add and subtract two-digit and three-digit whole numbers and £.p	**Crack the codes** At the start of the lesson, practise partitioning three-digit numbers in different ways, for example: 645 → 600 + 40 + 5 → 600 + 30 + 15 → 500 + 140 + 5 → 500 + 130 + 15 This type of partitioning is drawn upon when using the most common written method of subtraction, known as decomposition. **Suggested prompt/question:** • Show me how you completed that subtraction. • How could you check your answer?	**Written methods**	168
A bucketful of fun Marvel Mouse Escape from Planet Zog!	**Counting and understanding number** Use decimal notation for tenths and hundredths and partition decimals; relate the notation to money and measurement; position one-place and two-place decimals on a number line	**A bucketful of fun** This activity helps children to appreciate the value of each digit in a decimal. **Suggested questions:** • What happens if you have no tenths? How would you write the number? **Marvel Mouse** Children should have completed page 59 before attempting this worksheet. If desired, the worksheet can be masked and altered before photocopying to provide a more flexible resource. **Suggested questions:** • How many tenths has this number? • Can you find a number on your sheet with four hundredths/tenths/ones? **Escape from Planet Zog!** Before playing, explain the rules carefully, perhaps asking the children to colour the numbers on the line that have no hundredths in one colour and those with five hundredths in another colour. Encourage the children to say each number aloud as they move along the line. **Suggested questions:** • How do you say this number? • How many tenths/hundredths has this number? • What is one tenth more than the decimal you are on?	**Fractions and decimals**	169 170 171
Milking Milli	**Measuring** Choose and use standard metric units and their abbreviations when estimating, measuring and recording length, weight and capacity; know the meaning of 'kilo', 'centi' and 'milli' and, where appropriate, use decimal notation to record measurements (e.g. 1.3m or 0.6kg)	**Milking Milli** At the start of the lesson, remind the children that 1000 ml is the same as 1 litre and pass round a container, bottle or carton that holds a litre of liquid. This will help the children to begin to develop a sense of how much 1 litre or 1000 ml is. Explain that 1 ml is the amount of water that would fit into a centimetre cube (if that were possible). **Suggested questions:** • How many millilitres are there in a litre? • Can you suggest something that would hold about 1.5 l?	**Measures**	172
Fill it up! Potion pathways	**Measuring** Interpret intervals and divisions on partially numbered scales and record readings accurately, where appropriate to the nearest tenth of a unit	**Fill it up!** Explain that the aim of this game is to fill your container before your partner, adding new amounts and indicating this by colouring the new amount. Explain that at the end of each go the children should say exactly how much liquid they have in their container and also how much more or less they have than their partner. **Suggested questions:** • How much more liquid do you need to reach 1 litre? • How much liquid have you now? **Potion pathways** The following list explains the errors made if the children gave the answer as anything other than pot **H**. **Pot A**– *two errors: children have not noticed that the weighing scales at the start are marked in kilograms; they have given 75 ml as equivalent to ¾ of a litre (should be 750 ml).* **Pot B**– *three errors: children have not noticed that the weighing scales at the start are marked in kilograms; they have given 75 ml as equivalent to ¾ of a litre (should be 750 ml); they have read the scale on the minute timer incorrectly.* **Pot C**– *one error: children have not noticed that the weighing scales at the start are marked in kilograms.* **Pot D**– *two errors: children have not noticed that the weighing scales at the start are marked in kilograms; they have not realised that 5.5 kg is equivalent to 5500 g.* **Pot E**– *three errors: children have not noticed that the weighing scales at the start are marked in kilograms; they have not recognised that 500 ml is half a litre; they have read the temperature scale incorrectly as –6°C, rather than as –4°C.* *OR* *two errors: children have not recognised that 350 ml is not more than litre, they have read the temperature scale incorrectly as –6°C, rather than as –4°C.* **Pot F**– *one error: children have not recognised that 350 ml is not more than litre.* **Pot G**– *one error: children have read the right-hand weighing scales as 152 g (should be 170 g).* **Suggested questions:** • What is three-quarters of a litre? • What is three-quarters of a kilogram? • How do we read this scale where the level is between numbered marks?	**Measures**	173 174

Activity name	Strand and learning objectives	Notes on the activities	Assessment Focus	Page number
Poorly pets The number 56 bus	**Measuring** Read time to the nearest minute; use am, pm and 12-hour clock notation; choose units of time to measure time intervals; calculate time intervals from clocks and timetables	**Poorly pets** You can use this activity to assess the children's ability to read the time on analogue clocks as well as on digital clocks. Provide analogue clocks with movable geared hands to help the children with this activity. **Suggested questions/prompt:** • How did you work out that 45 minutes later than 2:21 is six minutes past three? • The time is a quarter to three. What time did the analogue clock show 23 minutes ago? **The number 56 bus** At the start of the lesson, demonstrate how a timetable of this type is used and encourage the children to notice that the different buses take the same time between stops on each of the routes. **Suggested questions:** • How long does it take to get from Pyramid Shopping Centre to the Swimming Pool? • Which bus would you get if you wanted to get to the Swimming Pool for 9:20?	**Measures**	175 176
Area llamas Fair and square	**Measuring** Draw rectangles and measure and calculate their perimeters; find the area of rectilinear shapes drawn on a square grid by counting squares	**Area llamas** The children will need 1 cm^2 paper for the extension activity. **Suggested questions:** • How many centimetre squares are in this shape? • What is its area? **Fair and square** At the start of the lesson, provide the children with the worksheet and demonstrate how a trail can be drawn around each shape to find the perimeter. Make sure that the children do not confuse this with the number of squares around the edge of the shape. Explain that even if a shape has the same perimeter as another, it does not mean that they have the same area inside the shape. The children will need 1 cm2 paper for the extension activity. **Suggested questions:** • What is the area of this shape? • What is its perimeter?	**Measures**	177 178
Angelina's angles	**Understanding shape** Know that angles are measured in degrees and that one whole turn is 360°; compare and order angles less than 180°	**Angelina's angles** It is useful if children have had experience of making turning angles using a piece of knotted wool through a hole in a circle. It can help them appreciate that angle is about turning, rather than only seeing angles as static representations. Once the children are aware that there are 90° in a right angle and 360° in a full turn they can begin to estimate the sizes of angles. **Suggested questions:** • About how many degrees do you think this angle is? • Is this angle larger or smaller than a right angle? • How can you check?	**Properties of position and movement**	179

Block E Securing number facts, calculating, identifying relationships Unit 1

Activity name	Strand and learning objectives	Notes on the activities	Assessment Focus	Page number
Quiz show Number sentences How? Measuring methods Field event	**Using and applying mathematics** Represent a puzzle or problem using number sentences, statements or diagrams; use these to solve the problem; present and interpret the solution in the context of the problem	**Quiz show** *Processes: explain, reason, make decisions* This worksheet provides the children with the opportunity to consider and identify which operations are necessary in solving each question. **Suggested questions:** • Why do you think you should use that calculation? • What words in the question show that it should be that operation? **Number sentences** *Processes: reason, make decisions, compare, explain* It is important that the children understand that more than one number sentence can represent each situation. Encourage discussion of each number sentence and ask the children whether they can think of further ways that the situation could be represented. **Suggested questions:** • Which of these are possible ways of showing the situation? **How?** *Processes: explain, reason, ask own questions, record* This activity encourages the children to describe the strategies they would use to answer a calculation and to consider the different ways that this could be done. Calculations can be altered to provide differentiation. **Suggested questions:** • What would you do? • Would you use any equipment? • Could you show me this on a number line/100-square? • What other ways could it be done? **Measuring methods** *Processes: visualise, make decisions, reason* During the plenary, ask the children to demonstrate the methods that they used. In particular, ask the children to explain any diagrams they drew to help them. Discuss the diagrams and relate them to calculations, for example if children drew -litre bottles and then counted them in fours until they had made 5 litres, you could write $\frac{1}{4} \times 4 + \frac{1}{4} \times 4 + \frac{1}{4} \times 4 + \frac{1}{4} \times 4 + \frac{1}{4} \times 4 + \frac{1}{4} \times 2 = 5\frac{1}{2}$. **Suggested question:** • How did you find this solution? **Now try this!** 80 cm **Field event** *Processes: visualise, make decisions, reason, test ideas, look for pattern* In the extension activity, encourage the children to try different multiples of 5 and to look for patterns in the solutions. More confident children may be able to begin to generalise and predict other solutions. **Suggested questions:** • How did you find this solution? • Have you checked each rule against your answers? • If you were to do this again, would you try a different way?	**Communicating** **Problem solving**	180 181 182 183 184
Chocolate chunks	**Counting and understanding number** Recognise the equivalence between decimal and fraction forms of one half, quarters, tenths and hundredths	**Chocolate chunks** This activity can help children to begin to build up a picture of the relative sizes of tenths and hundredths, and how they can be written as fractions or decimals. **Suggested questions:** • Which chocolate shows the biggest decimal on this page? • Which chocolate shows the biggest fraction on this page? Why is that also the biggest decimal?	**Fractions and decimals**	185

Activity name	Strand and learning objectives	Notes on the activities	Assessment Focus	Page number
Fraction Man Twins	**Counting and understanding number** Use diagrams to identify equivalent fractions (e.g. $\frac{6}{8}$ and $\frac{3}{4}$, or $\frac{70}{100}$ and $\frac{7}{10}$); interpret mixed numbers and position them on a number line (e.g. $3\frac{1}{2}$)	**Fraction Man** This worksheet can be used to assess how well the children understand the role of the numerator and the denominator. It may be necessary to revise the number of centimetres in a metre, millimetres in a centimetre, grams in a kilogram and millilitres in a litre. The answer to question 11 could be $\frac{3}{4}$ or $\frac{7}{8}$ depending on whether the children know four points of a compass or all eight. **Suggested questions:** • How many days are there altogether? How many of them begin with the letter T? How is this written as a fraction? **Twins** Children often believe that equivalent fractions are only formed by doubling, for example they may understand that and are equivalent, but they may not understand that and are equivalent. This worksheet is designed to provide examples of equivalent fractions formed in ways other than doubling. **Suggested question:** • Look at the fractions in each pair. Do you notice anything about the numerators and the denominators?	**Fractions and decimals**	186 187
Spelling fractions	**Calculating** Find fractions of numbers, quantities or shapes (e.g. $\frac{1}{5}$ of 30 plums, $\frac{3}{8}$ of a 6 by 4 rectangle)	**Spelling fractions** Check that the children remember how to find fractions of numbers. Explain that some of the squares will not be coloured in each letter. **Suggested questions/prompt:** • How did you know that $\frac{2}{3}$ of 12 is 8? • Colour of the letter $\frac{1}{10}$ N yellow. How many squares will be yellow?	**Fractions and decimals** **Mental methods**	188

Block E Unit 2

Activity name	Strand and learning objectives	Notes on the activities	Assessment Focus	Page number
Café life Coin contest Tent teaser	**Using and applying mathematics** Represent a puzzle or problem using number sentences, statements or diagrams; use these to solve the problem; present and interpret the solution in the context of the problem	**Café life** *Processes: reason, explain, record* This worksheet provides the children with the opportunity to consider and identify which operations are necessary in solving each question. It may be necessary for more than one number sentence to be used. Watch out for incorrect number sentences that merge two together, for example where a child incorrectly writes 32 ÷ 4 = 8 x 3 = 24, rather than 32 ÷ 4 = 8, 8 x 3 = 24. Draw attention to the need to be careful when dealing with pounds and pence. **Suggested questions:** • How did you find the answer? • Which questions did you find the hardest? Why? • How did you write this as a number sentence or number sentences? **Coin contest** *Processes: make decisions, predict, test ideas, be systematic, reason, look for pattern* All numbers from 6p to 60p can be made with six coins, and all but 38p, 39p, 48p and 49p can be made with only four coins. Encourage the children to work systematically, for example by swapping a 1p for a 2p in each of these solutions, and to look for patterns in the coins used. **Suggested questions:** • How could you present or report your findings to others? • What is the clearest way of showing the results to others? **Tent teaser** *Processes: visualise, make decisions, reason, be systematic, test ideas* Remind the children that they do not necessarily need to work through the clues in order. **Suggested questions:** • How did you find this solution? • Have you checked each rule against your answers? • If you were to do this again, would you try a different way?	**Communicating** **Problem solving**	189 190 191
Calculator cards	**Counting and understanding number** Recognise the equivalence between decimal and fraction forms of one half, quarters, tenths and hundredths	**Calculator cards** At the start of the lesson demonstrate how, by dividing the numerator (the number on the top) by the denominator (the number on the bottom), the equivalent decimal can be found. **Suggested questions:** • What patterns do you notice? • Can you predict what the decimal for $\frac{13}{100}$ will be? • Can you predict what the decimal for $\frac{11}{20}$ will be?	**Fractions and decimals**	192
'Wordsworth' Fraction wall	**Counting and understanding number** Use diagrams to identify equivalent fractions (e.g. $\frac{6}{8}$ and $\frac{3}{4}$, or $\frac{70}{100}$ and $\frac{7}{10}$); interpret mixed numbers and position them on a number line (e.g. $3\frac{1}{2}$)	**'Wordsworth' and Fraction wall** Provide the children with copies of both sheets and discuss the fraction wall together as a class. Show the children how equivalent amounts can be found on the wall and invite them to say equivalent pairs in words. Point out that not all the answers on the worksheet can be found on the wall and ask the children to suggest other ways of finding these answers. **Suggested questions:** • How can you work out this answer? Can you see a pattern in the other answers? • Talk to a partner about what you notice.	**Fractions and decimals**	193 194
Part and parcel	**Knowing and using number facts** Identify pairs of fractions that total 1	**Part and parcel** Before copying this page for higher-attaining children, you could delete the lines to the blank parcels. **Suggested questions:** • How do you know that $\frac{9}{20}$ and $\frac{11}{20}$ total 1? • How did you work out the fractions that should be on the blank parcels?	**Fractions and decimals** **Mental methods**	195

Activity name	Strand and learning objectives	Notes on the activities	Assessment Focus	Page number
Loads-a-money!	**Calculating** Find fractions of numbers, quantities or shapes (e.g. $\frac{1}{5}$ of 30 plums, $\frac{3}{8}$ of a 6 by 4 rectangle)	**Loads-a-money!** Children who find this activity difficult could exchange the coins of greater value for 1p coins, for example thirty-two 1p coins for 32p, and use grouping or sharing to find the unit fraction. When finding fractions that are not unit fractions, they could then use the numerator of the fraction to find the number of groups that they need and count, add or multiply to work out the required amount of money. SUGGESTED PROMPT/QUESTIONS: • Explain to me how you worked out the fractions of these numbers. • Did you divide first? By which number? Why?	**Fractions and decimals** **Mental methods**	196

Block E Unit 3

Activity name	Strand and learning objectives	Notes on the activities	Assessment Focus	Page number
Billy the baker's cakes Sour grapes Sheep and goats	**Using and applying mathematics** Represent a puzzle or problem using number sentences, statements or diagrams; use these to solve the problem; present and interpret the solution in the context of the problem	**Billy the Baker's cakes** *Processes: trial and improvement, test ideas, record, explain, reason* Encourage the children to notice patterns in the numbers, for example to realise that three rows of five will have the same number of buns as five rows of three. SUGGESTED QUESTIONS: • What patterns did you use to help you? • What patterns did you notice? • How do you know you have found all the solutions? **Sour grapes** *Processes: be systematic, generalise, compare, record, look for pattern, reason, predict, test ideas* Remind the children that they can check their solutions by ensuring the totals of each addition add to make the number of grapes. The children could compare solutions and collectively write a class list. Discuss strategies that the children used to help them find the solutions, for example: 'For six grapes I used the answers to five grapes and wrote out the 15 five-grape solutions with '1 +' in front of them. SUGGESTED QUESTIONS/PROMPT: • Could you do the same grapes but in a different order? • Do you notice any patterns? Explain them to us. • What strategies did you use? • What if there were seven or eight grapes? **Sheep and goats** *Processes: visualise, make decisions, reason, be systematic, test ideas* Encourage the children to use words or pictures to explain why each statement is true or false. SUGGESTED QUESTIONS/PROMPT: • Can you show me how you know whether this statement is true or false? • Look at Sam's explanation. Can you see how he worked this one out?	**Communicating** **Problem solving**	197 198 199
Connections World tour	**Knowing and using number facts** Derive and recall multiplication facts up to 10 × 10, the corresponding division facts and multiples of numbers to 10 up to the tenth multiple	**Connections** Write 12 on the board and ask what numbers are factors of 12, for example '12 is a multiple of 3', '12 is a multiple of 4'. SUGGESTED QUESTIONS: • Which times-tables have the answer 36? So 36 is a multiple of which numbers? **World tour** This activity encourages the children to quickly determine which numbers a number is a multiple of, for example recalling that 72 is a multiple of 8 and of 9. Display the multiplication tables to 10 × 10 on the classroom wall for the children to refer to. Each pair will require a dice, a counter and one activity sheet. SUGGESTED QUESTION: • Which other number could you have crossed off?	**Mental methods**	200 201
Life's a lottery	**Calculating** Develop and use written methods to record, support and explain multiplication and division of two-digit numbers by a one-digit number, including division with remainders (e.g. 15 × 9, 98 ÷ 6)	**Life's a lottery** This activity encourages the children to begin to appreciate the nature of remainders and to recall quickly which numbers are multiples of others. SUGGESTED QUESTIONS: • What multiplication fact helped you to work out the answer? • How could you check your answers?	**Written methods**	202
Odd one out	**Counting and understanding number** Recognise the equivalence between decimal and fraction forms of one half, quarters, tenths and hundredths	**Odd one out** Before cutting out the cards the children identify the odd one out in each row. To check their answers they could use a calculator to divide the numerator of the fraction by the denominator to find out its decimal equivalent. Once completed, the children can cut out the cards and play a 'pairs' game with a partner. SUGGESTED QUESTIONS: • What fractions are equivalent to 0.4? • Can you think of any other equivalent fractions?	**Fractions and decimals**	203
Cats' chorus Mixed up	**Counting and understanding number** Use diagrams to identify equivalent fractions (e.g. $\frac{6}{8}$ and $\frac{3}{4}$, or $\frac{70}{100}$ and $\frac{7}{10}$); interpret mixed numbers and position them on a number line (e.g. $3\frac{1}{2}$)	**Cats' chorus** This activity provides practice in building sequences of mixed numbers. It can help children to realise that there are numbers between the whole numbers on a number line, and that these are mixed numbers. SUGGESTED PROMPT: • Count on from 7 in steps of one third/one quarter/one half. **Mixed up** As a further extension, invite the children to make their own mixed-number number lines to be displayed on the classroom wall. Some children's lines could go up in thirds, others in fifths, etc. to create a range of different number lines. SUGGESTED QUESTION: • Which number comes exactly halfway between $3\frac{1}{2}$ and 4?	**Fractions and decimals**	204 205

Activity name	Strand and learning objectives	Notes on the activities	Assessment Focus	Page number
A spoonful of medicine Drink up!	**Calculating** Find fractions of numbers, quantities or shapes (e.g. $\frac{1}{5}$ of 30 plums, $\frac{3}{8}$ of a 6 by 4 rectangle)	**A spoonful of medicine** At the start of the lesson, ask the children a variety of times-table facts out of order, for example 6 × 4 = ?, 48 ÷ 8 = ? Check the children understand that to find a fraction of a number, they can divide to find a unit fraction and then multiply to find the number of parts specified. **SUGGESTED PROMPT/QUESTIONS:** • Explain to me how you worked out the fractions of these numbers. • Did you divide first? By which number? Why? **Drink up!** Ask the children to explain how they find fractions of two-digit numbers. Then ask them to discuss with a partner how they would find fractions of the three-digit numbers. Will they use similar methods or different methods? **SUGGESTED PROMPT/QUESTIONS:** • Explain to me how you worked out the fractions of these numbers. • Did you divide first? By which number? Why?	**Fractions and decimals** **Mental methods**	206 207
Nuts and raisins Pencil sharpeners Boxes of chocolates Puppy love Egghead Hungry Henry	**Counting and understanding number** Use the vocabulary of ratio and proportion to describe the relationship between two quantities (e.g. 'There are 2 red beads to every 3 blue beads, or 2 beads in every 5 beads are red'); estimate a proportion (e.g. 'About one quarter of the apples in the box are green')	**Nuts and raisins** This activity can help children to begin to appreciate the meaning of the term 'for every' and its multiplicative nature, for example that '2 for every 3' can be represented by 6 and 9 items or by 8 and 12 items etc. Begin by introducing the vocabulary 'for every', for example 'there are 2 nuts for every 3 raisins'. **SUGGESTED QUESTIONS:** • How many nuts are there? • Are there more nuts or more raisins? • In a bag there are 20 nuts and 30 raisins. Are there 2 nuts for every 3 raisins? How do you know? **Pencil sharpeners** In this activity, the children use 'for every' information to colour pencil sharpeners in correct ratios. It will be useful for assessing who has or has not understood the concept. **SUGGESTED QUESTIONS:** • How many blue/red sharpeners are there? • What patterns do you notice in the numbers you have written when you look at the statements? **Boxes of chocolates** When creating more puzzles of their own in the extension activity, explain to the children that the totals of the numbers in the ratio must divide exactly into the total number of chocolates in the box, for example 4:1 (total 5) must divide exactly into the number of chocolates in each box (15, 20 or 25, etc.) **SUGGESTED QUESTIONS:** • How did you work out how many milk chocolates there will be in that box? • Do you think that there will be more milk chocolates in the '2 milk for every 3 dark' box or in the '4 milk for every 1 dark' box? **Puppy love** This worksheet involves both ratio and proportion and encourages the children to begin to understand the difference. At the start of the lesson, ask 3 boys and 2 girls to come to the front of the class. Explain that we can say 'There are 3 boys for every (or to every) 2 girls' (ratio); '3 out of the 5 children are boys' (proportion). **SUGGESTED QUESTIONS:** • Show me how you worked out that 1 out of 4 puppies are black. • Draw me a picture that shows 3 out of 4 puppies are black. How did you know what to draw? **Egghead** Some children may begin to appreciate that Nest A can be described more simply as '1 brown for every 1 white', rather than '4 brown for every 4 white', thus demonstrating some understanding that ratios can be written in a simplest form. **SUGGESTED QUESTION:** • How many white eggs are there for every 2 brown eggs? **Hungry Henry** As the children's answers are estimates they will vary considerably. **SUGGESTED QUESTION:** • Can the fraction of this shape be described in more than one way?	**Fractions, decimals, ratio and proportion**	208 209 210 211 212 213

Number puzzles

Each grid shows part of a number square.
Some numbers are shaded to form a sequence.

- **Write the rule for each sequence.**

1

95	96	97	98
105	106	107	108
115	116	117	118
125	126	127	128

____

2

56	57	58	59
66	67	68	69
76	77	78	79
86	87	88	89

____

3

102	103	104	105
112	113	114	115
122	123	124	125
132	133	134	135

____

4

84	85	86	87	88	89
94	95	96	97	98	99
104	105	106	107	108	109
114	115	116	117	118	119

____

5

171	172	173	174	175	176
181	182	183	184	185	186
191	192	193	194	195	196

____

6

134	135	136	137
144	145	146	147
154	155	156	157
164	165	166	167

____

Teachers' note Explain how rules for sequences can be written, for example 'adding 10' or 'counting on in tens'. Encourage the children to discuss each sequence with a partner and to look at the different ways of describing each rule. As an extension, ask the children to make up their own number grid puzzle for a partner to solve.

Full stretch

This number is being expanded.

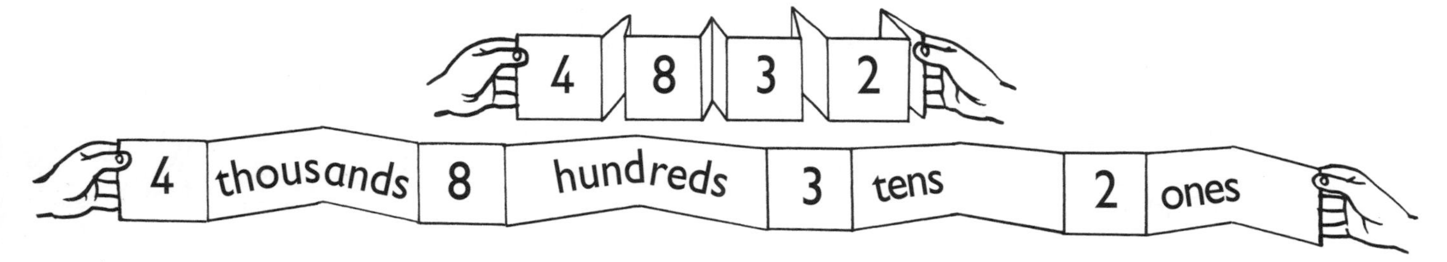

- **Fill in the missing numbers.**

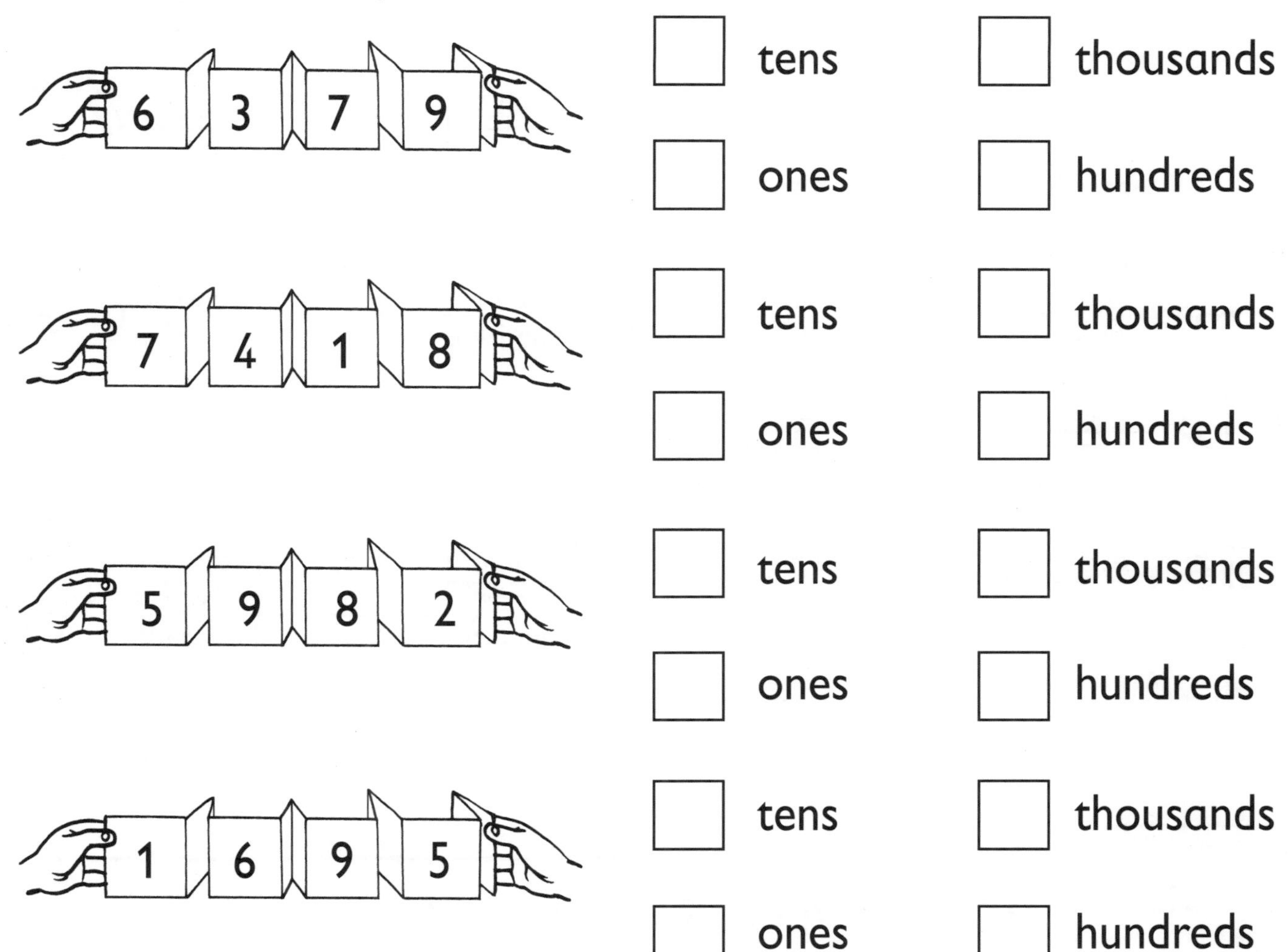

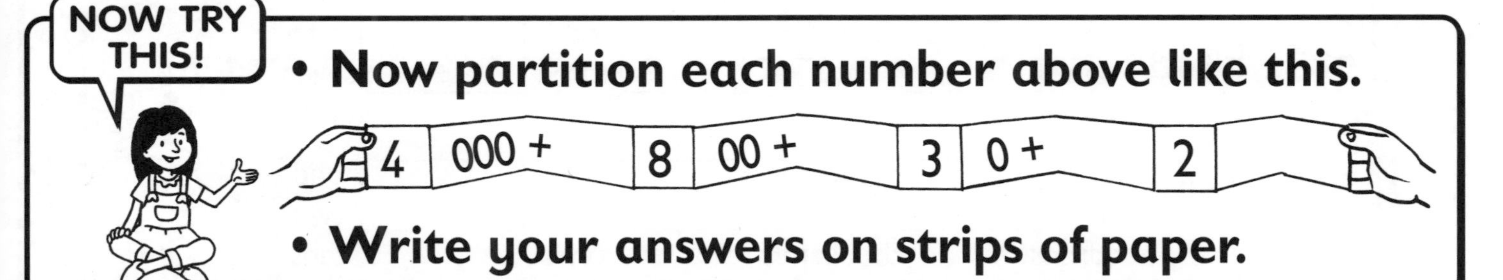

- **Now partition each number above like this.**
- **Write your answers on strips of paper.**

Teachers' note Children who find it difficult to split numbers could 'make' the numbers from place value materials or cards so that they can see how the numbers are formed.

Metamorphosis

- **Change one digit each time to get from the number at the start to the number at the end.**

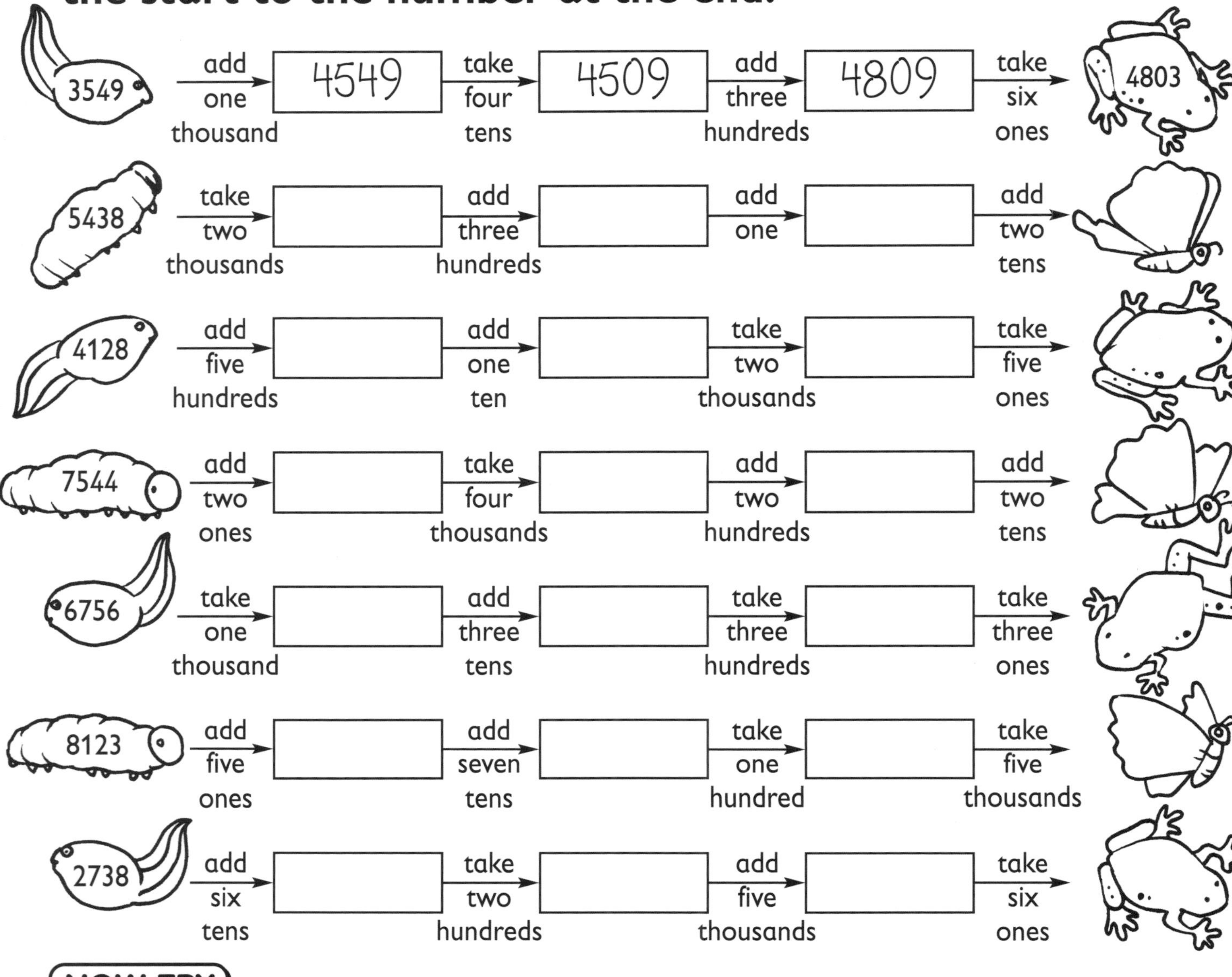

NOW TRY THIS!

- **Try changing these numbers. For some, more than one digit might need to be changed.**

9148 → take one thousand → ☐ → add four ones → ☐ → add three tens → ☐ → add seven hundreds →

3698 → add five hundreds → ☐ → add five thousands → ☐ → take six ones → ☐ → add two tens →

Teachers' note For the extension activity, the addition of ones, for example, results in more than nine ones and thus the tens digit will need to be increased by one. If pupils experience difficulty with this it indicates that their understanding of place value is not fully developed. Show how when there are more than nine in a column this results in the column to the left going up one.

Partition penguins

- **Play this game with a partner.**

☆ You will each need a copy of this sheet.

☆ Take turns to pick two numbers from the iceberg to find the total. Record the question and answer and partition your answer into multiples of 1000, 100, 10 and 1.

☆ Colour the penguins showing each part of the partition.

☆ The winner is the first player to colour all of the penguins.

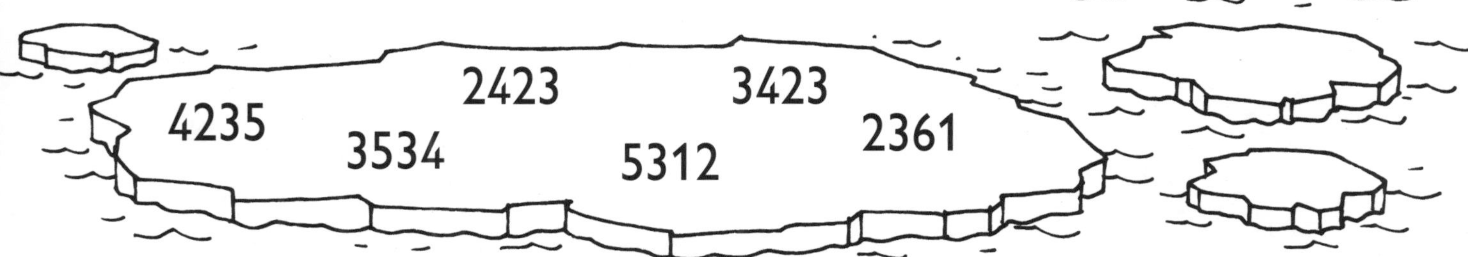

Record your answers here or on the back of this sheet.

3423 + 2423 = 5846 5846 = 5000 + 800 + 40 + 6

Teachers' note Children will need a coloured pencil for this activity. At the start of the lesson practise adding four-digit numbers using partitioning methods, for example when adding 3423 to 2423, start with 3423, add 2000, then 400, then 20 and then 3 changing each digit at a time. Note that none of these additions cross a multiple of 1000, 100 or 10 boundary.

Rounding puzzle

- **Play this game with a partner.**

☆ Your teacher will tell you how to make this puzzle and use it to practise rounding.

☆ Cut along the dotted line.

☆ As you use the puzzle, cross off the answers.

☆ When you have crossed off four in a row, lift the flap to find out how well you have done.

3300	1990	2500	4400
3380	7700	1710	7470
4350	3900	5250	4390

Round 3263 to the nearest 100 (move 3)

Round 1994 to the nearest 10 (move 2)

COOL!

Brain-box!

Round 4385 to the nearest 10 (move 7)

Round 4381 to the nearest 100 (move 4)

Round 3384 to the nearest 10 (move 5)

What a star!

Round 7695 to the nearest 10 (move 6)

GENIUS!

You're amazing!

Round 1707 to the nearest 10 (move 3)

You've got style!

Round 5253 to the nearest 10 (move 2)

Round 3919 to the nearest 100 (move 5)

Round 4354 to the nearest 10 (move 4)

Top of the class!

Whizz kid!

Round 7465 to the nearest 10 (move 5)

Round 2450 to the nearest 100 (move 6)

Teachers' note The children may already be familiar with this playground puzzle. Here the puzzle encourages them to practise rounding four-digit numbers to the nearest 10/100. See the notes on page 6 for information about how to introduce this activity and to extend it further.

Hotel lift

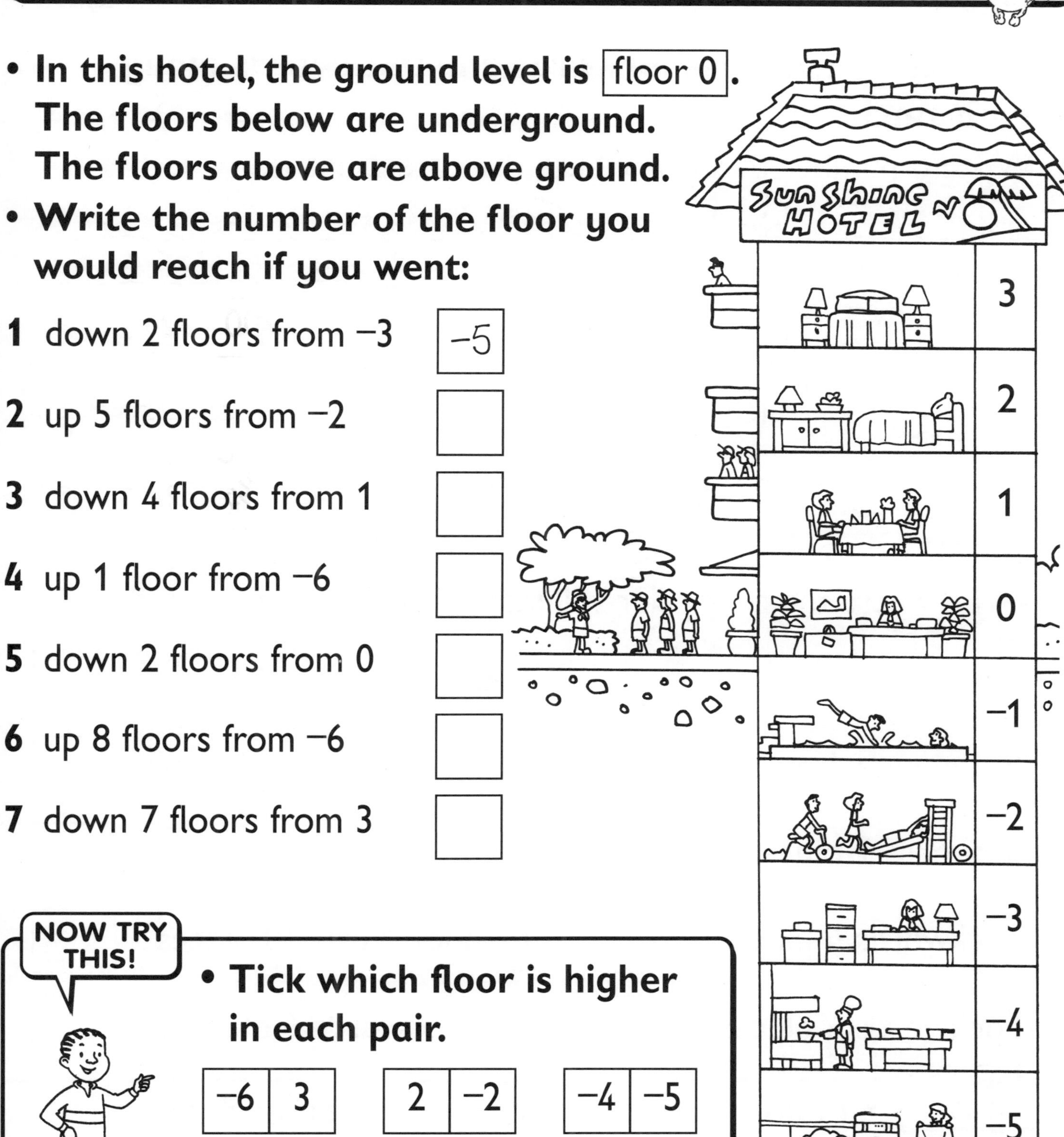

- **In this hotel, the ground level is floor 0. The floors below are underground. The floors above are above ground.**
- **Write the number of the floor you would reach if you went:**

1	down 2 floors from −3	−5
2	up 5 floors from −2	
3	down 4 floors from 1	
4	up 1 floor from −6	
5	down 2 floors from 0	
6	up 8 floors from −6	
7	down 7 floors from 3	

NOW TRY THIS!

- **Tick which floor is higher in each pair.**

−6	3	2	−2	−4	−5
−1	−3	−5	1	−4	3
−5	−6	2	−1	0	−6

Teachers' note Ensure the children realise that ground level is floor zero and that everything below this is described using negative numbers. As an extra challenge, children could write their answers to the extension activity using the 'greater than' (>) and 'less than' (<) symbols.

Caterpillar crawl

- **The caterpillar goes forwards and backwards along the branch.**

1 Write a number to show where the caterpillar is.

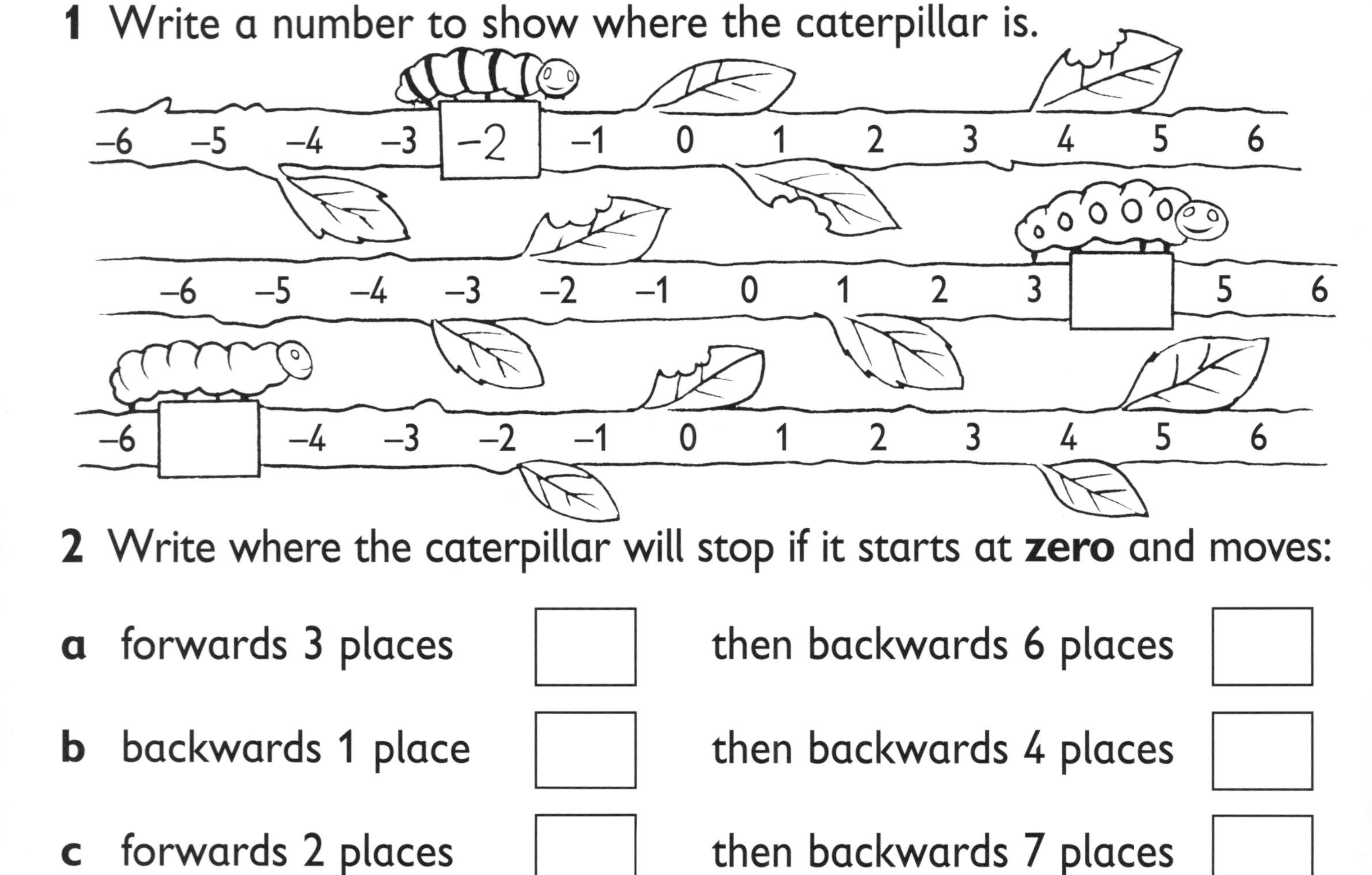

2 Write where the caterpillar will stop if it starts at **zero** and moves:

a	forwards 3 places	☐	then backwards 6 places	☐
b	backwards 1 place	☐	then backwards 4 places	☐
c	forwards 2 places	☐	then backwards 7 places	☐
d	backwards 6 places	☐	then forwards 10 places	☐
e	backwards 4 places	☐	then forwards 6 places	☐

NOW TRY THIS!

- **Follow this trail. Where do you end up?**

Start at zero, go backwards 3, then forwards 8, then backwards 2, then forwards 1, then backwards 4.

- **Make up some more trails like this for your partner to solve.**

Teachers' note If the children find these activities difficult, they could draw out their own number line from -6 to 6 and use an object to represent the caterpillar, physically moving it forwards and backwards along the line.

Signs of a thaw

The temperature of each snowman is shown.

1 Write them in order, coldest to warmest.

_____°C _____°C _____°C _____°C _____°C _____°C _____°C

2 Write the > or < sign between each pair.

- **Choose six whole numbers smaller than 3.**
- **Now write them in order, smallest first.**

_____ _____ _____ _____ _____ _____

Teachers' note Provide the children with a number line that includes negative numbers between −15 and 15. Ensure they understand the 'greater than' (>) and 'less than' (<) signs and that they appreciate that whilst 5 is greater than 4, −5 is less than −4.

Difference walls

- **Colour touching pairs with the difference shown. Number pairs can touch vertically or horizontally but not diagonally. Each wall will show a letter that spells a word.**

1. Difference of 20

120	90	110
100	30	80
160	90	150
140	20	180
170	150	130

2. Difference of 30

180	260	390
210	190	360
240	120	330
400	280	320
370	340	290

You need different-coloured pencils.

3. Difference of 40

880	920	720
530	590	670
490	450	630
360	720	590
400	440	240

4. Difference of 50

280	330	540
420	290	490
370	410	510
440	500	460
390	650	600

5. Difference of 60

440	520	590
400	510	530
330	590	470
570	640	620
500	550	560

6. Difference of 70

540	470	500
330	500	340
260	320	410
190	380	480
650	580	420

- **What word do the letters spell?** ________

NOW TRY THIS!

- **Draw your own wall on squared paper.**
- **Colour it to show a different letter of the alphabet. Then write numbers into the coloured squares that have a difference of 80.**

Teachers' note Ensure the children check all sets of adjacent numbers as a number may match with two numbers, for example for difference of 20, 150 matches with 170 and 130. The children should colour in the touching pairs in different colours. That way it will be obvious which adjacent numbers do not have the difference given.

Spot the dice

In a game, each spot on a dice is worth 8 points.

- **Write how many points are scored for each pair of dice.**

1. 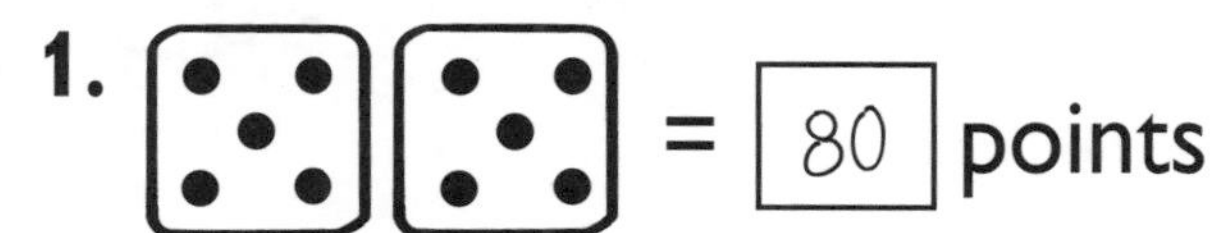 = 80 points
2. = ___ points
3. = ___ points
4. = ___ points
5. = ___ points
6. = ___ points
7. = ___ points
8. = ___ points
9. = ___ points
10. = ___ points
11. = ___ points
12. = ___ points

NOW TRY THIS!

- **Play the game with a partner.**

☆ Take turns to roll two dice. Score 8 points for each spot.

☆ Roll four times each. Record your points here.

Player 1

Total = ______

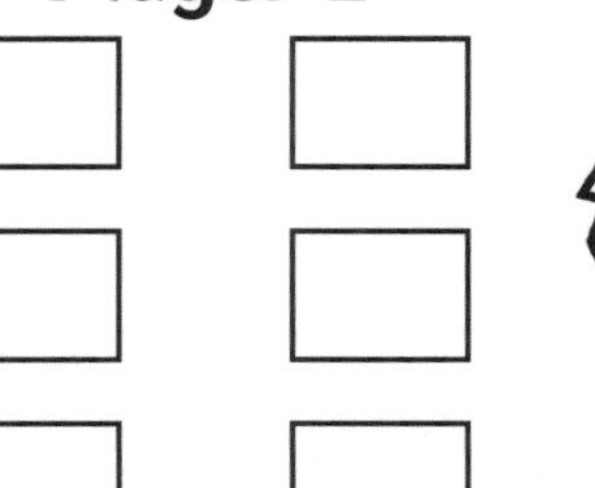

Player 2

Total = ______

Teachers' note This sheet can be used to practise other tables facts than the 8 times-table. Change the number 8 to any number to 10 before copying. (Also change the answer to question 1.) For the extension activity, the children could be given a calculator to check their total. The player with the most points is the winner.

Fingers of fun

☆ Hold your palms towards you. For **3** × 9 hold down your **third** finger from the left.

☆ **The fingers to the left of the bent finger are each worth 10.**

☆ **The fingers to the right of the bent finger are each worth 1.**

☆ For **4** × 9 or 9 × **4** hold down your **fourth** finger and so on.
It works for all the 9 times-table!

- **Cut out the cards. Write the answers on the back of each card and test yourself to see how quickly you can learn the facts.**

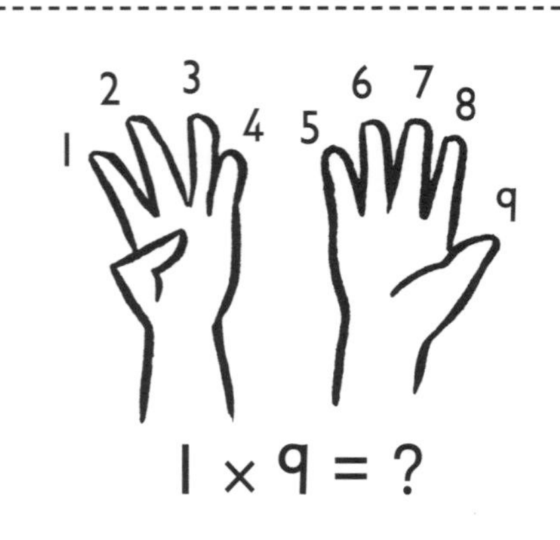

1 × 9 = ?

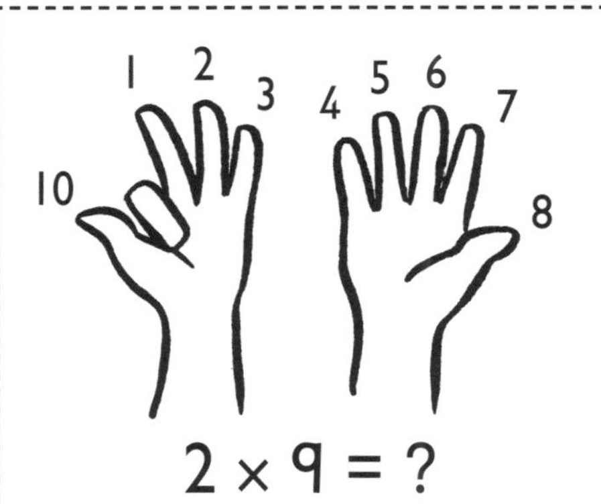

2 × 9 = ?

3 × 9 = ?

4 × 9 = ?

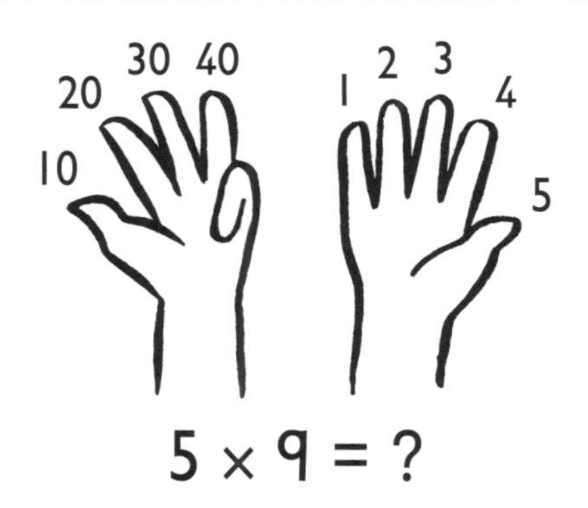

5 × 9 = ?

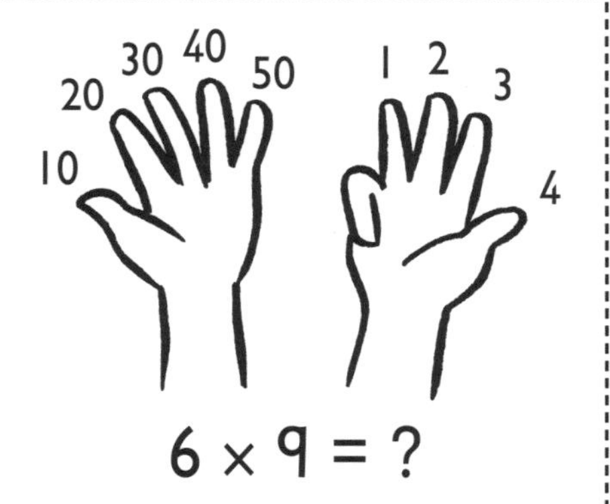

6 × 9 = ?

7 × 9 = ?

8 × 9 = ?

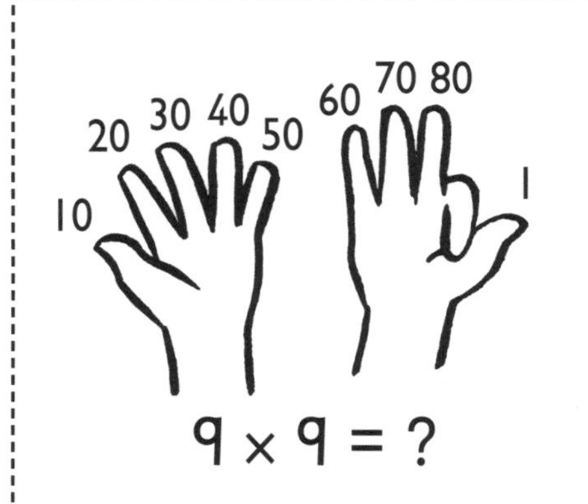

9 × 9 = ?

Teachers' note Show the children how to hold their hands to make each of the facts and include 10 × 9 = 90, which works by holding down the 10th finger (i.e. the right-hand thumb) leaving 9 fingers held up to the left of it, making 90.

Under the microscope

When this super microscope is set to $\times 10$, each length appears 10 times longer.

- Write how long each bug appears if its original length is:

1. 5 mm

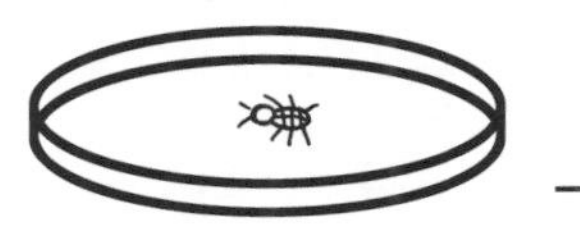

______ mm

2. 7 mm

______ mm

3. 11 mm

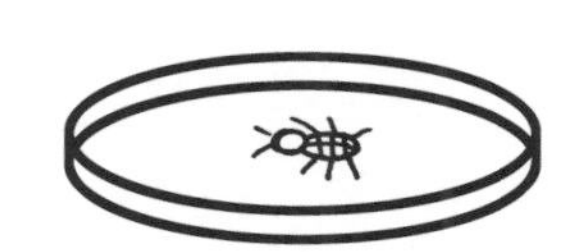

______ mm

4. 14 mm

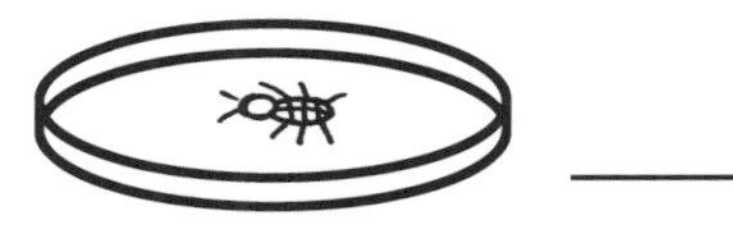

______ mm

5. 19 mm

______ mm

6. 23 mm

______ mm

7. 27 mm

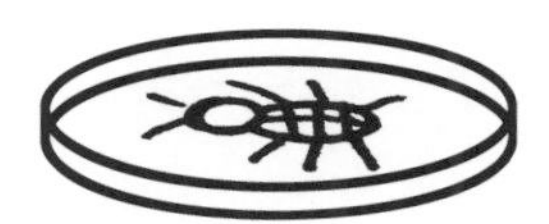

______ mm

8. 31 mm

______ mm

NOW TRY THIS!

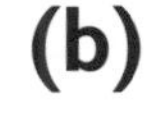

- When this super-duper microscope is set to $\times 100$, each length appears 100 times longer.
- Write how long each bug appears if its original length is:

(a) 6 mm

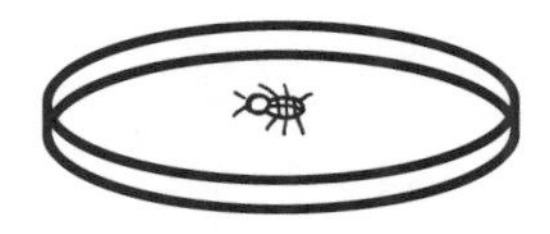

______ mm

(b) 10 mm

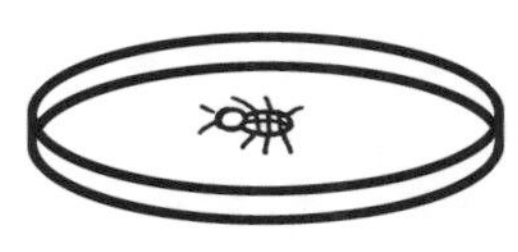

______ mm

(c) 14 mm

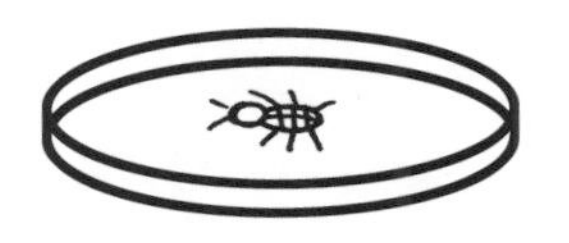

______ mm

(d) 17 mm

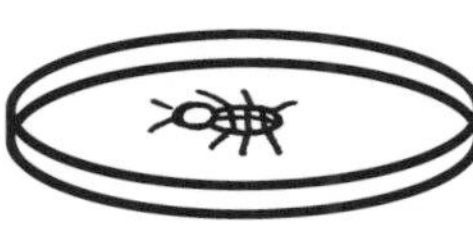

______ mm

Teachers' note Encourage the children to appreciate the movement of the digits rather than focusing on 'putting a zero on the end', as this will cause them difficulties when multiplying decimals in the future, for example $3.5 \times 10 = 35$, not 3.50.

Double or halve

- **Use this sheet to help you double or halve two-digit numbers.**

1.

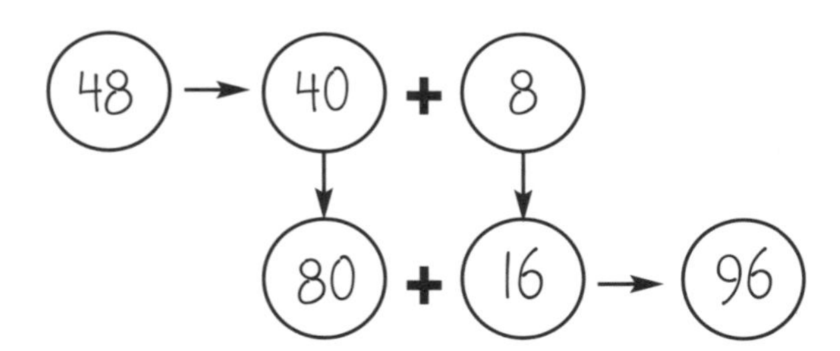

2.

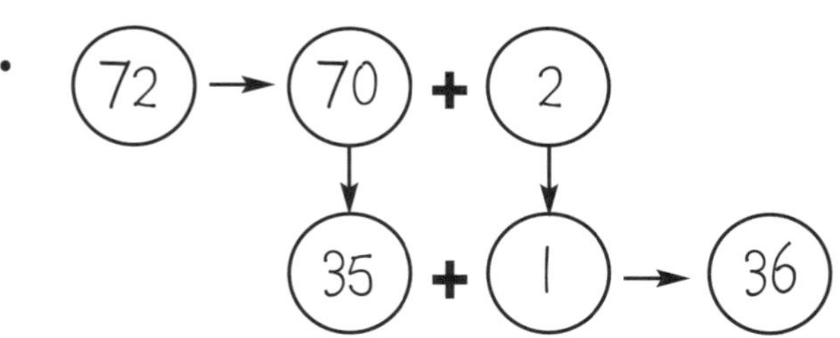

3.

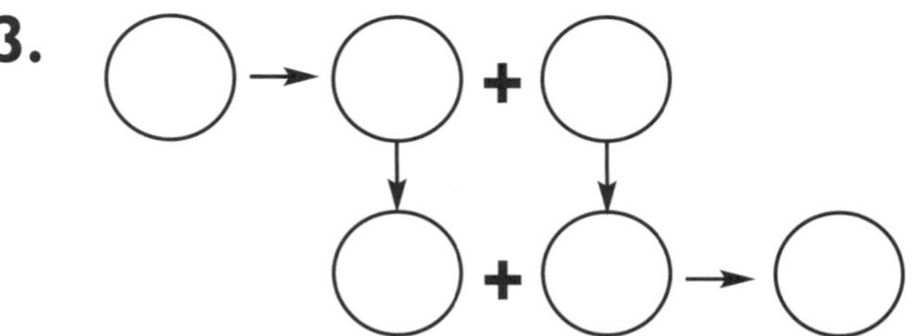

4.

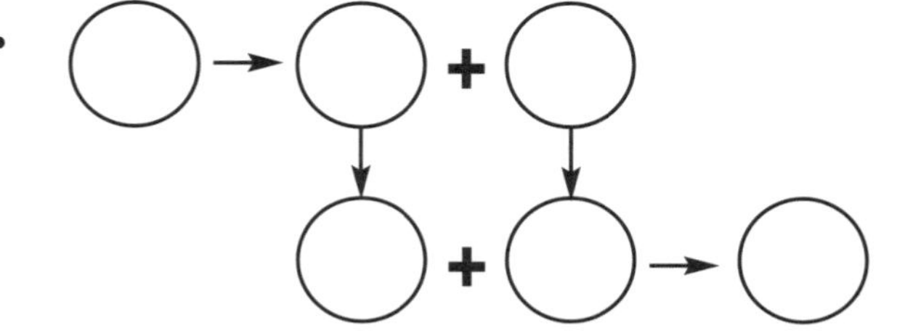

5.

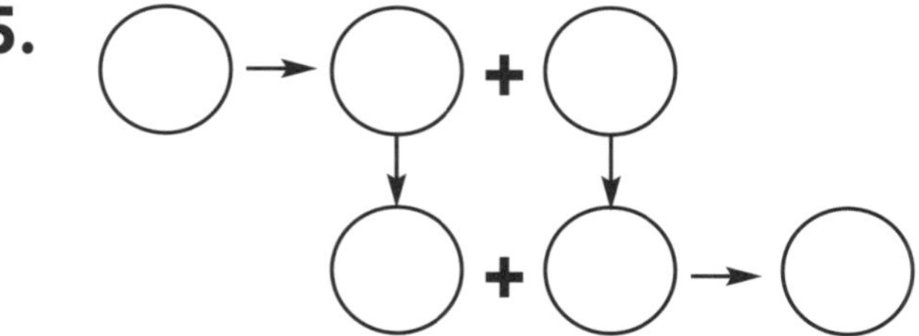

6.

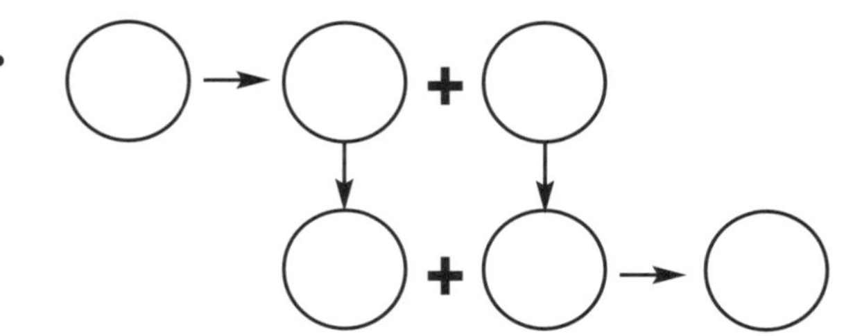

7.

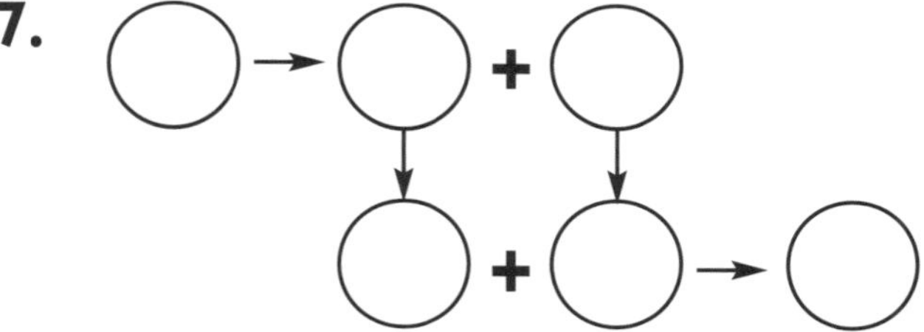

8.

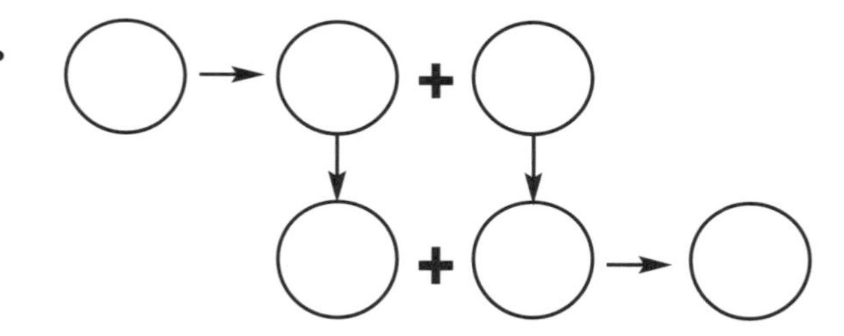

9.

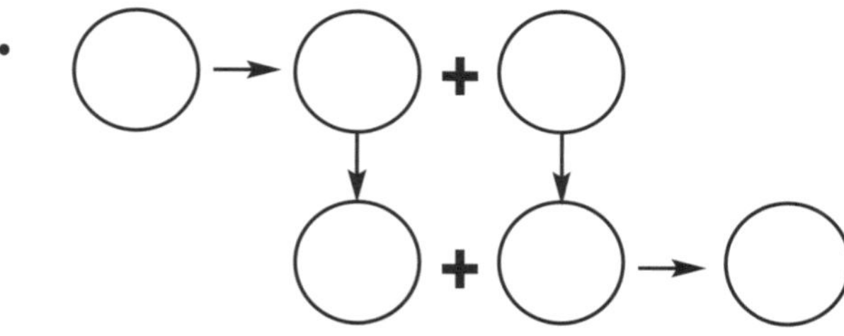

10.

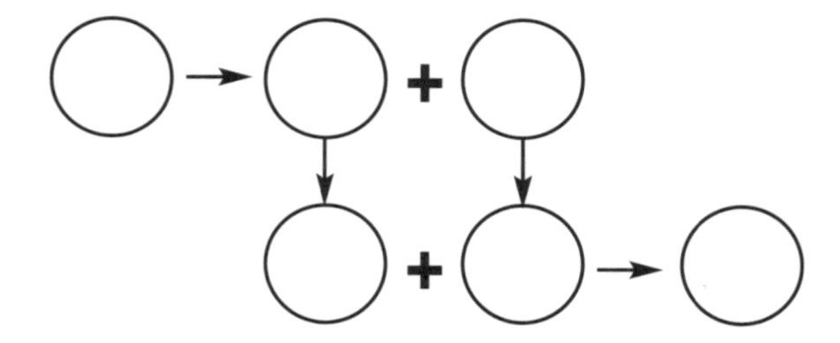

11.

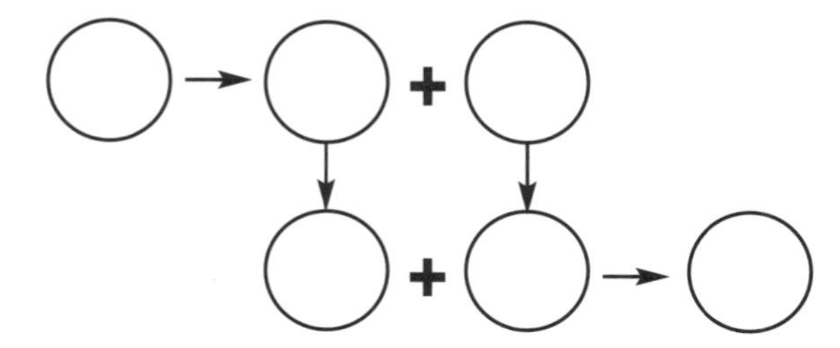

12.

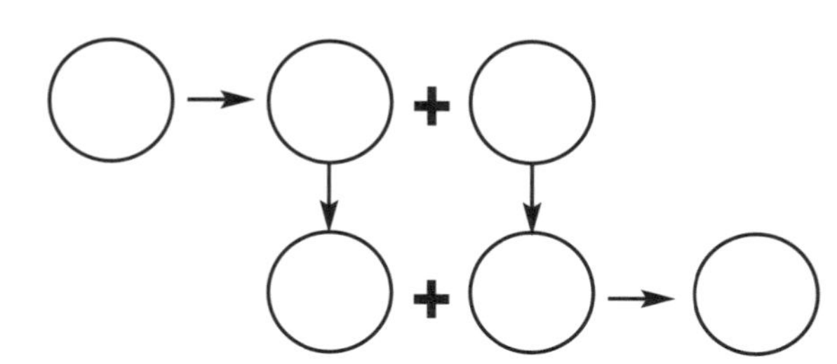

Teachers' note This sheet can be used to introduce the children to partitioning before doubling and halving each part separately. It can be given to children in conjunction with any of the following doubling or halving sheets.

Calculator calamities: 1

These children have been making mistakes on the calculator.

- **Help them to correct their mistakes.**

1 Freya wanted to add 472 and 386.
She entered 172 + 386 by mistake.
Tick to show what she should press next to correct the mistake in one go.

- **+ 3** ☐
- **– 300** ☐
- **+ 300** ☐
- **– 386** ☐

2 Ben wanted to subtract 185 from 468.
He entered 468 – 85 by mistake.
Tick to show what he should press next to correct the mistake in one go.

- **+ 100** ☐
- **– 1** ☐
- **+ 185** ☐
- **– 100** ☐

3 Chloe wanted to add 489 to 392.
She entered 392 + 469 by mistake.
Tick to show what she should press next to correct the mistake in one go

- **+ 20** ☐
- **– 200** ☐
- **+ 2** ☐
- **– 20** ☐

4 Anoop wanted to take 384 from 927.
He entered 727 – 384 by mistake.
Tick to show what he should press next to correct the mistake in one go.

- **+ 2** ☐
- **– 200** ☐
- **+ 200** ☐
- **– 2** ☐

NOW TRY THIS!

- **Try this multiplication mistake.**

Daisy wanted to multiply 567 by 14.
She entered 567 × 13 by mistake.
Tick to show what she should press next to correct the mistake in one go.

- **× 1** ☐
- **+ 1** ☐
- **+ 567** ☐
- **× 567** ☐

Teachers' note Use in conjunction with 'Calculator calamities: 2', which can be used as further extension work and includes multiplication and division calculator mistakes to be undone. The numbers on this worksheet can be altered to provide differentiation.

Calculator calamities: 2

These children have been making mistakes on the calculator.

- **Help them to correct their mistakes.**

1 Sam wanted to multiply 12 by 34.
He entered 12 × 33 by mistake.

Tick to show what he should press next to correct the mistake in one go.

+ 1 ☐
× 1 ☐
+ 33 ☐
+ 12 ☐

2 Meena wanted to subtract 245 from 449.
She entered 449 – 205 by mistake.

Tick to show what she should press next to correct the mistake in one go.

+ 4 ☐
– 40 ☐
+ 40 ☐
– 205 ☐

3 Dan wanted to multiply 378 by 17.
He entered 378 × 18 by mistake.

Tick to show what he should press next to correct the mistake in one go.

+ 378 ☐
+ 1 ☐
– 378 ☐
– 1 ☐

4 Kimberley wanted to divide 368 by 4.
She entered 368 ÷ 2 by mistake.

Tick to show what she should press next to correct the mistake in one go.

× 2 ☐
+ 2 ☐
÷ 2 ☐
– 2 ☐

- **Try this division mistake.**

David wanted to divide 252 by 3.
He entered 252 ÷ 6 by mistake.

Tick to show what he should press next to correct the mistake in one go.

÷ 2 ☐
× 2 ☐
÷ 3 ☐
× 3 ☐

Teachers' note Use in conjunction with 'Calculator calamities: 1', which can be used as an introductory worksheet. The numbers on this worksheet can be altered to provide differentiation.

3 for 2!

- **For each question, tick to show which is the better offer and work out how much you would save.**

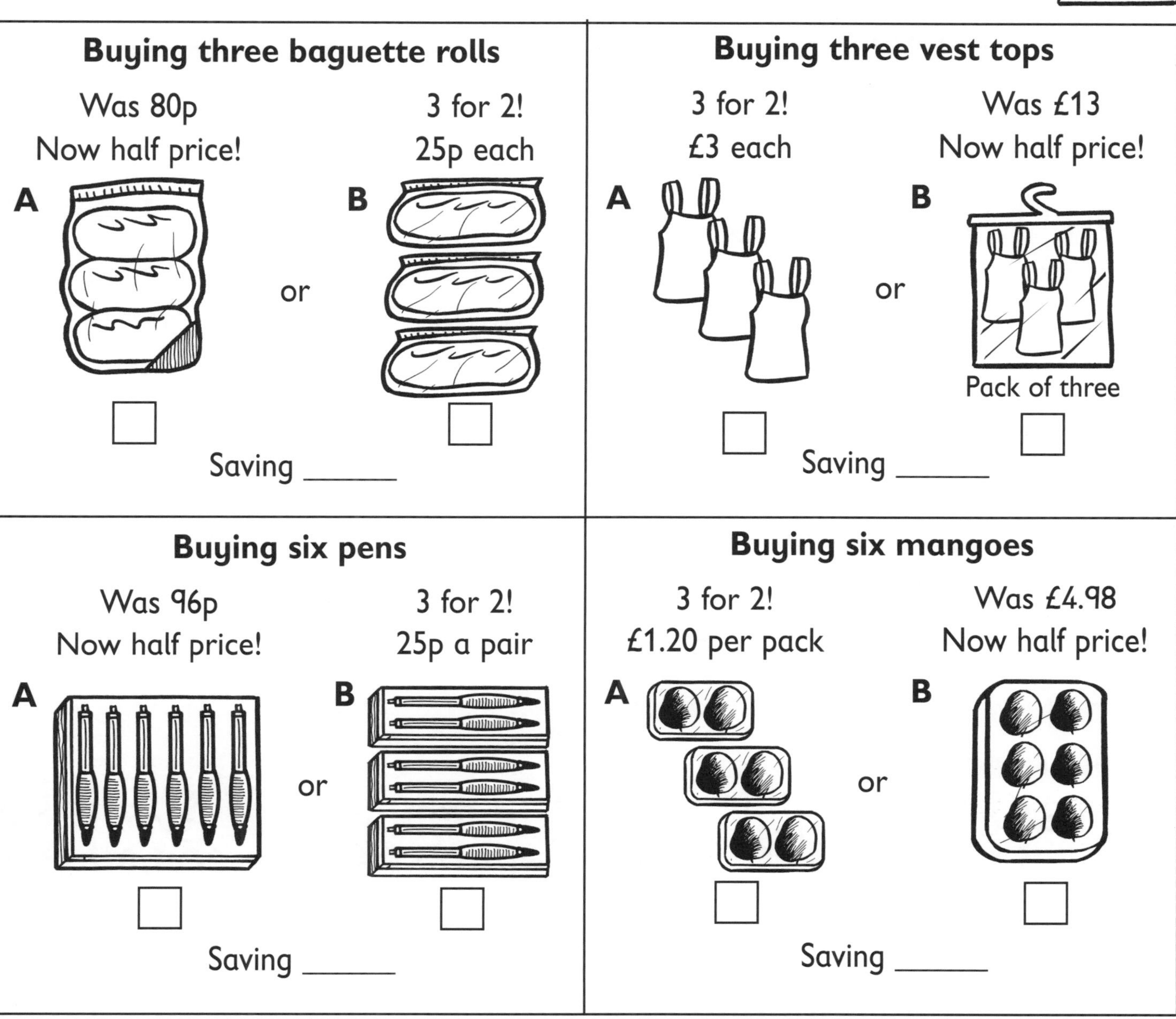

Buying three baguette rolls

A: Was 80p Now half price!
or
B: 3 for 2! 25p each

Saving ______

Buying three vest tops

A: 3 for 2! £3 each
or
B: Was £13 Now half price! Pack of three

Saving ______

Buying six pens

A: Was 96p Now half price!
or
B: 3 for 2! 25p a pair

Saving ______

Buying six mangoes

A: 3 for 2! £1.20 per pack
or
B: Was £4.98 Now half price!

Saving ______

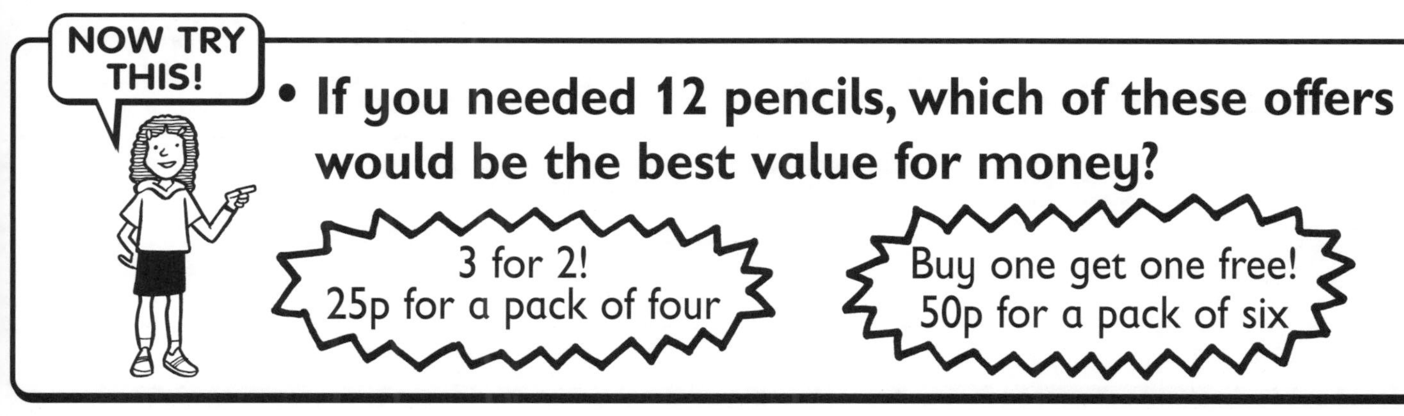

- **If you needed 12 pencils, which of these offers would be the best value for money?**

3 for 2!
25p for a pack of four

Buy one get one free!
50p for a pack of six

Teachers' note Before beginning the activity, ensure that the children understand what is meant by the offer '3 for 2'. Encourage the children to discuss each offer with a partner and to make judgements about which offer is the best value for money.

Animal walkabout

- **Count on or back to write the first six terms of each sequence. Write on the animals.**

1 Count on in fours.

2 Count back in threes.

3 Count on in sixes.

4 Count on in nines.

5 Count back in eights.

6 Count on in sevens.

NOW TRY THIS!

- **Count back in fours from 101.**

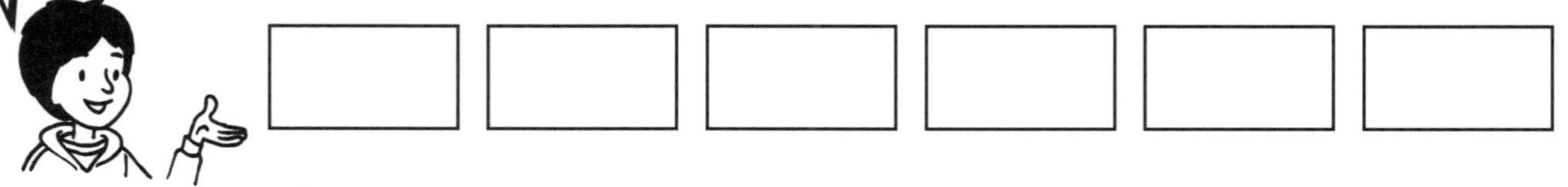

Teachers' note The start numbers can be altered before copying to create differentiation. It may be more suitable for some children to work with three-digit or even two-digit numbers for this activity. For a more advanced sheet, negative start numbers could also be introduced.

Decimal snap!

- **Play this game with a partner.**

You need a pack of playing cards with the Jokers, Jacks, Queens and Kings removed...

...and a copy of this worksheet each.

☆ Share out the cards.

☆ Together say 'turn' and each put three cards on your sheet.

☆ Shout 'snap!' if your decimal has the same number of ones, tenths or hundredths as your partner's.

☆ The first to shout 'snap!' and say correctly which digits are the same wins all the cards.

☆ Record both decimals on your sheets.

☆ The winner is the player with all the cards, or with the most cards when 15 decimal pairs have been recorded.

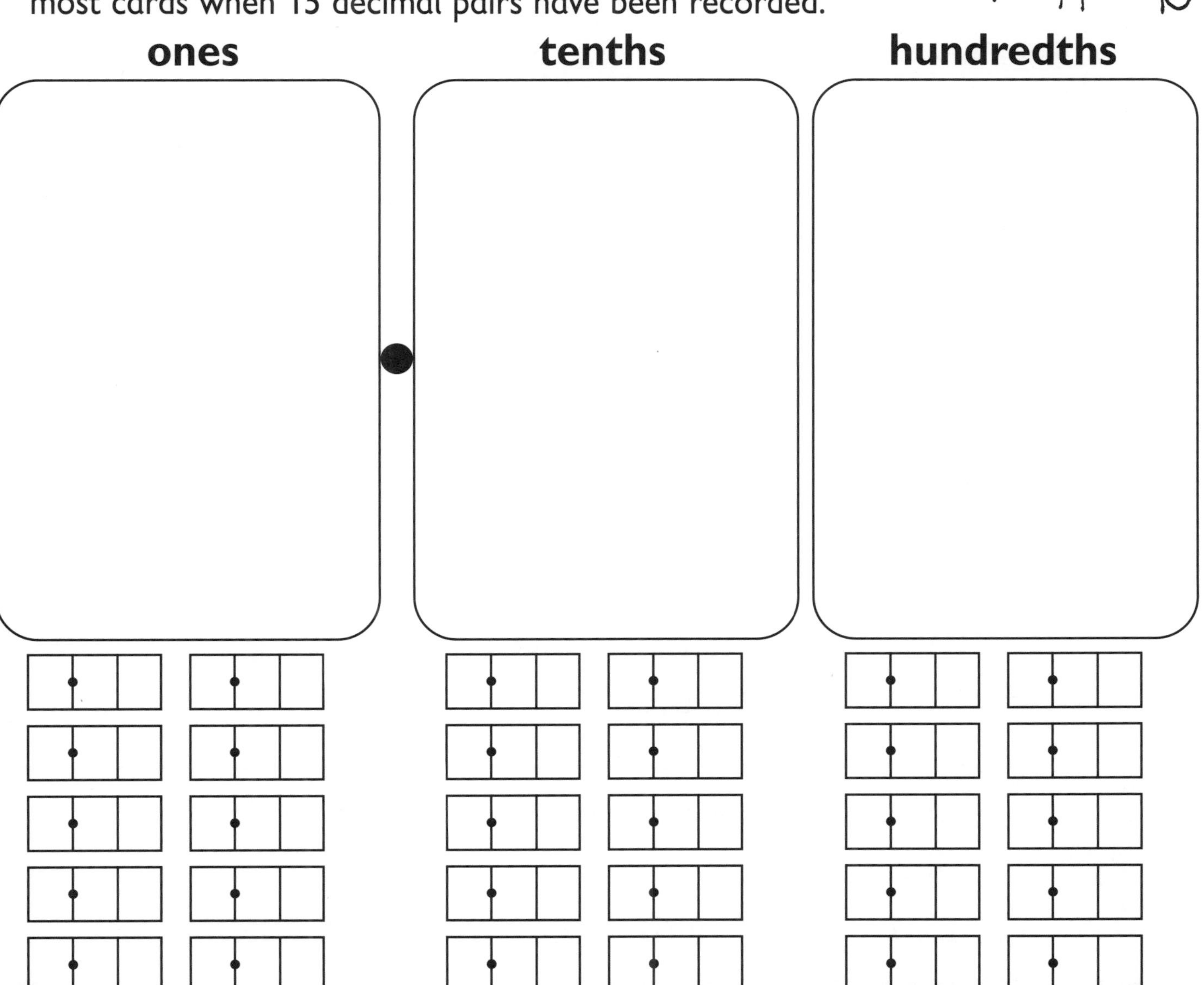

Teachers' note Ensure the children realise that an ace stands for the digit 1. Demonstrate how to play the game and explain that the children should continue turning new cards, placing them on top of the others, until someone calls 'snap'. Encourage them to say the decimals aloud and to name the digit (or digits) which are the same, rather than just pointing to the card.

Pocket money

- **Write a decimal to show the amount of money in each pocket.**

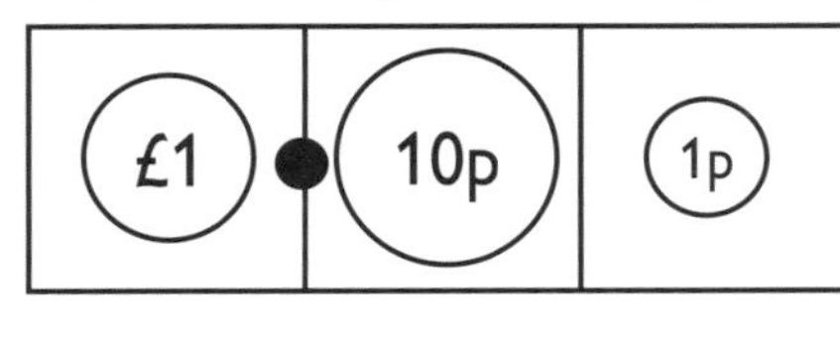

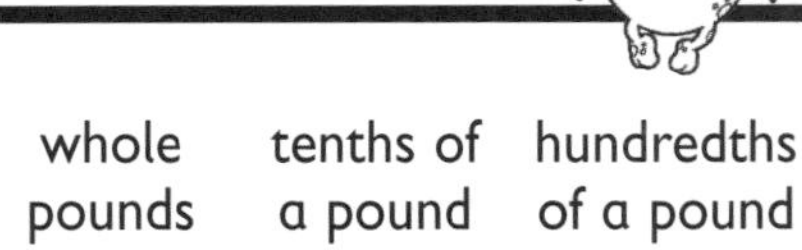

1

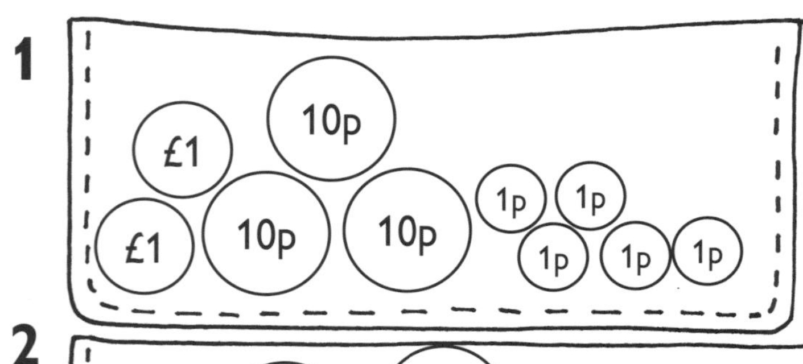

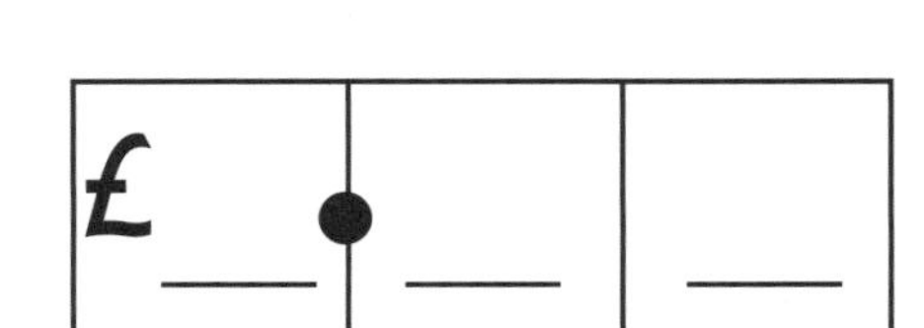

2

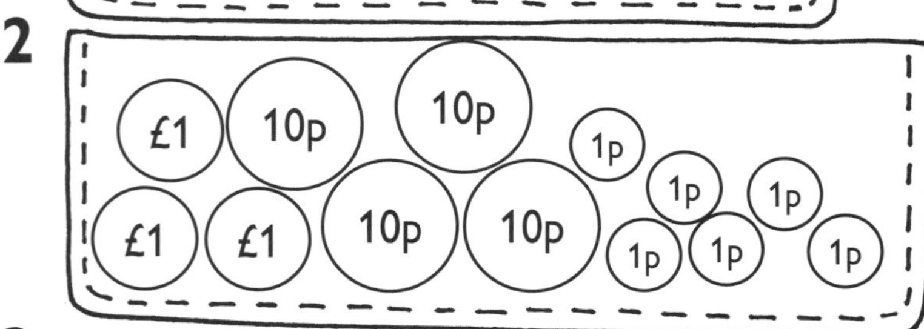

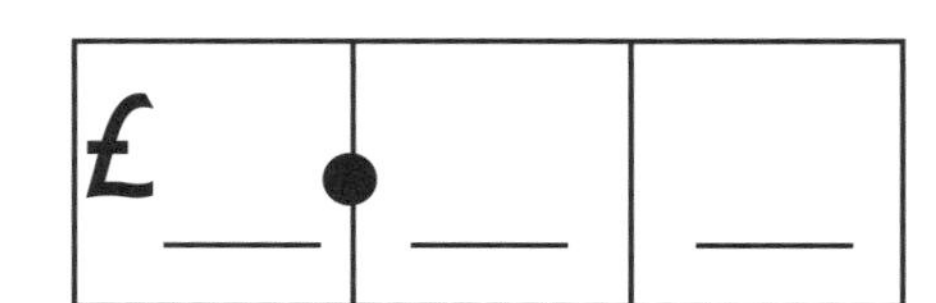

3

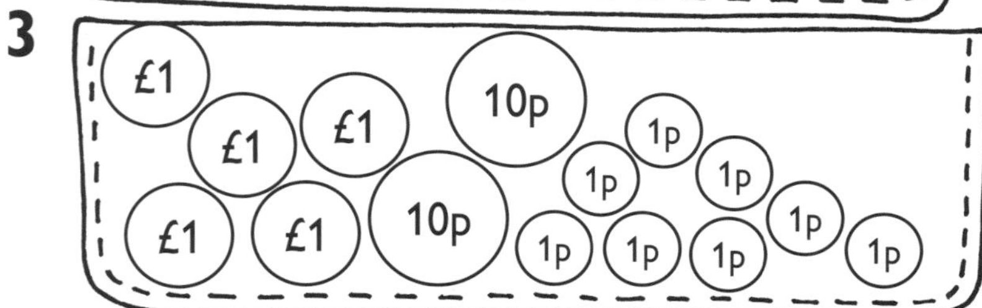

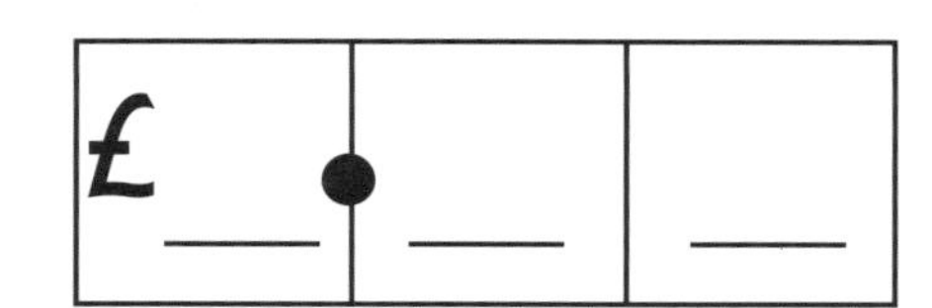

4

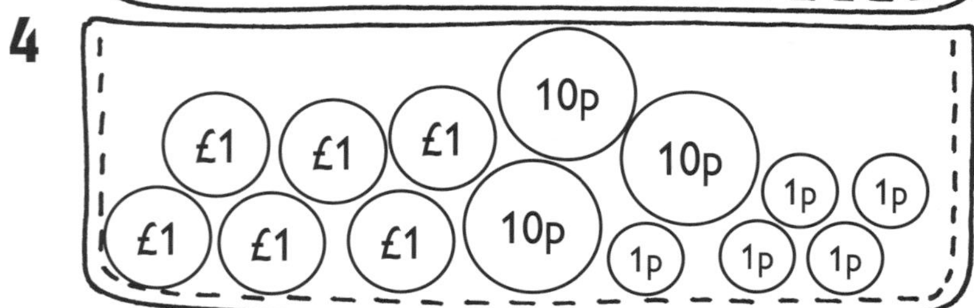

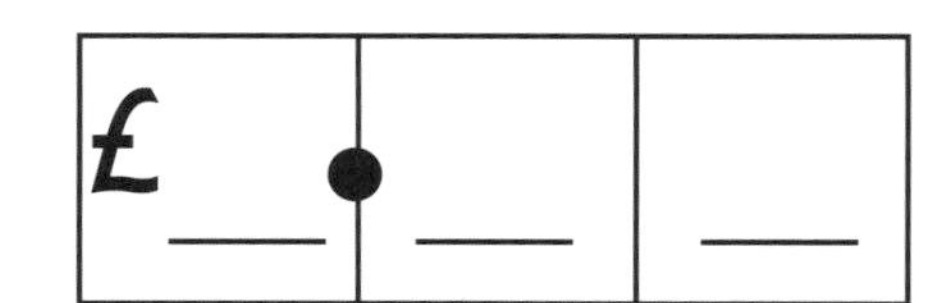

5

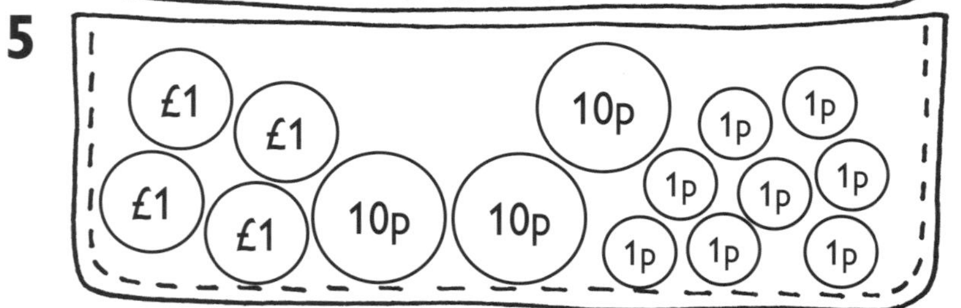

NOW TRY THIS!

- **Write ten amounts and partition them like this:**

£2.74 = 2 pounds, 7 ten pences and 4 pennies

Teachers' note This activity encourages the children to appreciate that the digits of a decimal refer to tenths and hundredths of a whole, in this case whole pounds. Point out that one tenth of a pound is 10p, as ten of them make one pound, and that one hundredth of a pound is 1p, as 100 of them make one pound.

Exploding numbers

- **Partition each exploding number and show the value of the digits.**

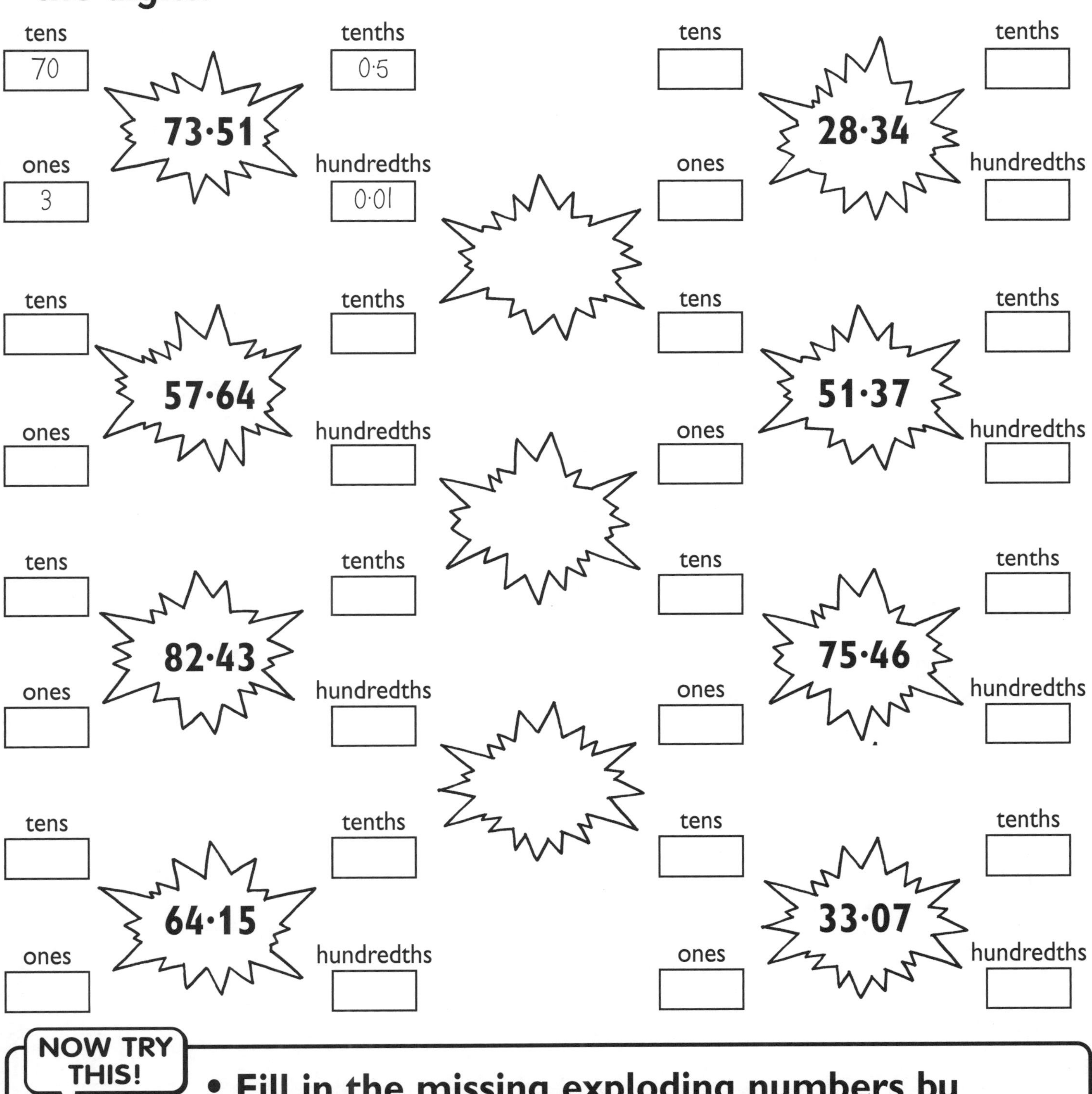

- **Fill in the missing exploding numbers by adding together the tens, ones, tenths and hundredths boxes.**

Teachers' note Demonstrate how to find the appropriate digit of each number and then state its value, for example the 'tenths' digit of the number 32·45 is four-tenths or 0·4. For the extension activity, the children should find the three missing exploding numbers by carefully combining the four parts that surround each number.

Sleepover dreamtime

- **Play this game with a partner.**

You need
a dice, a cube
and 20 counters.

☆ Cover each number on the bedspread with a counter.
☆ Place the cube anywhere on the pillow trail.
☆ Take turns to roll the dice and move the cube on.
☆ Answer the question. Lift a counter and see if the answer is beneath. If it is, keep the counter. If not, replace it.
☆ The winner is the player with the most counters at the end.

7	49	14	28
35	21	56	63
70	0	42	28
49	42	63	56
14	35	21	0

7 × 5 | 4 × 7 | 8 × 7 | 7 × 3 | 7 × 7 | 7 × 2 | 10 × 7

3 × 7 | 1 × 7

7 × 7 | 5 × 7

9 × 7 | 7 × 6

0 × 7 | 7 × 4 | 7 × 8 | 6 × 7 | 2 × 7 | 7 × 0 | 7 × 9

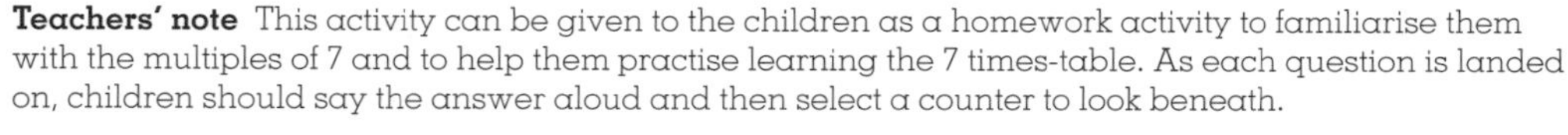
Teachers' note This activity can be given to the children as a homework activity to familiarise them with the multiples of 7 and to help them practise learning the 7 times-table. As each question is landed on, children should say the answer aloud and then select a counter to look beneath.

Curious cube

☆ Choose pairs of three-digit numbers from the curious cube that will have a total that is a multiple of 10.

☆ Numbers can be taken from any face, reading across or down.

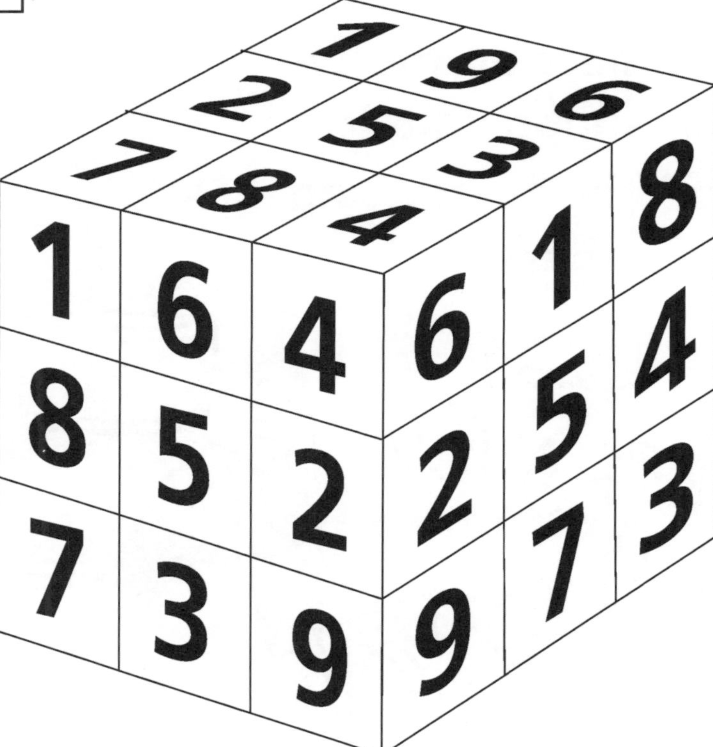

187 + 973

$$\begin{array}{r} 187 \\ +\ 973 \\ \hline 1160 \end{array}$$

☆ Find ways to make these totals.

(a) 360 196 + 164 360	**(b)** 380	**(c)** 410	**(d)** 440
(e) 450	**(f)** 830	**(g)** 840	**(h)** 970
(i) 1000	**(j)** 1030	**(k)** 1470	**(l)** 1810

Teachers' note The children can use any appropriate method of written addition, such as using the traditional column method without partitioning. Provide scrap paper for the children's jottings.

Supermarket stacks

The number on each tin is the total of the numbers on the two tins supporting it.

- **Fill in the missing numbers.**

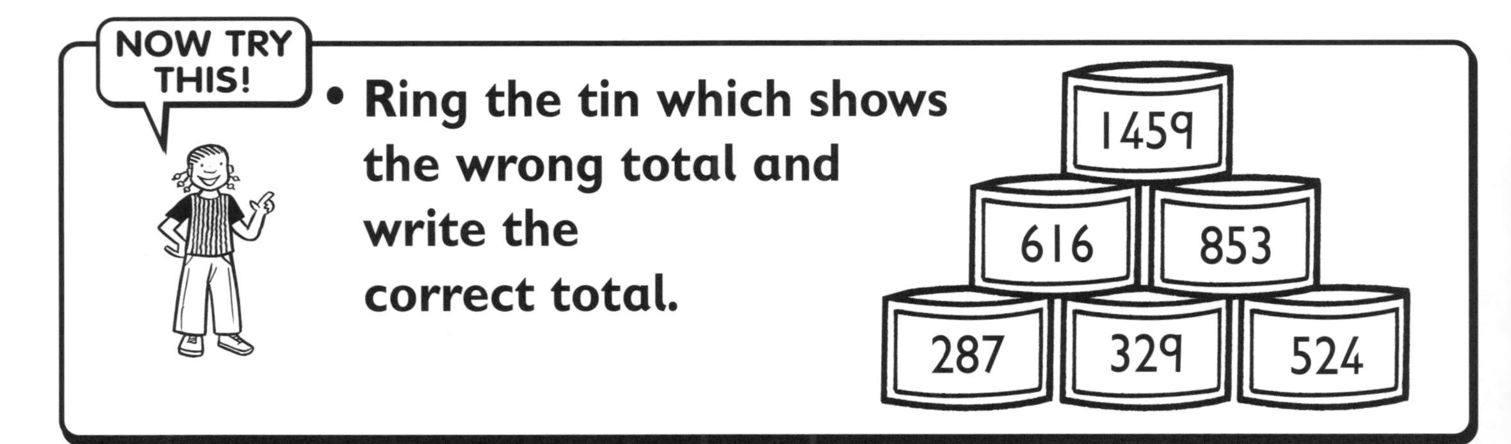

- **Ring the tin which shows the wrong total and write the correct total.**

Teachers' note The children could use any appropriate method for these additions, including partitioning, drawing number lines, or using written methods leading towards the traditional column method of addition. Encourage children tackling the extension activity to explain which methods they used to check the totals.

Animal antics

- **Time yourself to see how quickly you can answer the tables questions in each block.**

Time ____________

Teachers' note Edit this page on the CD-ROM or mask and alter the numbers before photocopying in order to provide more variety or differentiation. The most difficult tables facts up to 10 × 10 are included in each of these tests. As an extension activity, the children could colour the facts that they find hardest and which they need to revise further.

Tidying up

• **Write each slip of paper onto the correct bin to show how the number has been changed.**

840 → 84 (crossed out)

2 → 200

4100 → 41

600 → 6

300 → 3000

60 → 6000

9800 → 980

23 → 230

170 → 17

58 → 5800

34 → 3400

400 → 40

9700 → 97

57 → 570

67 → 6700

11 → 110

5000 → 50

70 → 700

84 → 8400

768 → 7680

500 → 50

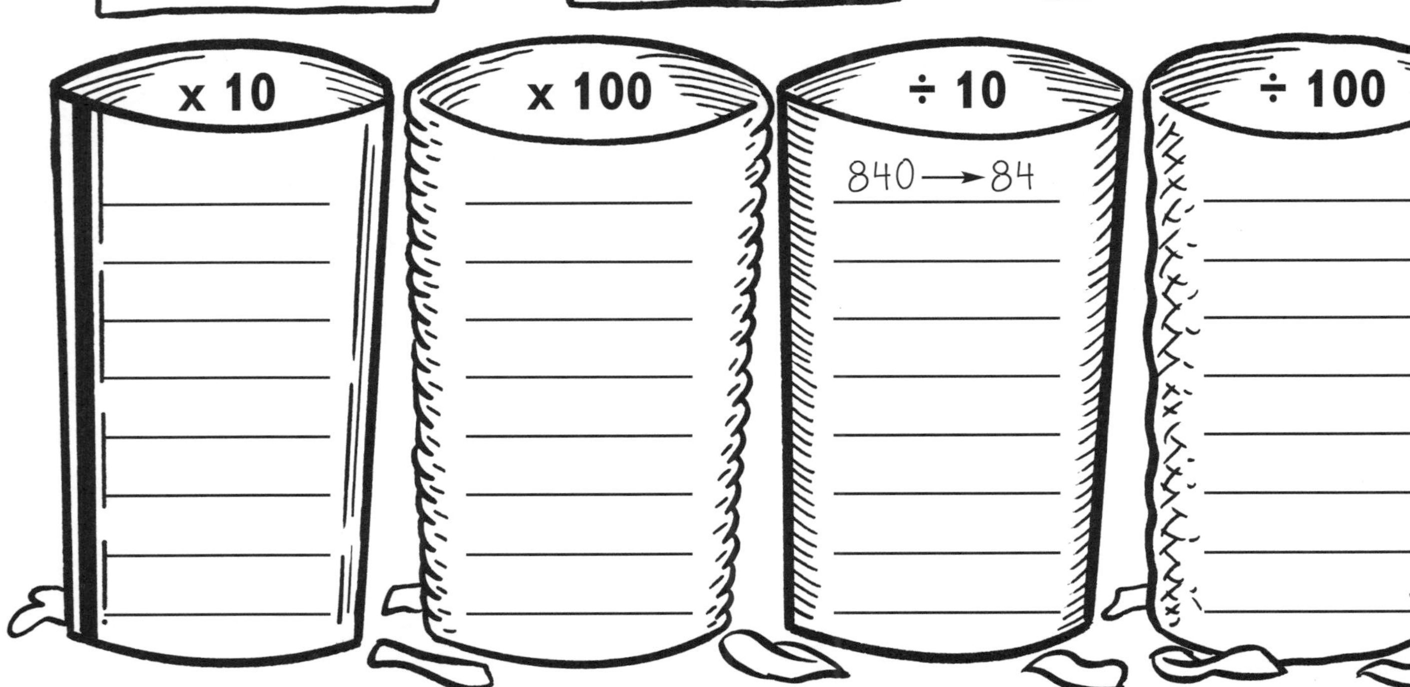

• **Write two more true facts on each bin.**

Teachers' note The children should cross off the slip of paper as they write it onto a bin. Encourage them to appreciate the movement of the digits rather than focusing on 'putting a zero on the end or removing it', as this will cause them difficulties when multiplying and dividing decimals in the future, for example 3.5 × 10 = 35, not 3.50.

Dicing with dinosaurs

- **Play this game with a partner.**

☆ Take turns to roll the dice three times.

☆ Multiply the numbers together.
If the answer is **even** score **1 point**.
If it is **odd** score **0 points**.

Dice numbers	Answer to multiplication	Odd or even?	Points scored
2 × 5 × 3 =	30	even	1
☐ × ☐ × ☐ =			
☐ × ☐ × ☐ =			
☐ × ☐ × ☐ =			
☐ × ☐ × ☐ =			
☐ × ☐ × ☐ =			
☐ × ☐ × ☐ =			
☐ × ☐ × ☐ =			
☐ × ☐ × ☐ =			
☐ × ☐ × ☐ =			
☐ × ☐ × ☐ =			
		Total	

- **Play again, but this time take the answer to the multiplication and divide it by 2.**
- **Is it easier or harder to score points?**

Teachers' note Multiplying three numbers provides practice of recalling multiplication facts and also of using informal mental or written methods for multiplying larger numbers. Ensure that the children appreciate the commutative and associative nature of multiplication (see page 8).

Codebreaker

- **Find each answer in the grid and write the number and letter.**

10 E	148 D	324 U	9 O
19 N	100 R	55 V	45 I
46 C	102 E	8 A	60 R

1 A coach holds 54 people. If six full coaches go to a football match, how many people go by coach? [324 / U]

2 Ali swims 32 lengths and Jo swims 51 lengths. What is the difference?

3 Sam has 37 stickers and Kai has three times as many. How many stickers do they have altogether?

4 One-quarter of 136 children eat school meals. How many children do **not** eat school meals?

5 There are 150 children in a school. If two-thirds of the children are girls, how many girls are there?

6 How many apples are needed so that 91 children can each have half an apple?

7 In a class of 32, five children are away. If the others are put into three equal groups, how many children are in each group?

8 A book has 96 pages. If Kim reads 12 pages on day 1 and 29 on day 2, how many pages has she left to read?

9 A factory makes 99 bottles every day. How many days will it take the factory to make over 900 bottles?

10 If there are 15 sheep in a field, how many legs are there altogether?

Code word: U __ __ __ __ __ __ __ __ __

Teachers' note Encourage the children to show their working out on a separate piece of paper. As an extension, ask the children to say which of the following questions will give the largest answer: 26 × 5, 600 ÷ 4, 42 + 79, 200 – 57.

Pebble positions

- **Write the numbers on the pebbles in order, starting with the smallest.**

3463	4518	6238	2645	2645	3463	4518	6238
1638	3672	6349	8902				
1785	5871	7158	6371				
5678	8765	6578	7658				
1875	7815	1758	1587				
2345	5432	4325	5324				
1693	6391	9316	3916				
4782	7824	2847	8742				
1745	5471	7451	4517				
2468	4682	8642	6428				
1234	3241	2314	4123				
6457	7546	7564	5467				

NOW TRY THIS!

- **Write a number on each pebble so that the numbers are in order in each row.**

3145		3415	4351	6789		6987	7896
4378	4387		4873	5687	5786		5876

Teachers' note Revise place value to thousands for this activity, and encourage children who are struggling to write the numbers in columns and to compare from the left.

Raffle tickets

- **Put each set of numbers in order, smallest first.**

Numbers	Smallest first
3623	1274
4075	2847
5726	
1274	
2847	

Numbers	Smallest first
6472	
4278	
3803	
5789	
3008	

Numbers	Smallest first
7624	
6582	
7934	
6912	
4998	

Numbers	Smallest first
8765	
6785	
5768	
7685	
8756	

Numbers	Smallest first
2918	
3826	
1589	
3428	
5310	

Numbers	Smallest first
4268	
2784	
9573	
8367	
4383	

Numbers	Smallest first
5831	
5743	
5924	
5108	
5099	

Numbers	Smallest first
9452	
9542	
9425	
9254	
9245	

NOW TRY THIS!

- **Write four numbers that lie between:**

3798    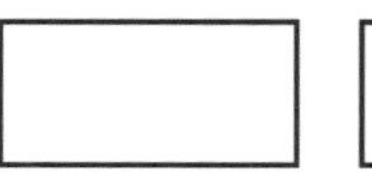 3809

Teachers' note For this activity, revise place value of four-digit numbers, and encourage children who are struggling to write the numbers in columns and to compare from the left.

Join the dots

- **In each box, join the numbered dots in order, smallest to largest. If you are right, you will spell a word in each row.**

4267	2689	3824	6659	5893	7891	6582	7038
5682	6723	3929	6580	3903	8032	8853	8761
9729	7896	4074	5582	1643	9738	4392	

5689	6291	4829	5657	6478	6950	5245	5038
7045	6834	4729	6584	5764	6905	7730	
4727		4719	7582	5673	6509	8522	8587

5764	5298	3821	4659	4884	4896	6004	
6656	9872	3929	4580	3955	7062	6010	
7729	7896	4070	4558	3699	7738	8009	8341

5669	5691	4730	3887	5403	6783	4628	8887
		5874		8938	7674	5399	7459
5833	6823	7292	8640	4671	9643	6284	6653

4525	4425	4544		2651	5612	6976	7045
4552		7689		2561	5621	7061	7054
4787	9896	8078	8581	1562	6512	6893	

6758	6785	3645	3654	5768	5678	6798	6789
6875	6857	3546	4356	5876	6857	6879	6897
5678	6900	3456	4365	6758	6785	6987	6978

NOW TRY THIS!

- **Make up a puzzle like this for a partner to solve.**

Teachers' note Children may need to write column headings and enter the numbers underneath. Encourage them to compare digits by working from the left.

Integer dominoes

• **Cut out these dominoes and play with a partner.**

>	–5	<	7	>	–3
<	–1	>	–4	<	0
>	–8	<	6	>	–2
<	1	>	–9	<	–6
>	–12	<	8	>	–7
<	4	>	–11	<	–10
>	–15	<	3	>	–13
<	5	>	–14	<	10

Teachers' note Ensure that the children are familiar with the 'greater than' and 'less than' signs. When playing dominoes the children should lay one domino on the table and should take turns to try to lay a domino so that the correct sign lies between the two numbers on adjacent dominoes, for example if the domino [< 7] is on the table the domino [> –3] could be laid to its right.

Little Miss Moneybags!

- **How much money in each purse?**

1 Count on in steps of £1.

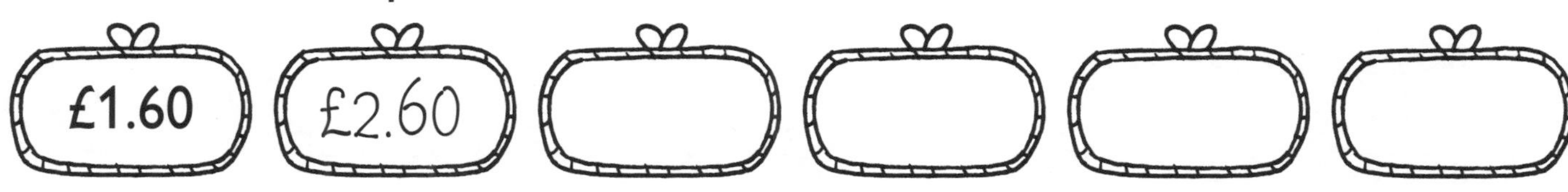

2 Count on in steps of 10p.

3 Count back in steps of 50p.

4 Count on in steps of 20p.

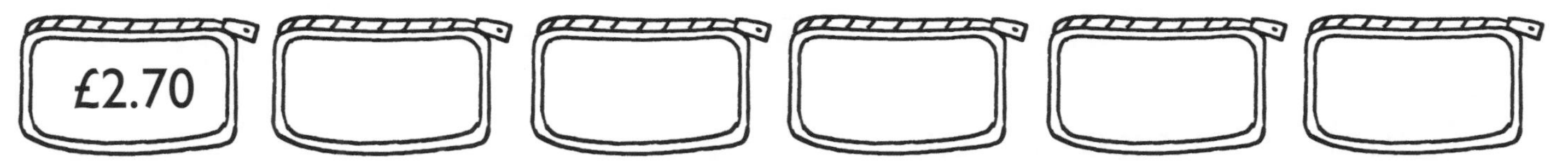

5 Count back in steps of 10p.

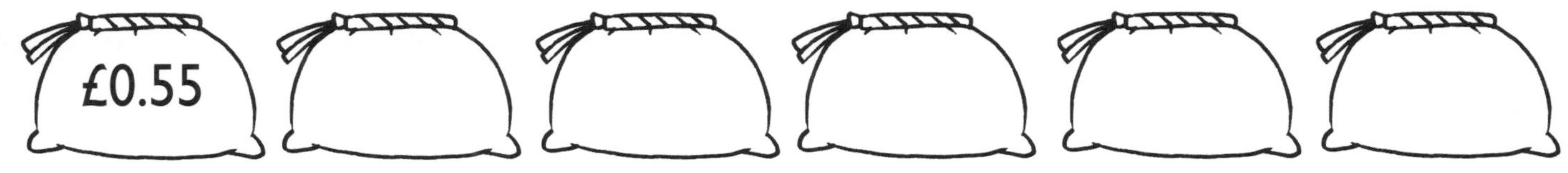

6 Count on in steps of £2.

Teachers' note Children who are having difficulty could use play money to make the amounts and then count on or back by adding or taking away coins.

Animal hospital

- **Continue the sequence in each row.**

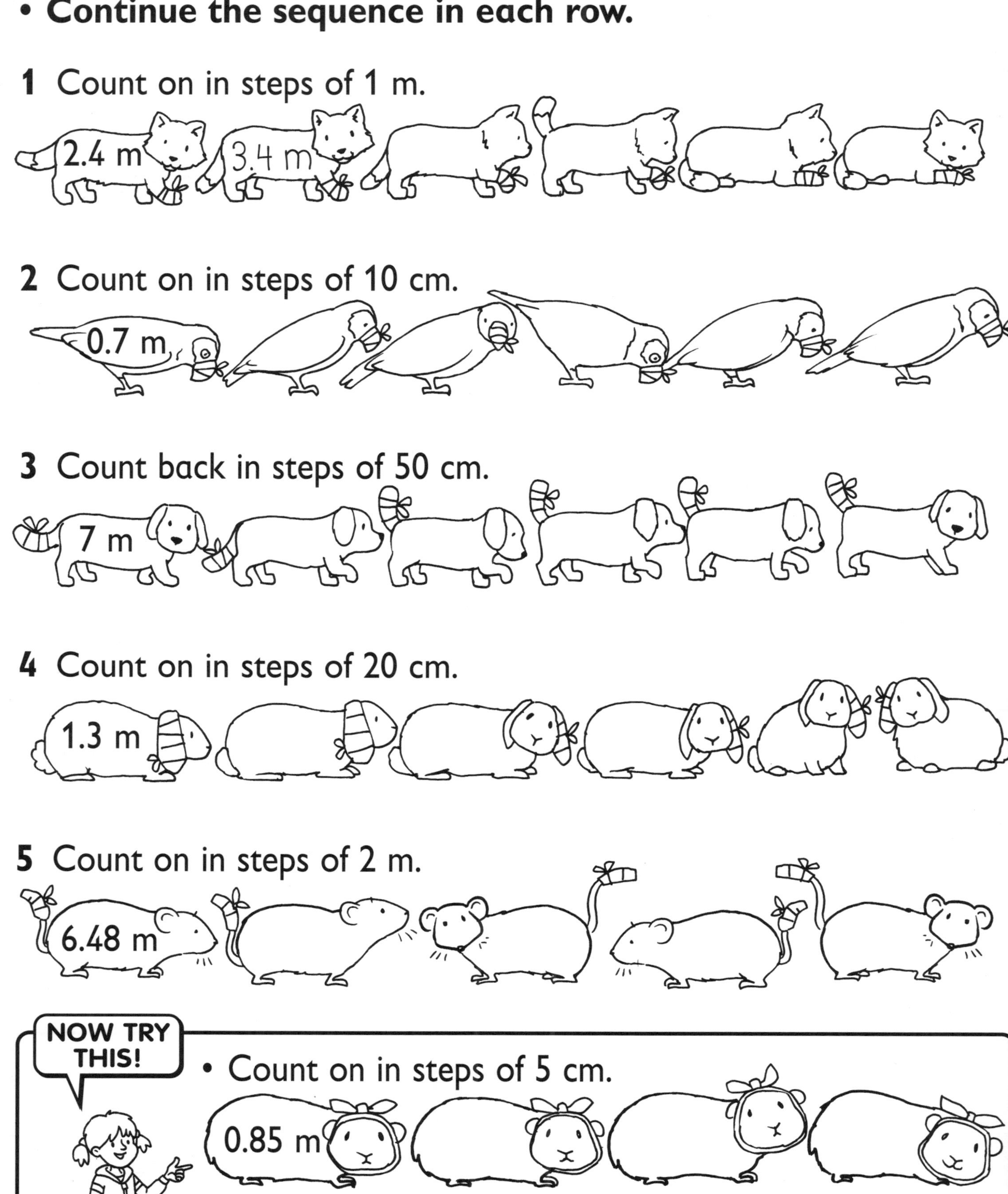

Teachers' note Children who are having difficulty could use place value equipment (units for centimetres, sticks for 10 cm and flats for metres) to make the lengths and then count on or back by adding or taking away equipment.

Shooting stars

- **Fill in the missing numbers in each trail.**

+3 16

+5 25

+10 19

−6 79

+5 50

+6 79

−3 94

+8 125

+7 90

+2 121

−5 85

+4

+11 48

- **Use the constant function on a calculator to check your sequences.**

Teachers' note Show the children how to use the constant function on a calculator to help them to generate or check the numbers in these sequences. Begin by keying in the first number followed by ++ or – – and the step size (on most calculators). By continuing to press the = key the display will show the numbers in the sequence.

Nature trails

• **Fill in the decimals on each trail.**

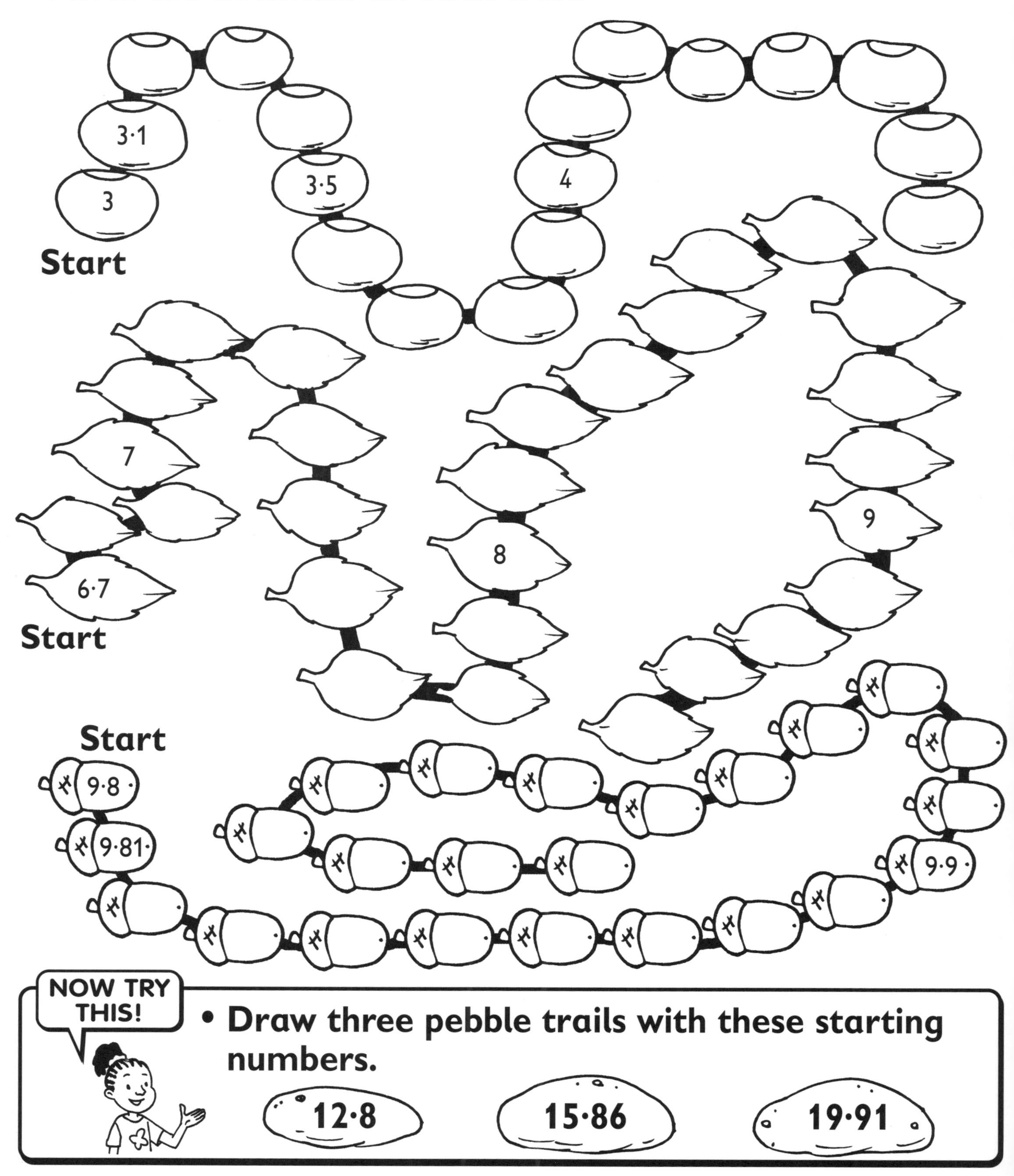

NOW TRY THIS!

• **Draw three pebble trails with these starting numbers.**

12·8 15·86 19·91

Teachers' note At the start of the lesson, practise counting on in steps of one tenth (0·1) or one hundredth (0·01) from any small number. The numbers written on each of the trails can be masked and altered to provide a more flexible resource.

Super Squirrel

- **How full is Super Squirrel's powerpack?**
- **Write your answer as a decimal.**

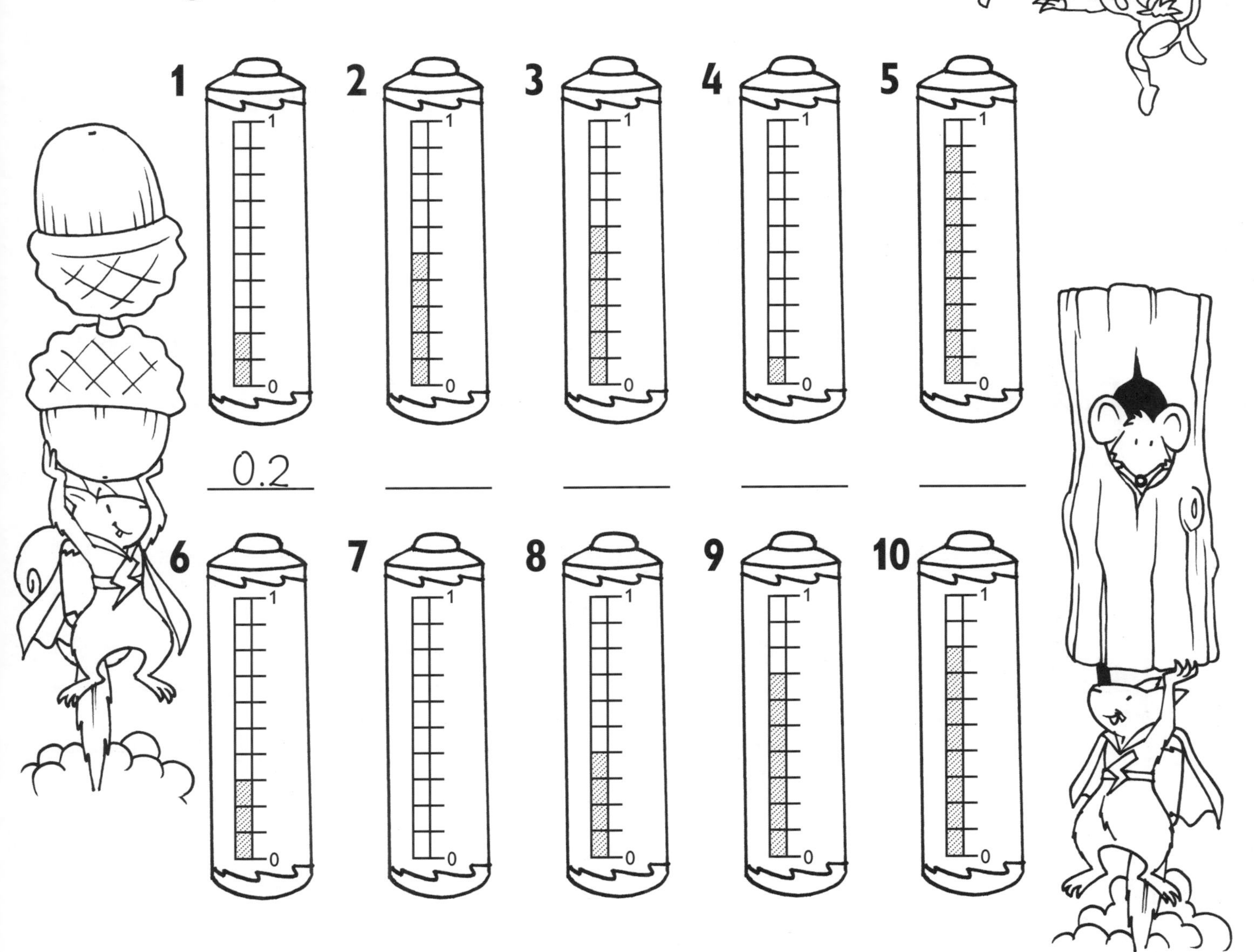

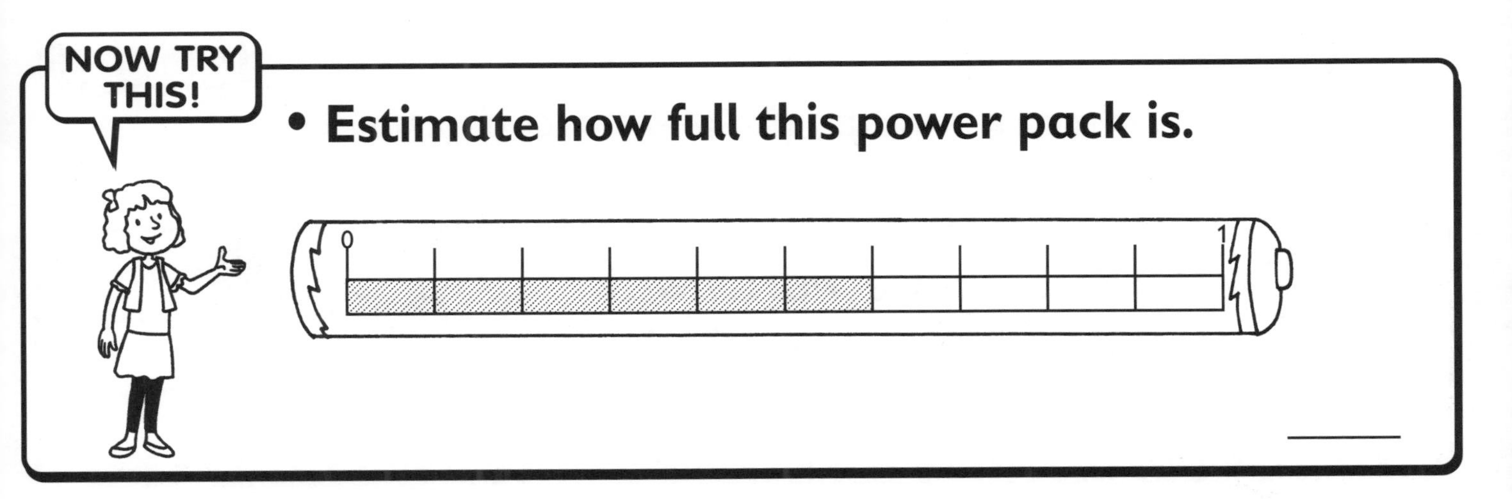

- **Estimate how full this power pack is.**

Teachers' note Explain that empty is 0 (zero) and full is 1. If the battery is split into ten parts, each part is one tenth, which can be written as a fraction ($\frac{1}{10}$) or a decimal (0·1). The extension activity also encourages the children to consider what lies between tenths, i.e. hundredths. Page 170 can be used to extend these ideas further.

Animal additions

a	b	c	d	e	f	g	h	i	j	k	l	m
28	214	351	531	67	672	833	777	89	369	473	794	335
n	**o**	**p**	**q**	**r**	**s**	**t**	**u**	**v**	**w**	**x**	**y**	**z**
646	64	951	506	748	357	729	26	631	542	914	54	467

- **Find the letters in the key and add the numbers to find the value of each animal.**

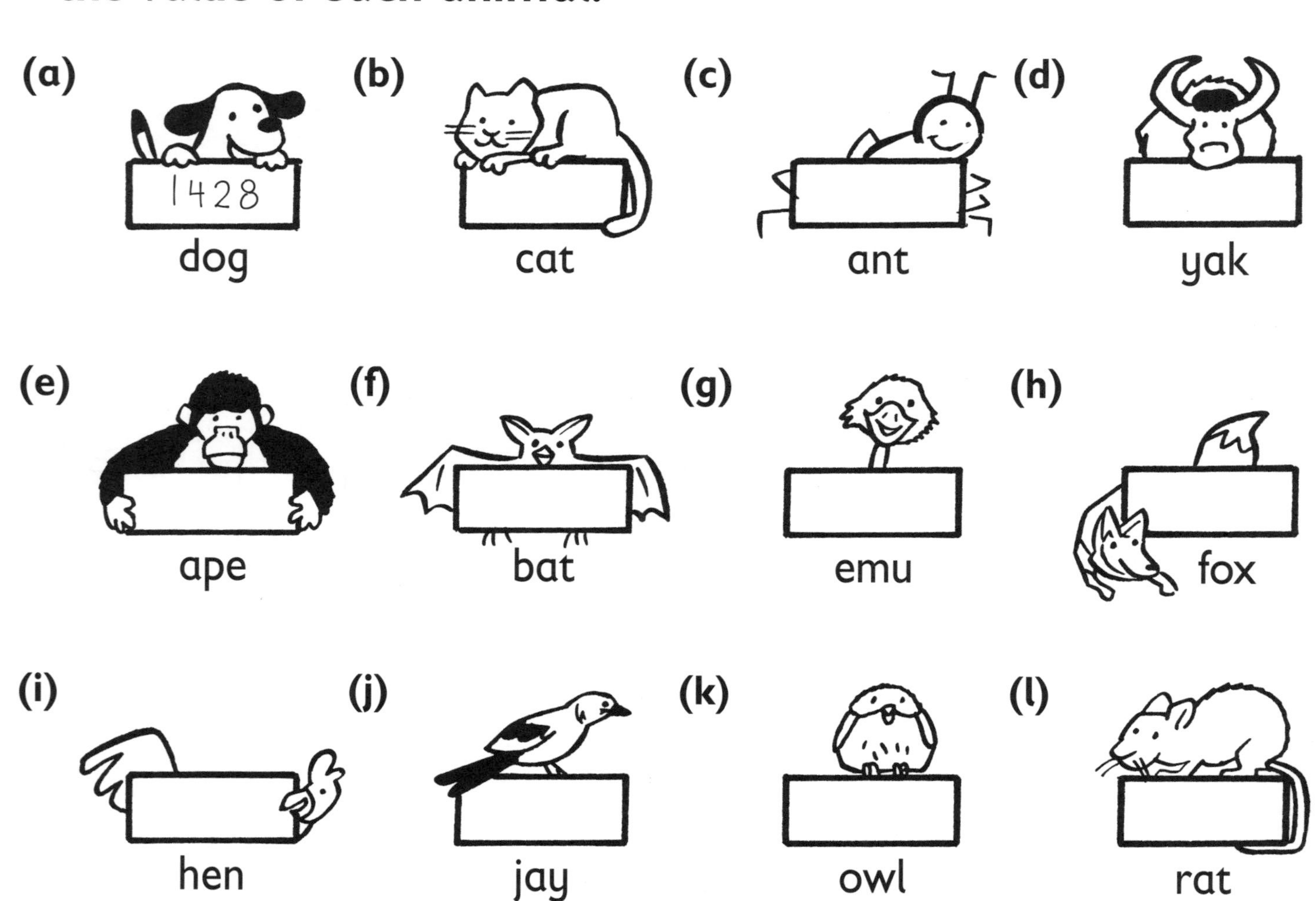

- **Write some words with** four **letters and find their values.**

Teachers' note For the extension activity, encourage the children to choose different four-letter words. Alternatively, they could find the value of the letters in their own name. Discuss appropriate written methods that could be used to add the numbers, for example using the traditional column method of addition.

Captain Dynamic

Captain Dynamic uses subtraction to choose an eight-digit code to keep his superhero identity safe!
He thinks of 573 – 86 = 487, so his code is | 5 | 7 | 3 | 8 | 6 | 4 | 8 | 7 |

- **Use subtraction to find the last three digits of each code. Show your workings.**

(a) 4 3 9 7 4 _ _ _

(b) 8 4 5 9 2 _ _ _

(c) 6 5 3 6 7 _ _ _

(d) 9 1 2 5 9 _ _ _

(e) 8 0 7 7 5 _ _ _

(f) 6 1 7 7 5 _ _ _

- **Make up two more codes using subtraction.**

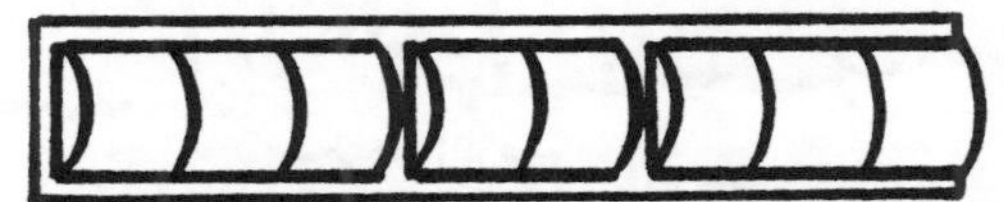

Teachers' note Encourage the children to use an appropriate written method of subtraction to find each answer, such as using a vertical column method involving partitioning or drawing a number line.

Movin' on

☆ Pick a starting position: 1, 2, 3 or 4. Answer the question.

☆ Move on the same number of places as the answer.

☆ Answer the question you land on and move on. Keep going until you reach the end.

☆ Do you escape or do you get eaten by a crocodile?

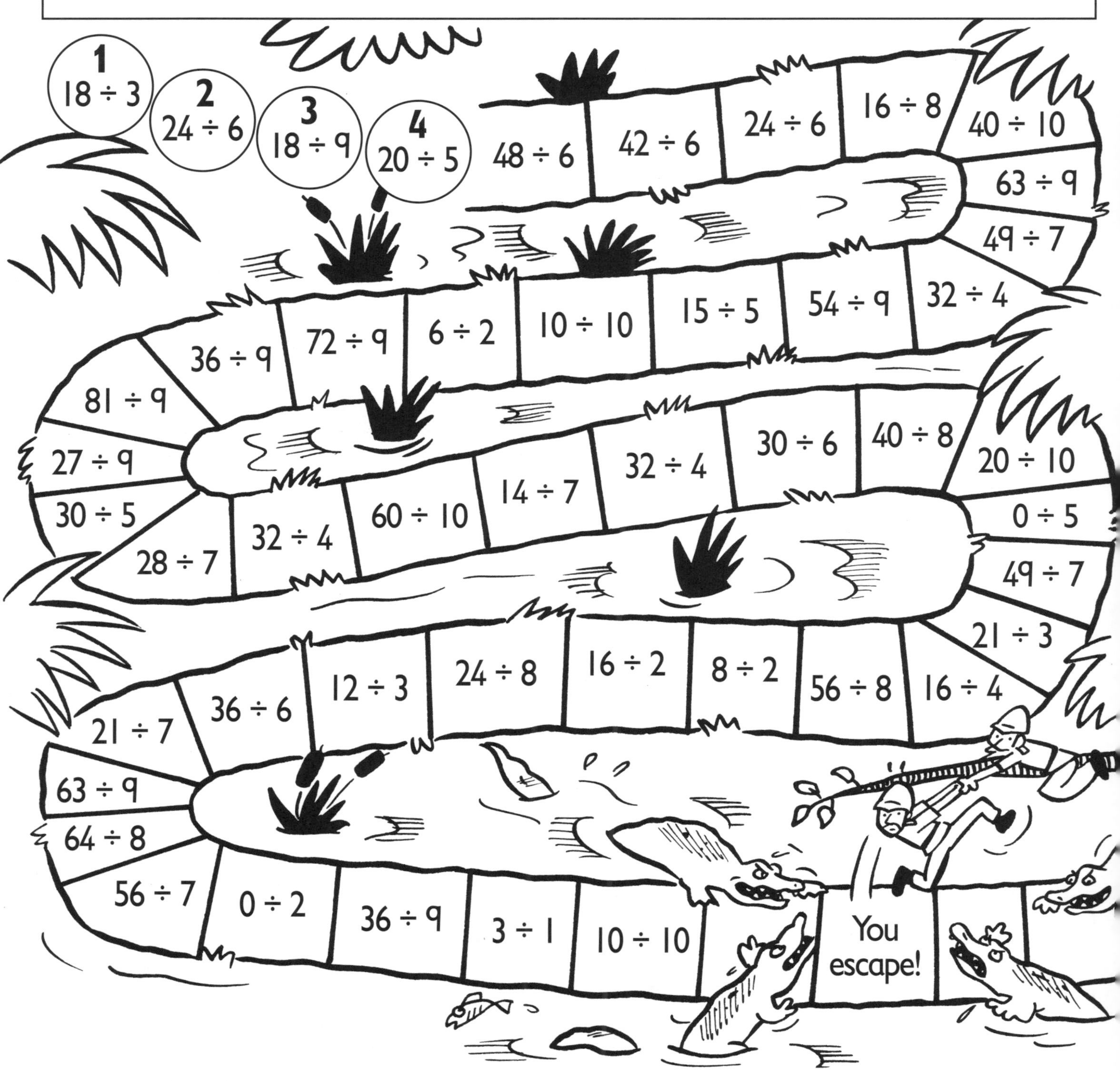

Teachers' note Encourage the children to make the link between multiplication facts and division facts. It might be useful for the tables facts to be displayed on the classroom wall for children to refer to. As an extension activity, ask the children on which number they have to start to escape.

Crazy calculations

☆ Cut out the cards.

☆ Pick an input card, for example 58, and an operation card, for example x 3.

☆ Work out the answer to the multiplication. Show your workings on a separate piece of paper.

☆ Try to find the six pairs of cards which will give these output numbers.

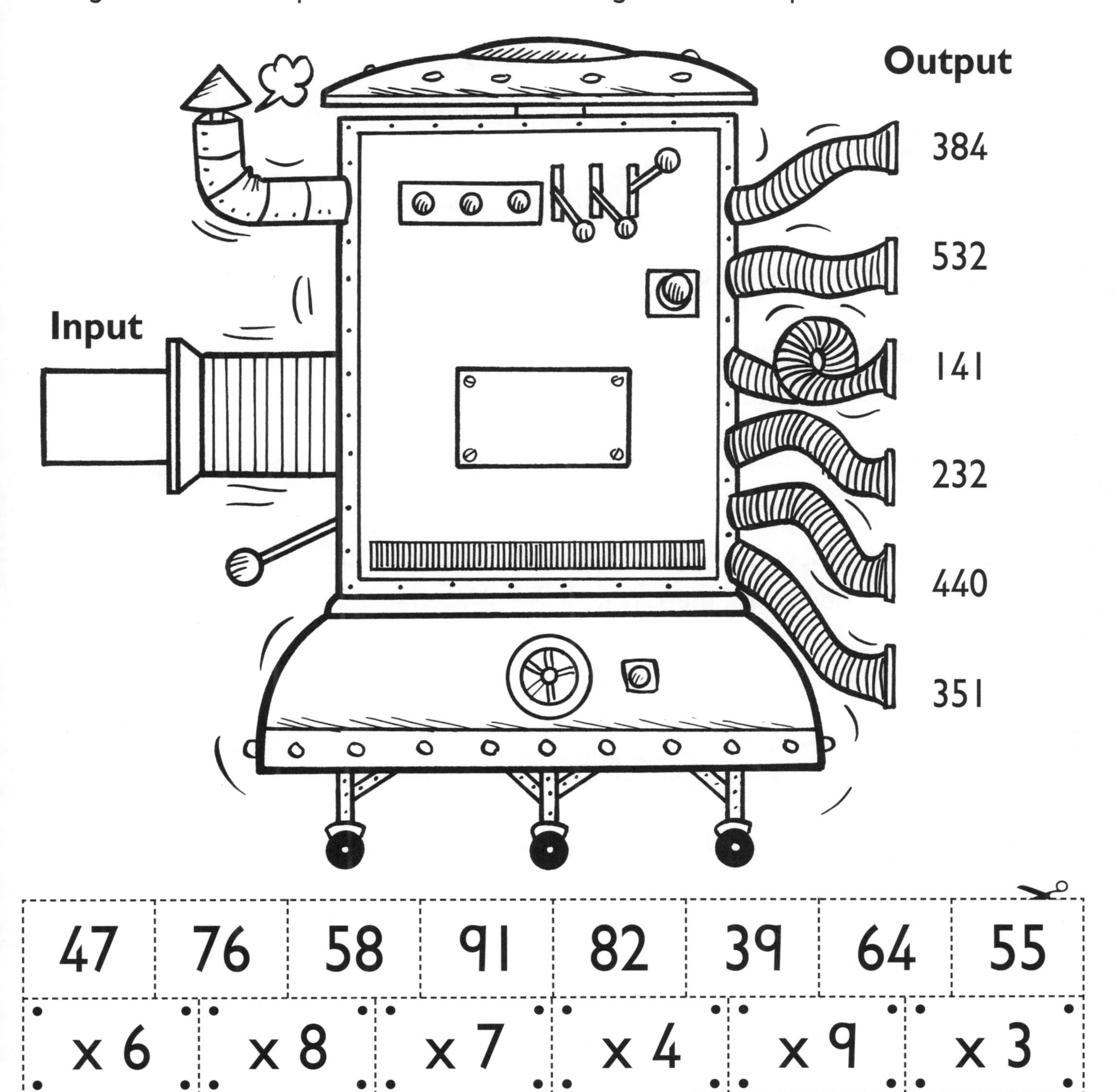

Teachers' note The children can use any appropriate method of multiplication, such as using the grid method based on partitioning each two-digit number and multiplying each part separately.

Detective Dog

- **Cut out the cards.**
- **Read each clue and together help Detective Dog solve the division puzzle.**

1. The number is between 40 and 50.
When it is divided by 5 there is a remainder of 3.
When it is divided by 7 there is a remainder of 6.
The number is

2. The number is between 30 and 40.
When it is divided by 3 there is a remainder of 1.
When it is divided by 4 there is a remainder of 1.
The number is

3. The number is between 60 and 70.
When it is divided by 6 there is a remainder of 1.
When it is divided by 4 there is a remainder of 3.
The number is

4. The number is between 70 and 80.
When it is divided by 4 there is a remainder of 3.
When it is divided by 5 there is a remainder of 0.
The number is

5. The number is between 70 and 80.
When it is divided by 7 there is a remainder of 2.
When it is divided by 6 there is a remainder of 1.
The number is

6. The number is between 60 and 70.
When it is divided by 7 there is a remainder of 6.
When it is divided by 8 there is a remainder of 5.
The number is

7. The number is between 80 and 90.
When it is divided by 9 there is a remainder of 5.
When it is divided by 4 there is a remainder of 2.
The number is

8. The number is between 80 and 90.
When it is divided by 8 there is a remainder of 1.
When it is divided by 7 there is a remainder of 5.
The number is

Teachers' note Cutting out the cards will help the children to focus on one puzzle at a time. Some children will benefit from having a number line and multiplication tables to refer to. As an extension, ask the children to make up some puzzles of their own for another pair to solve.

Sponsored spell

- **Use a calculator to help you answer these questions.**

1. Ryan is sponsored 17p for each word. He spells 24 words correctly.

How much money does he raise?

2. Baljit raises £17.25 and Claire raises £15.35.

How much money do they raise altogether?

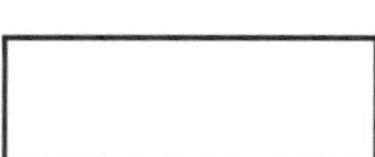

3. Three children raise exactly the same amount. Together they raise £53.67.

How much money does each child raise?

4. Four children raise these amounts:

£14.76 £25.64
£21.17 £9.34

How much less than £100 do they raise altogether?

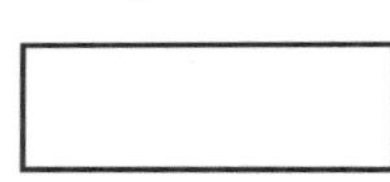

5. Amber raises £19.84. Afterwards, her Dad gives her an extra 87p.

How much money does she raise in total?

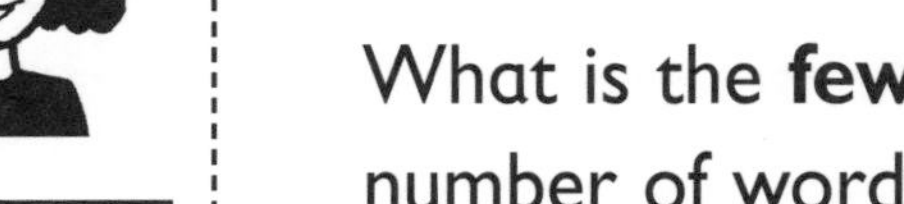

6. Kieran wants to raise £50. He is sponsored 75p for each word.

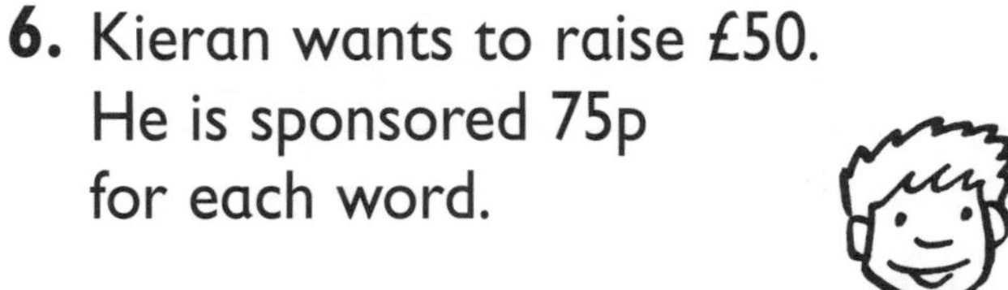

What is the **fewest** number of words he must spell correctly?

7. Chloe spells 19 words correctly at £1.13 per word. Jay spells 26 words correctly at 94p per word.

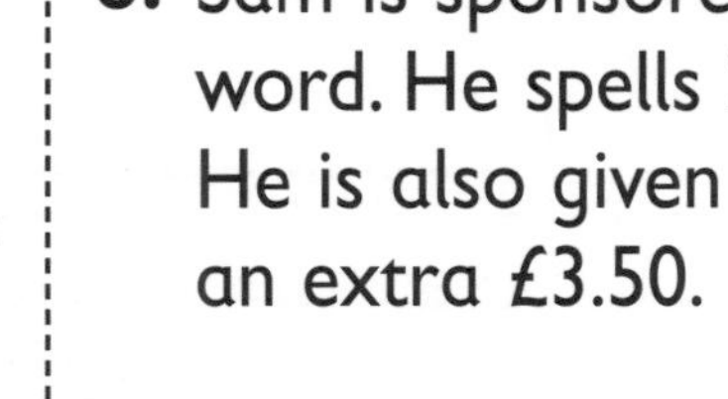

Who raises more money, Chloe or Jay?

8. Sam is sponsored 19p for each word. He spells 24 words correctly. He is also given an extra £3.50.

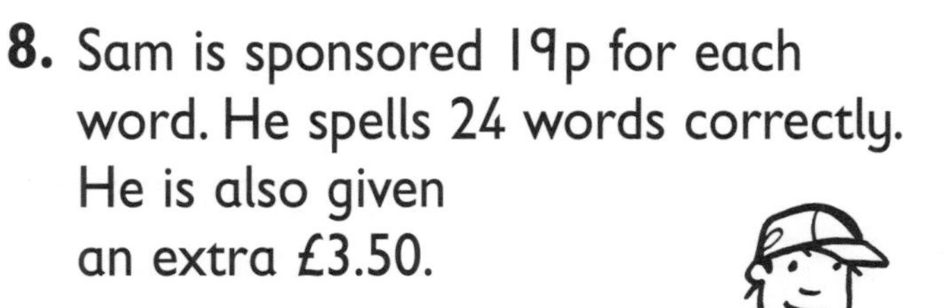

How much money does he raise in total?

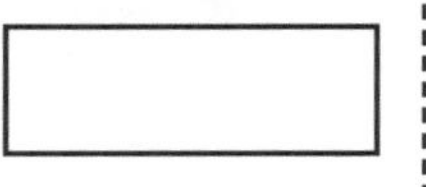

Teachers' note Encourage the children to discuss how each question can be solved. Draw attention to the importance of putting two digits after the decimal point for amounts such as 7.2 £7.20, and of not mixing up amounts in pounds and in pence. As an extension, ask the children to make up some sponsored spell puzzles of their own for another pair to solve.

Spend, spend, spend!

- **Work with a partner.**
- **Use a calculator to help you answer the questions.**

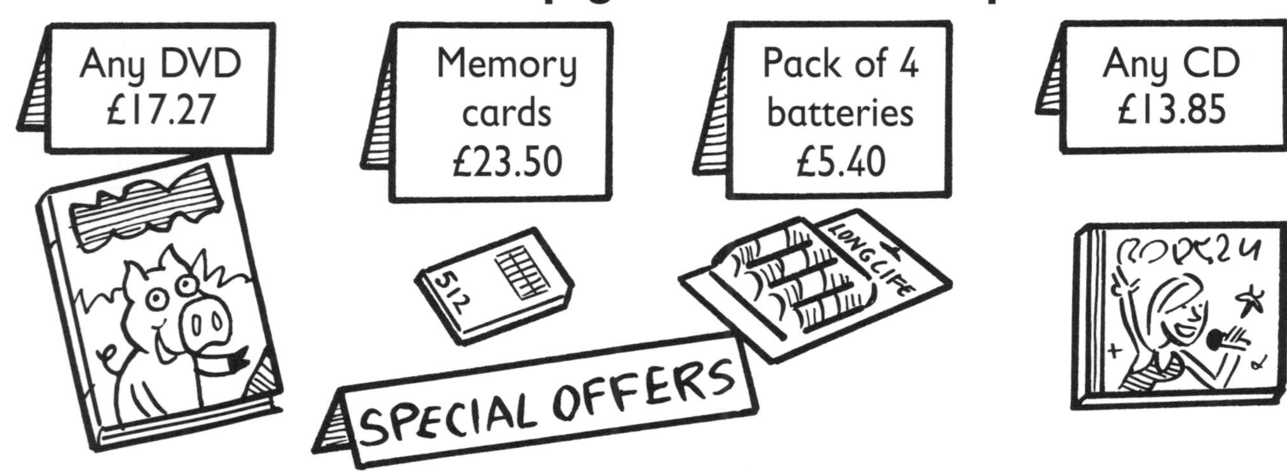

1. Abdou bought one DVD, two CDs and four packs of batteries. How much did he spend? £ ________	**2.** Leanne bought eight CDs. How much did they cost? £ ________
3. Luca spent £83.10 on CDs. How many did he buy? £ ________	**4.** Six of which item costs £103.62? ________
5. How many CDs can Ella buy for £100? ________	**6.** How much change from £150 would Dan get if he bought four DVDs and two packs of batteries? £ ________
7. Five CDs cost more than four DVDs. How much more? £ ________	**8.** Kayla bought two items. She spent £31.12. What did she buy? ________

- **Make up some more puzzles for another pair to solve.**

Teachers' note Provide children with calculators and encourage them to discuss their strategies for solving the problems. Encourage estimating and checking.

Splish! Splash! Splosh!

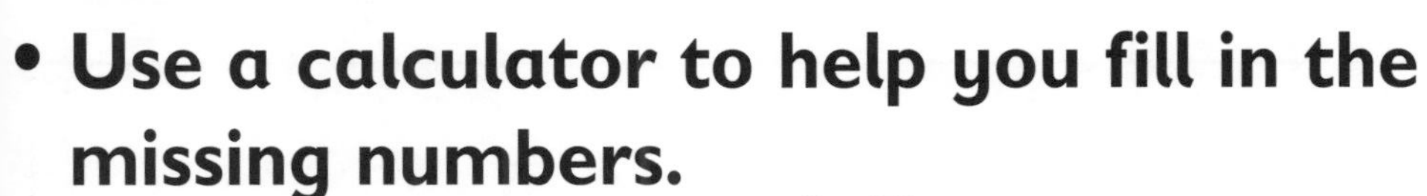

Jess the dog has shaken water all over Connor's calculations.

- **Use a calculator to help you fill in the missing numbers.**

1. $358 + 375 =$ ___
2. $57 \div 3 =$ ___
3. $48 \times 9 =$ ___
4. $312 - 253 =$ ___
5. $466 +$ ___ $= 578$
6. $52 \div$ ___ $= 13$
7. $37 \times$ ___ $= 592$
8. $466 -$ ___ $= 375$
9. ___ $+ 46 = 824$
10. ___ $\div 7 = 32$
11. ___ $\times 3 = 87$
12. ___ $- 467 = 238$

NOW TRY THIS!

- **Check each answer using the calculator.**

Teachers' note Demonstrate how missing numbers can be found using the same operation or its inverse. Point out which number is the largest in each calculation, as this can help the children to decide which operation to use: for addition and multiplication, the answer is the largest; for division and subtraction, the first number in the question is the largest.

Confetti colours

- **Use the clues to help you colour each pattern in the correct way.**

Work with a partner.

1

Blue is not next to yellow.
One heart is yellow.
Red is between pink and blue.
Both stars are the same colour.
Green is under blue.

2

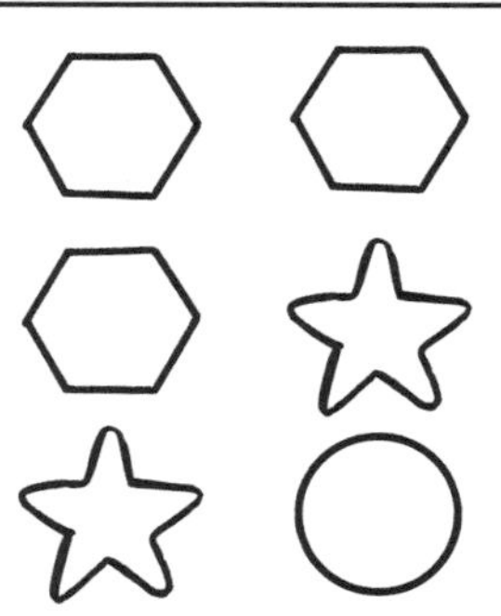

Green is not next to blue.
Three shapes are blue.
One hexagon is orange.
Red is under blue.
Orange is to the left of blue.

3

No heart is red.
Red is between pink and blue.
Both stars are the same colour.
Green is not next to red.
Pink is not next to green.
Yellow is above red.

4

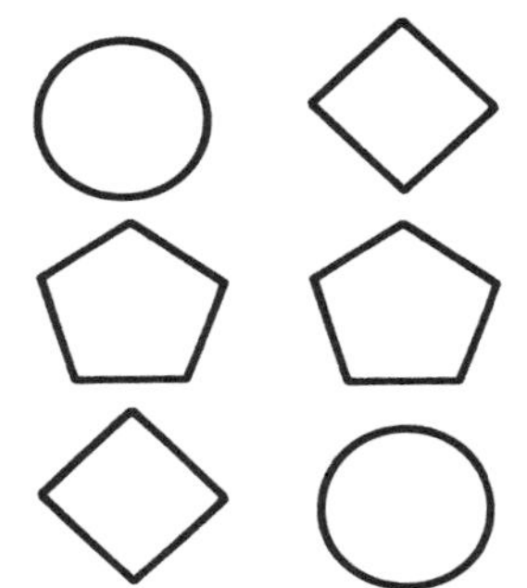

Blue is between yellow and red.
Both circles are the same colour.
Orange is to the right of blue.
Yellow is under orange.
There are two red shapes.

NOW TRY THIS!

- **Make up some confetti colour puzzles of your own for a partner to solve.**

Teachers' note Ask the children to work in pairs to solve these puzzles and provide them with a range of coloured pencils. Before colouring their final solutions they should be encouraged to check that each clue works.

The rules of the rows

- **Fill in the missing numbers to match these rules.**

☆ The square is always five more than the triangle in the same row.

☆ The circle is always double the triangle in the same row.

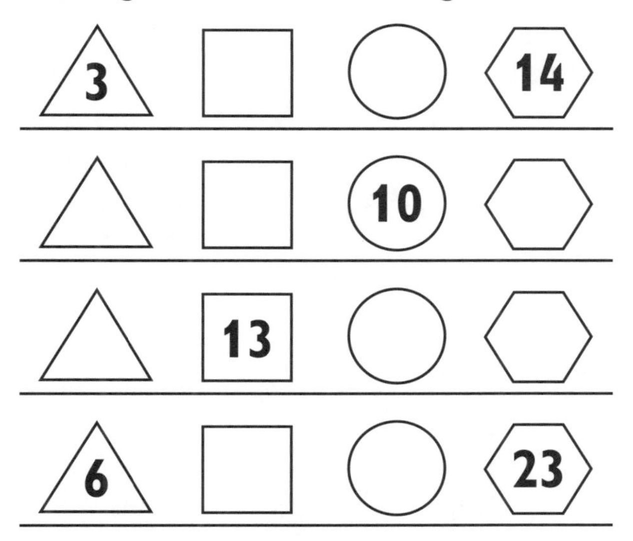

Explain it to a partner.

- **What is the rule for the hexagon?**

NOW TRY THIS!

- **Fill in the missing numbers to match these rules.**

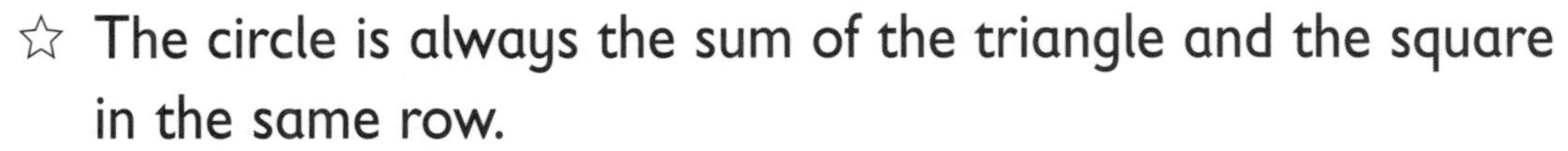

☆ The triangle is always half the square in the same row.

☆ The circle is always the sum of the triangle and the square in the same row.

- **Can you find different rules for the hexagon?**

Teachers' note Encourage the children to look for relationships in the completed grids, for example writing a new rule to compare the triangle and circle numbers or the triangle and hexagon numbers of the second grid. The children could also make up their own rules and devise puzzles for a partner to solve.

Hard cards

☆ Cut out the cards and turn them face down.

☆ Take turns to pick a card and answer the question.

☆ Ask your partner to check your answer.

Work with a partner.

1

The numbers on these cards are both **odd**. If I add them together, will the answer be odd or even?

______

2

One of these cards is **odd**. One is **even**. If I find the difference between them, will the answer be odd or even?

______

3

One of these cards is **odd**. One is **even**. If I add them together, will the answer be odd or even?

______

4

The numbers on these cards are both **odd**. If I multiply them together, will the answer be odd or even?

______

5

If I double the number on this card, will the answer be odd or even?

______

6

The numbers on these three cards are all **odd**. If I add them together, will the answer be odd or even?

______

7

If I multiply the number on this card by four, will the answer be odd or even?

______

8

The numbers on these cards are both **even**. If I add them together, will the answer be odd or even?

______

9

The numbers on these four cards are all **odd**. If I add them together, will the answer be odd or even?

______

10

One of these cards is **odd**. The other is **even**. If I find the product of them, will the answer be odd or even?

______

Teachers' note If necessary, remind the children how to recognise odd and even numbers before they begin this activity. The children could be given sets of number cards, from 1–9 or 1–100, to help them realise that these general statements apply to all sizes of numbers. As an extension, ask the children to write four examples on the back of each card to prove the answer.

Be a detective

• With a partner, find the number that matches the clues.

1 **Clues**

The number is between 40 and 50.
When it is divided by 5 there is a remainder of 2.
When it is multiplied by 2 the answer is more than 90.

The number is

2 **Clues**

The number is between 50 and 70.
When it is divided by 4 there is no remainder.
The sum of its digits is 6.

The number is 

3 **Clues**

The number is between 61 and 79.
It is a multiple of 5.
The product of its digits is 0.

The number is 

4 **Clues**

The number is between 40 and 60.
When it is doubled the answer is a multiple of 10.
When it is divided by 6 there is a remainder of 3.

The number is

5 **Clues**

The number is between 40 and 90.
When it is divided by 7 there is a remainder of 4.
It is a square number.

The number is

6 **Clues**

The number is between 20 and 99.
The number is a square number.
The product of its two digits is a square number.

The number is 

7 **Clues**

The number is between 76 and 86.
The sum of the digits is odd.
The product of the digits is a multiple of 10.

The number is 

8 **Clues**

The number is between 40 and 60.
When it is divided by 5 there is no remainder.
When it is divided by 7 there is a remainder of 3.

The number is 

Teachers' note Some children will benefit from having a number line and multiplication tables displayed, to which they can refer. If preferred, the worksheet can be cut into cards so that the children can concentrate on one set of clues at a time.

Market stall

- **Work out how much each person spent.**

Teachers' note As an extension, the children can make up their own questions for a partner to solve. Remind them to think carefully about whether the amounts are given in pence or pounds. The prices can be altered to more difficult numbers, for example £1.37 for a pineapple and 79p per kilogram for tomatoes, to provide more challenging calculations.

Sheila's shopping basket

- **How many of each item must Sheila buy?**

1 Sheila needs 1 kg of flour.

She needs ____ bags.

2 Sheila needs 500 g of chocolate.

She needs ____ bars.

3 Sheila needs 775 g of butter.

She needs ____ packs.

4 Sheila needs 800 g of sugar.

She needs ____ bags.

5 Sheila needs 1 kg of raisins.

She needs ____ bags.

6 Sheila needs 650 g of cocoa.

She needs ____ tins.

7 Sheila needs 575 ml of cream.

She needs ____ pots.

8 Sheila needs 1 litre of custard.

She needs ____ cartons.

- **On the back of this sheet, work out how much of each ingredient Sheila will have left over.**

Teachers' note Ensure the children understand that, most of the time, Sheila must buy more than the amount she actually needs so that she has sufficient for the recipes she is following. Encourage the children to explain their methods and to describe the strategies that they used for finding the answers.

In a flap

- **Work out which number is hidden beneath each flap.**

The first one has been done for you.

1	$36 + 17 = $ 53	**2**	$12 \times 3 = \square$
3	$45 - 13 = \square$	**4**	$36 \div 4 = \square$
5	$25 + 19 = \square$	**6**	$41 - 17 = \square$
7	$16 + \square = 39$	**8**	$13 \times \square = 39$
9	$24 \div \square = 3$	**10**	$47 - \square = 29$
11	$\square \div 4 = 8$	**12**	$\square + 38 = 81$
13	$\square - 40 = 63$	**14**	$\square \times 10 = 270$

103 ~~53~~ 36 23 27 32 3 32 9 8 24 43 44 18

- **Check your answers using a different method.**

NOW TRY THIS!

- **Write four more missing number questions for a partner to solve.**

Teachers' note Encourage the children to explain how they worked out each answer, drawing particular attention to when inverse operations are used. The calculations can be altered to provide differentation.

Cheese triangles

The three angles in each triangle total 180°.

- **Add the two given angles and subtract your answer from 180° to find the missing angle.**

1. 70° 70° 40°

2. 60° 80°

3. 90° 50°

4. 60° 70°

5. 50° 60°

6. 60° 90°

7. 80° 70°

NOW TRY THIS!

This set of four angles adds to make 360°.

- **Fill in the missing angle.**

70° 90° 80° ☐°

Teachers' note This activity involves children adding two multiples of 10 and then subtracting the answer from 180. Encourage them to use their knowledge of number facts for single-digit numbers and to see the relationships between those and multiples of 10, e.g. 8 + 7 = 15 so 80 + 70 = 150. Children who complete the extension activity could make up two more puzzles of their own.

Square dance

☆ Cut out the cards at the bottom of the page. Arrange them in a square so that each side has the total shown.

☆ Write in the boxes to record your answers.

Each side adds up to 1200

Each side adds up to 1300

Each side adds up to 1400

Each side adds up to 1500

100	200	300	400	500	600	700	800

Teachers' note As an extension activity, ask the children to arrange the cards in a line where the differences between adjacent numbers are always 300 or 400. As a further extension activity, invite children to see which of the following are possible: to arrange the cards in a line where the differences between adjacent numbers are always: a) 100 or 200, b) 200 or 300, c) 400 or 500 etc.

Proper properties game

- **Cut out a set of property cards each.**
- **Play this game with a partner.**

You also need the cards from Shapes: 1 and 2.

☆ Put your property cards face up in front of you and the shape cards face down in a pile.

☆ Take turns to turn over a shape card and choose one of your property cards that describes the shape, if you can.

☆ Read it aloud and if your partner agrees, turn the property card face down.

☆ The winner is the first player to turn all their property cards face down.

Player one's property cards

It has exactly three right angles. **1**	It is symmetrical about a horizontal mirror line. **2**	It has four right angles. **3**	It is symmetrical about a vertical mirror line. **4**	It is a quadrilateral. **5**
All its sides are of equal length. **6**	It is a pentagon. **7**	It has eight lines of symmetry. **8**	It has two vertical sides. **9**	It is a triangle. **10**

Player two's property cards

It has exactly three right angles. **1**	It is symmetrical about a horizontal mirror line. **2**	It has four right angles. **3**	It is symmetrical about a vertical mirror line. **4**	It is a quadrilateral. **5**
All its sides are of equal length. **6**	It is a pentagon. **7**	It has eight lines of symmetry. **8**	It has two vertical sides. **9**	It is a triangle. **10**

Teachers' note Use this sheet in conjunction with 'Shapes: 1 and 2'. The children should cut out these cards so that they have ten property cards each. The shape cards should also be cut out (ideally having been copied onto thin card) and placed in a pile.

Shapes: 1

• **Cut out the cards.**

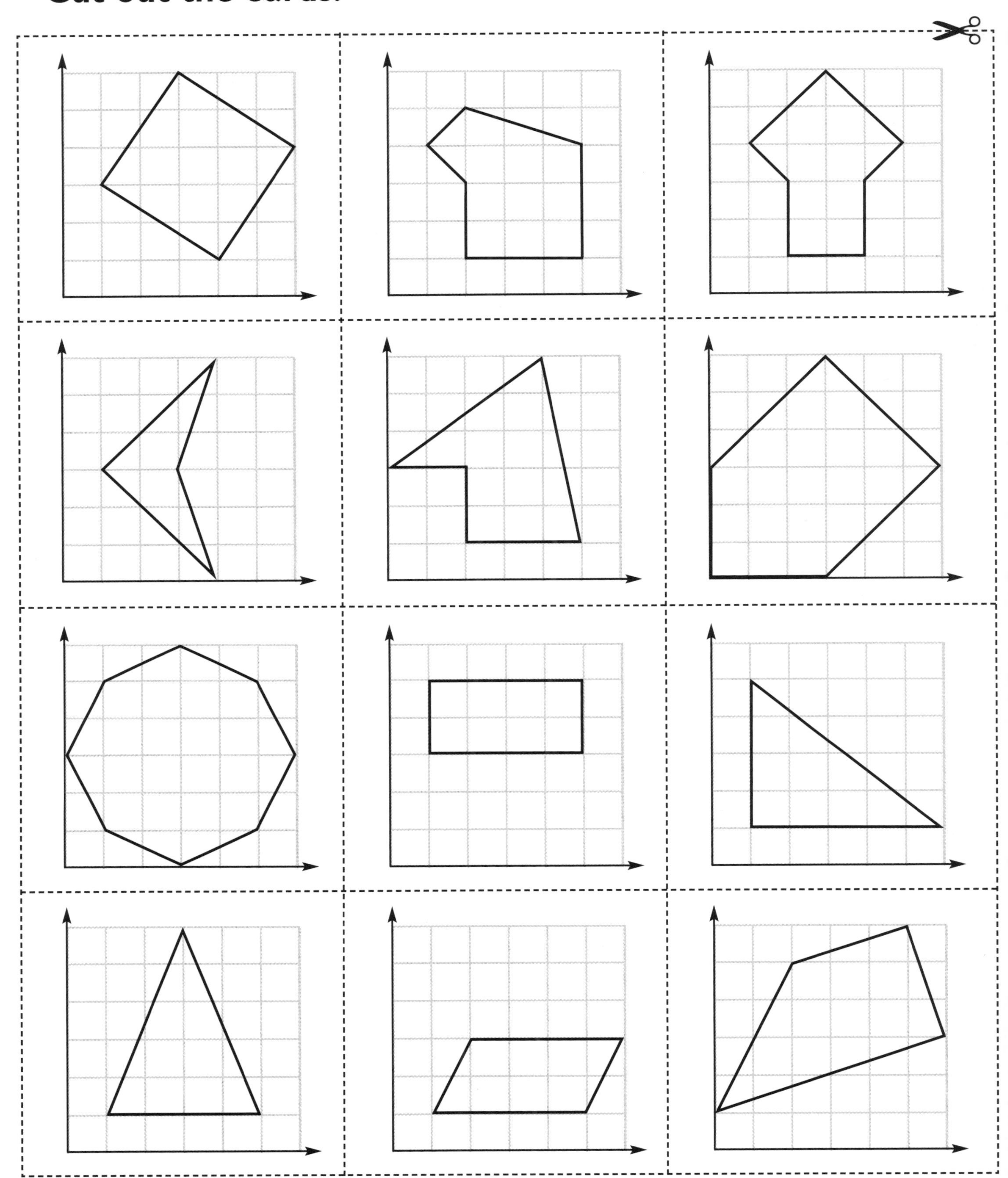

Teachers' note Use this sheet in conjunction with 'Proper properties game' and 'Shapes: 2'. Copy the sheet onto thin card and ask the children to cut out the cards. The cards could be laminated to provide a more permanent classroom resource. Explain that the arrows on the shape cards show the horizontal and vertical directions.

Shapes: 2

• **Cut out the cards.**

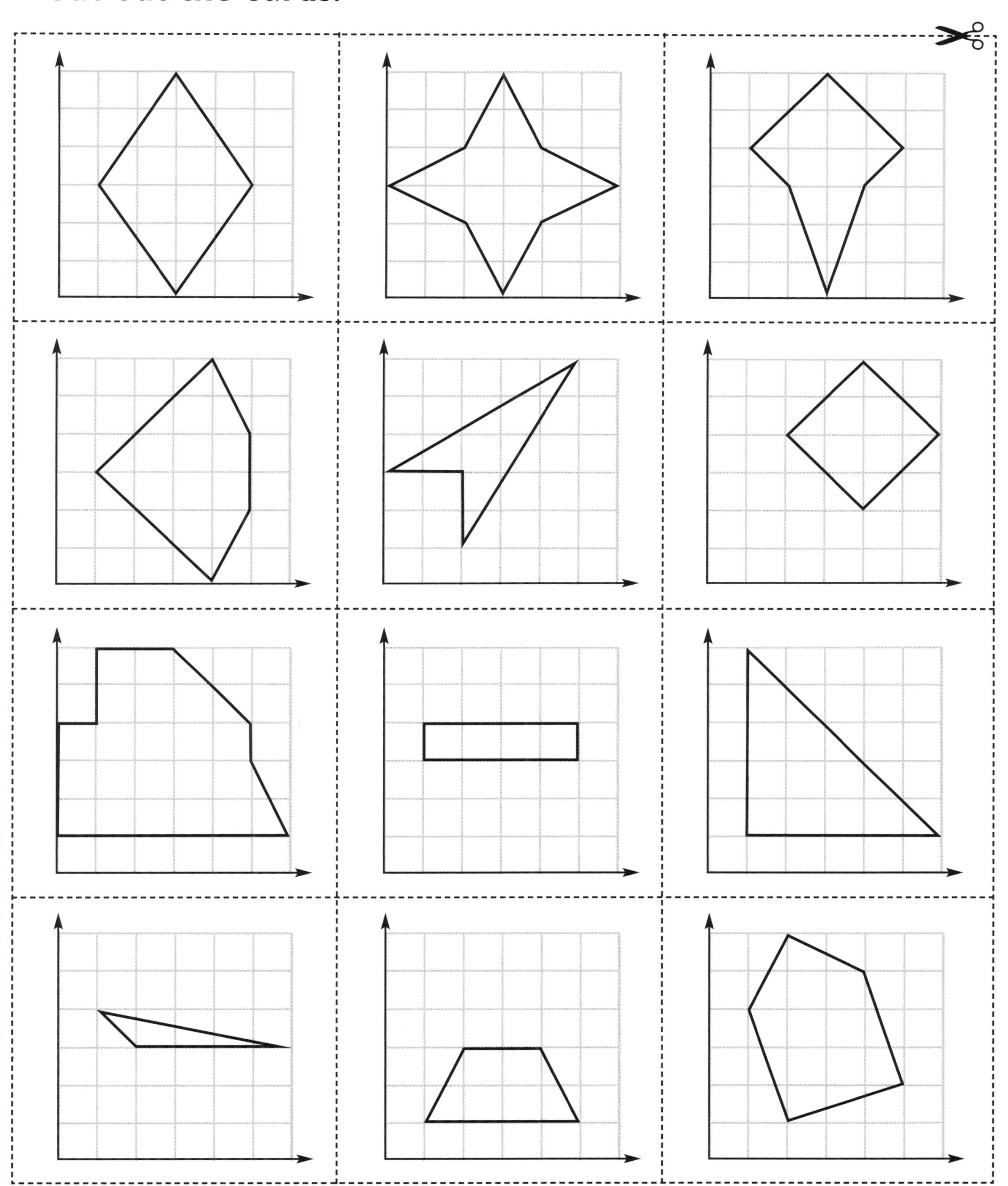

Teachers' note Use this sheet in conjunction with 'Proper properties game' and 'Shapes: 1'. Copy the sheet onto thin card and ask the children to cut out the cards. The cards could be laminated to provide a more permanent classroom resource. Explain that the arrows on the shape cards show the horizontal and vertical directions.

Party presents

- **Colour the presents that are** prisms **.**

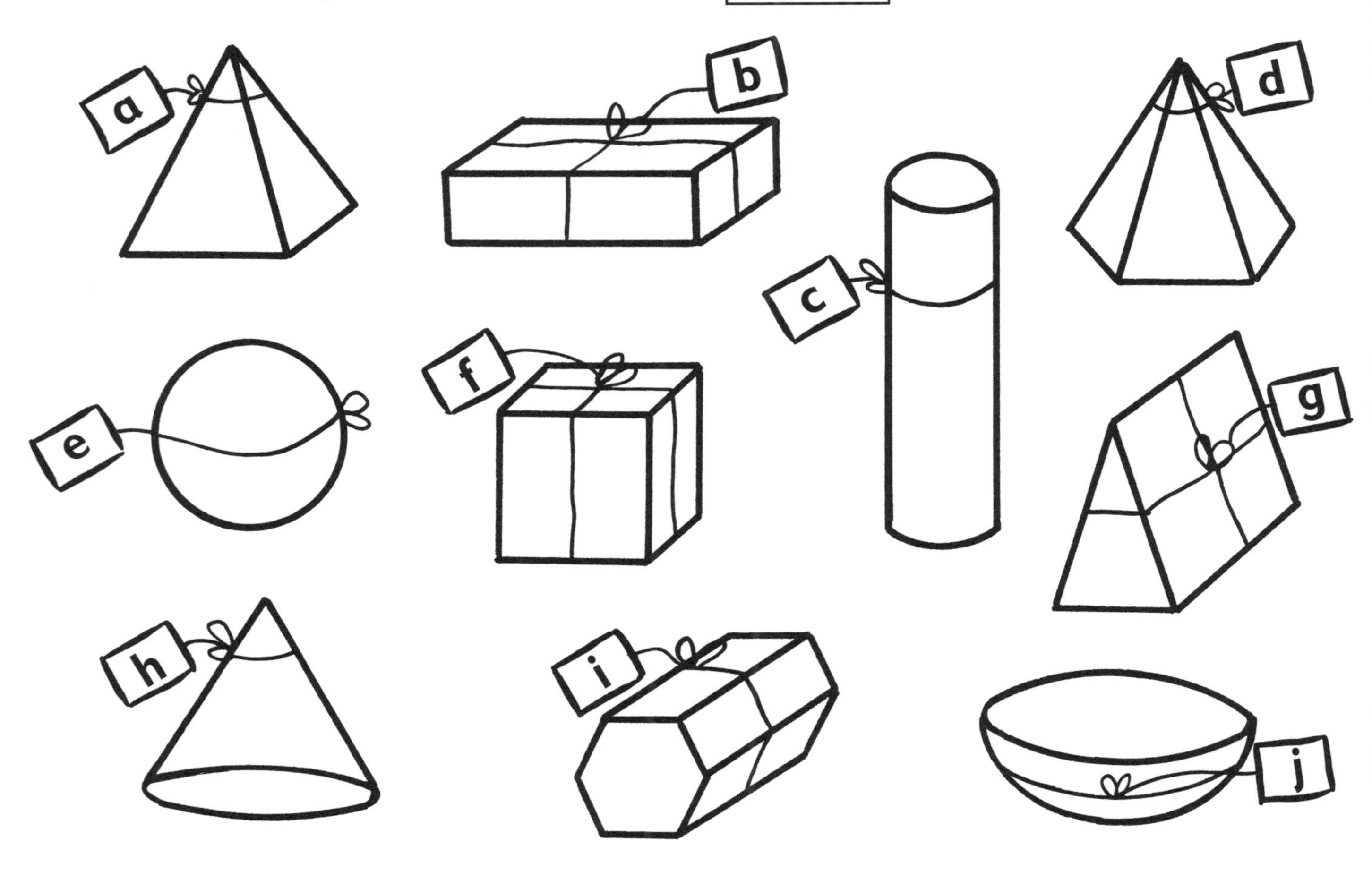

- **Write which present each child brought.**

1. h — My present has one circular face and one vertex.

2. My present has six triangular faces and one hexagonal face.

3. My present has one circular face, one curved edge and no vertices.

4. My present has six rectangular faces and two hexagonal faces.

5. My present has two circular faces, two curved edges and no vertices.

6. My present has six square faces, eight vertices and twelve edges.

Teachers' note Remind the children that prisms have the same cross-section throughout their length. Provide the children with matching solid shapes to enable them to count and examine the properties. As a further extension, the children could write descriptions of the other shapes, referring to faces, edges and vertices.

Cube challenge

- **Make each shape in the colours shown.**

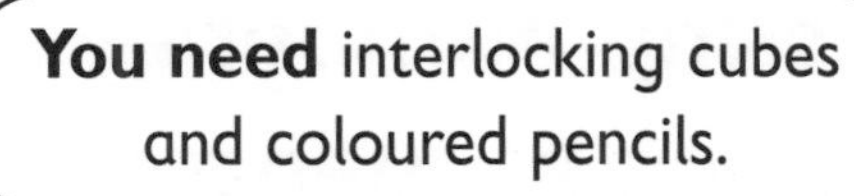

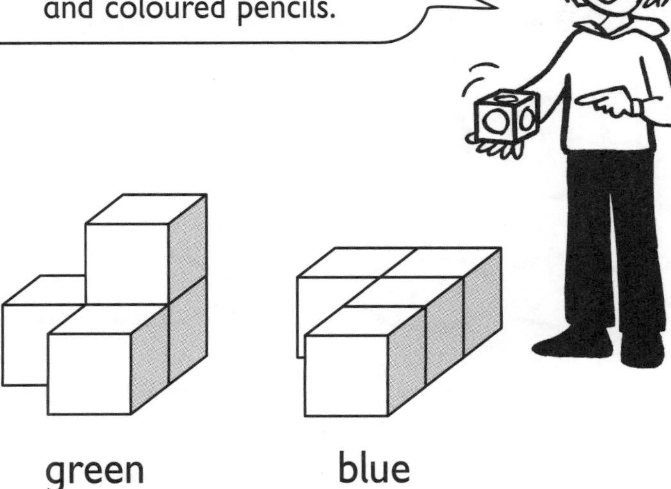

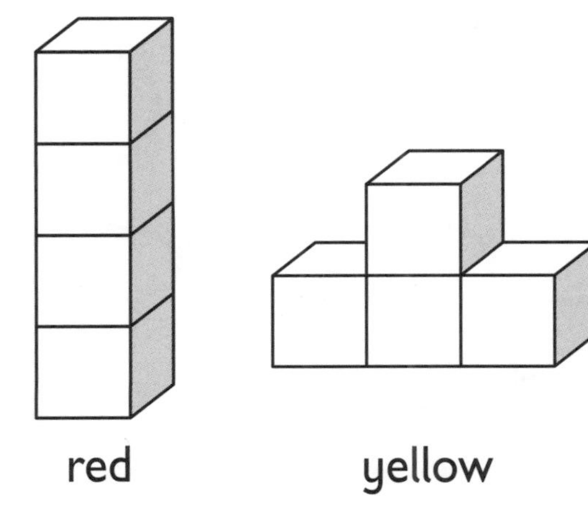

- **Now make each model below using two of your shapes.**
- **Colour the faces of each picture to show how you did it.**

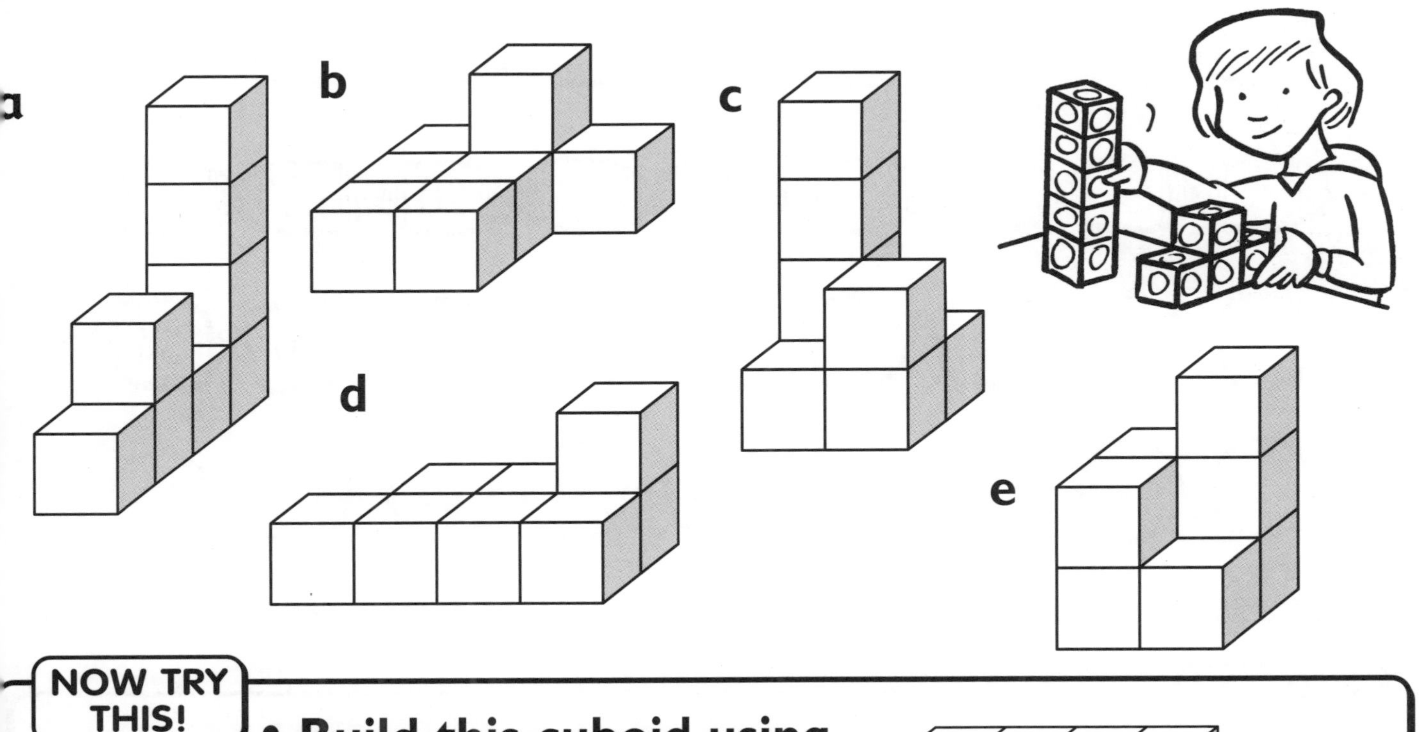

NOW TRY THIS!

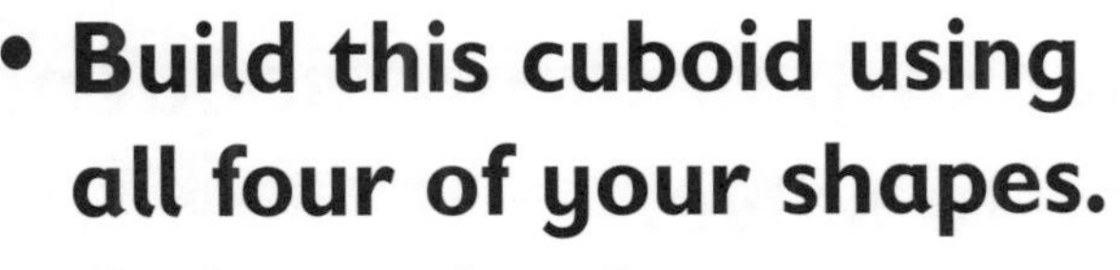

- **Build this cuboid using all four of your shapes.**
- **Colour the faces to show how you did it.**

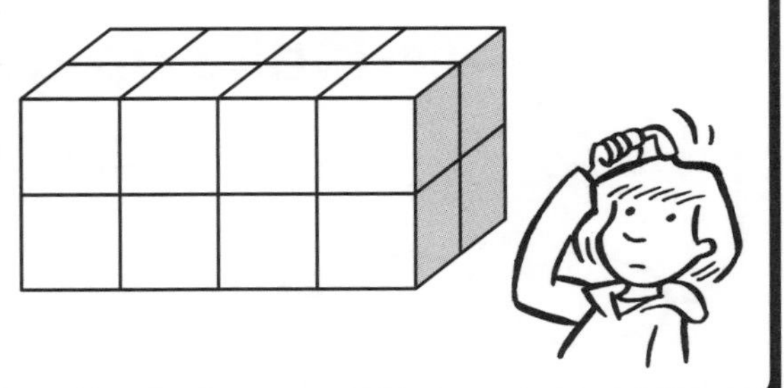

Teachers' note Ensure that the children have a range of coloured Multilink cubes to make these shapes and the appropriate coloured pencils. As a further extension, the children could make a model using two of the shapes and try to draw a picture of it.

Necklace numbers

- **Fill in the missing numbers in these necklace sequences.**

1	17	20	23						
2		13	17	21					
3				18	23	28			
4				19	25	31			
5		7		17	22				
6			8		14		20		
7							46	50	54
8					29		41		53

- **Discuss the rule for each sequence with a partner.**

NOW TRY THIS!

- **Make up your own necklace sequence for a partner to solve.**

Teachers' note Encourage the children to find the difference between adjacent numbers in each sequence where possible, and then to extend the sequences in the directions necessary. Where there are no adjacent numbers, the children can find the difference between given numbers and halve the answer to find the intermediate number.

Sticks

Ali and Sally have been making shapes using sticks of different lengths.

- **Use the clues below to work out which shapes each child made.**
- **Colour Ali's shapes red, and Sally's shapes blue.**

Teachers' note Ensure the children understand that when a rule applies to one person it does not necessarily mean that the opposite is true for the other person, for example because Ali only makes shapes with an odd number of sides, it does not mean that Sally only makes shapes with an even number of sides.

Dividing exactly

- **Which number from this board is each child talking about?**
- **Write it in the box.**

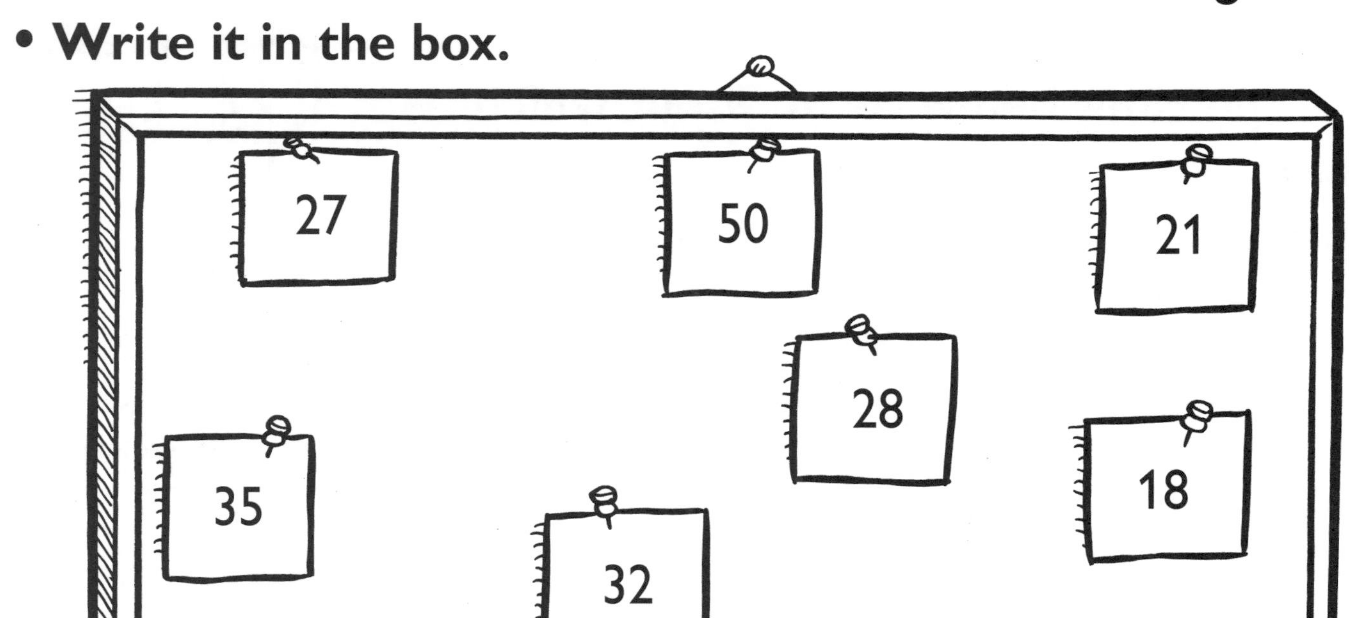

My number divides exactly by 2, by 5 and by 10.

☐ Hussain

My number divides exactly by 3, but **not** by 6 or by 9.

☐ Jane

My number divides exactly by 2 and by 4, but **not** by 8.

☐ Jermaine

My number divides exactly by 9 and by 3, but **not** by 6.

☐ Benny

My number divides exactly by 5, but **not** by 10.

☐ Jenny

My number divides exactly by 2, by 3 and by 6.

☐ Penny

NOW TRY THIS!

- **Which of the numbers is not described?** ____
- **Write all the numbers that divide exactly into it.**

____

Teachers' note The numbers can be altered to provide differentation. Encourage the children to discuss the nature of different multiples of a number, for example that multiples of 10 end in zero, and to write their own descriptions about other numbers given.

Andy, Sandy and Mandy

Andy, Sandy and Mandy are taking part in a maths quiz.

- **Tick who says the best approximation.**

1. 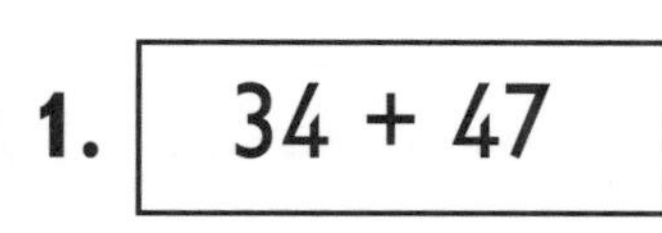
34 + 47

2. 67 – 48

3. 127 + 52

4. 171 – 28

5. 173 + 249

6. 64 × 5

NOW TRY THIS!

- **Estimate the answers to these questions.**

(a) 268 – 43 ☐ (b) 53 × 8 ☐ (c) 94 ÷ 9 ☐

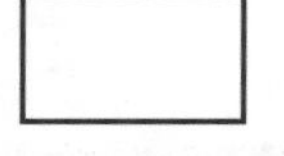

Teachers' note When estimating the size of an answer encourage the children to round the numbers appropriately or to use their knowledge of tables and number facts to find a fact close to the one in the question.

What a puzzle!

- **Find the missing digits to make each calculation correct.**
- **Solve each puzzle and write a report on how you worked it out.**

No two digits in a puzzle can be the same.

You may use a calculator.

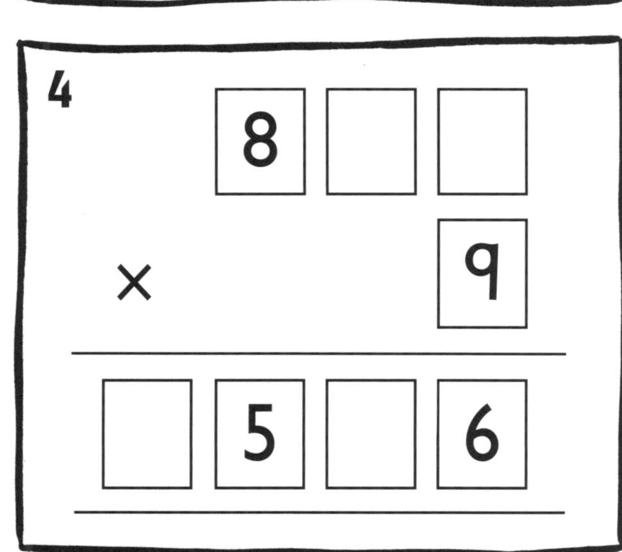

- **Write more missing number questions for a partner to solve.**

Remember, no two digits can be the same.

Teachers' note The focus of this activity should be on reporting back to the rest of the class about the strategies and reasoning used to solve the puzzles.

Double trouble

1. Double all the numbers between 26 and 50. Write the original number in the correct section of the grid.

51	52 26	53	54	55	56	57	58	59	60
61	62	63	64	65	66	67	68	69	70
71	72	73	74	75	76	77	78	79	80
81	82	83	84	85	86	87	88	89	90
91	92	93	94	95	96	97	98	99	100

2. Double all the numbers between 76 and 100. Write the original number in the correct section of the grid.

151	152 76	153	154	155	156	157	158	159	160
161	162	163	164	165	166	167	168	169	170
171	172	173	174	175	176	177	178	179	180
181	182	183	184	185	186	187	188	189	190
191	192	193	194	195	196	197	198	199	200

- **Talk to a partner about patterns you notice in both grids.**

Teachers' note Encourage the children to choose a number, double it and find the answer rather than to choose a number from the grid and halve it, as this will enable them to begin to see connections between numbers between 26 and 50 and those between 76 and 100.

At the sales

Everything in the sale is half price!

- **Write the new prices on the labels.**

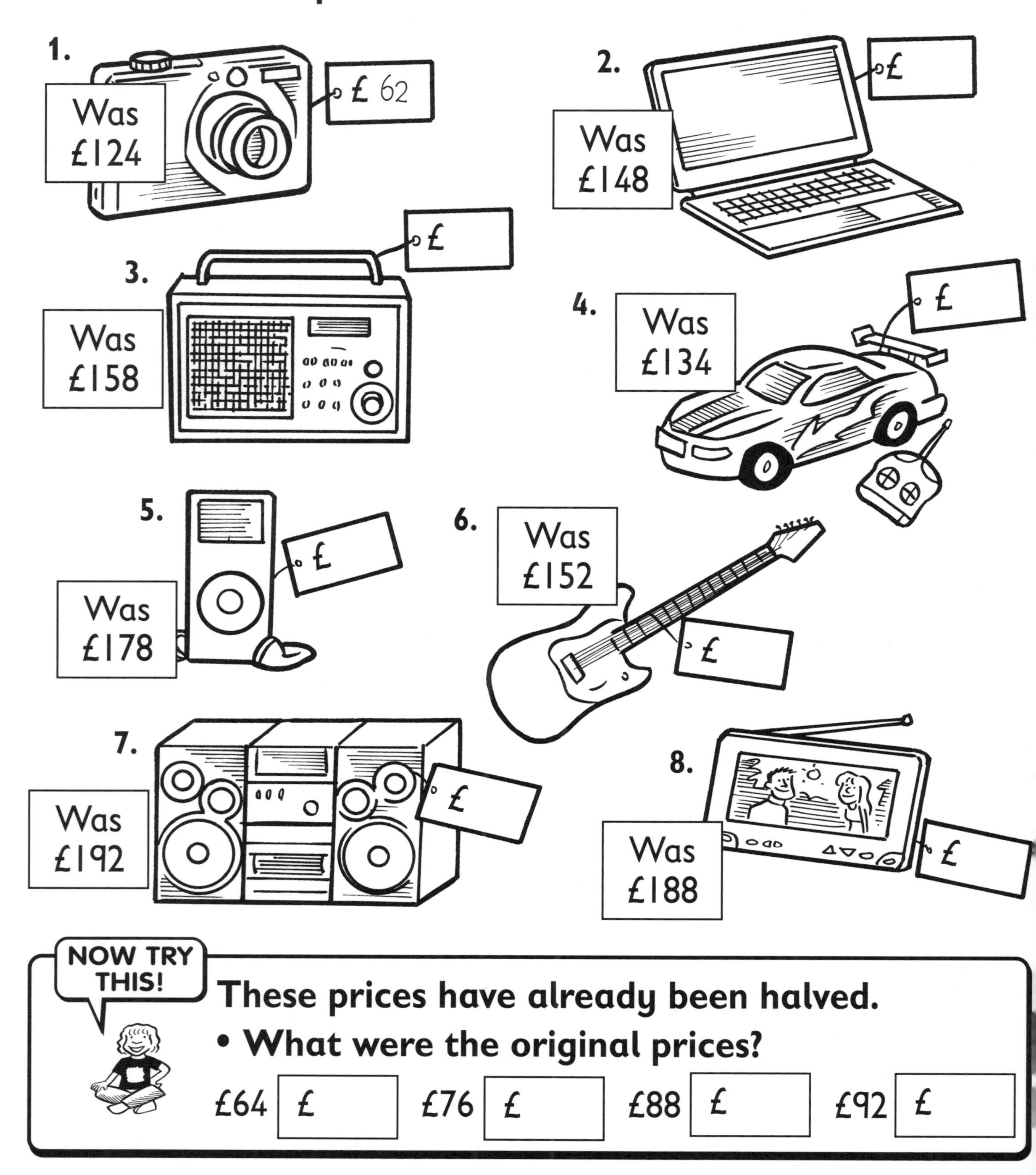

NOW TRY THIS!

These prices have already been halved.

- **What were the original prices?**

£64 £ £76 £ £88 £ £92 £

Teachers' note Children can be given the 'Double or halve' sheet on page 37 to help them to partition the numbers being halved.

Brooches

- **Draw all the lines of symmetry on each brooch. Some are <u>not</u> symmetrical.**

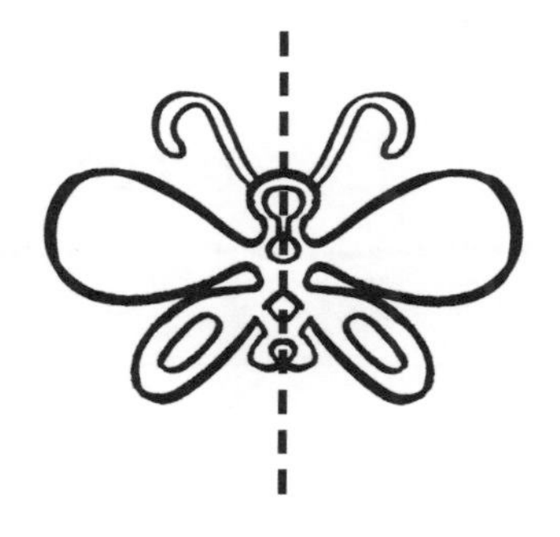

- **Design your own brooch with three or six lines of symmetry.**

Teachers' note Some of these brooches have rotational but not reflective symmetry. Watch out for children who may mistakenly think that lines of symmetry can be drawn on such brooches. Demonstrate where shapes are not symmetrical by tracing or cutting out the brooch and showing how the halves do not match when folded.

Decorations

Here are some festival decorations.

- **Use this key to colour them.**

Key	
triangles	blue
quadrilaterals	red
pentagons	yellow
hexagons	green

a 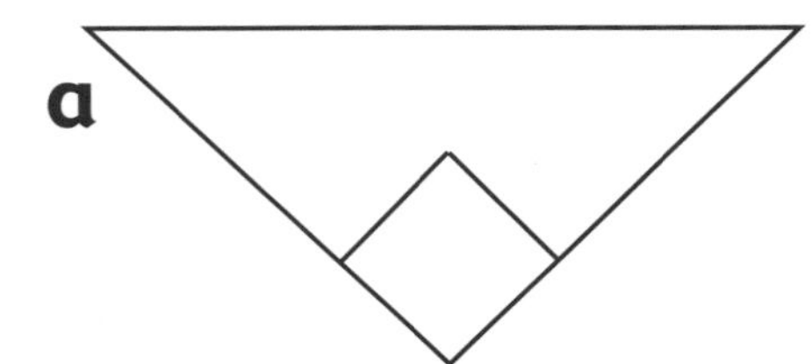

b 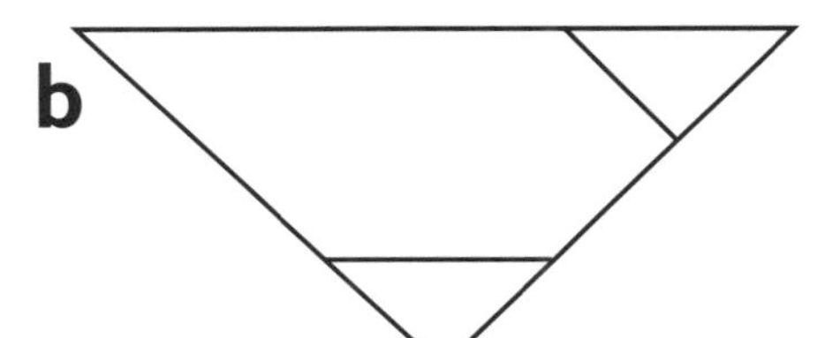

c 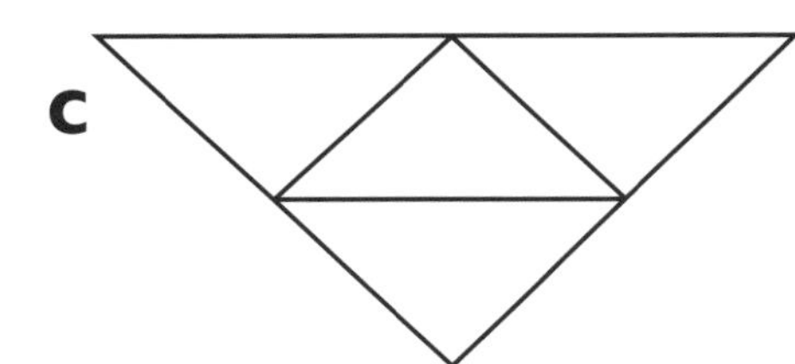

d 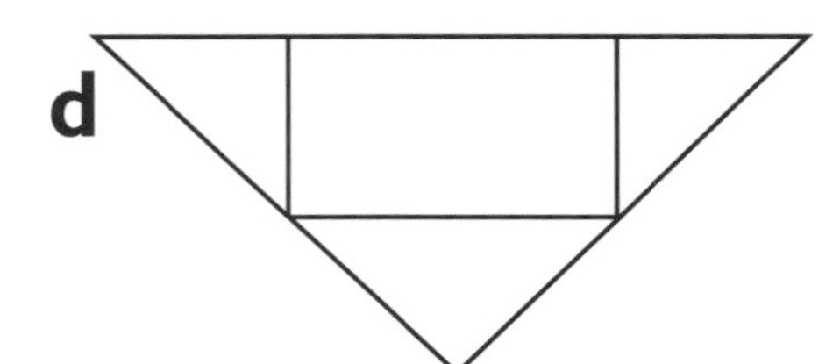

e 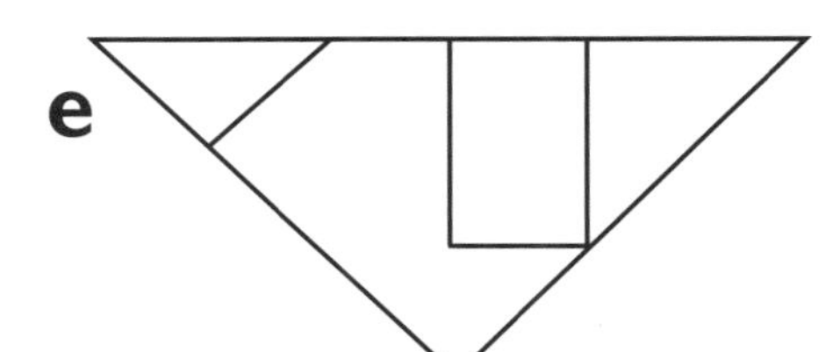

f 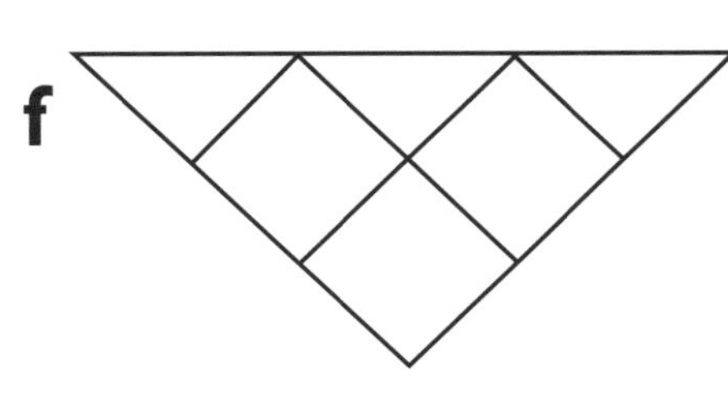

g 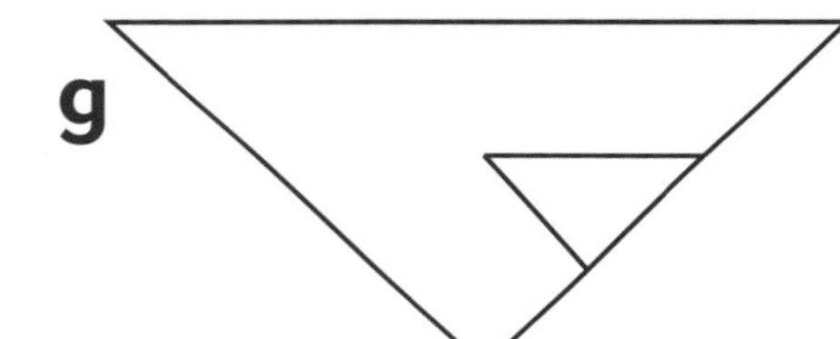

h 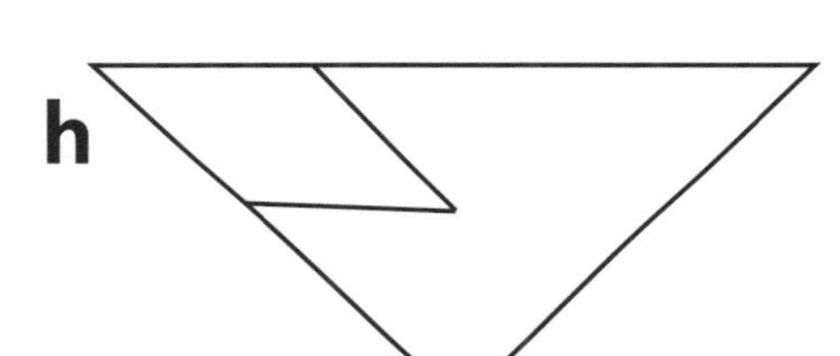

i 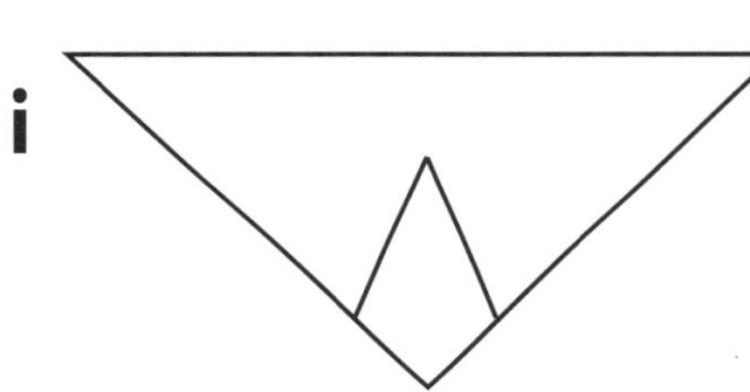

NOW TRY THIS!

- **Write the matching letter in the correct section of the** Venn diagram **.**

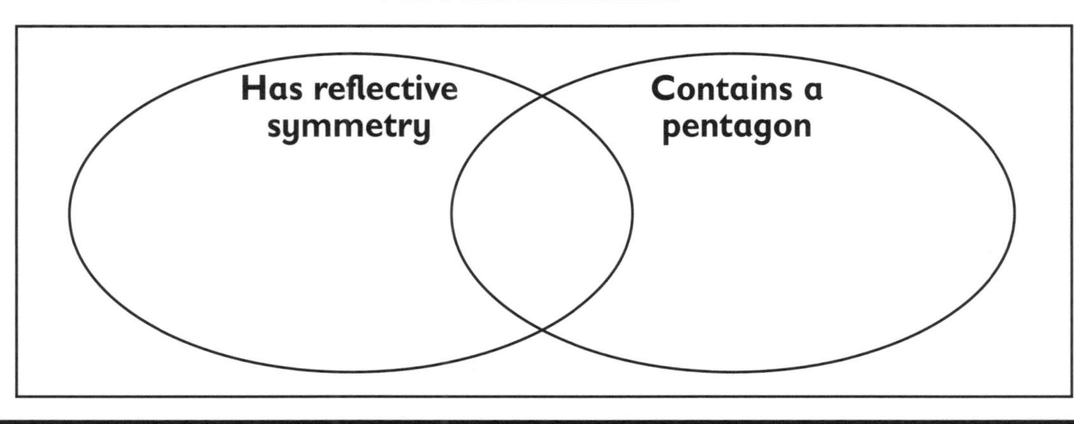

Teachers' note As a further extension, the children could draw and complete another Venn diagram and label it 'Is not symmetrical' and 'Has vertical sides'.

Crazy cubes

- **Tick the cube that you think matches each net.**

1.

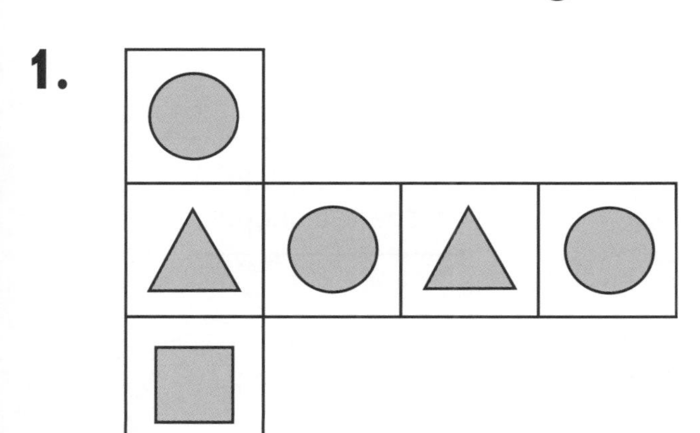

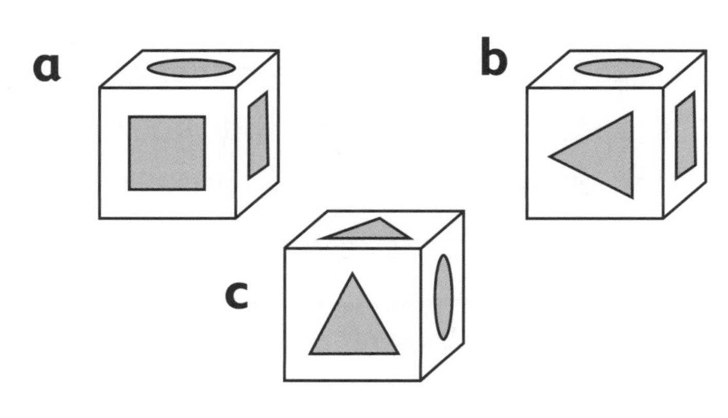

2.

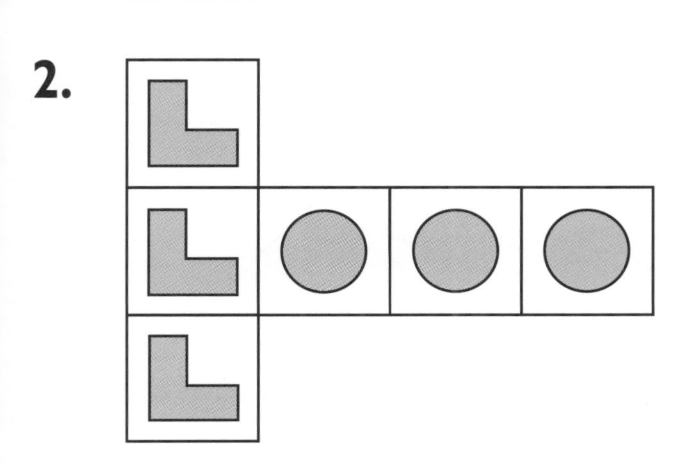

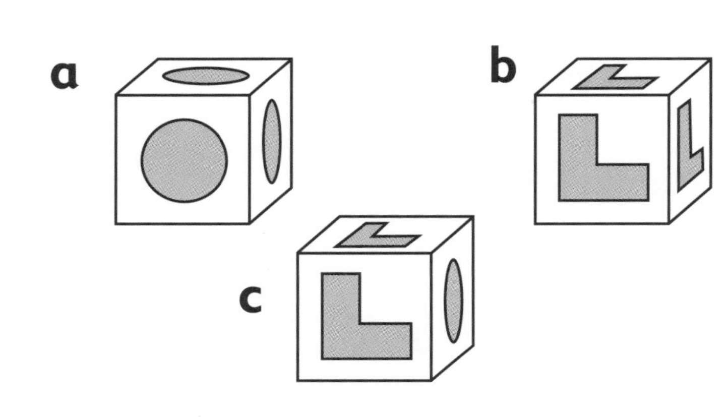

3.

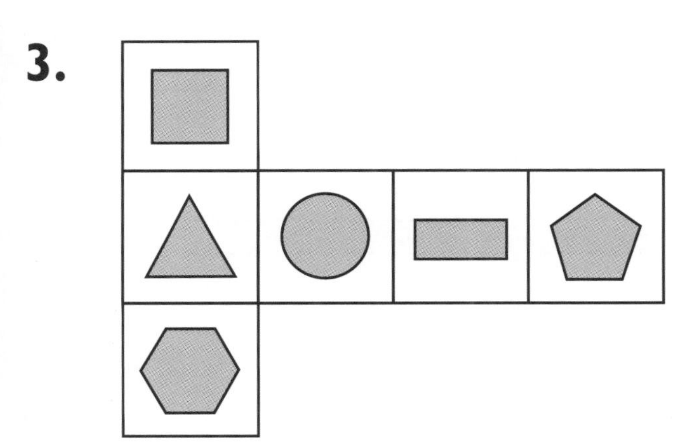

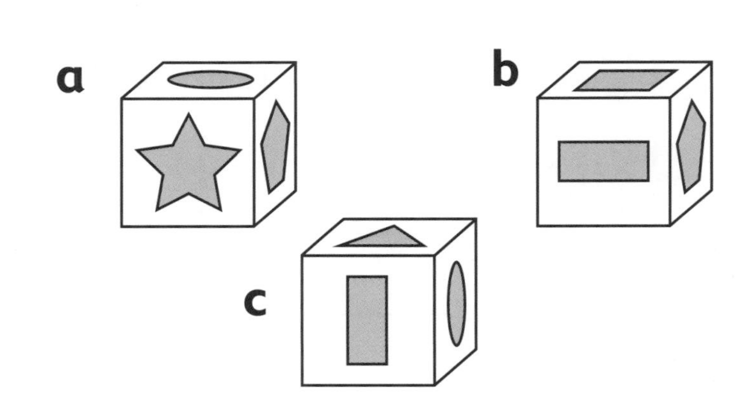

- **Now cut out the nets to check your answers.**

NOW TRY THIS!

- **Make your own cube net with shapes on it.**
- Sketch **the cube from different angles.**

Teachers' note Some children may find it difficult to visualise the cubes from the nets and will need to make up each cube and match it to a picture. The children could use sticky tape to hold the faces of the cubes together. The sheet could be enlarged to A3 size and stuck onto card to make the nets more permanent.

Tell me

☆ Work with a partner.

☆ Cut out the cards and place them face down in a pile.

☆ Take turns to pick a card and describe the shapes on the card so that your partner can draw them exactly onto a piece of paper.

☆ Use these words to help you.

Don't let your partner see the shapes!

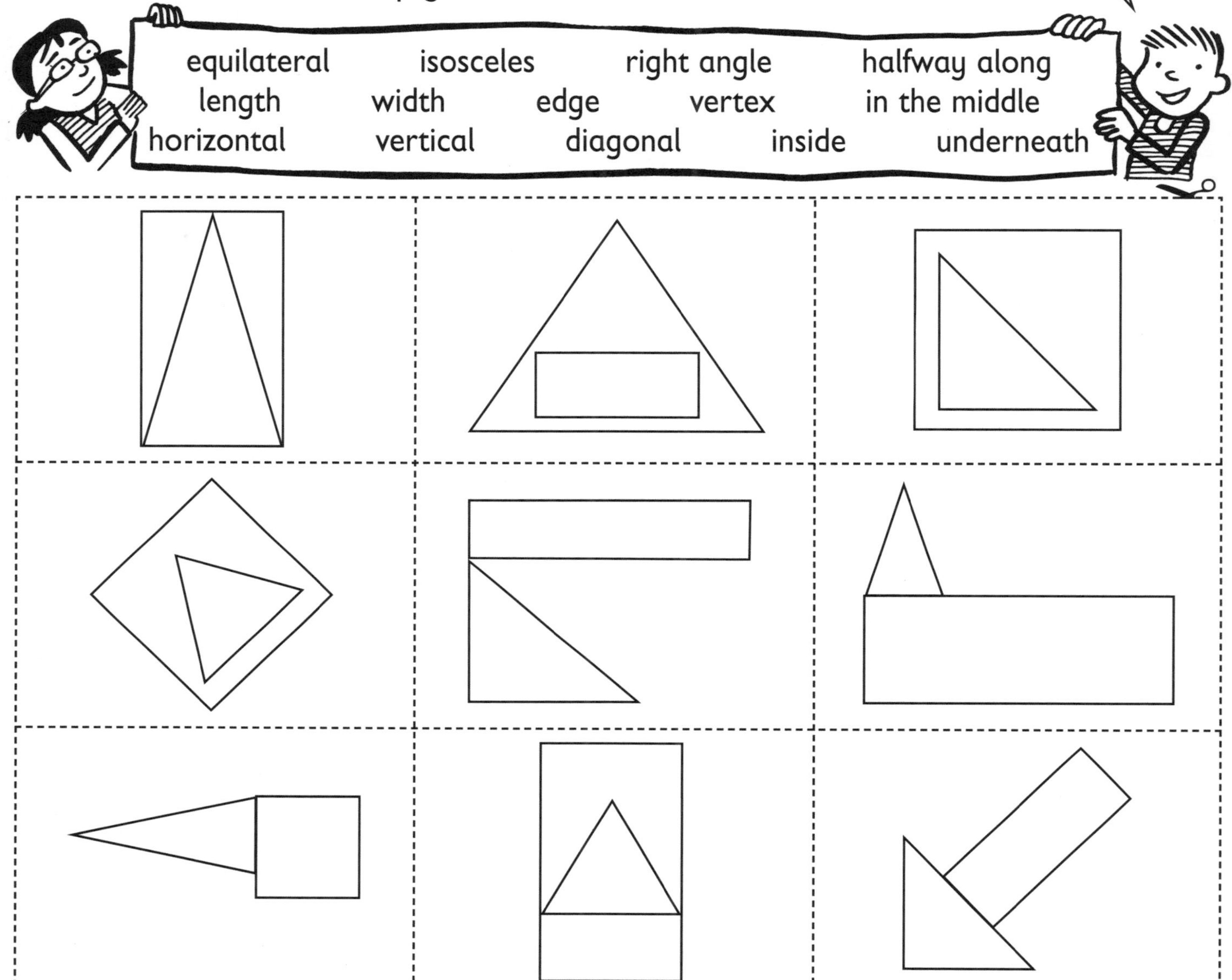

- **Write descriptions of three of the cards so that someone else could pick them from this set.**

Teachers' note Ideally, this worksheet should be copied onto card so that the shapes cannot be seen through the paper. As a further extension, encourage the children to talk to each other about the shapes and to decide how they would like to sort them into groups. Accept any ways of sorting, encouraging the children to explain their reasoning to others.

True statements

☆ Cut out the cards.
☆ How many true statements can you make using the cards?
☆ You do not have to use all the cards in a statement.
☆ Record your answers below.

6 is a factor of 54

is a factor of				is the product of
multiplied by				is a multiple of
6	9	54	=	divided by

Teachers' note The numbers can be altered to provide differentiation. Encourage the children to work systematically to find all the possible solutions. As an extension, the children could record all possible number sentences that can be made with those numbers.

Halfway house

- Colour true or false for each statement.
- Write examples on the houses to prove it.

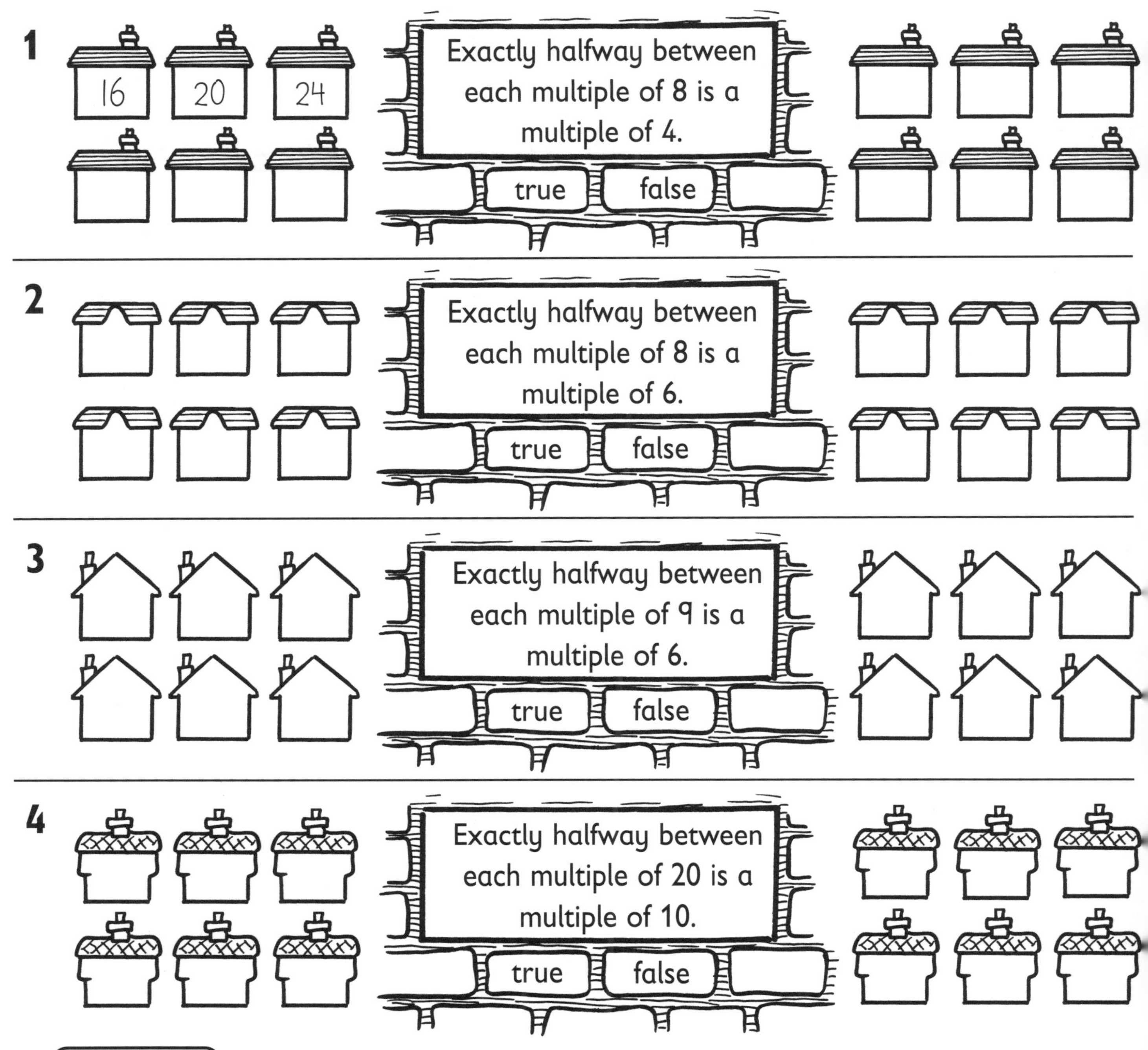

- On the back of this sheet, make up a halfway statement that is true.
- Write four examples to prove it.

Teachers' note Remind the children of the meaning of the word 'multiples' and identify some on a number line. Emphasise that the halfway number must be exactly halfway, and demonstrate this on a number line if necessary. Ensure the children understand that giving one example is insufficient to prove a general statement, although one example can be enough to disprove it.

Badge sale

The children of Hawsker school have made badges to sell at the school fête.

	Shields	Stars	Flowers	Circles
large				
small				

1 Three small shields cost 60p. How much do five small shields cost? ☐

2 Two large circles cost £1.60. How much do three large circles cost? ☐

3 Three large stars cost £4.50. How much do two large stars cost? ☐

4 Four small flowers cost 48p. How much do five small flowers cost? ☐

5 Five small circles cost £1. How much do three small circles cost? ☐

6 Four large shields cost £5.20. How much do three large shields cost? ☐

7 Three small stars cost 75p. How much do seven small stars cost? ☐

8 Five large flowers cost £5.50. How much do three large flowers cost? ☐

NOW TRY THIS!

James buys one of each badge.

- **How much does it cost?**

Teachers' note Ensure that the children understand that the price given for several items is the total price for that number, and not the price for one of the items. Encourage the children to describe the strategies that they used for solving the problems, using words, diagrams or calculations.

Fair share: 1

Mrs Joseph puts £10 notes into six envelopes. She puts £10 in the first envelope, £20 in the second envelope, and so on.

£10 £20 £30 £40 £50 £60

1 How much money is there in total? _______

2 Mrs Joseph gives two envelopes to each of her three nieces. Which envelopes does she give each child so that they each have the same amount?

_____________________ _____________________ _____________________

3 If Mrs Joseph had eight envelopes, how much money would there be in total? _______

£10 £20 £30 £40 £50 £60 £70 £80

4 How could she give each child the same amount this time?

_____________________ _____________________ _____________________

NOW TRY THIS!

- **Find other ways of sharing out the eight envelopes to give each child the same amount of money.**

Teachers' note Use in conjunction with 'Fair share: 2'. Encourage the children to decide for themselves how to work out the solutions, for example using a cube to represent each £10 note or writing the amounts on slips of paper. Compile a class list of all the possible solutions to the eight envelopes problem.

Fair share: 2

Mr Barber puts £10 notes into envelopes. He puts £10 in the first envelope, £20 in the second envelope, and so on.

£10 £20 £30 £40 £50 £60 £70 £80

1 How much money is there in total? _______

2 Mr Barber gives two envelopes to each of his four children. Which envelopes does he give each child so that they each have the same amount?

_______________ _______________ _______________ _______________

3 If Mr Barber had nine envelopes, how much money would there be in total? _______

£10 £20 £30 £40 £50 £60 £70 £80 £90

4 How could he give **three** of his children the same amount?

_____________________ _____________________ _____________________

NOW TRY THIS!

- **Find other ways of sharing out the nine envelopes to give three of his children the same amount of money.**

Teachers' note Use in conjunction with 'Fair share: 1'. Encourage the children to decide for themselves how to work out the solutions, for example using a cube to represent each £10 note or writing the amounts on slips of paper. Compile a class list of all the possible solutions to the nine envelopes problem.

Computer glitch

A computer keeps making mistakes.

- **Check which are wrong using inverses.**

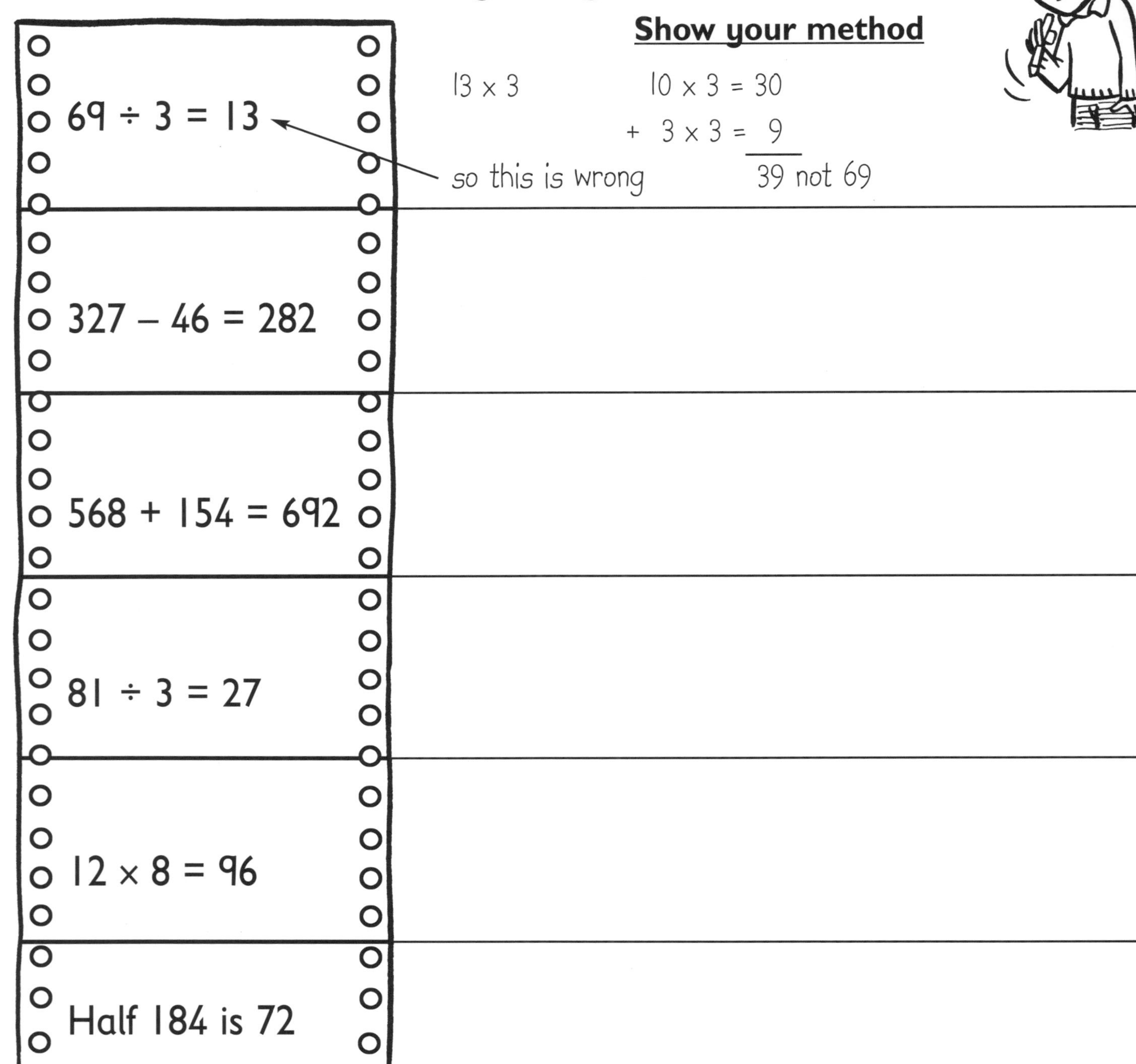

- **Talk to a partner about how you checked each one.**

Teachers' note At the start of the lesson discuss the meaning of the word 'inverse' and determine which operations are inverse to which. Demonstrate how calculations can be checked using the answer and the inverse calculation, for example to check 354 – 32 = 322 we can add 322 and 32 to see if the answer is 354.

Grid reasoning

- **Place counters on two or more numbers in each row so that the remaining numbers in each row and column add up to 20.**

You need counters.

6	2	5	3	5	4	4	1
4	6	1	2	1	6	1	5
5	1	3	4	2	2	1	4
2	3	4	3	7	9	1	5
1	3	6	8	3	2	6	5
7	9	2	4	6	2	2	4
2	2	4	4	3	4	4	1
4	4	7	2	1	5	8	1

NOW TRY THIS!

- **Write a report on what you did and the strategies that you used.**

Teachers' note The focus of this activity should be on reporting back to others in the class about the thinking and reasoning that took place when solving the puzzle.

Water slide

- Start at the top and write the answers as you go.
- Try to reach the finish as quickly as you can.

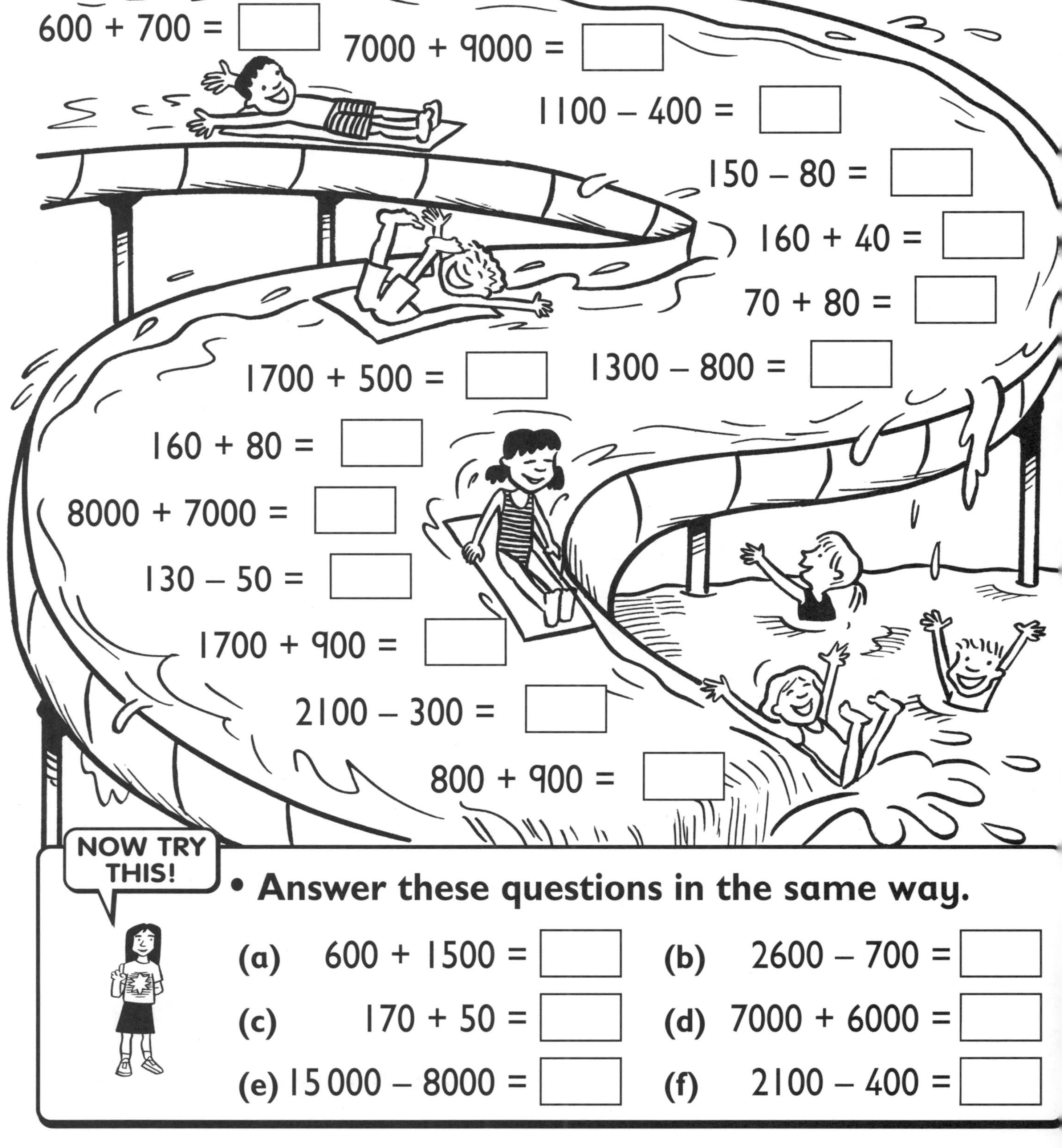

NOW TRY THIS!

- Answer these questions in the same way.

(a) 600 + 1500 = ☐ (b) 2600 – 700 = ☐

(c) 170 + 50 = ☐ (d) 7000 + 6000 = ☐

(e) 15 000 – 8000 = ☐ (f) 2100 – 400 = ☐

Teachers' note Encourage the children to see the link between the addition and subtraction facts for totals to 20 and the facts of multiples of 10, 100 and 1000, for example 6 + 7 = 13 so 600 + 700 = 1300. Discuss that subtraction and addition are inverses and encourage the children to use addition facts they know to help them quickly derive subtraction facts and vice versa.

Sitting ducks

There are six ways of moving from 'start' to 'finish' where you land on three multiples of 1000.

- **Find all six routes. Add the numbers you land on to find the total for each route.**

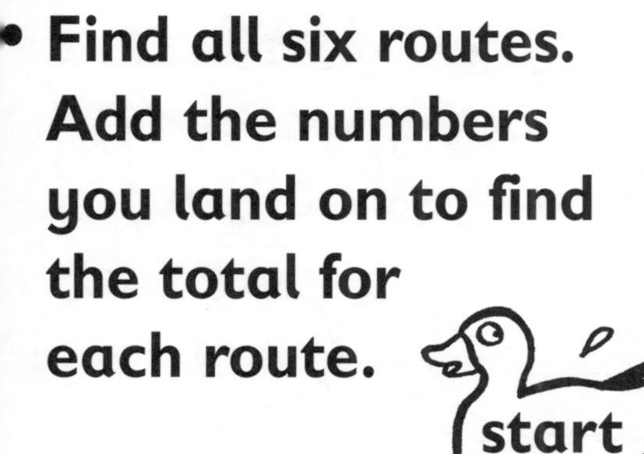

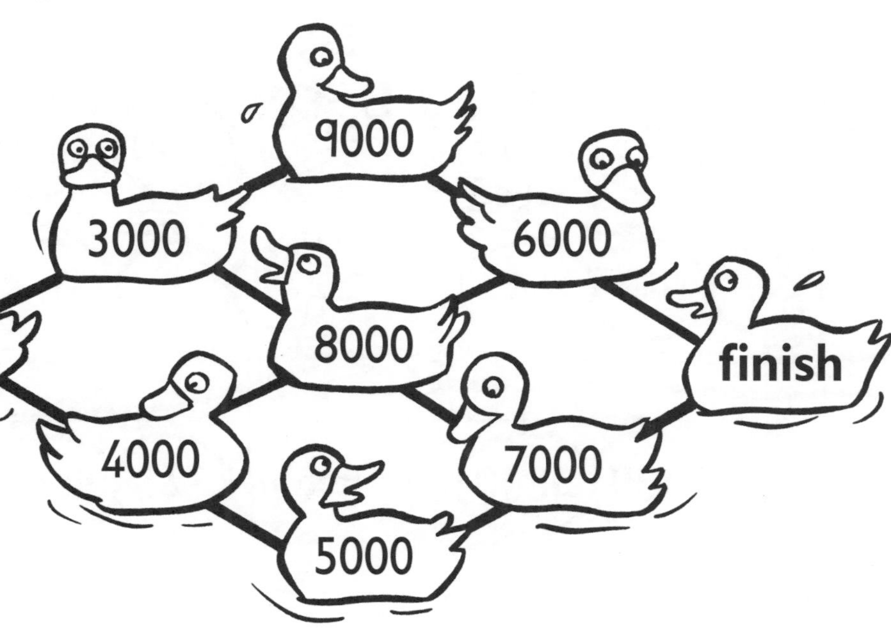

3000 + 9000 + 6000 = 18 000

NOW TRY THIS!

- **Find three ways of moving from 'start' to 'finish' where you land on five multiples of 1000. Find the total for each route.**

Teachers' note Encourage the children to be systematic when finding different possible routes. Ask further questions about the totals such as, 'Which three-multiple route has the highest total?' 'Which five-multiple route has the lowest total?' 'Can you find a route that has a total of 42 000?'

Double bugs

- **Double the numbers on the first bug and write them on the second bug.**

1.

2.

3.

4.

5.

6.

7.

8.

9.

10.

11.

12.

- **Draw a pair of double bugs of your own to display on the classroom wall.**

Teachers' note This activity draws the children's attention to the relationships between doubling two-digit numbers and multiples of 10 and 100. The 'Double or halve' sheet could be given to the children to help them partition the two-digit number first.

Half bugs

- **Halve the numbers on the second bug and write them on the first bug.**

1. 12 | 120 | 1200
   24 | 240 | 2400
2. 36 | 360 | 3600
3. 42 | 420 | 4200
4. 66 | 660 | 6600
5. 84 | 840 | 8400
6. 48 | 480 | 4800
7. 72 | 720 | 7200
8. 56 | 560 | 5600
9. 74 | 740 | 7400
10. 86 | 860 | 8600
11. 92 | 920 | 9200
12. 98 | 980 | 9800

NOW TRY THIS!

- **Draw a pair of half bugs of your own to display on the classroom wall.**

Teachers' note This activity draws the children's attention to the relationships between halving numbers and multiples of 10 and 100. The 'Double or halve' sheet could be given to the children to help them partition the two-digit number first.

Stick 'em up

The children always put the same number of stickers on each page of their books.

- **How many stickers are on each page?**

1. 54 stickers, 6 pages

Answer: 9

2. 49 stickers, 7 pages

Answer: ☐

3. 64 stickers, 8 pages

Answer: ☐

4. 63 stickers, 9 pages

Answer: ☐

5. 56 stickers, 7 pages

Answer: ☐

6. 72 stickers, 9 pages

Answer: ☐

7. 56 stickers, 8 pages

Answer: ☐

8. 72 stickers, 8 pages

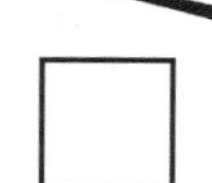

Answer: ☐

9. 63 stickers, 7 pages

Answer: ☐

NOW TRY THIS!

- **Use the answers above to help with these.**

(a) ☐ × 8 = 72 (b) 9 × ☐ = 63 (c) 7 × 8 = ☐

(d) ☐ × ☐ = 81 (e) 9 × ☐ = 54 (f) 6 × ☐ = 48

Teachers' note Ensure the children realise that, because of the commutative law, if they know one multiplication fact, for example 7 × 8 = 56, they also know that 8 × 7 = 56. An understanding of this effectively halves the number of facts a child has to learn.

The great shape game

- **This is a game for 2 or 4 players.**

Teachers' note The children cut out the cards and share them out. The first player puts down a card, chooses a grey shape and names it. The number of sides equals the number of points scored. The next player then places a card alongside it (with a whole side touching) to make a new grey shape. The winner is the player with the most points when all the cards have been placed.

Nets with pentagons

- **Cut out the** nets **.**
- **Fold along the lines to make** 3-D **shapes.**

You need scissors, glue and sticky tape.

tab

tab

tab

tab

tab

tab

tab

tab

tab

tab

tab

tab

tab

tab

Teachers' note Copy this worksheet onto thin card, or glue the sheet onto thicker card. Once constructed, the shapes could be coloured so that no two touching faces are the same colour.

Nets with triangles

- **Cut out the** nets **.**
- **Fold along the lines to make** 3-D **shapes.**

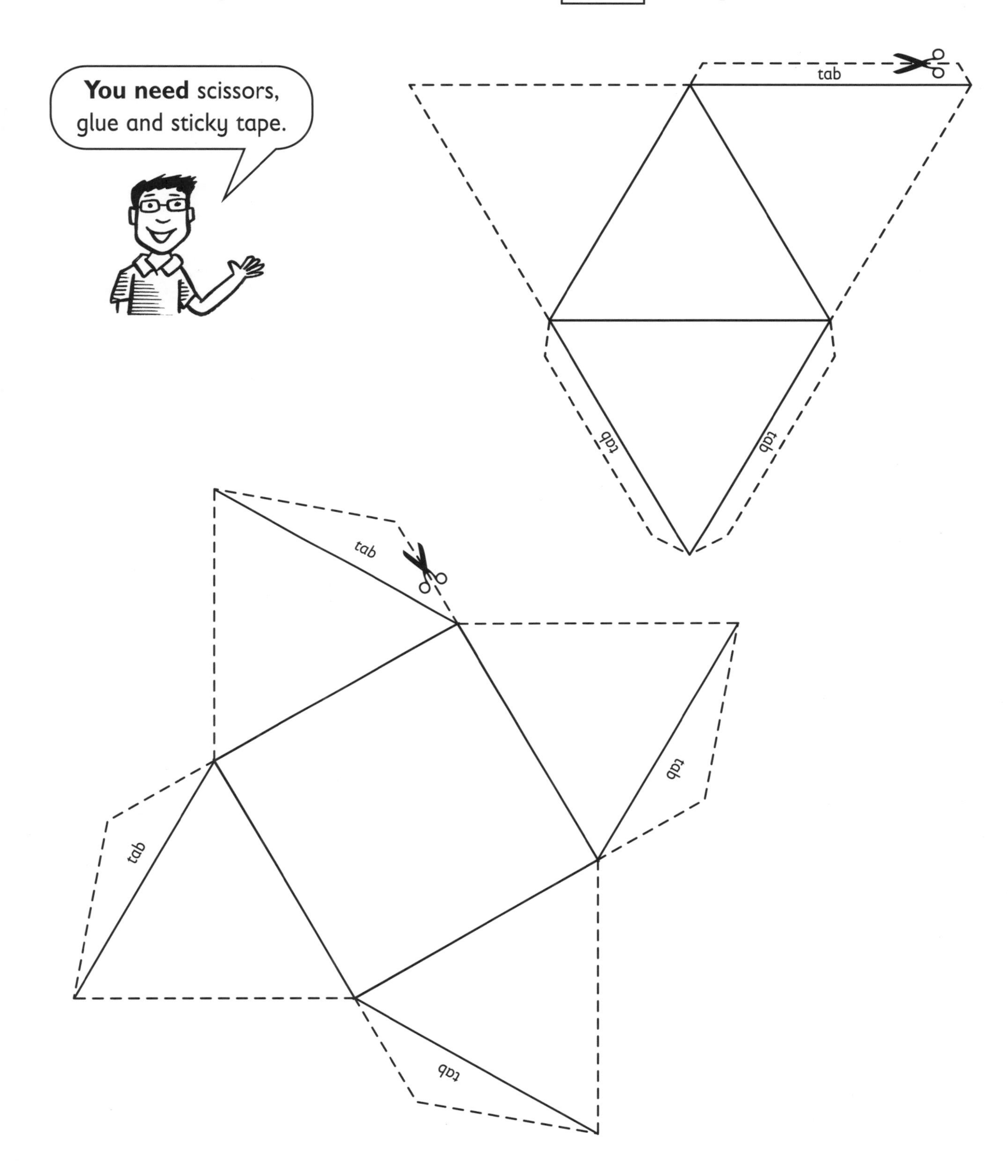

Teachers' note Copy this worksheet onto thin card, or glue the sheet onto thicker card. Once constructed, the shapes could be coloured so that no two touching faces are the same colour.

Nets with rectangles

- **Cut out the** nets **.**
- **Fold along the lines to make** 3-D **shapes.**

You need scissors, glue and sticky tape.

Teachers' note Copy this worksheet onto thin card, or glue the sheet onto thicker card. Once constructed, the shapes could be coloured so that no two touching faces are the same colour.

Nets with circles

- **Cut out the nets.**
- **Fold along the lines to make 3-D shapes.**

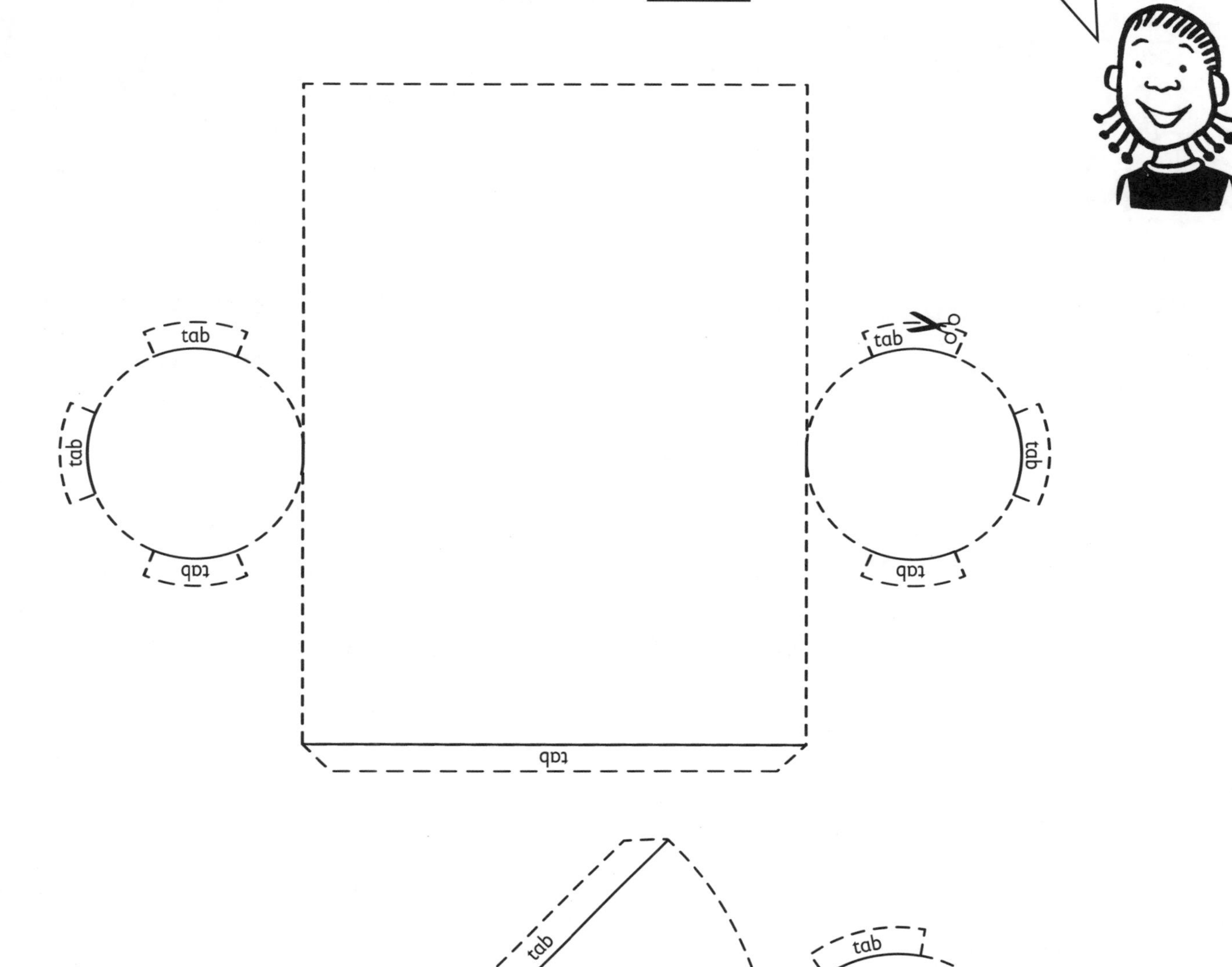

Teachers' note Copy this worksheet onto thin card, or glue the sheet onto thicker card. Be prepared to help children who accidentally cut off the circles from the main net.

Fruit segments

There are 24 children.

Each child eats the same amount of fruit.

There are four apples and six satsumas.

Each apple can be cut into halves or quarters.

Each satsuma has 12 segments.

- **Write four questions about the information above for a partner to answer. You could start your questions with:**

How many ..?

What is the most ..?

What is the fewest ..?

If all the apples are shared ..?

If four satsumas are shared ..?

How many segments ..?

What fraction of the apples ..?

1 ______________________________

____

2 ______________________________

____

3 ______________________________

____

4 ______________________________

____

- **Swap worksheets with your partner and answer his/her questions.**

Teachers' note This activity encourages the children to make up their own questions using appropriate vocabulary. When the children exchange worksheets for the extension activity, encourage them to describe how they decided what to do and to use number sentences to show the operation used. The numbers could be altered to provide differentiation.

Thinking thimbles

Li collects thimbles and wants to display some on a shelf with three sections. In each section she could put no thimbles, one thimble or two thimbles.

- How many different ways do you think Li could do this?
- Draw the thimbles to show the ways.

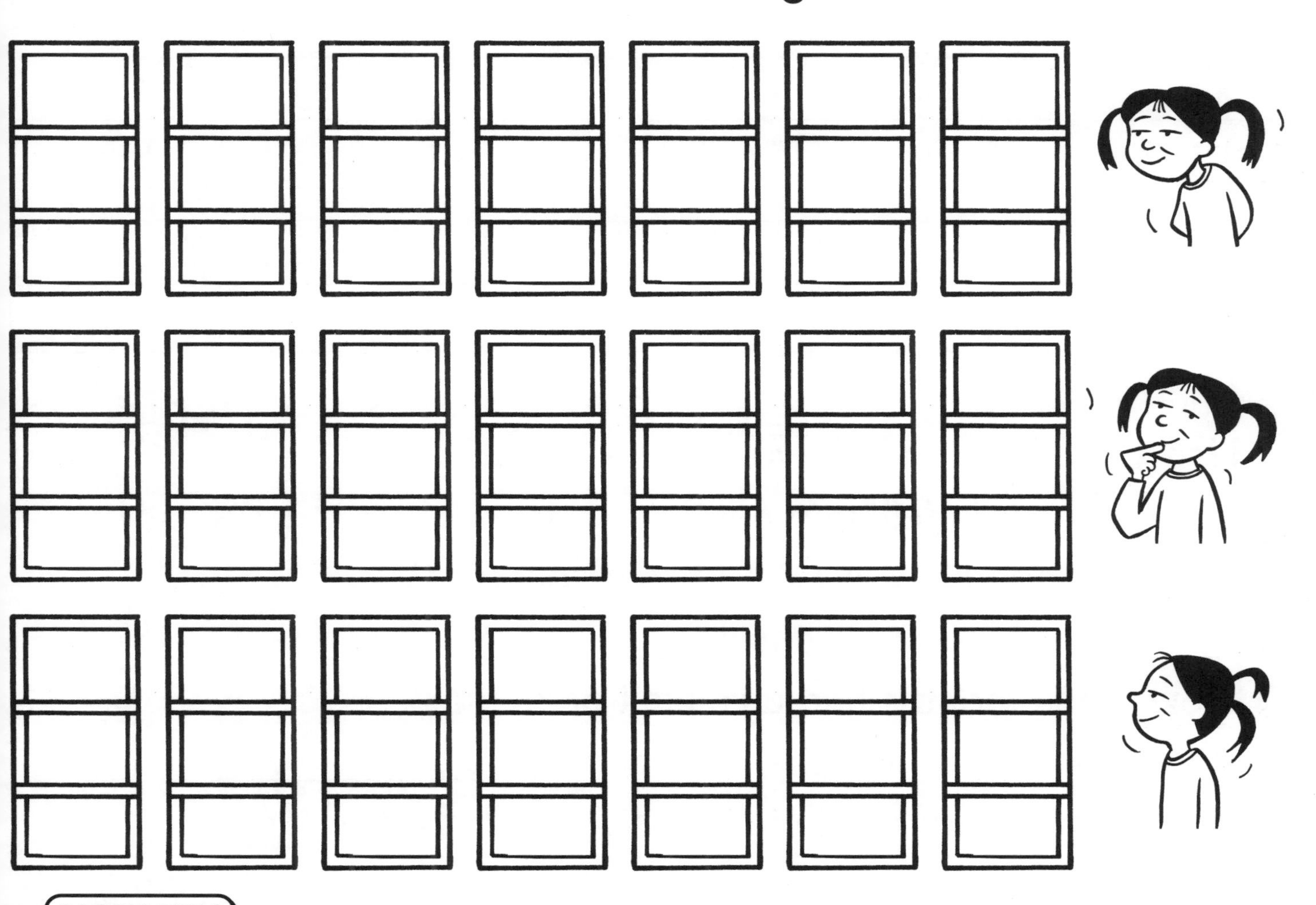

NOW TRY THIS!

Li keeps three gold thimbles on a special 3-section shelf. Each section can hold up to three thimbles.

- What arrangements are possible?

Teachers' note Ensure the children understand that a 0, 1, 2 shelf is the same as a 2, 1, 0 shelf, just with the shelves in different places. Discuss alternative ways of recording solutions to the extension activity, for example 012, 222, 121. Some children may, however, prefer to have a second blank sheet, or squared paper, on which to record the solutions.

Rain recorder

The Isle of Wight is an English island off the south coast of England.

The table below shows typical rainfall on the island, rounded to the nearest centimetre.

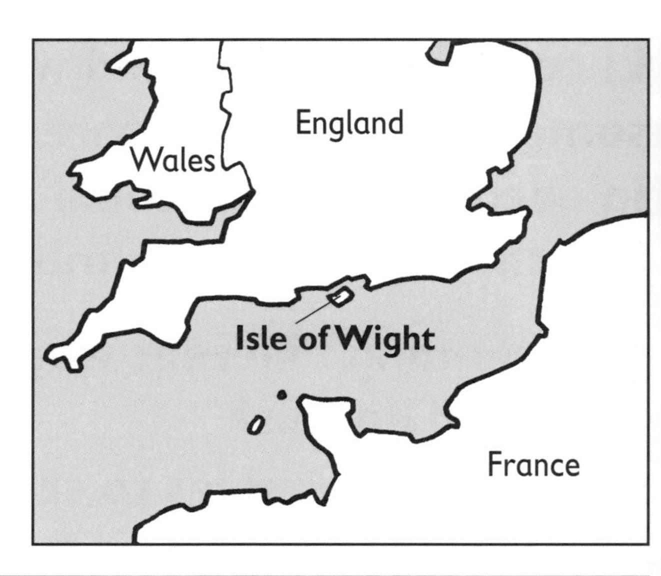

January	February	March	April	May	June
8 cm	5 cm	7 cm	5 cm	9 cm	5 cm

July	August	September	October	November	December
6 cm	8 cm	5 cm	13 cm	7 cm	9 cm

- **Use the table to answer these questions.**

1 How much rain fell in August? ____ cm

2 In which months was 7 cm of rain collected?

__________________ and __________________

3 How many months had a rainfall of 5 cm? ____

4 a In which month did the most rain fall? __________________

b How much more rain fell in this month than in May? ____ cm

5 How much rain fell in the month of your birthday? ____ cm

NOW TRY THIS!

- **How much rain was collected over the whole of the year?** ____ cm

Teachers' note This data is taken from http://www.isleofwightweather.com/ The data is rounded to the nearest centimetre. Calculators could be made available for the extension activity.

No shoes allowed!

Jemima was asked to make sure that children took off their footwear before going on the bouncy castle.

1 Complete the 'total' column in the **tally chart** to show how many pairs of each type of footwear were recorded during the time Jemima was in charge.

Type of footwear	Tally (number of pairs)	Total
Flip-flops	𝍸 𝍸 𝍸 ||	17
Plimsolls	𝍸 ||	
Trainers	𝍸 𝍸 𝍸 𝍸 |||	
Boots	|	
Wellies	||||	
School shoes	||	

2 How many children wore wellies? ____

3 How many pairs of flip-flops were there? ____

4 There were **exactly** seven pairs of which type of footwear?

____

5 **a** Which type of footwear did **fewest** children wear? ______________

b Why might this be? ________________________________

NOW TRY THIS!

Two children came in bare feet.

- **Add these bare-footed children to the tally chart.**
- **How many children in total went on the bouncy castle whilst Jemima was in charge? ____**

Teachers' note If necessary, revise how to record using a tally system. Explain to the children that each child has one go only on the bouncy castle.

Rock, paper, scissors

Your teacher will explain the rules of 'Rock, paper, scissors'.

Rock beats scissors, scissors beat paper and paper beats rock.

☆ Play the game with a partner.

☆ In the first column of the chart, write your name and the name of your partner.

☆ Keep a tally of who wins each game.

☆ Finally, add up the total number of wins for each player and complete the chart.

Name	Tally of wins	Total number of wins

- **Use the tally chart to answer these questions.**

1 How many games were played altogether? ____

2 Who won the most games? ________________

3 What is the difference between the scores? ____

NOW TRY THIS!

- **Write each of these tally results in numbers.**

Tally of wins	Total number of wins
𝍸 𝍸 𝍸 𝍸 𝍸 𝍸 |||	
𝍸 𝍸 𝍸 𝍸 ||||	
𝍸 𝍸 𝍸 𝍸 𝍸 𝍸 𝍸 𝍸 |||	

Teachers' note Ensure that the children are familiar with the rules of 'Rock, paper, scissors', which should be played in pairs (this could be done in mixed-ability pairs). Give the children a time limit or specify a number of games to play. A stopwatch could be used if the children are playing for a set number of minutes.

Sorting symmetry

1 Write each letter in the correct section of the Venn diagram.

~~a~~ b C D e F G H I J k L M N o P Q r s T U v w x Y Z

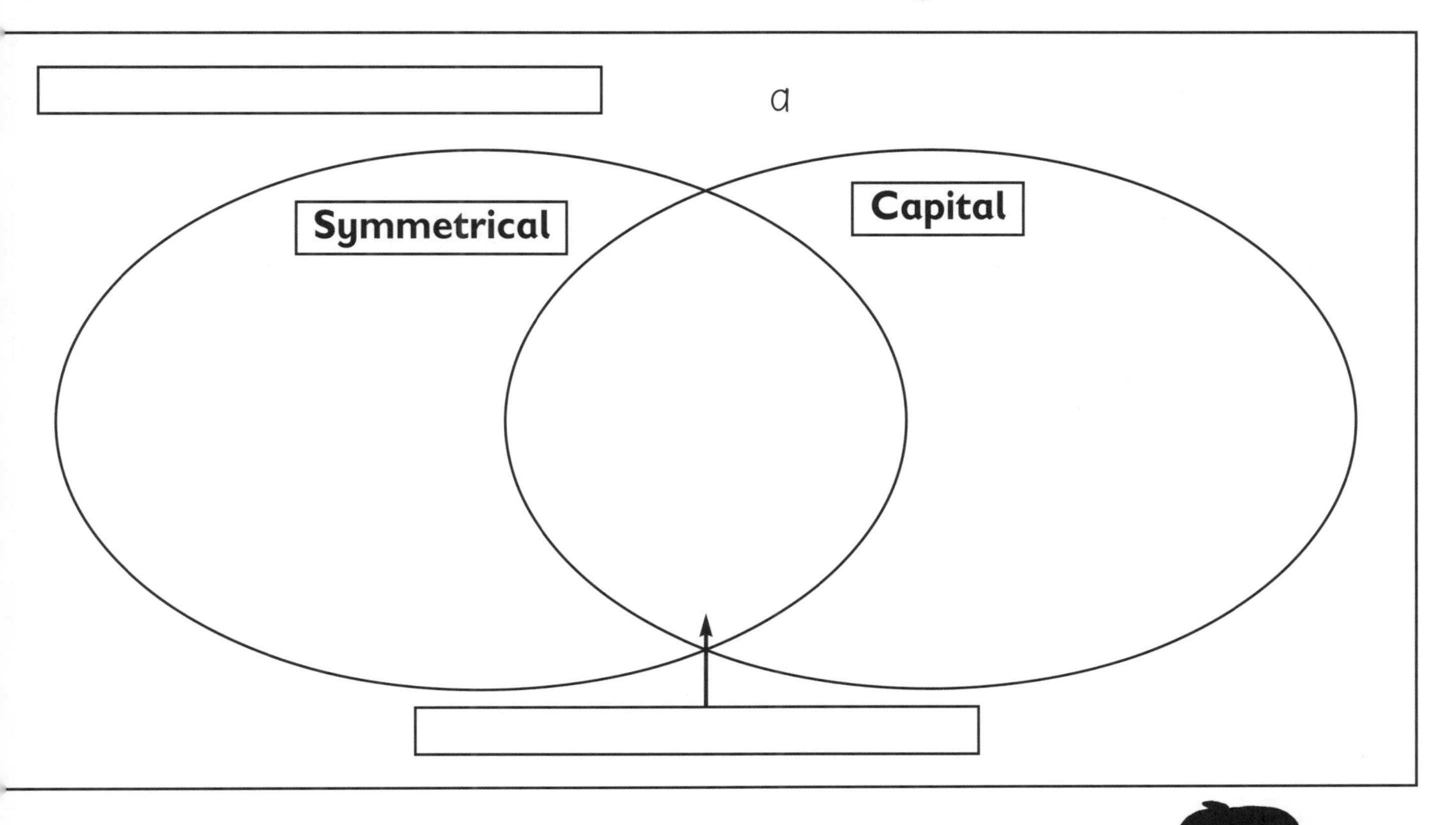

2 There are 26 letters above. How many are:

a capital? ____ **b** symmetrical? ____

3 How many letters are in the middle section? ____

4 How did you decide which letters to put in the middle section?

____

5 There are six letters inside the rectangle and outside the circles. How would you describe this data? ______________________________

- **Fill in the empty labels to complete the Venn diagram.**

Teachers' note Ensure the children understand that the alphabet shows some capital and some lowercase letters. Some children might find it helpful to have a small mirror to help them decide whether the letters are symmetrical. Remind them that letters can have vertical or horizontal lines of symmetry.

Monsters' tea party

This Carroll diagram shows data from the monsters' tea party.

	Chocolate cake	Not chocolate cake
Orange juice	Elmo, Nessie, Ziggy, Cleo, Dino, Percy, Mitzi	Cornelius, Minnie
Not orange juice	Taz, Wolfy, Slimy, Bogle	Howie, Stinker, Flower

1 How many monsters were at the tea party? ____

2 How many monsters had chocolate cake **and** orange juice? ____

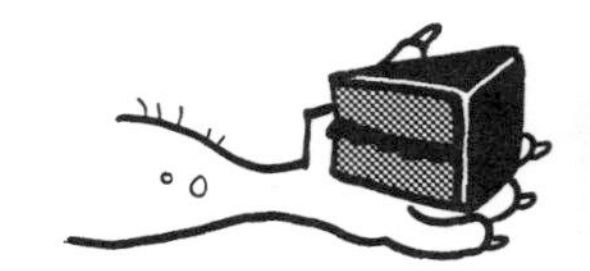

3 How many monsters did **not** have orange juice? ____

4 Who had orange juice but did not have chocolate cake?

____

5 How many monsters had chocolate cake? ____

6 Did Taz have orange juice? Yes ☐ No ☐

NOW TRY THIS!

Do you like chocolate cake and orange juice?

- **Write your name on the diagram to show what you would have.**

Teachers' note Discuss the diagram before the children answer the questions. Ensure that they understand the layout. The same data could be presented on a Venn diagram and comparisons made between the two diagrams.

Odd one out: 1

In each set, two of the charts show the same data and one shows different data.

- **Which is the odd one out in each set? Put a tick in the box.**

Set 1 Number of pets sold in one day at Pets 'R' Us

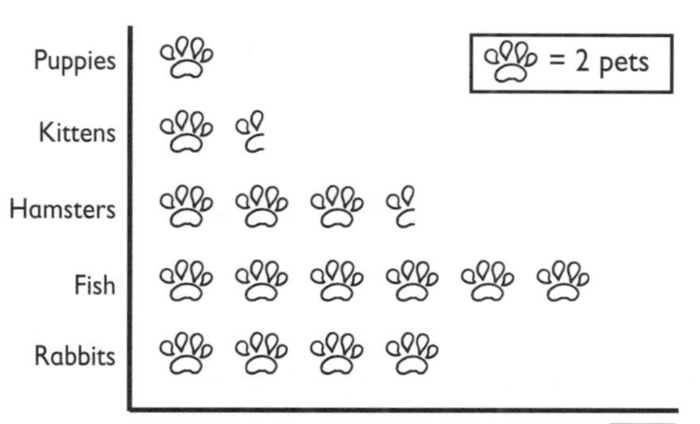

Pet	Tally
Puppies	||
Kittens	|||
Hamsters	𝍸 |
Fish	𝍸 𝍸 ||
Rabbits	𝍸 ||

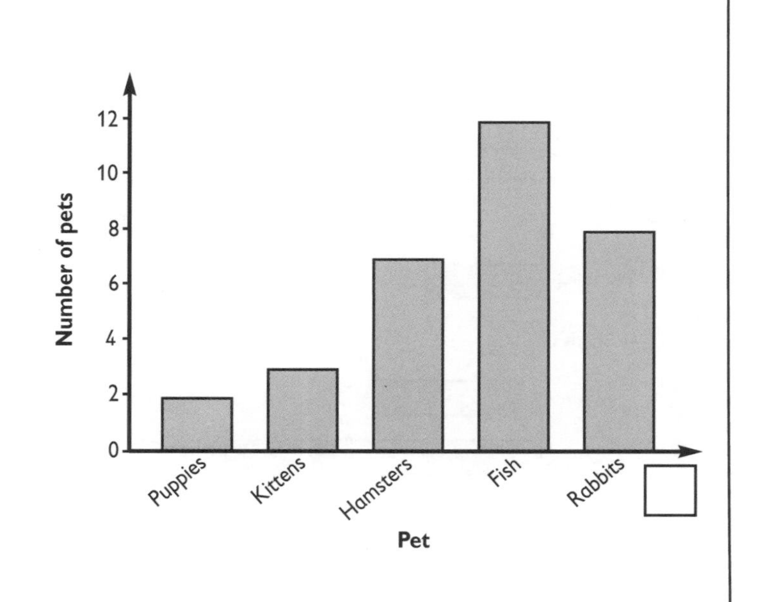

- **Use a coloured pencil to make changes to the odd one out in each set so that all three charts show the same data.**

eachers' note Use in conjunction with 'Odd one out: 2'. The children will need to be familiar with in-erpreting and constructing tally charts, pictograms and bar charts. Encourage them to use a ruler to ead across from the bar to the numbered axis. Coloured pencils are needed for the extension activity.

Odd one out: 2

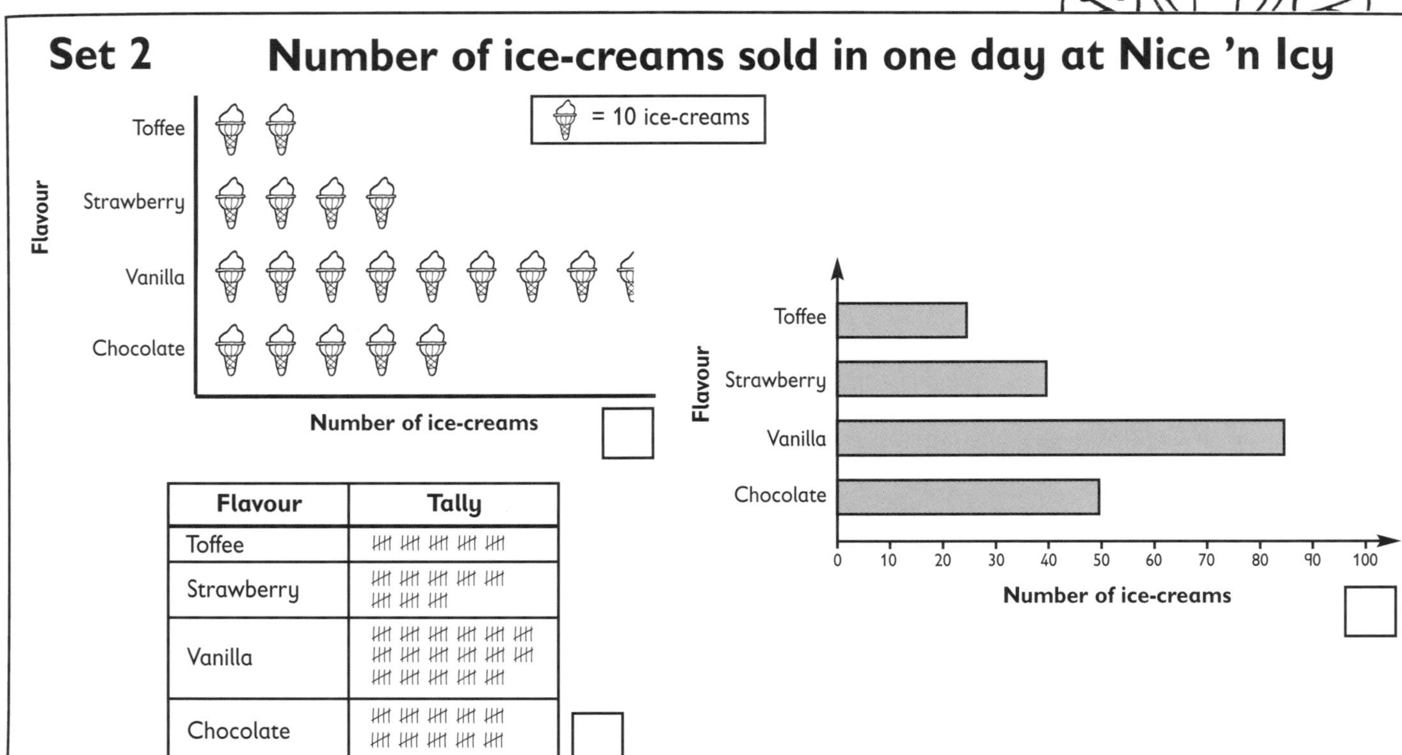

Flavour	Tally
Toffee	卌 卌 卌 卌 卌
Strawberry	卌 卌 卌 卌 卌 卌 卌 卌
Vanilla	卌 卌 卌 卌 卌 卌 卌 卌 卌 卌 卌 卌 卌 卌 卌 卌 卌
Chocolate	卌 卌 卌 卌 卌 卌 卌 卌 卌 卌

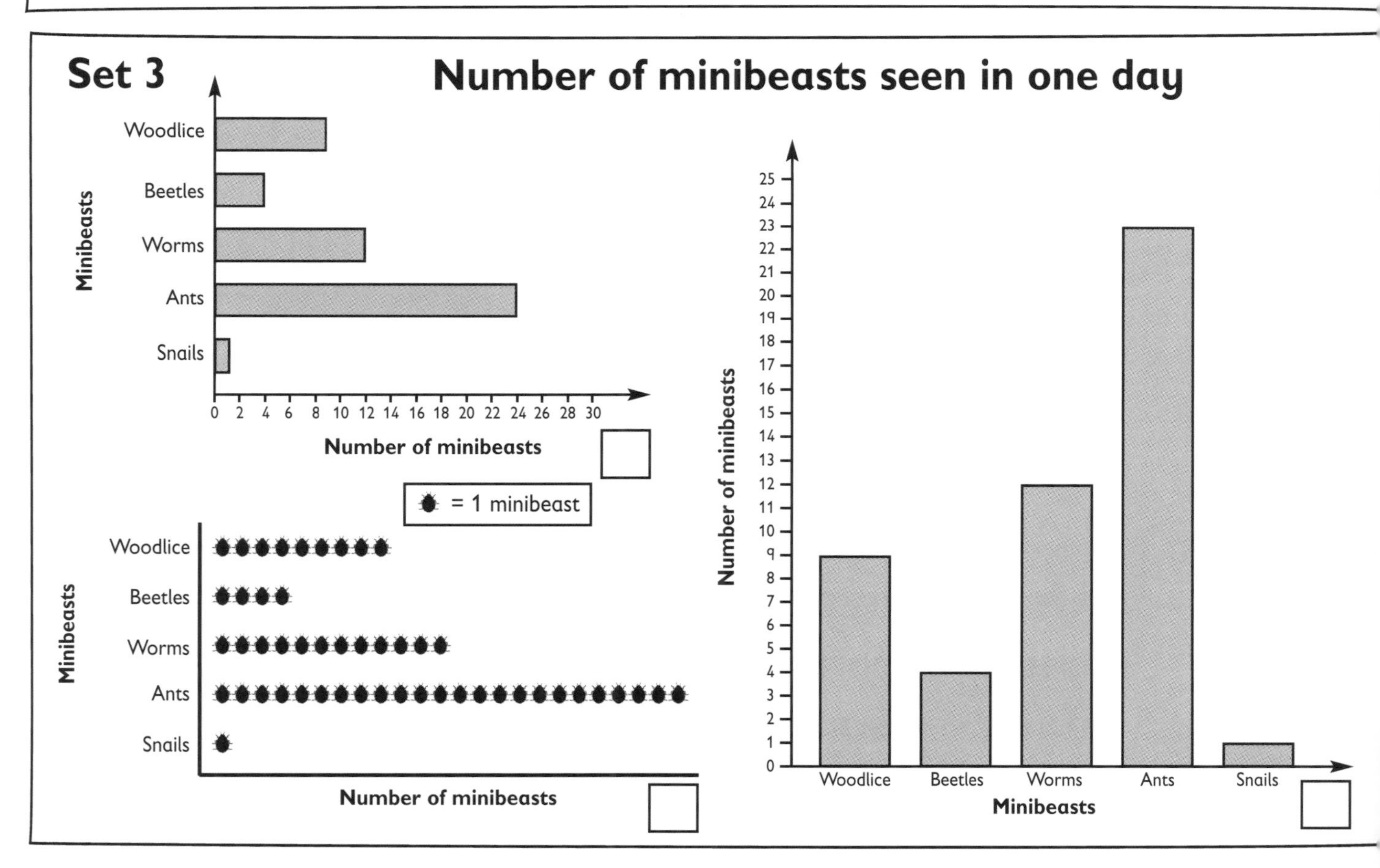

Teachers' note Use in conjunction with 'Odd one out: 1'.

Marble run

On the marble run there are sections that can be opened or closed to allow the marble to carry on or to drop down.

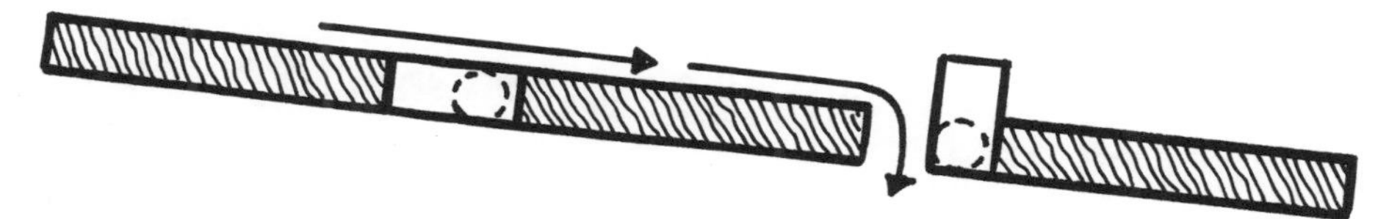

- **Find different ways that the marble can go and work out its total when it drops into a container.**

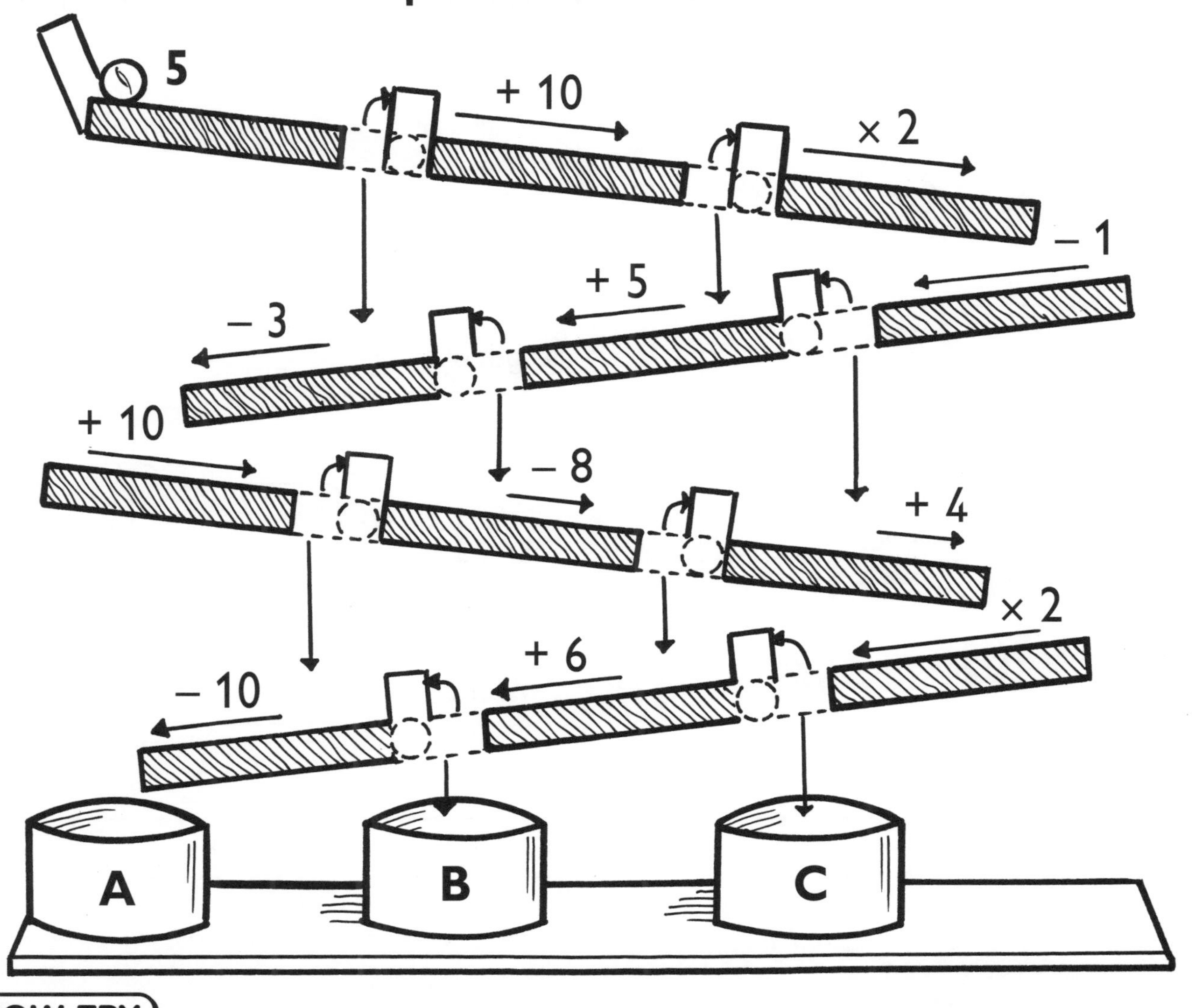

- **Can you find ways of making any of these numbers?**

10 16 32 0 12 80

Teachers' note There are many different possible numbers that can be made, starting with the marble number 5. This number could be changed to create more challenging calculations. Encourage the children to persevere to find the numbers in the extension activity, and to predict which routes are likely to give the highest or lowest numbers.

Measure for measure

Work with a partner or in a small group.

You need some measuring equipment and:
a shoe
a T-shirt
a jumper or a sweatshirt
a trainer or a plimsoll

- **Measure each item and record the measurements below. You should measure to the nearest centimetre and to the nearest gram.**

1. length ____ width ____ mass ____
area of sole ____

2. length of sleeve ____
width of chest ____
mass ____

3. length of sleeve ____
width of chest ____
mass ____

4. length ____ width ____ mass ____
area of sole ____

NOW TRY THIS!

- **Do you think the shoe or the trainer has the larger capacity? Or do they have the same capacity?**

Teachers' note Explain that a shop is advertising these items on the Internet and wants to describe them fully. Provide tape measures, rulers and scales, together with squared paper for measuring the area of the soles. Encourage the children to realise the importance of saying what unit is being used.

Book counting

- **Names of the children in our group.**

Work in a group of three or four.

______________________ ______________________

______________________ ______________________

- **How many books are there in our school library?**

We estimate that there are about _______ books.

- **How are we going to find out?**

____

____

____

- **What information do we need?**

____

____

____

- **What do we think we will find, and why?**

____

____

____

- **How will we find the information?**

____

____

____

Teachers' note This activity should be done in small groups. The children should plan how they would go about answering the question. The focus should be on planning the investigation, and time should be spent discussing all the children's work.

2s and 3s

1 Write each of these numbers in the correct section of the Carroll diagram.

~~16~~ 21 33 12 101 2 10 35 30 18 1 6 8 14

	Multiple of 2	Not a multiple of 2
Multiple of 3		
Not a Multiple of 3	16	

2 a How many numbers in the diagram are a multiple of 2 **and** a multiple of 3? ___

b Write them here: ______________________________

3 How many numbers in the diagram are a multiple of 2 but **not** a multiple of 3? ___

4 In a different colour, write two more numbers that you think should be included in each section of the Carroll diagram.

NOW TRY THIS!

- **How could you check whether you have placed the numbers correctly?**
- **Talk to a partner about your ideas.**

Teachers' note Children who find it difficult to remember their 2 times- and 3 times-tables could use tables grids to help them. As a further extension, the children could draw a Venn diagram of the same data.

Sweet success

You need: two blank Venn diagrams, two blank Carroll diagrams, some scissors and glue.

☆ Cut out the sweets, one set at a time.

☆ Sort each set of sweets onto a Venn diagram or a Carroll diagram.

☆ Try to find four **different** ways to sort the sweets.

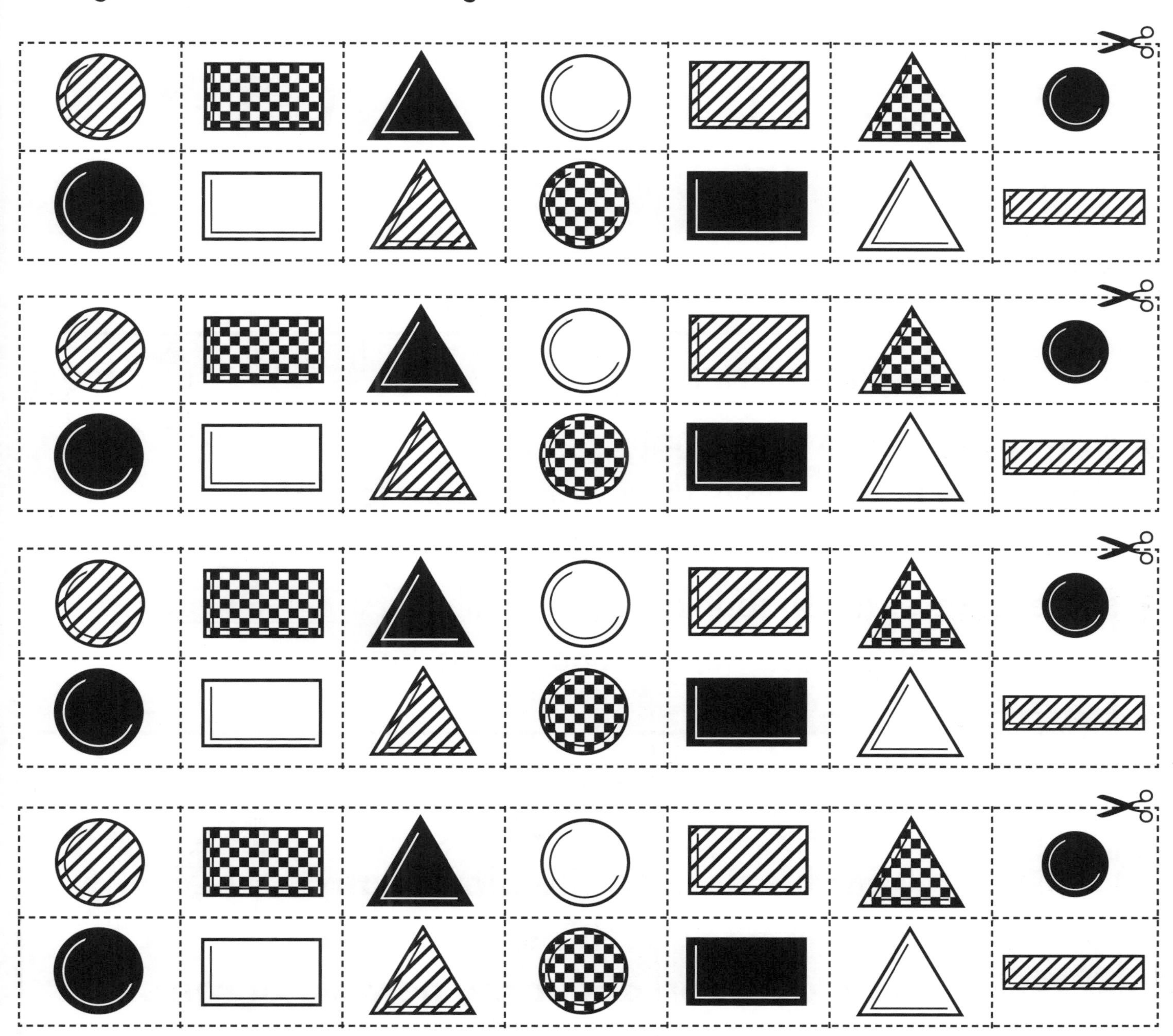

Teachers' note There are more than four ways to sort the sweets so you could demonstrate one way of sorting first, for example 'triangular sweets' and 'checked sweets'. Encourage the children to think about how they can check that they have found all the ways to sort the sweets.

Minibeasts

This pictogram shows how many minibeasts were found during a class investigation.

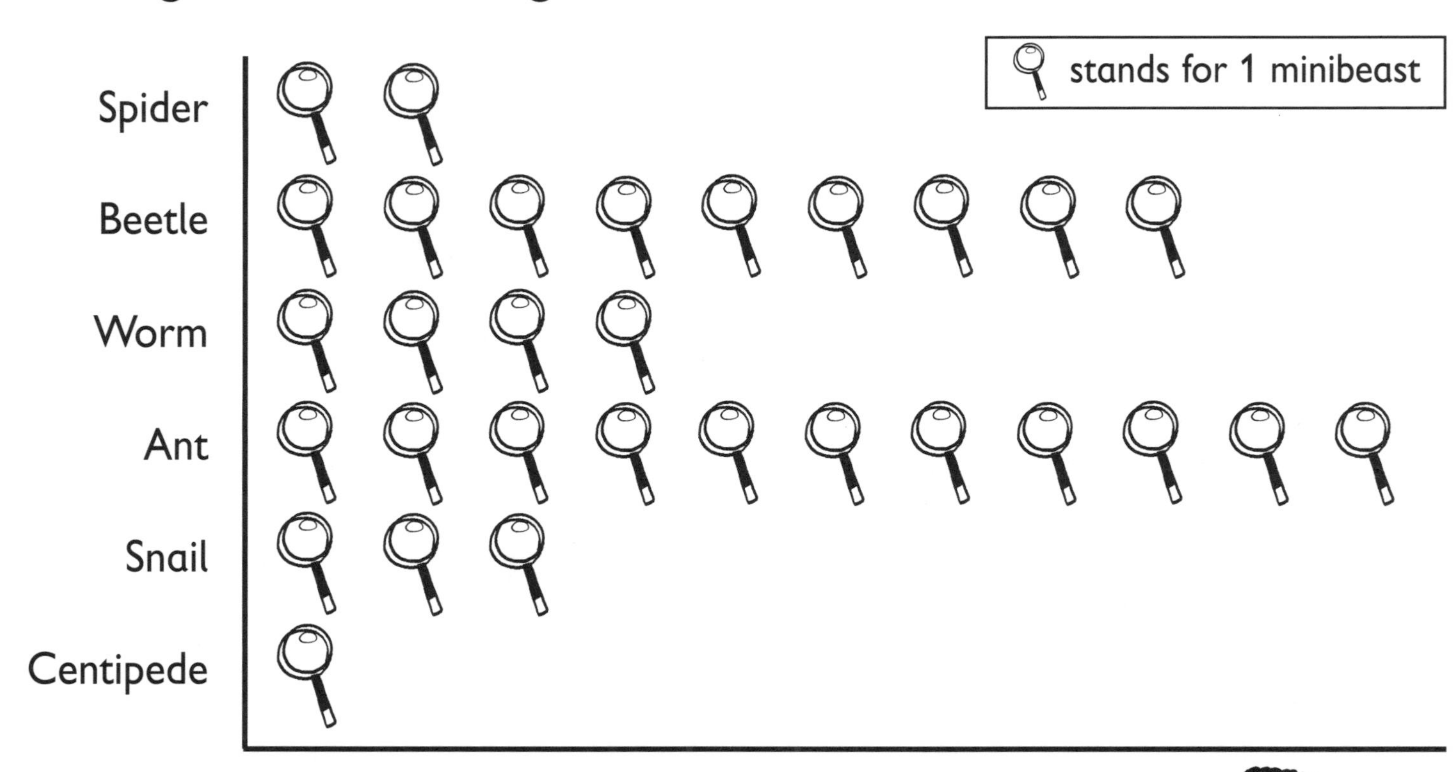

1 How many spiders were found? ____

2 How many ants were found? ____

3 How many more beetles than worms were found? ____

4 How many fewer spiders than snails were found? ____

5 There were **exactly** four of which minibeast? ____________

6 How many minibeasts were found altogether? ____

Kajwast found two snails stuck to the lid of her container.

- **Add this data to the pictogram.**
- **On the back of this sheet, make up a question about the new pictogram.**

Teachers' note Talk about the pictogram before the children answer the questions. Explain that the symbol of the magnifying glass is used to represent any minibeast.

Summer fête

This pictogram shows the number of people who took part in different activities at the school fête.

🞮 stands for 10 people

Coconut shy

Tug-of-war

Beat the goalie

Skittles

Hook-a-duck

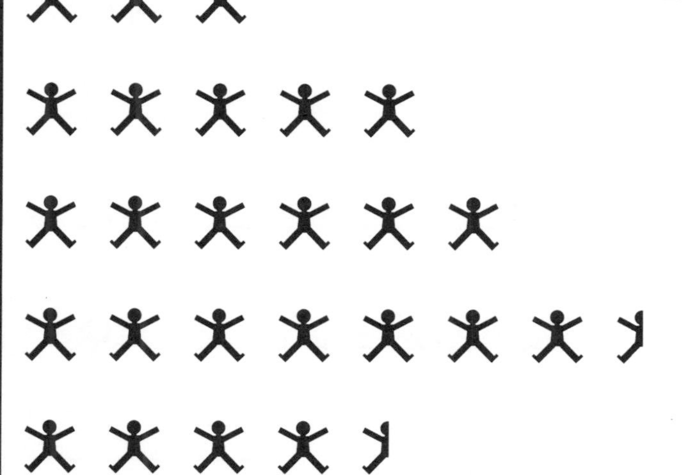

1 How many people had a go on the Coconut shy? ____

2 How many people took part in Hook-a-duck? ____

3 Fifty people took part in which activity?

____

4 How many more people took part in Skittles than Hook-a-duck? ____

5 How many fewer people took part in Beat the goalie than Skittles? ____

NOW TRY THIS!

Thirty-five people guessed how many sweets there were in a jar.

- **How would you show this on the pictogram?**

Guess how many ______________________

Teachers' note Ensure that the children understand the vocabulary for the different activities. Draw attention to the symbol and explain that each one represents ten people.

Mr Folly's lollies

This tally chart shows how many lollies Mr Folly sold during one week.

Monday	Tuesday	Wednesday	Thursday	Friday	Saturday	Sunday
卌 卌 卌 卌 卌	卌 卌 卌	卌	卌 卌	卌 卌 卌 卌 卌 卌	卌 卌 卌 卌 卌 卌 卌 卌 卌 卌 卌	卌 卌 卌 卌 卌 卌 卌 卌

- **Use the data to construct a pictogram.**

Think about how many lollies your picture will stand for.

A pictogram to show the number of lollies sold in one week

stands for [ ] lollies

Monday	
Tuesday	
Wednesday	
Thursday	
Friday	
Saturday	
Sunday	

NOW TRY THIS!

- **Why do you think that the number of lollies sold on Wednesday was so low?**

Talk to a partner about your ideas.

Teachers' note The children could be given some paired discussion time to consider how many lollies will be represented by the symbol used in the pictogram.

Game, set and match: 1

You need a copy of Game, set and match: 2.

- **Look at the four descriptions below.**
- **Match each description to the chart that you think represents the data.**

1 James and his five friends from football had a penalty shoot-out. They had eight shots each. ☐
2 Six local schools took part in a netball championship. Each team played five games. ☐
3 A tennis competition was held where each person played ten games. Four players took part. ☐
4 Four wrestlers entered the annual wrestling match. Each wrestler took part in eight matches. ☐

- **Compare your answers with those of a partner.**
- **Explain to your partner why you think your answers are correct.**

NOW TRY THIS!

- **Fill in the missing labels on each chart.**

Teachers' note Use in conjunction with 'Game, set and match: 2'. There is one correct representation for each scenario. Ensure that the children appreciate that the charts on page 00 show the games and matches won and the goals scored. Encourage the children to explain why they think the other three representations cannot be correct, as well as giving a rationale for their chosen one.

Game, set and match: 2

You need a copy of Game, set and match: 1.

- **Look carefully at the charts.**

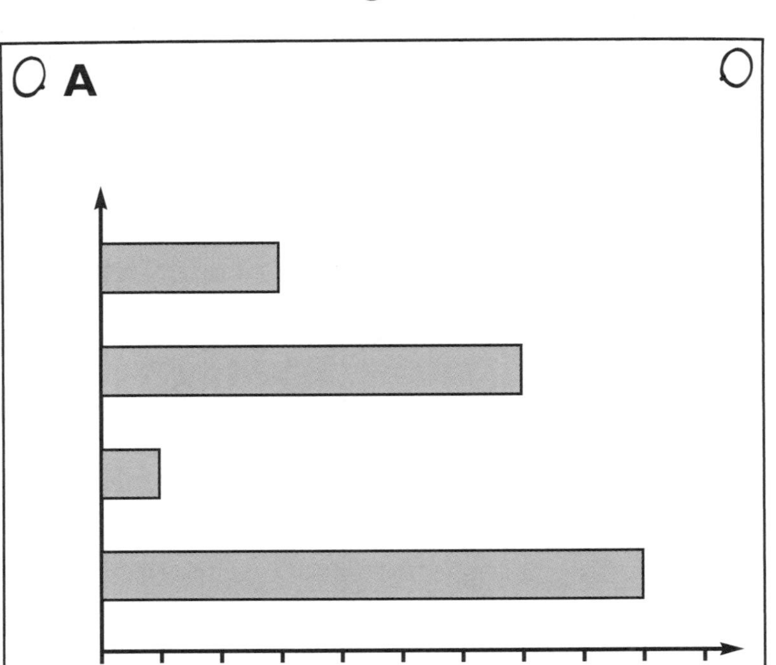

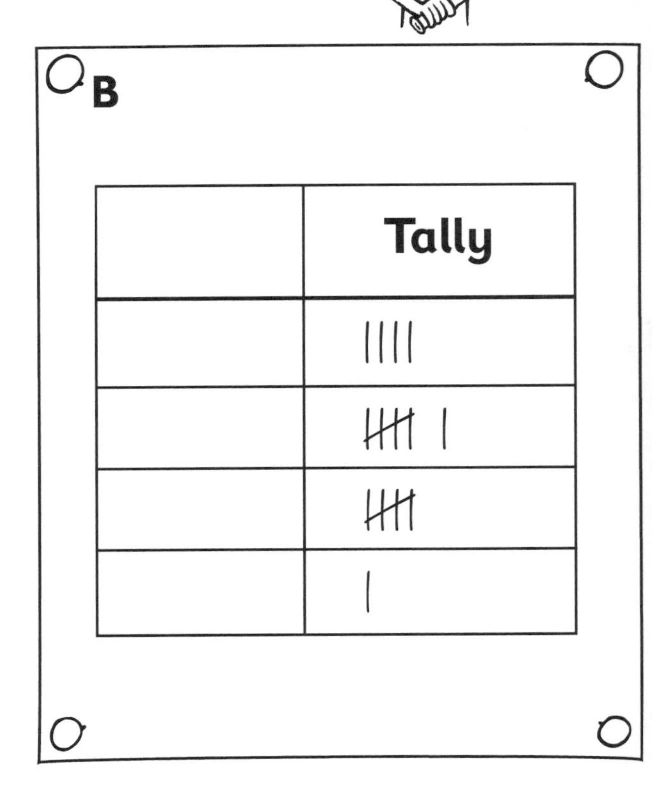

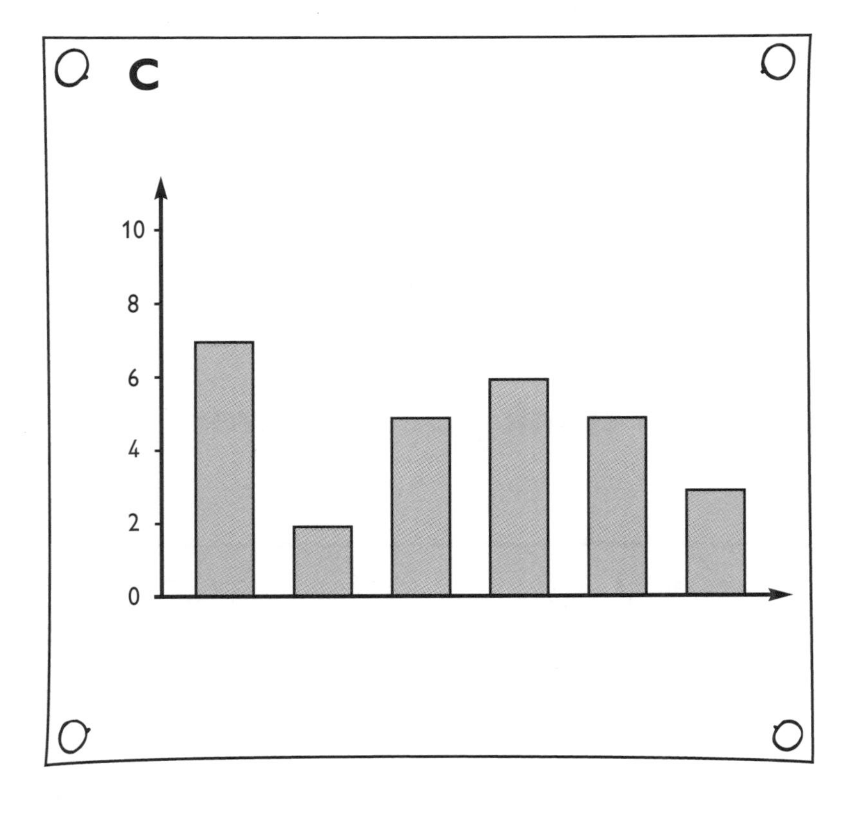

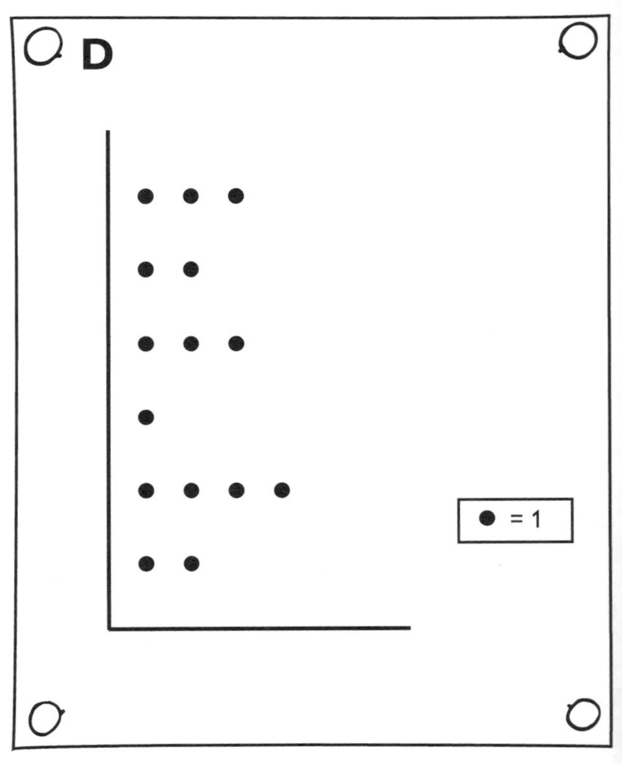

Teachers' note Use in conjunction with 'Game, set and match: 1'.

Measure together

- **Cut out the cards.**
- **Decide which unit of measurement would be best to use in each answer.**
- **Then try to find the answers to some of the cards.**

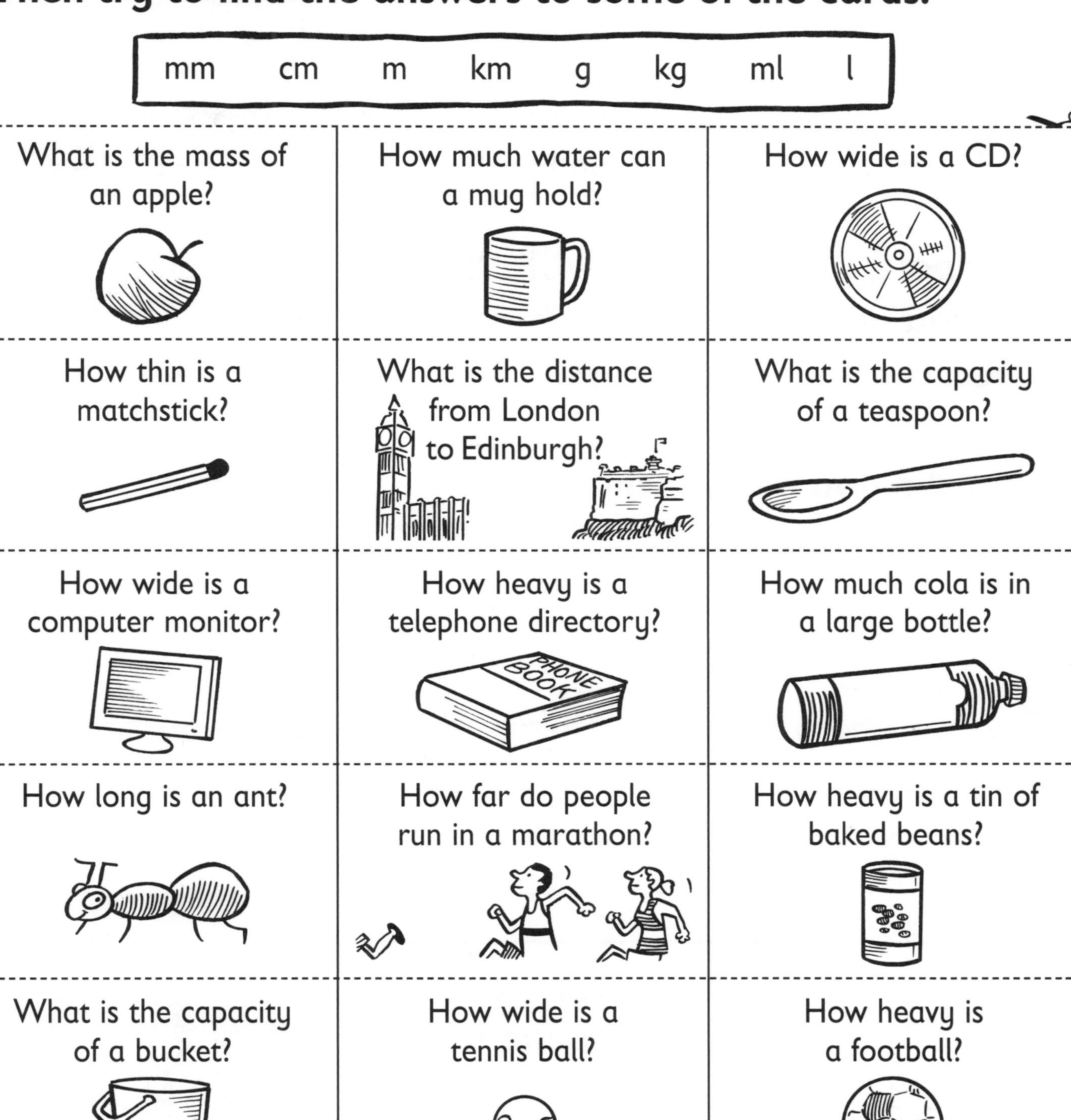

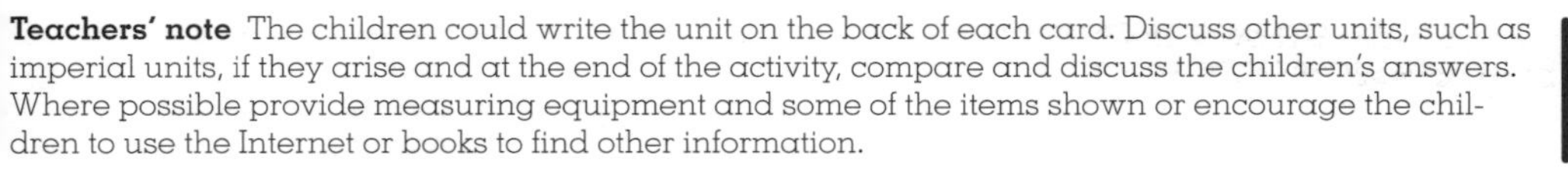

Teachers' note The children could write the unit on the back of each card. Discuss other units, such as imperial units, if they arise and at the end of the activity, compare and discuss the children's answers. Where possible provide measuring equipment and some of the items shown or encourage the children to use the Internet or books to find other information.

Mix and match: 1

You need the cards cut from Mix and match: 2.

- **Sort the bar charts into pairs which show the same data.**
- **Record the letters of the bar charts that you think are pairs.**

- **Compare your answers with those of a partner.**
- **Did you get the same answers?** Yes ☐ No ☐

If not, check your answers.

- **How did you decide which bar charts showed the same data?** ____________________

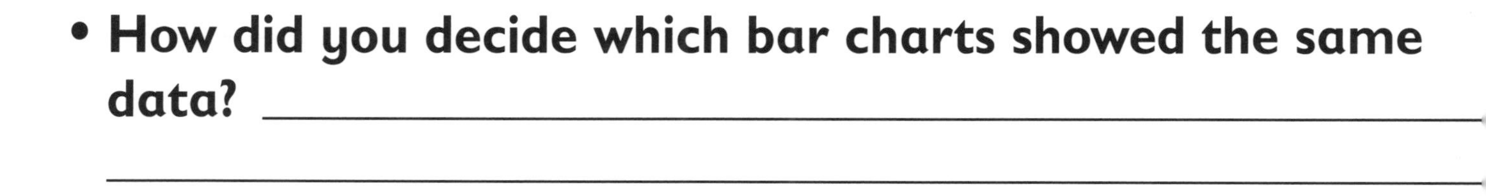

- **Choose one pair of bar charts. Explain how you know this is a pair?** ____________________

NOW TRY THIS!

- **Construct a tally chart to show the data from one pair of cards.**
- **Ask a partner to work out which pair it matches.**

Teachers' note Use in conjunction with 'Mix and match: 2'. Check that children understand that the pairs of bar charts show the same data but represent it differently.

Mix and match: 2

- **Cut out the cards below.**
- **Match the pairs of data and record on Mix and match: 1.**

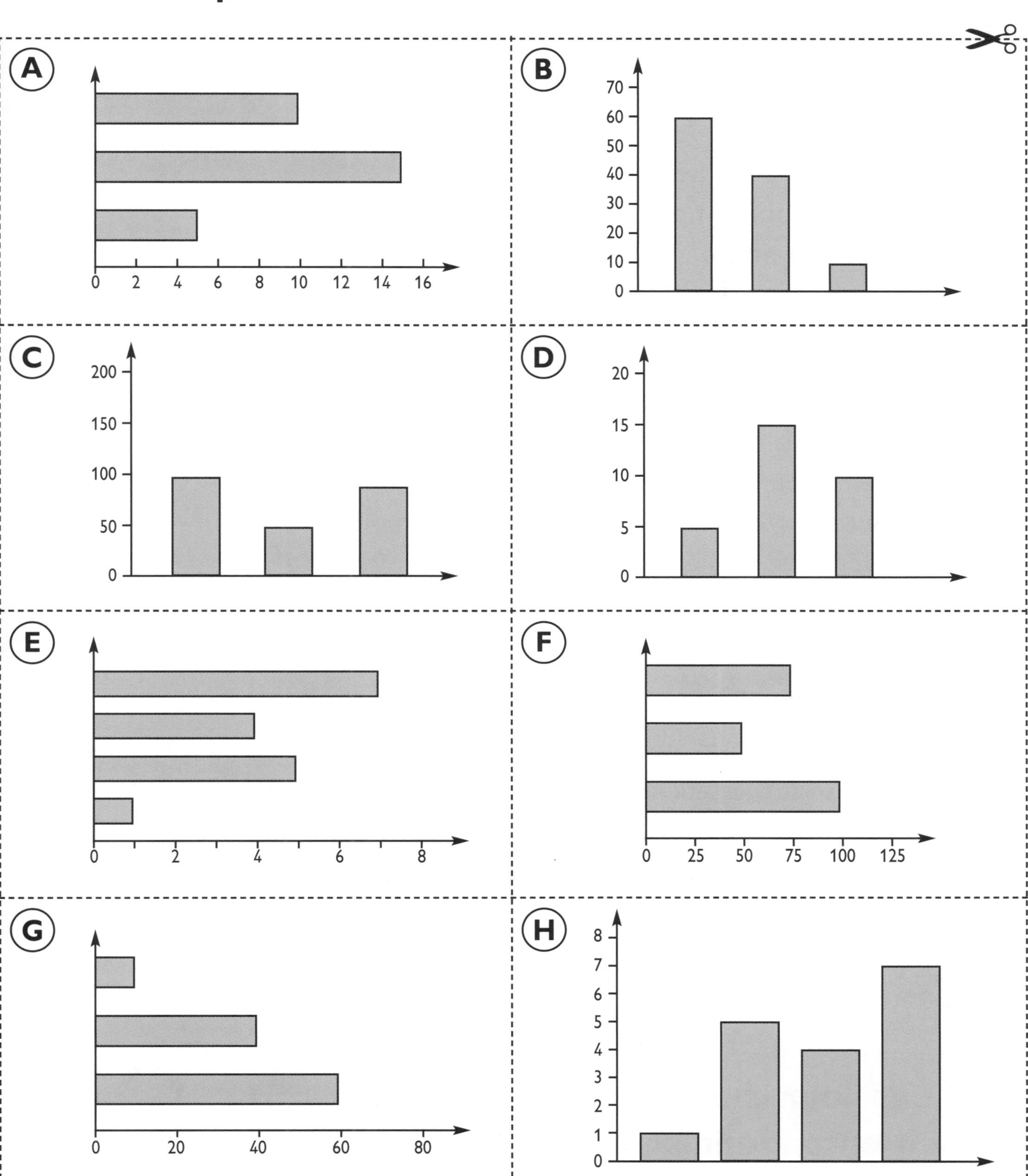

Teachers' note Use in conjunction with 'Mix and match: 1'.

Planning enquiries: 1

- **Work with a partner.**
- **Read through the questions and choose one question to work with.**

You need Planning enquiries: 2.

Is it true that the height of the school is more than six metres?

Is it true that fewer than half of the children in our class like cauliflower?

It is true that most of the children in our class have more than six letters in their first name?

Is it true that more than one-third of the children in our class have had chickenpox?

Is it true that the teachers in our school drink more coffee than tea?

Is it true that three-quarters of the children in our class are in bed by 9 o'clock?

- **Cut out your chosen question and stick it onto Planning enquiries: 2**

Teachers' note Use in conjunction with 'Planning enquiries: 2'. Working in pairs, the children should choose a question and then stick it onto the following worksheet. They should then plan how they would go about answering the question. The focus should be on planning the investigation, and time should be spent discussing all the children's work.

Planning enquiries: 2

- **Our names:**

____

____

Stick your chosen question here.

- **Show how you could find out whether your statement is true.**

1 What information do we want to collect?

2 How are we going to collect the information?

3 What equipment do we need, or what do we need to prepare before collecting the information?

4 What do you think the information will tell us, and why?

Teachers' note Use in conjunction with 'Planning enquiries: 1'. As an extension, ask the children to discuss any problems that they think they might encounter.

After-school sports

A new after-school sports club is to be set up. This bar chart shows how many children voted for each sports club.

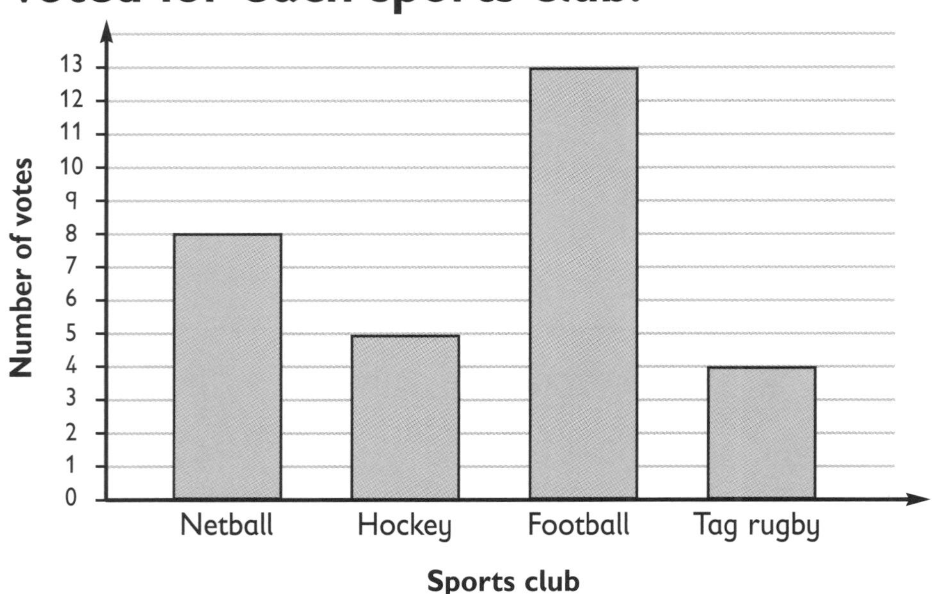

1 Which is the most popular choice of sport? ____________

2 a From looking at the results, which sports club do you think should be set up? ____________

b What are your reasons for this?

Talk to a partner about your ideas.

c How many votes did this sport get? ____

d How many children did **not** vote for this club? ____

3 Have you changed your mind about which club should be set up? Yes ☐ No ☐

Talk to a partner about your reasons.

NOW TRY THIS!

- **What would you suggest the school does to solve this problem?**

Talk to a partner about your ideas.

Teachers' note The emphasis here is on analysing the data to solve a problem. The children need to consider the proportion of votes that a particular sport did and did not get.

Splish, splash

This table shows the number of babies in the small pool on each day of the week.

Day	Number of babies
Monday	14
Tuesday	10
Wednesday	7
Thursday	5
Friday	16
Saturday	19
Sunday	9

- **Construct a bar chart to show this data.**

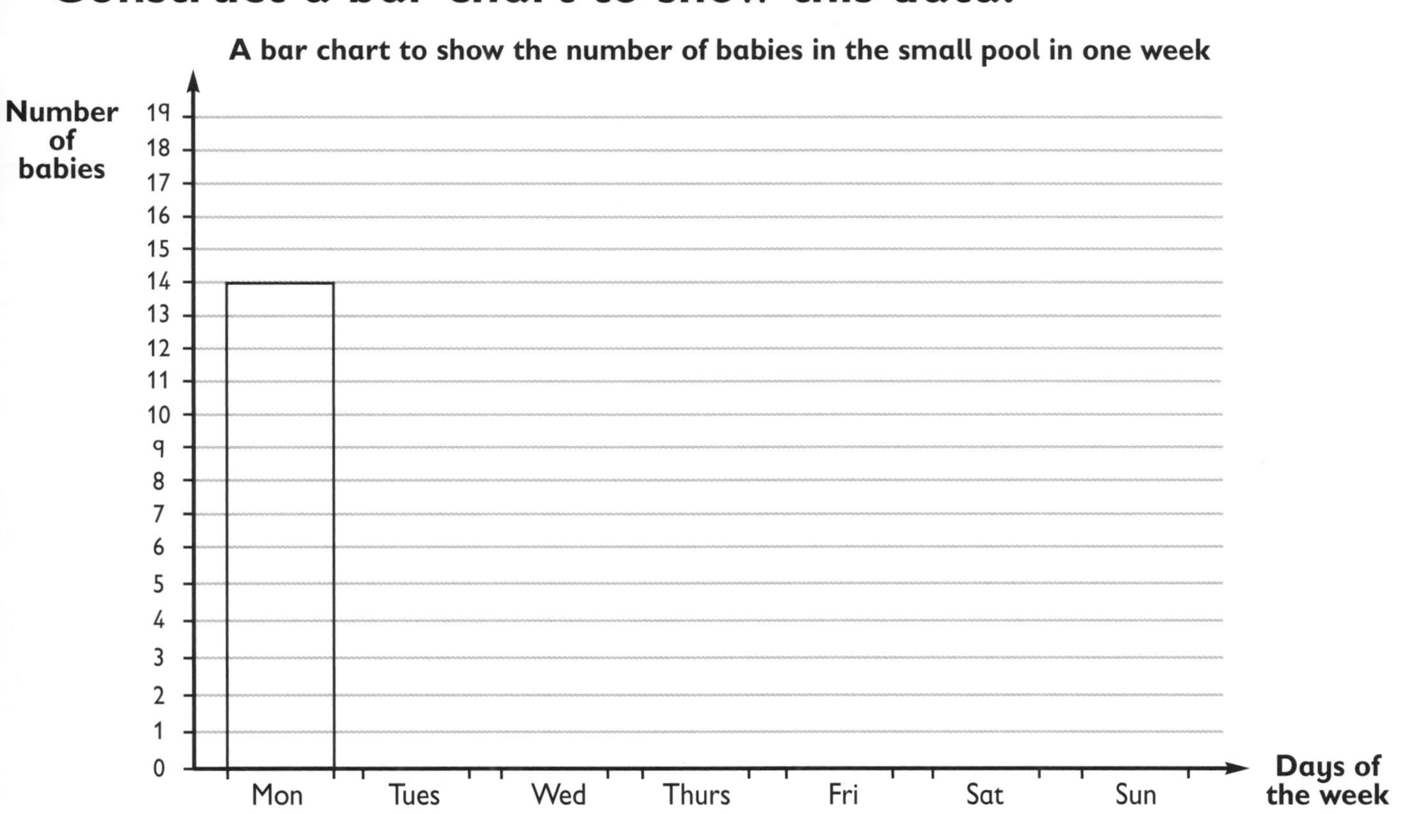

- **On a separate piece of paper, write four questions to ask a partner about the data in your chart.**

Teachers' note Ensure the children understand that the height of each bar shows how many babies were in the small pool that day.

What a smoothie!

This table shows the number of fruits needed to make different smoothies.

- **Use this data to complete the bar chart.**

Type of smoothie	Number of fruits needed
Pineapple	3
Peach	7
Banana	8
Strawberry	10
Mango	2

A bar chart to show the number of fruits needed to make different smoothies

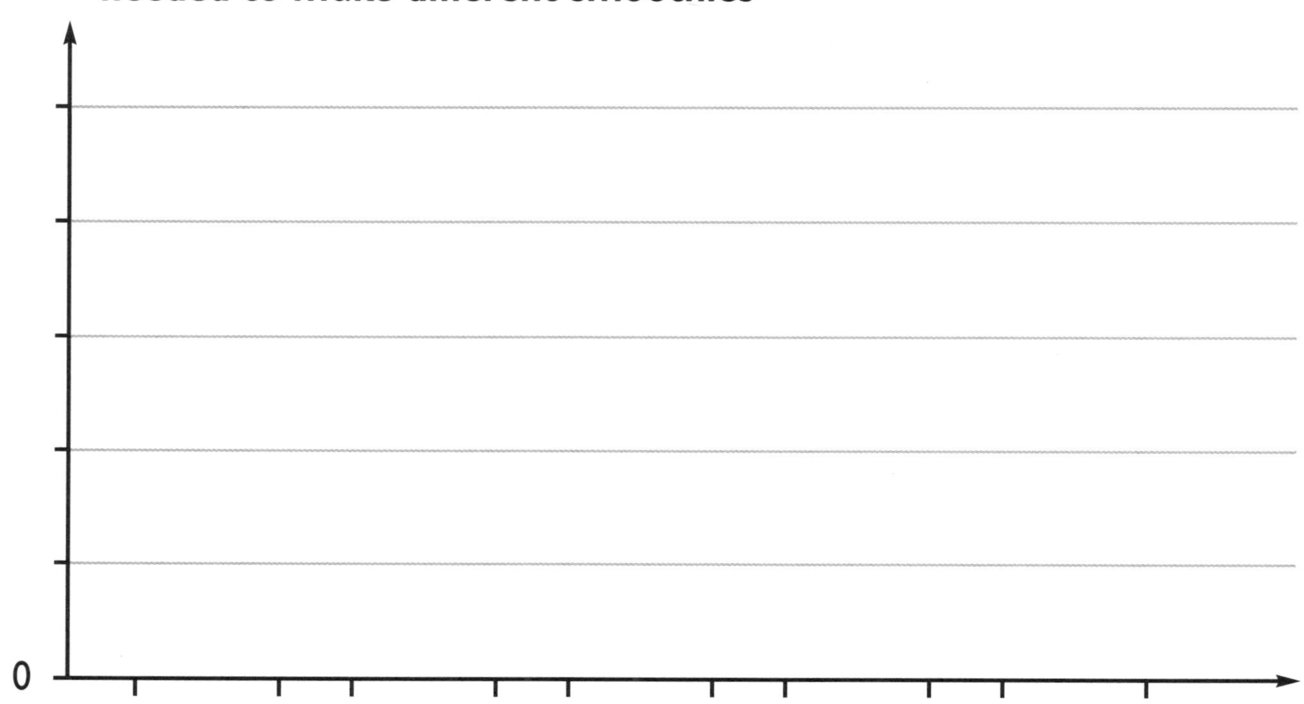

NOW TRY THIS!

- **Talk to a partner:**

a Did you both use the same scale? Yes ☐ No ☐

b What made you decide to use this scale?

Teachers' note If preferred, the children could draw the fruit on the horizontal axis, rather than writing the names of the fruit. The extension activity requires the children to work in pairs or small groups.

Bounce 4 charity

William and his friends organised a sponsored trampoline event called 'Bounce 4 charity.' This bar chart shows the amount of money raised by each class.

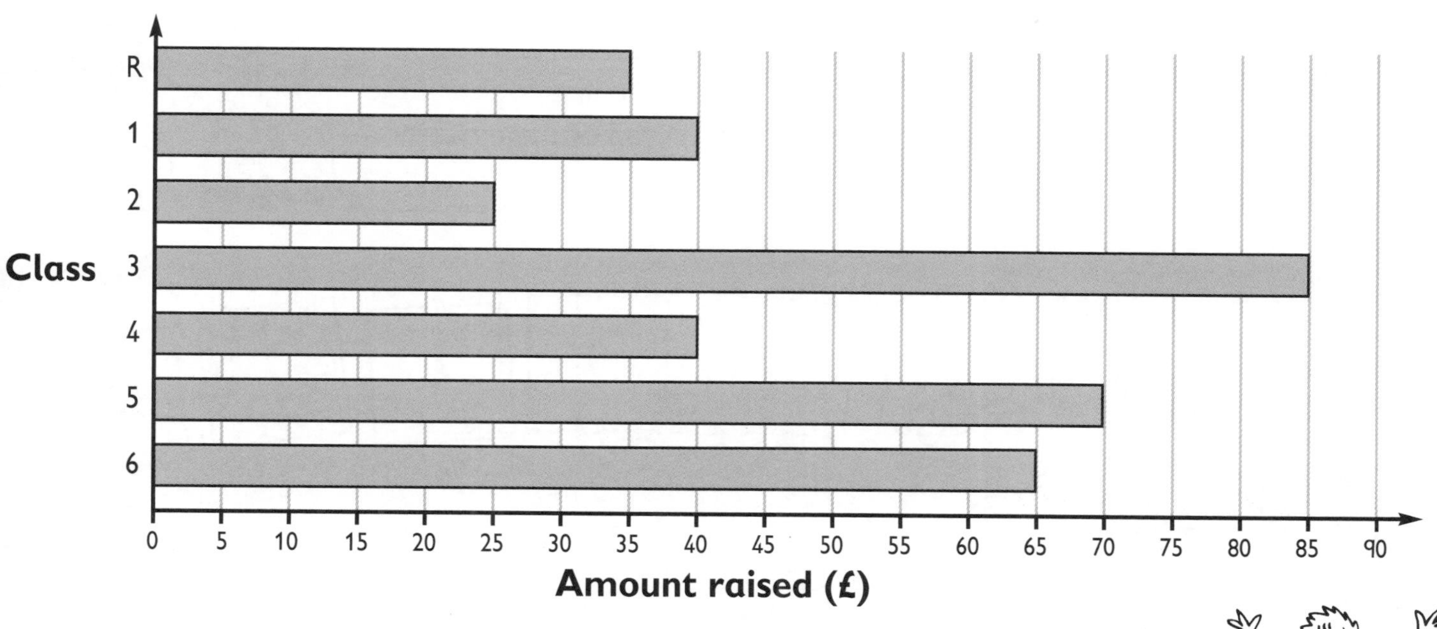

1 How much money did Class 5 raise? _____

2 Which class raised £25? ______________

3 a Which two classes raised the same amount of money?
______________ and ______________

b How much did these two classes raise altogether? _____

4 a What do you notice about the amount raised by Class 3?

b What might explain this?

Talk to a partner about your ideas.

NOW TRY THIS!

- **William and his friends counted the money raised by all the classes. Ring the correct total.**

£260 £340 £360

Teachers' note Discuss the scale used for the bar chart. The children should discuss their ideas for question 4 with a partner before a whole-class discussion.

Top of the mountain: 1

- **Play this game with a partner.**

☆ Shuffle the cards and put them in a pile face down.

☆ Take turns to roll the dice and move your counter.

☆ If you land on a slimy square, pick up a card.

☆ If you get the answer right, slide forward one space.

☆ If you get it wrong, stick where you are.

☆ Return your card to the bottom of the pile.

You need the cards cut from Top of the mountain: 2, a dice and two counters.

SWAMP CREATURE

The first to reach the top of the mountain is the winner.

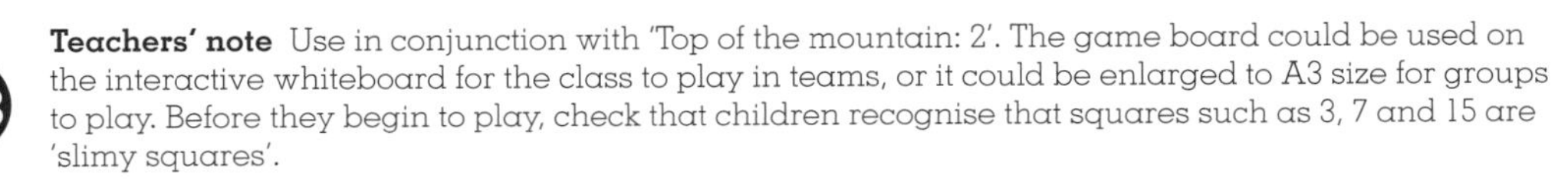
Teachers' note Use in conjunction with 'Top of the mountain: 2'. The game board could be used on the interactive whiteboard for the class to play in teams, or it could be enlarged to A3 size for groups to play. Before they begin to play, check that children recognise that squares such as 3, 7 and 15 are 'slimy squares'.

Top of the mountain: 2

- **Cut out the cards.**

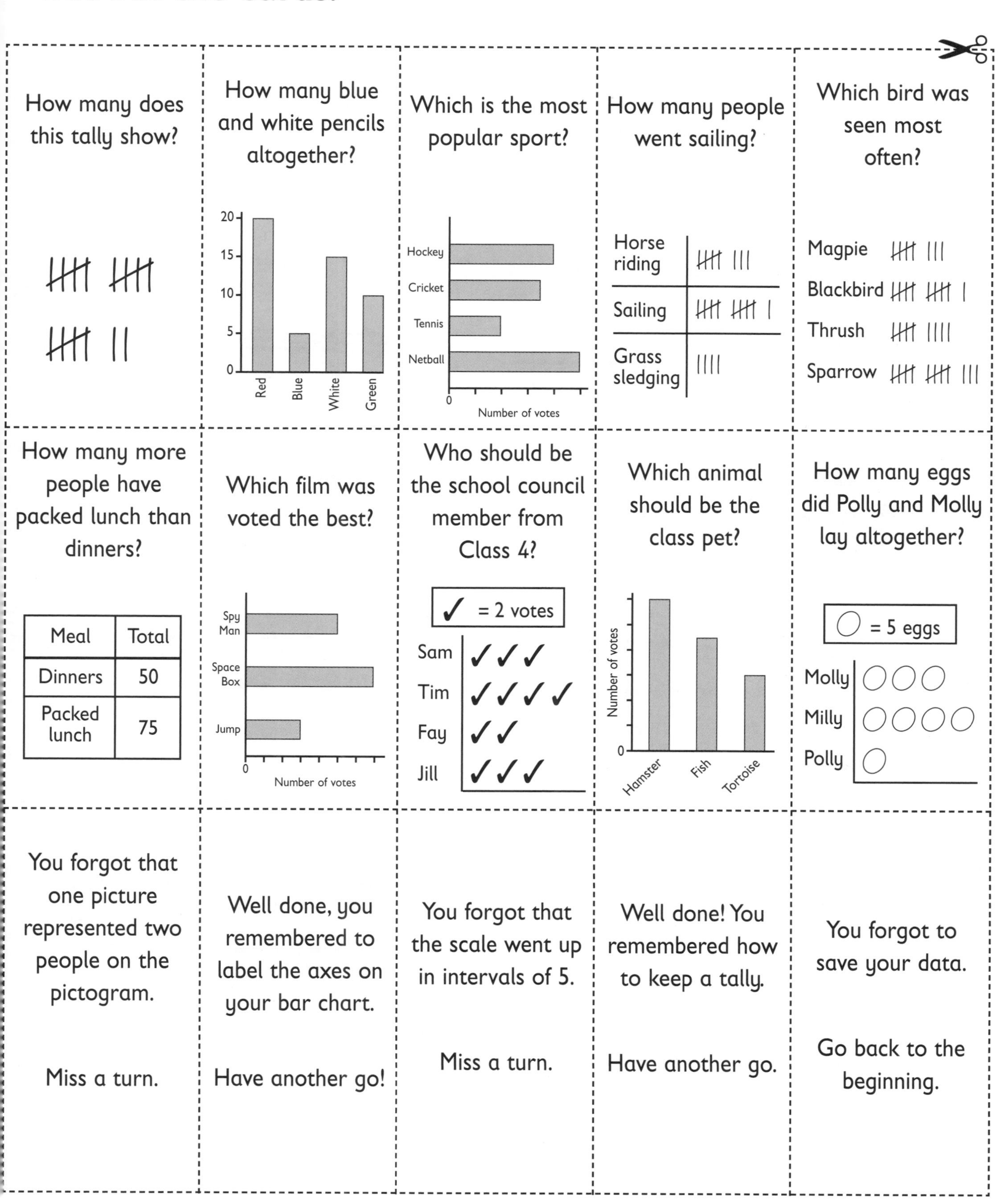

How many does this tally show?

How many blue and white pencils altogether?

Which is the most popular sport?

How many people went sailing?

Which bird was seen most often?

How many more people have packed lunch than dinners?

Meal	Total
Dinners	50
Packed lunch	75

Which film was voted the best?

Who should be the school council member from Class 4?

Which animal should be the class pet?

How many eggs did Polly and Molly lay altogether?

You forgot that one picture represented two people on the pictogram.

Miss a turn.

Well done, you remembered to label the axes on your bar chart.

Have another go!

You forgot that the scale went up in intervals of 5.

Miss a turn.

Well done! You remembered how to keep a tally.

Have another go.

You forgot to save your data.

Go back to the beginning.

Teachers' note Use in conjunction with 'Top of the Mountain: 1'. Additional cards could be written by the children and added to the game resource.

Made to measure

These scarves are different lengths.

- **Write the missing numbers on the scarves.**

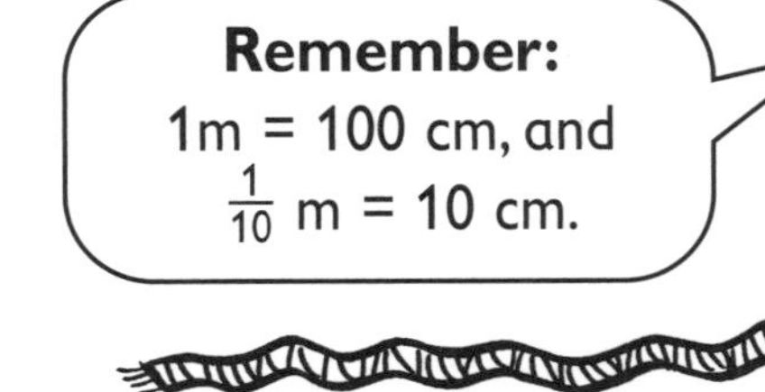

Centi is the Latin word for **hundred**.

1.

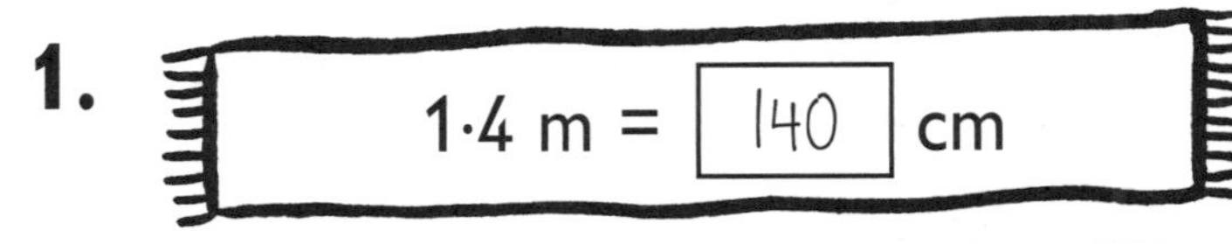

2.

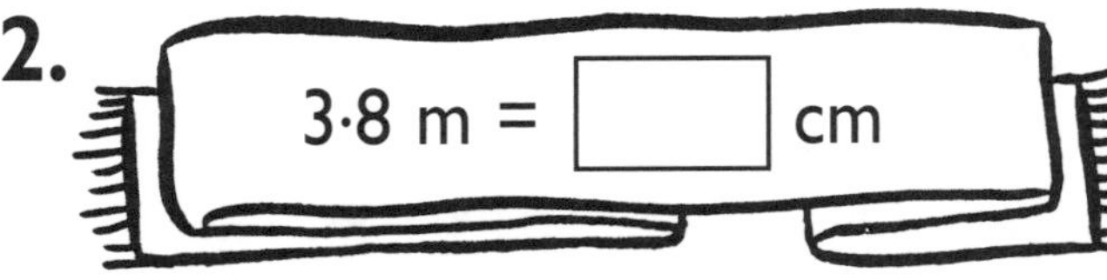

3.

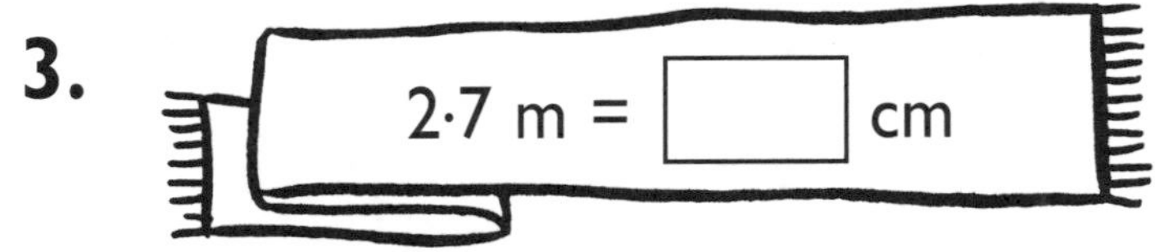

4.

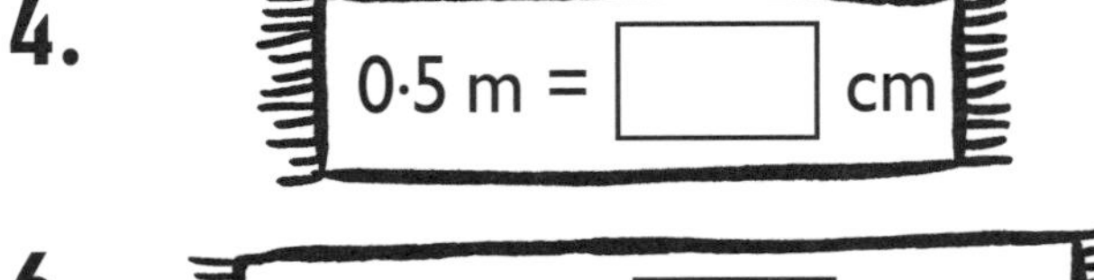

5.

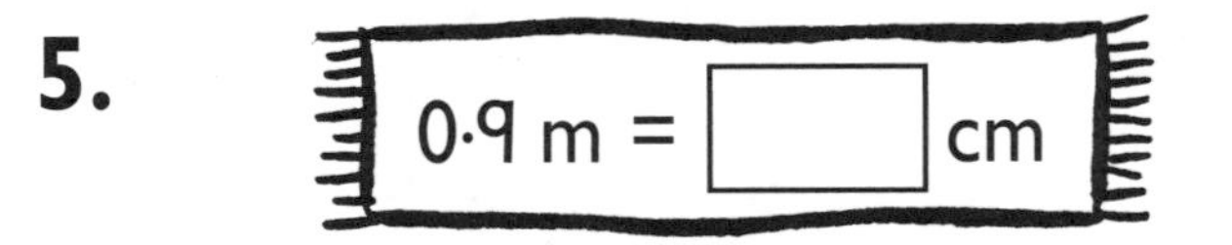

6.

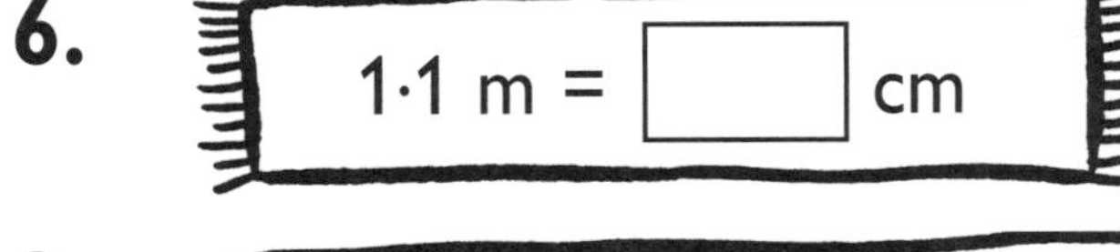

7.

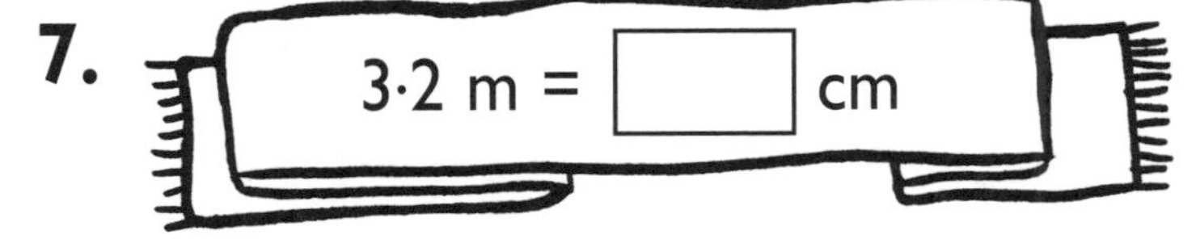

8.

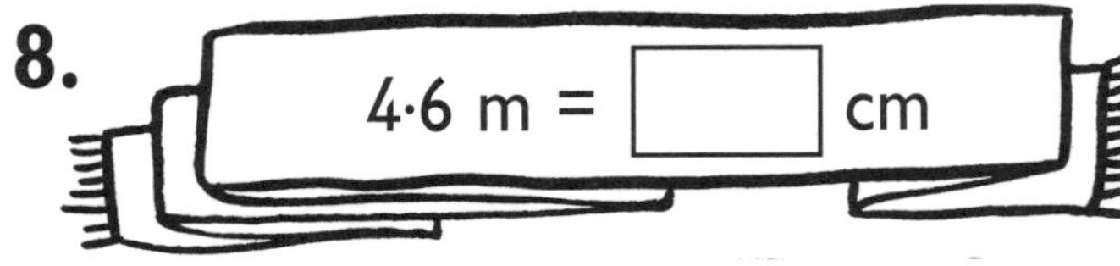

9.

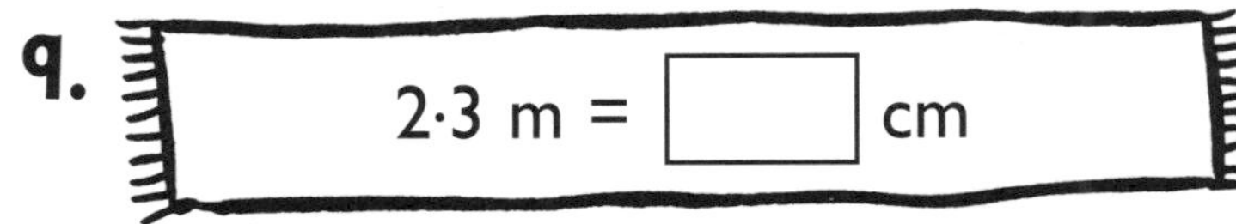

10.

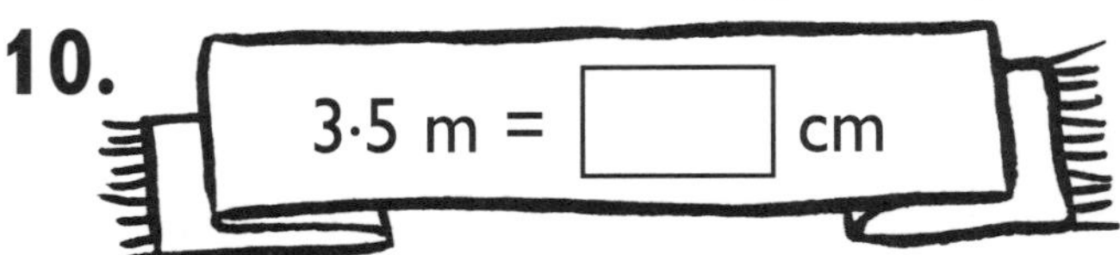

NOW TRY THIS!

- **Write these missing numbers.**

a.

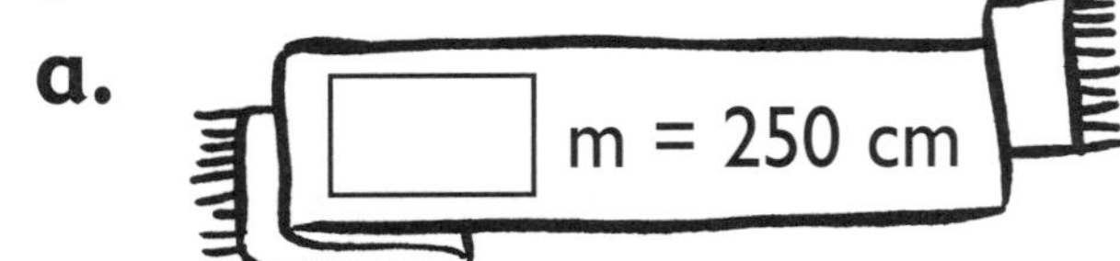

b.

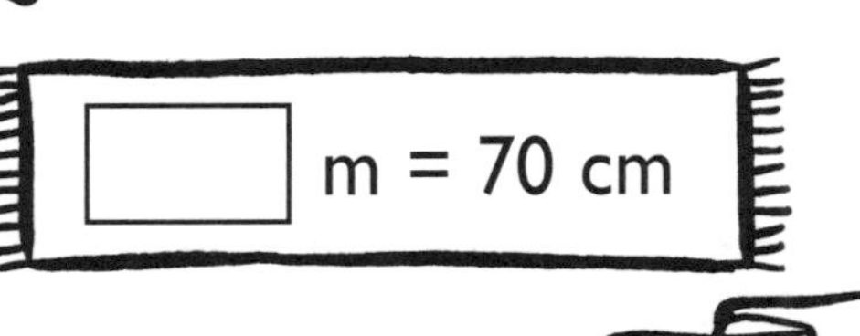

c.

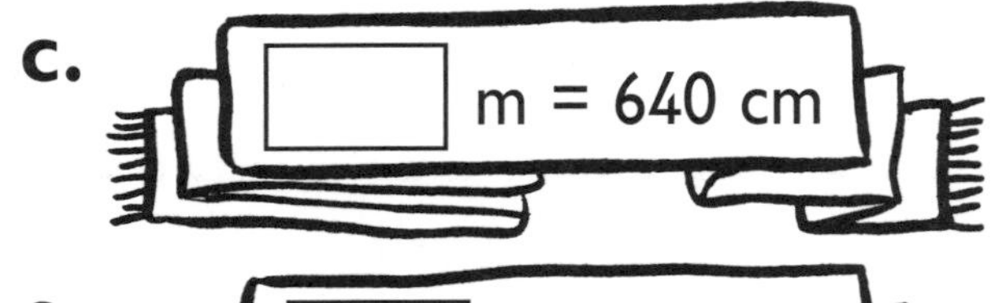

d.

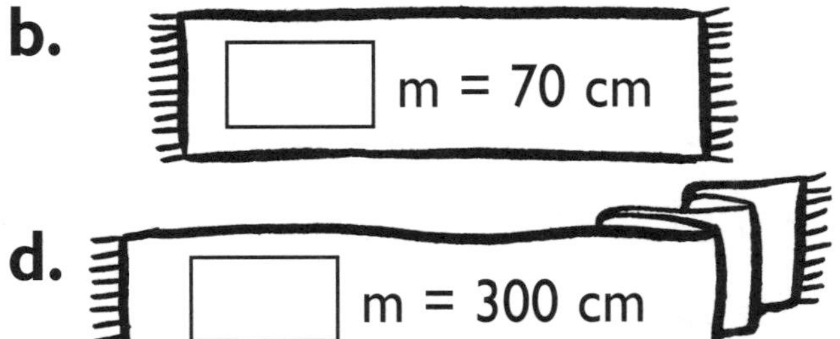

e.

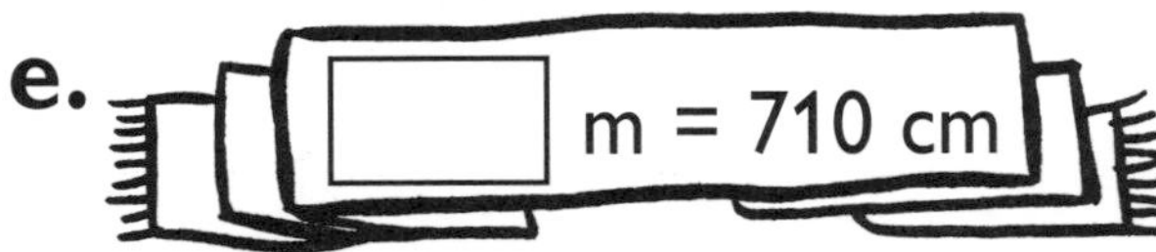

Teachers' note As the children become more familiar with the relationships between the units they can begin to convert between them, including using decimals. Remind the children that the column after the decimal point tells you how many tenths of a metre (or how many lots of 10 cm) there are.

Scaly fish: 1

This table shows the number of each type of fish in Mika's aquarium.

Type of fish	Number of fish
Rainbow fish	4
Zebra fish	9
Neon tetra	23
Angelfish	15

- **Construct four vertical bar charts to show this data.**

A

B

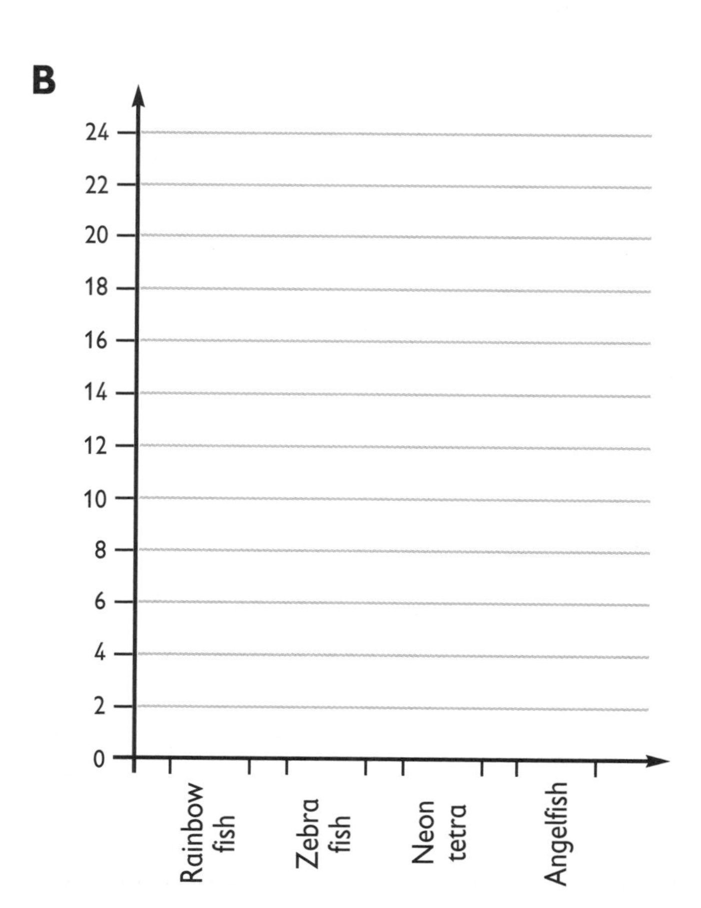

Teachers' note Use in conjunction with 'Scaly fish: 2'. Draw the children's attention to the different scales on each of the four vertical axes. Ensure the children understand that they are plotting the same data on each bar chart.

Scaly fish: 2

C

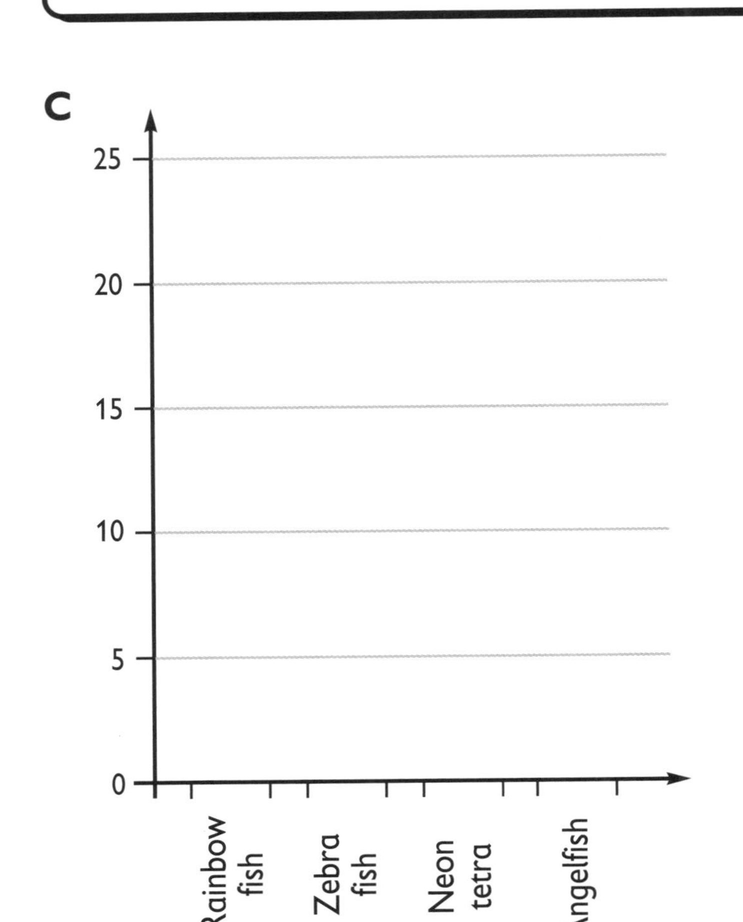

D

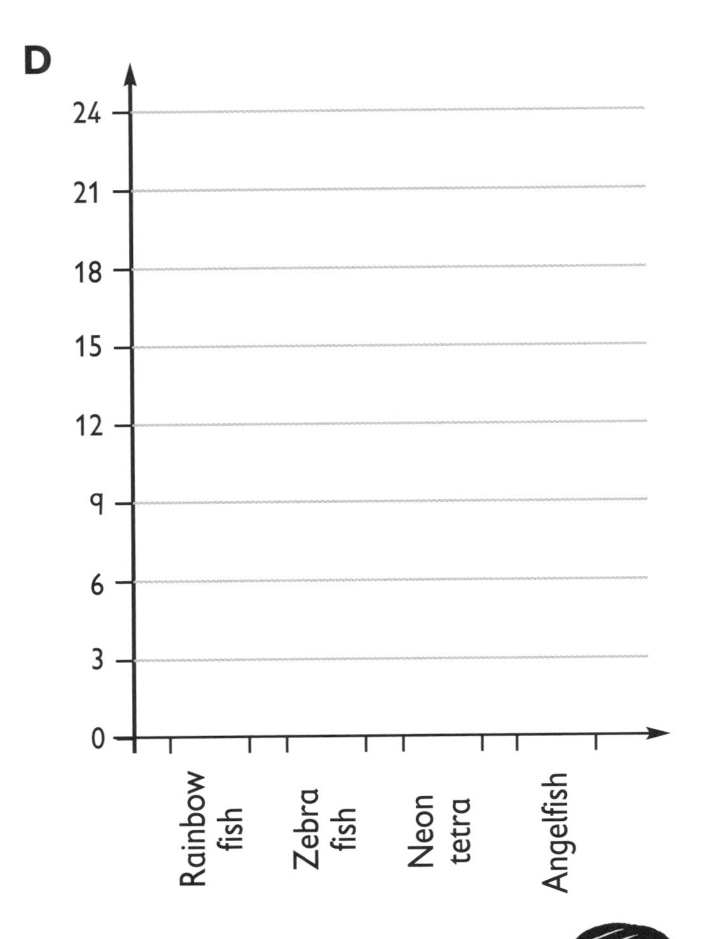

1 How did you work out where to draw the end of each bar?

Talk to a partner about how you did this.

2 Which bar chart was the easiest to draw? ___

3 Do you think the data looks the same in each bar chart?

Talk to a partner about your ideas.

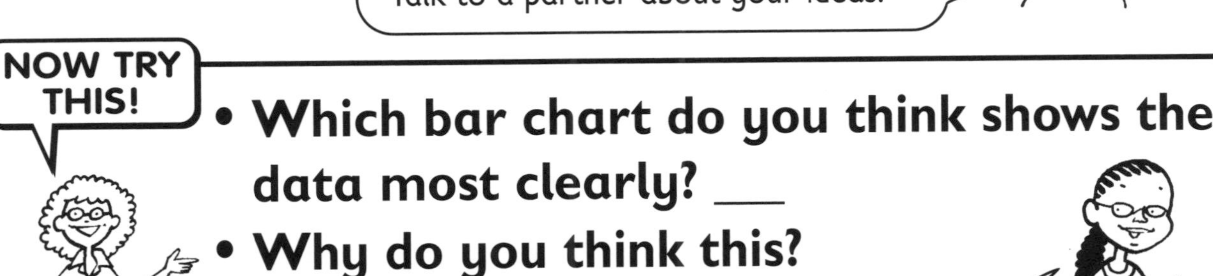

NOW TRY THIS!

- **Which bar chart do you think shows the data most clearly? ___**
- **Why do you think this?**

Talk to a partner about your ideas.

Teachers' note Use in conjunction with 'Scaly fish: 1'.

Time teaser

☆ Work with a partner.
☆ Cut out the cards.
☆ Match a clock to each question card.

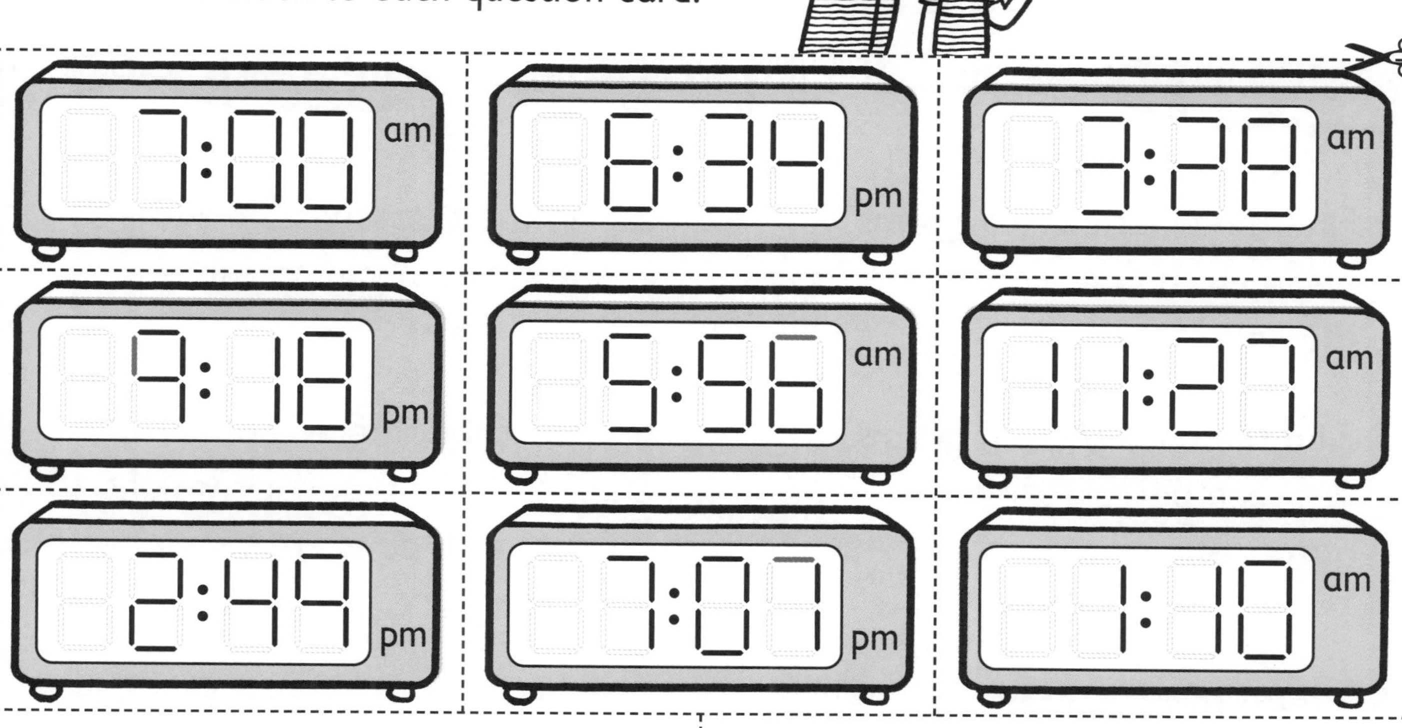

A	Which of these times is nearest to twenty past six in the evening?	**B**	Which of these times is nearest to ten past seven in the morning?
C	Which of these times is between 1 o'clock and 3 o'clock in the afternoon?	**D**	Which of these times shows four minutes to six in the morning?
E	Which of these times is nearest to 8 o'clock in the evening?	**F**	Which of these times is nearest to midnight?
G	Which of these times is just before half past three in the morning?	**H**	Which of these times comes next after nine-thirty in the morning?

Teachers' note As an extension, ask the children to write a question card for the remaining time, using vocabulary such as 'between', and saying whether the time is in the morning, afternoon or evening. Some children may benefit from having geared analogue clocks to help them with this activity.

Post office problems

The mass of each parcel is shown.

A	B	C	D
$\frac{1}{2}$ kg	700 g	1·1 kg	0·3 kg

1 Find the difference, in grams, between the heaviest and the lightest parcels. ______ g

2 Find the total mass, in kilograms, of the two heaviest parcels. ______ kg

3 Find the difference, in grams, between parcel A and parcel B. ______ g

4 In parcel D there is a pair of shoes. If the box itself weighs 100 g, how much does each shoe weigh? ______ g

5 Which three parcels together weigh 1.5 kg? ____ , ____ and ____

6 In parcel B there are three identical mugs. If the box itself weighs 100 g, how much does each mug weigh? ______ g

7 In parcel A there are eight identical ornaments. If the box itself weighs 100 g, how much does each ornament weigh? ______ g

8 Find the total mass, in kilograms, of all four parcels. ______ kg

NOW TRY THIS!

- **Put the parcels into pairs so that one pair is exactly 1 kg heavier than the other pair.**

☐ and ☐ ☐ and ☐

Teachers' note Remind the children that 1000 g are equivalent to 1 kg, and revise equivalent masses of decimals to one decimal place, for example 0.7 kg or 1.3 kg. Ask the children to explain the strategies that they used to solve these problems.

The banker's game

- **Play this game with a partner.**

You need
1 'Banker's game' sheet each and the 'Save and spend cards'.

☆ Each player starts with £50 in the bank.
☆ Spread the cards face down on the table.
☆ Take turns to pick a card and fill in your banking sheet to show how much you have now.
☆ The winner is the player with the most money when all the cards have been used.

Save (add to your balance)	**Spend** (subtract from your balance)	**Balance**
		£50

Teachers' note Use this sheet in conjunction with the cards on 'Save and spend cards'. Ensure that the children understand how a balance sheet works and demonstrate how it is filled in. The children can play in pairs or small groups and require a recording sheet each.

Save and spend cards

• **Cut out the cards and use them with 'The banker's game'.**

It's your birthday! Add £27	Buy a pizza Subtract £9	Clean your dad's car Add £15	Take dog to the vet Subtract £28
Pocket-money day! Add £12	Buy an ice cream Subtract £2	Help your gran Add £13	Buy a DVD Subtract £17
Do a paper round Add £25	Break your mum's vase Subtract £32	Win a prize! Add £37	Take cat to the vet Subtract £16
Pocket-money day! Add £12	Buy a book Subtract £7	The bank pays you interest Add £5	Buy presents for the family Subtract £29
Help your mum Add £17	Lose your purse Subtract £16	Do some babysitting Add £19	Buy a CD Subtract £14

Teachers' note This sheet should be used in conjunction with 'The banker's game'.

Fi's fruitcake

Fi is making a fruitcake. She keeps adding new ingredients to the scales.

- **Read each new measurement.**

NOW TRY THIS!

- **How much of each ingredient does Fi put onto the scales?**

cocoa ______ g flour ______ g raisins ______ g

sugar ______ g butter ______ g sultanas ______ g

Teachers' note Begin the lesson by looking at the scales and determining the value of each interval. Encourage the children to read the scales as accurately as they can. The arrows can be adjusted to provide a range of different scales to read and to provide differentiation.

Time dominoes

- **Cut out the cards.**
- **Play time dominoes with a partner.**

Teachers' note Enlarge the sheet to A3 size and laminate for a more permanent resource. Encourage the children to read the times on the two matching clocks aloud as they lay a domino. As a further activity the children could also pick a domino and work out the time interval between the times shown on the two clocks.

Time bingo

- ☆ Tick eight of the times from the list below and draw them onto the blank clocks.
- ☆ Swap sheets with a partner and check that their clocks match their chosen times.
- ☆ Now you are ready to play Time bingo!

- quarter past one ☐
- nine fifty-eight ☐
- ten to twelve ☐
- two thirty-nine ☐
- eleven twenty-two ☐
- seven minutes past one ☐
- seventeen minutes past four ☐
- ten past three ☐
- twenty to two ☐
- six thirty ☐
- eight fifty ☐
- twenty-five to seven ☐
- ten forty-seven ☐
- half past ten ☐
- twelve fifteen ☐
- six minutes to five ☐

Teachers' note When the times have been drawn on the clocks and checked by a partner, call out times from the list, ideally altering the way they are described, for example 'six thirty' could be read out as 'half past six', or 'eight fifty' as 'ten to nine'.

Dan's day

It is Monday.

- Colour the box that shows what Dan is most likely to be doing at these times.

Time		
12:15 pm	Going to bed	Getting up
	Eating lunch	In bed
10:10 am	At school	Eating lunch
	Getting up	In bed
1:00 am	Watching TV	At school
	Eating lunch	In bed
4:15 pm	In bed	Getting up
	Eating lunch	Watching TV
3:30 am	Going home	In bed
	Watching TV	Eating lunch
7:30 am	Going to bed	Getting up
	Eating lunch	At school
1:00 pm	At school	Getting up
	Eating breakfast	In bed

NOW TRY THIS!

- Choose any six am and pm times.
- Write what you are usually doing at those times on a weekday.

Teachers' note It is important that children are able to interpret 'am' and 'pm' times, and are not just taught that 'am' represents the hours between midnight and midday and 'pm' the hours between mid-day and midnight. Encourage the children to talk about the activities they might be doing at different times of the day.

Optical illusions

Look carefully at these designs.

- **Colour** horizontal **lines blue.**
- **Colour** vertical **lines red.**

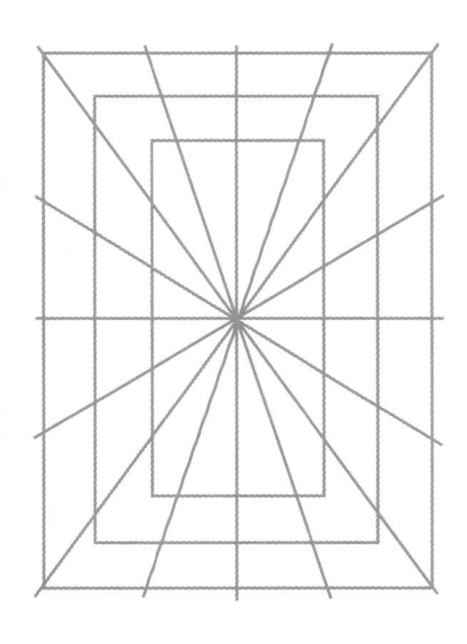

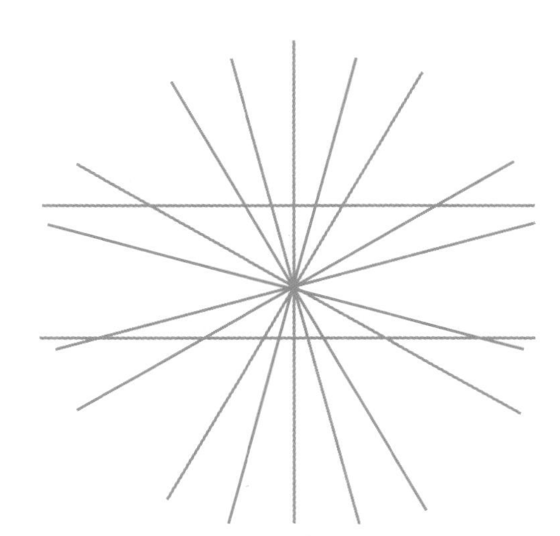

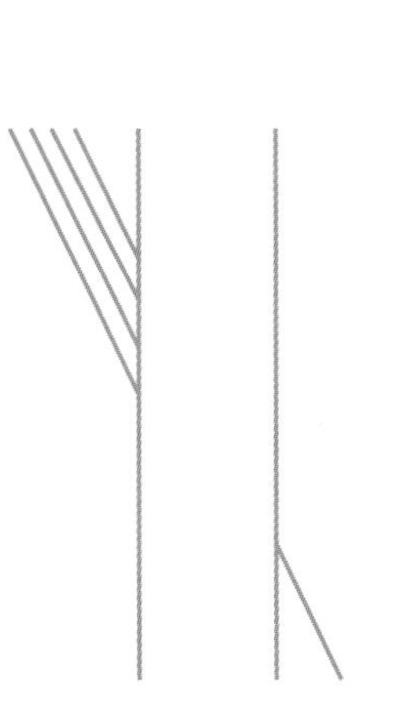

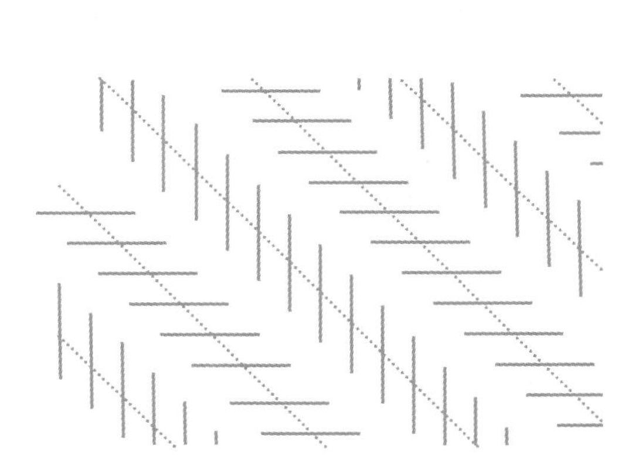

- **Now try this design.**

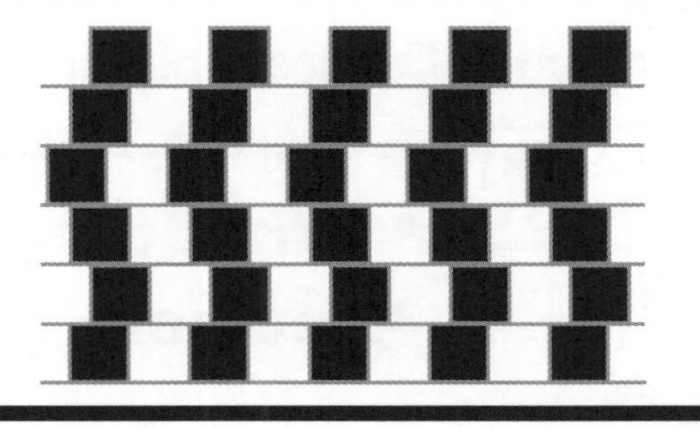

Teachers' note Optical illusions are an interesting way to introduce discussion about the terms 'vertical' and 'horizontal'. Explain that sometimes your eyes deceive you when looking at patterns and lines that look wavy can sometimes be straight. Encourage the use of rulers to check the direction and straightness of the different lines.

Cinema seating

- **Colour the people's T-shirts to match these descriptions.**

The man in **C4** has a **green** T-shirt.

The girl in **D3** has a **blue** T-shirt.

The people in **E2** and **F2** have **red** T-shirts.

The boy in **A6** has a **yellow** T-shirt.

The woman in **B3** has an **orange** T-shirt.

The girl in **F6** has a **pink** T-shirt.

The woman in **F5** has a **purple** T-shirt.

The woman in **D5** has a **black** T-shirt.

- **Write the positions of the people whose T-shirts you have <u>not</u> coloured.** ______________________

Teachers' note When introducing this activity, remind the children that the letter is given first and then the number to indicate the position of a square in a grid.

Counter attack

A counter is placed on a square and then moved.

- **Write where the counter ends up each time.**

7							
6							
5							
4							
3							
2							
1							
	A	B	C	D	E	F	G

N, NE, E, SE, S, SW, W, NW

1. The counter starts on B4. It moves 1 square NE, then 4 squares SE. It is now on ☐

2. The counter starts on D6. It moves 3 squares SE, then 2 squares SW. It is now on ☐

3. The counter starts on C3. It moves 1 square NW, then 2 squares NE. It is now on ☐

4. The counter starts on F6. It moves 3 squares SW, then 2 squares NE. It is now on ☐

5. The counter starts on B5. It moves 2 squares SE, then 2 squares NW. It is now on ☐

6. The counter starts on C4. It moves 2 squares NW, then 3 squares SE. It is now on ☐

NOW TRY THIS!

- **Make up three puzzles of your own for a partner to solve.**

Teachers' note You may wish to enlarge this sheet to A3. Remind the children of the eight compass directions at the start of the lesson and ensure that the children are confident in locating a square on a grid.

Reading the signs

Jack likes to drive his car.
He sees lots of road signs on his trips.

- **Work with a partner to answer the questions.**

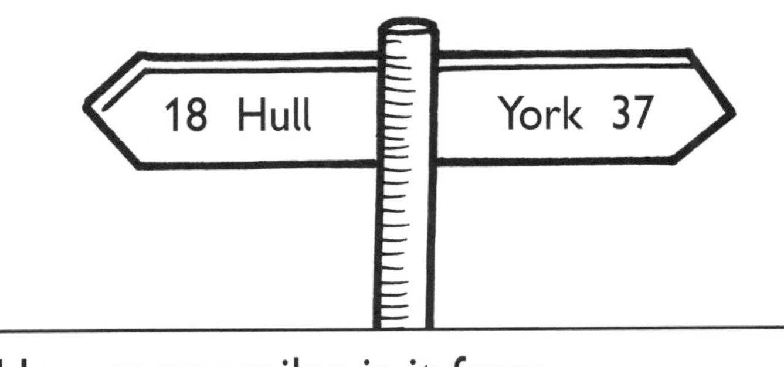

1 How many miles is it from Hull to York along this road?

_____ miles

2 How many miles is it from Cambridge to London along this road?

_____ miles

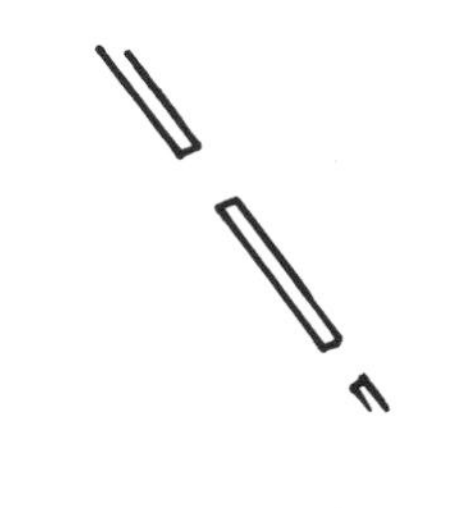

Whitby 48

3 If Jack drives one-quarter of the way to Whitby, how many more miles does he still have to drive?

_____ miles

4 Last week Jack drove to Manchester and back each weekday. How far did he drive in total?

_____ miles

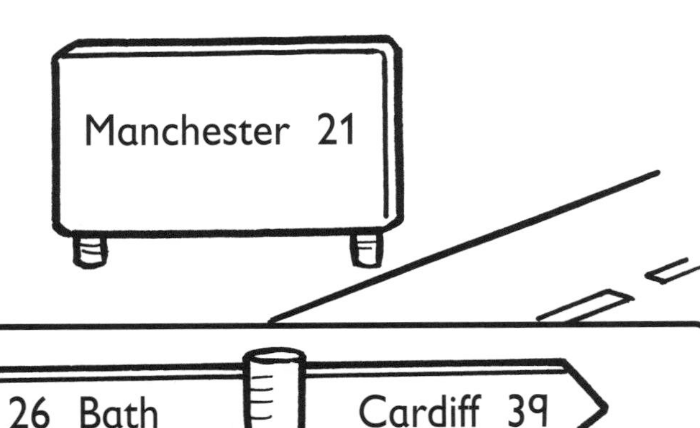

Leeds 34
Oldham 67

26 Bath
Cardiff 39

- **Use these signs to make up four questions for another pair to solve.**

Teachers' note Draw attention to the fact that different types of signposts work in different ways. For example when on a motorway, the signs show only the towns in one direction, whereas a two-armed signpost shows towns in two different directions. Talk about how this affects the operation used to solve the problem.

Tallest man ever

The tallest man that ever lived, Robert Wadlow, was 272 cm **tall!**

- **Use a written method to find the difference between his height and the heights of these people.**

1.

2.

3.

4.

5.

1.	2.	3.	4.	5.
Zeng Jinlian (tallest woman ever) **248 cm**	Roald Dahl **198 cm**	Elvis Presley **183 cm**	Queen Victoria **152 cm**	Joan of Arc **149 cm**
______ cm	______ cm	______ cm	______ cm	______ cm

- **Work in a group of three or four.**
- **Measure your heights and fill in the table.**

Name	Height (cm)	Difference between 272 cm and this height

Teachers' note Encourage the children to use an appropriate written method, such as a vertical column method involving partitioning or the more traditional decomposition method. Provide a separate piece of paper for their workings. The children will require a tape-measure, metre sticks or height measurer for the extension activity.

Magic ingredients

Griselda is recording the boxed ingredients in her cupboard. She counts the boxes.

- **Use multiplication to work out how many of each ingredient she has.**

4 boxes of warts

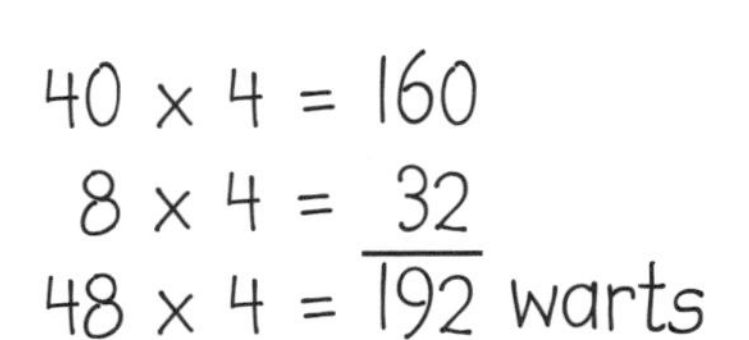

7 boxes of slugs

6 boxes of hairballs

8 boxes of maggots

9 boxes of eyeballs

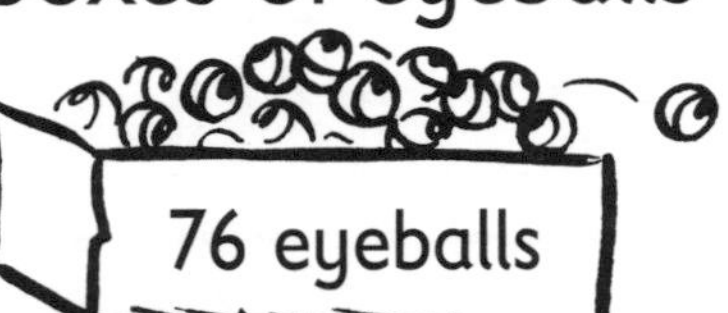

NOW TRY THIS!

- **Use a calculator to work out how many ingredients there are altogether.** ______

Teachers' note Encourage the children to use an appropriate method of multiplication, such as partitioning in the way shown or using a grid method of multiplication.

Beautiful brooches

A jeweller cuts a length of wire into equal-sized pieces to make a brooch. The more pieces of wire that a brooch contains, the more expensive it is.

A	B	C	D	E	F
6 pieces	7 pieces	8 pieces	9 pieces	11 pieces	12 pieces

1. He uses a wire **57 cm** long. What is the most expensive brooch he can make, if the wire is cut into:

(a) 6 cm pieces?	**(b)** 7 cm pieces?	**(c)** 9 cm pieces?
$57 \div 6 = 9$ r3 9 pieces D		

2. He uses a wire **74 cm** long. What is the most expensive brooch he can make, if the wire is cut into:

(a) 6 cm pieces?	**(b)** 8 cm pieces?	**(c)** 9 cm pieces?

3. He uses a wire **65 cm** long. What is the most expensive brooch he can make, if the wire is cut into:

(a) 7 cm pieces?	**(b)** 8 cm pieces?	**(c)** 9 cm pieces?

Teachers' note Encourage the children to use an appropriate practical, informal or written method of division. As an extension, ask the children to use their answers to work out how much wire was wasted altogether.

From 'metre' you

- **This metre stick is marked in** tenths.

1 Write each length as a decimal.

a $\frac{3}{10}$ of a metre = 0·3 m

b $\frac{6}{10}$ of a metre = ☐ m

c $\frac{7}{10}$ of a metre = ☐ m

d $\frac{5}{10}$ of a metre = ☐ m

e $\frac{8}{10}$ of a metre = ☐ m

f $\frac{9}{10}$ of a metre = ☐ m

- **This metre stick is marked in** hundredths.

2 Write each length as a decimal.

a $\frac{6}{100}$ of a metre = 0·06 m

b $\frac{1}{100}$ of a metre = ☐ m

c $\frac{15}{100}$ of a metre = ☐ m

d $\frac{19}{100}$ of a metre = ☐ m

e $\frac{78}{100}$ of a metre = ☐ m

f $\frac{93}{100}$ of a metre = ☐ m

NOW TRY THIS!

Talk to a partner about what you notice.

- **Write these lengths as decimals. What do you notice?**

$\frac{8}{10}$ of a metre = ☐ m

$\frac{80}{100}$ of a metre = ☐ m

$\frac{7}{10}$ of a metre = ☐ m

$\frac{70}{100}$ of a metre = ☐ m

Teachers' note This sheet can be used as an introduction to tenths and hundredths of a metre. Show the children a metre stick and discuss how one tenth of a metre is 10 cm and one hundredth of a metre is 1 cm to help the children get a sense of the size of the measurements. Encourage them to make the link between, for example, 0·6 and 0·60, using the metre stick.

Guinea pig food

These sacks of guinea pig food have been weighed.
Pairs of sacks weigh the same.

- **Fill in the missing weights on the sacks.**

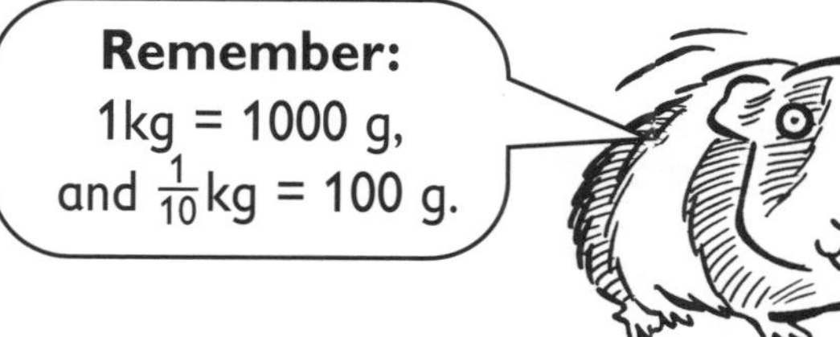

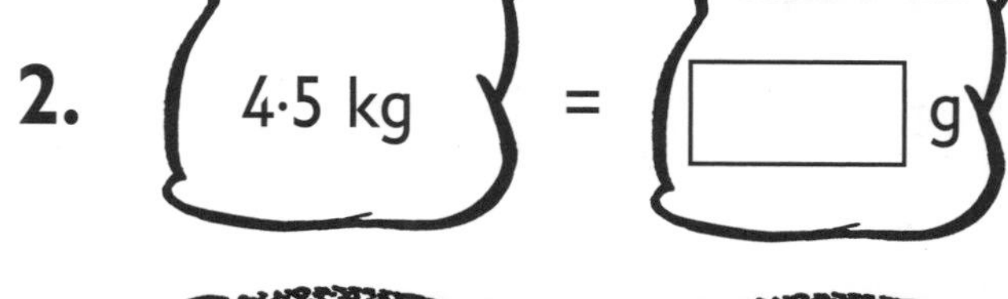

1. 2 kg = 2000 g

2. 4·5 kg = ☐ g

3. 1·5 kg = ☐ g

4. 7·3 kg = ☐ g

5. 2·8 kg = ☐ g

6. 5·9 kg = ☐ g

7. 7 kg = ☐ g

8. 0·1 kg = ☐ g

- **Fill in these missing weights.**

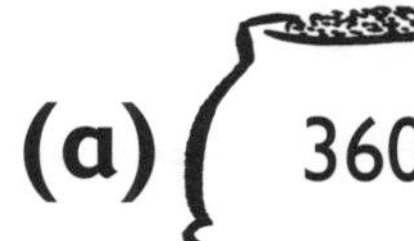

(a) 3600 g = ☐ g

(b) 5800 g = ☐ g

(c) 700 g = ☐ g

Teachers' note As the children become more familiar with the relationships between units they can begin to convert between them, including using decimals. Remind the children that the column after the decimal point tells you how many tenths of a kilogram (or how many lots of 100 g) there are.

Scale shapes

- **Match up each letter with a shape in the key below.**

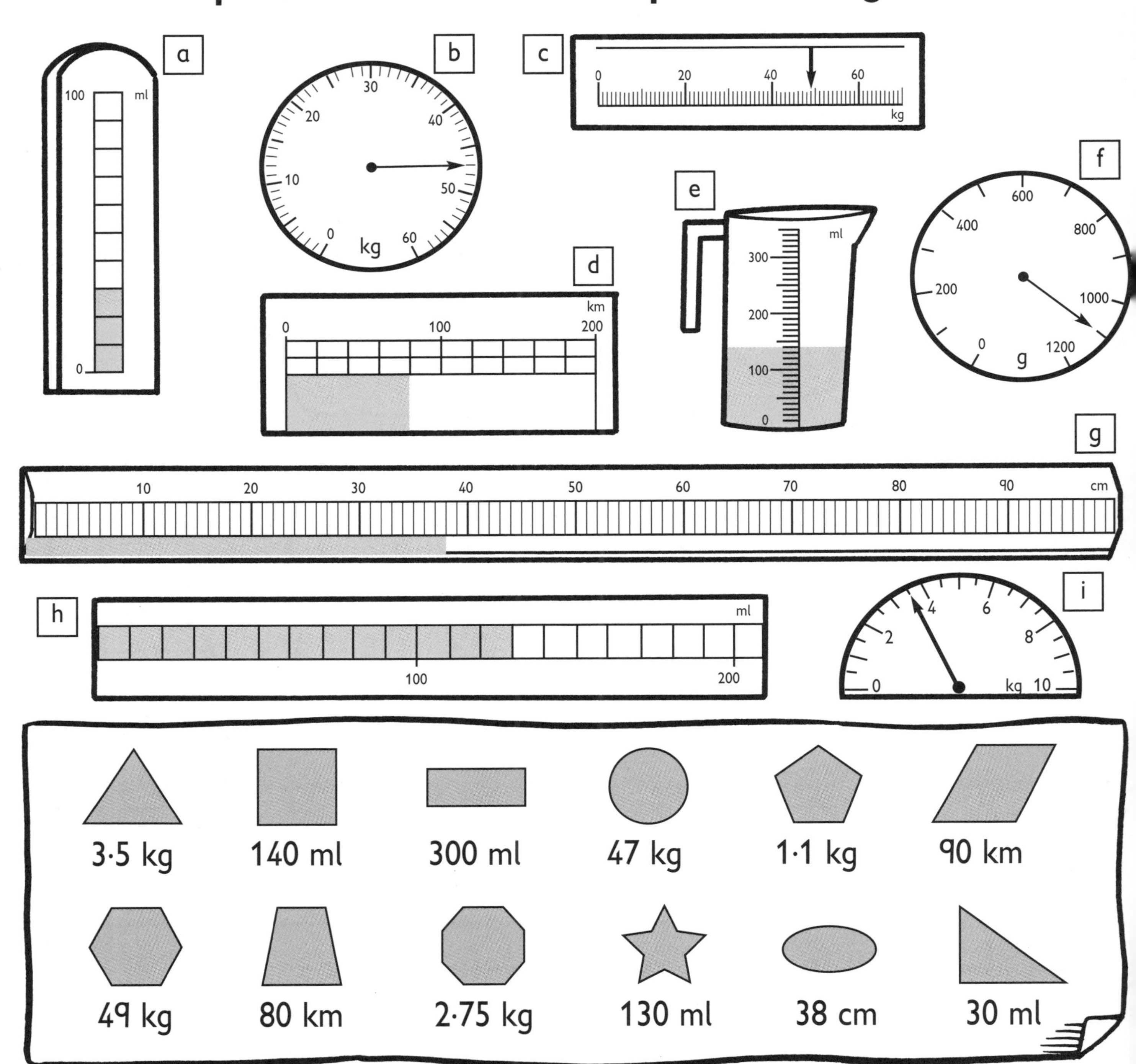

- **Record your answers here.**

a =

Teachers' note Encourage the children to discuss their answers at the end of the lesson and examine scales that have caused difficulties. Draw attention to the fact that some scales are marked in grams but the reading is shown in kilograms, and remind the children of the relationship between these units.

Spot the rectangles

- ☆ Using a ruler, join four dots to make a rectangle with horizontal and vertical sides.
- ☆ Measure the sides of the rectangle and record its perimeter in the box below.
- ☆ Do this for three more rectangles.

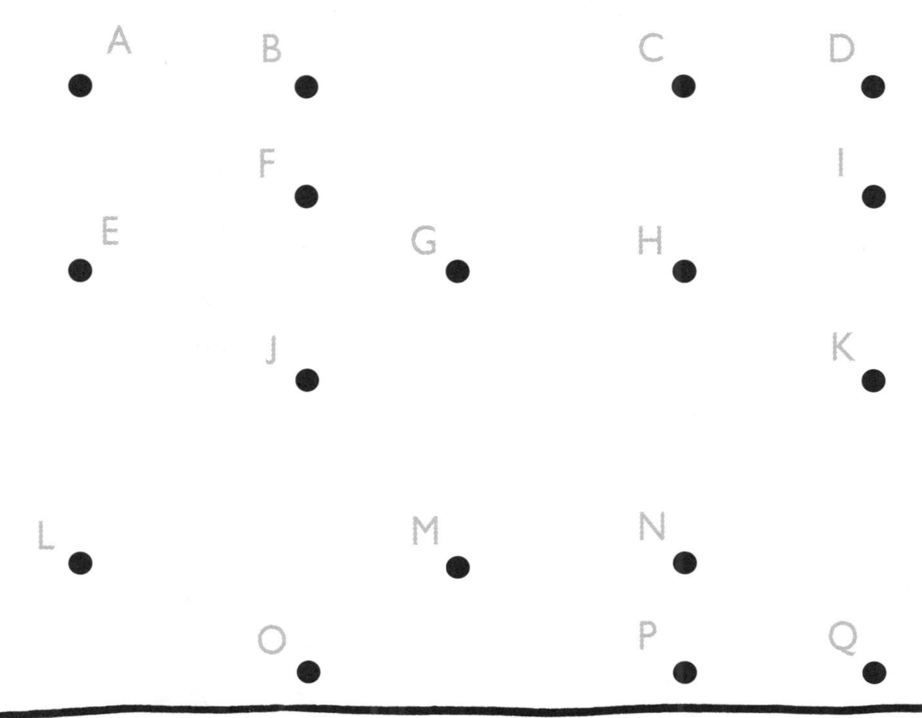

- **On the back of the sheet, draw three different rectangles, each with a perimeter of 24 cm.**

Teachers' note During the plenary, investigate how many different perimeters the class have found.

Hickory, dickory, dock

These clocks show each o'clock **time from 1 o'clock to 12 o'clock.**

- **Complete the table to show the angles between the hands.**

o'clock	1	2	3	4	5	6	7	8	9	10	11	12
angle			90°									

- **Talk to a partner about any patterns you notice.**

This clock shows half past 6.

- **What do you think the angle between the hands is here?_____**

Teachers' note When introducing this activity, begin by exploring the angle between the hands at 3 o'clock, which the children should recognise as a right angle. Then show how the right angle can be split into three equal parts and discuss the angle between the hands at 1 o'clock. Encourage the children to look for patterns in the numbers and to discuss these with a partner.

Magic spell

Maurice faces the first letter of the word. He turns through an angle to face the next letter, and so on.

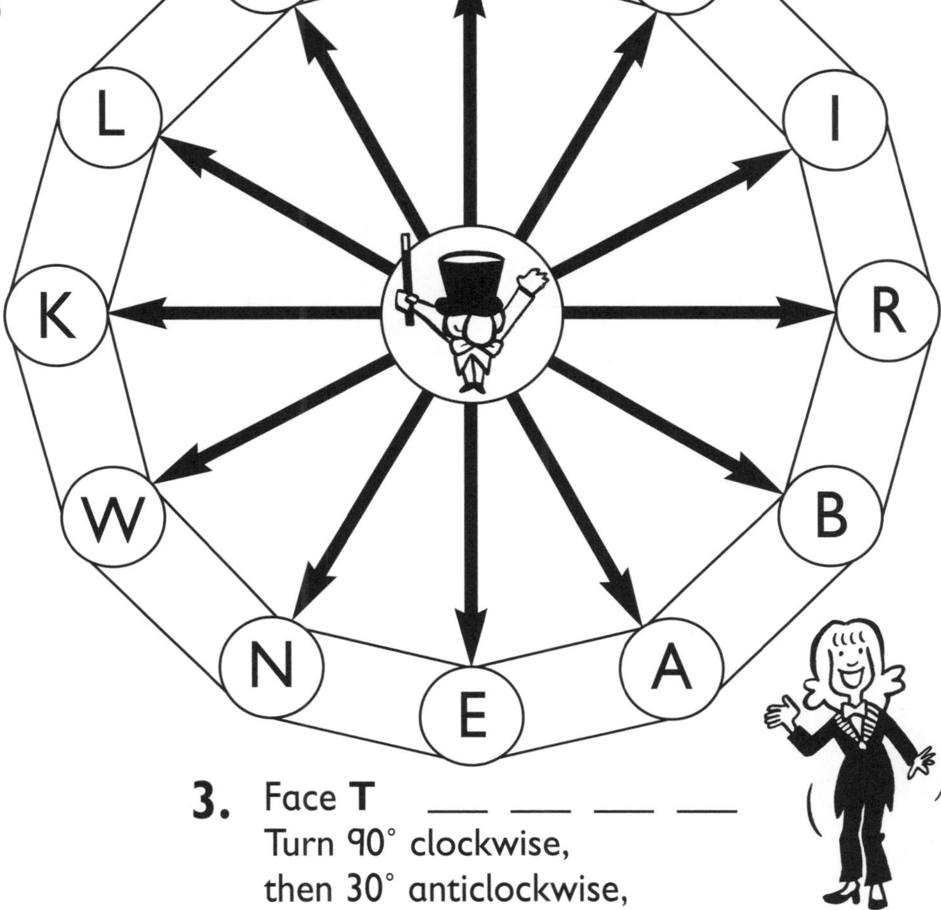

- **Follow the instructions to spell a word.**

1. Face **W** A ___ ___
Turn 90° anti-clockwise,
then 60° clockwise,
then 180° clockwise.

2. Face **C** ___ ___ ___
Turn 180° clockwise,
then 60° anticlockwise,
then 60° anticlockwise.

3. Face **T** ___ ___ ___ ___
Turn 90° clockwise,
then 30° anticlockwise,
then 90° anticlockwise,
then 60° anticlockwise.

4. Face **R** ___ ___ ___ ___ ___
Turn 60° clockwise,
then 30° anticlockwise,
then 360° clockwise,
then 60° anticlockwise,
then 60° anticlockwise.

5. Face **C** ___ ___ ___ ___ ___
Turn 90° clockwise,
then 30° clockwise,
then 120° anticlockwise,
then 30° anticlockwise,
then 120° anticlockwise.

- **Write instructions for some words of your own for a partner to solve.**

Teachers' note Begin the lesson by demonstrating this activity practically (see page 19). Remind the children of the directions **clockwise** and **anticlockwise**, and demonstrate the sizes of different turns, including 90°, 45°, 30°, 60°, 180° and 360°.

That's an order!

- **Put each set of angles in order of size, starting with the smallest.**

1.

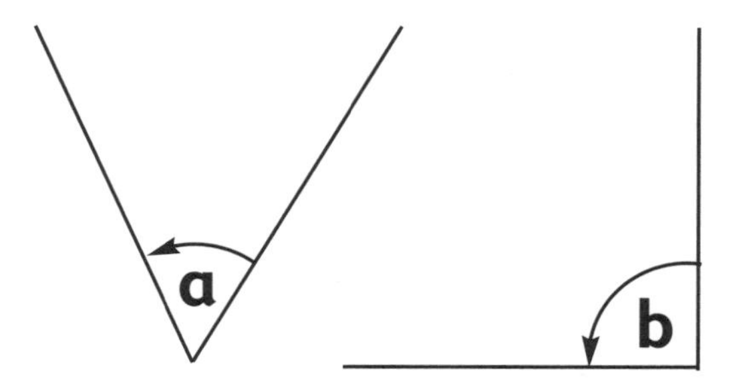

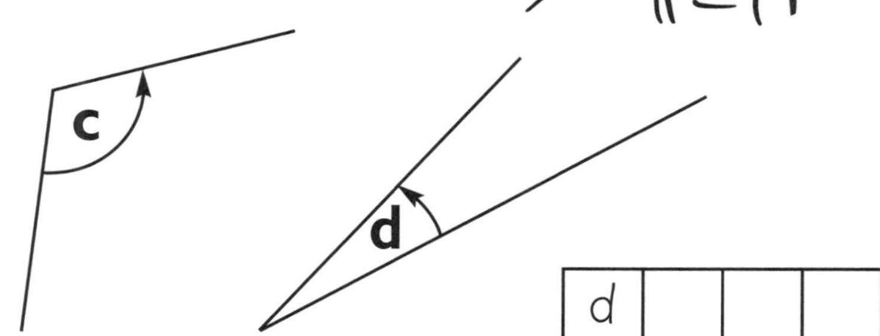

d			

2.

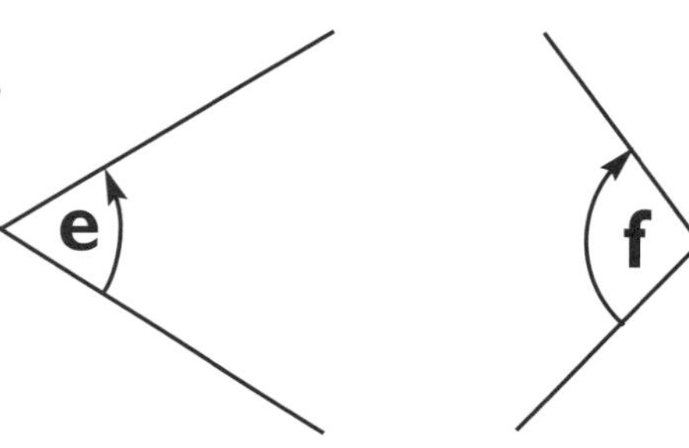

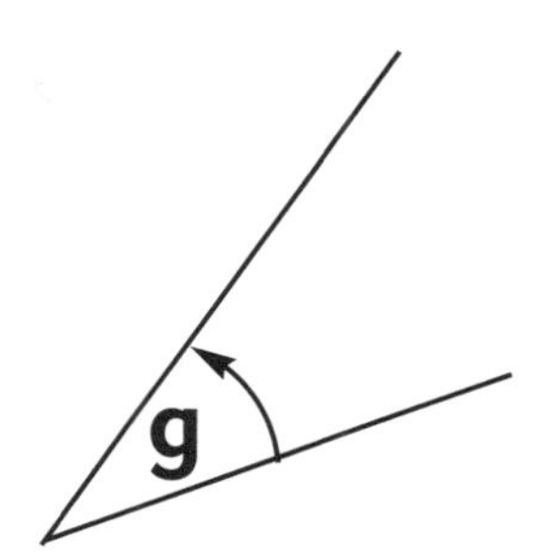

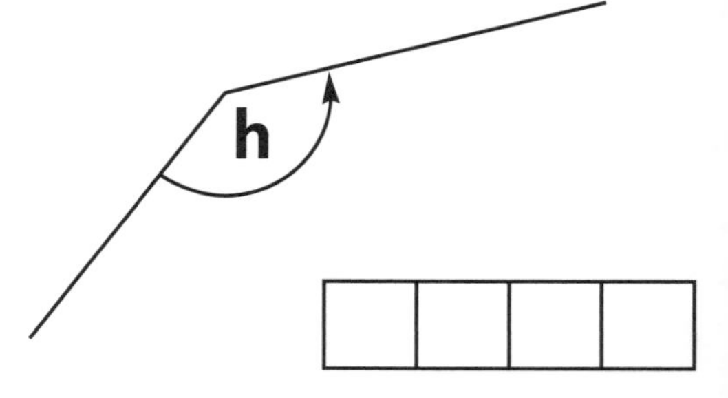

3.

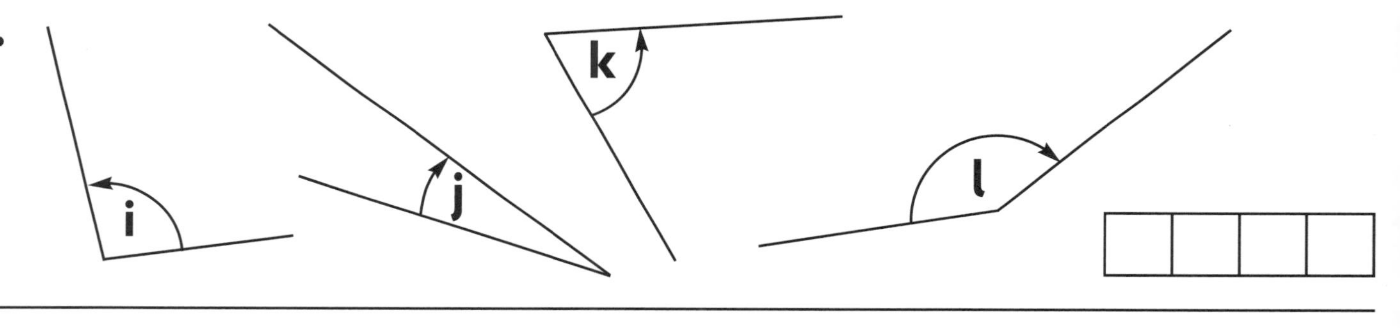

4.

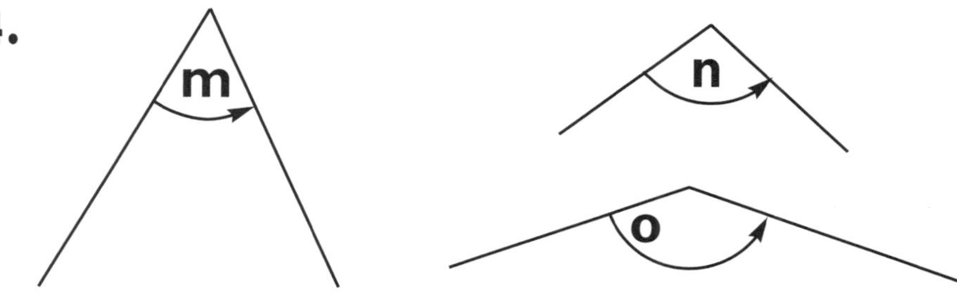

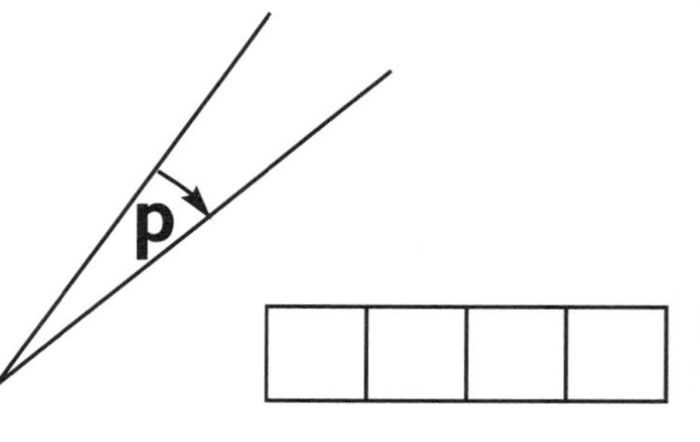

NOW TRY THIS!

- **Draw four angles for a partner to order.**

Teachers' note Encourage the children to begin ordering the angles by seeing which are greater than, equal to or less than a right angle. Draw attention to the fact that angle is the amount of turn from one line to the other, and is not related to line length, area inside the arc or distance between the two end-points of the lines.

Zap 'em: 1

- **Cut out the cards and use them to play the game on Zap 'em: 2.**

Zap a counter if it is **NE** of yours	Zap a counter if it is **SW** of yours	Zap a counter if it is **S** of yours	Zap a counter if it is **NW** of yours
Zap a counter if it is **E** of yours	Zap a counter if it is **SE** of yours	Zap a counter if it is **NE** of yours	Zap a counter if it is **S** of yours
Zap a counter if it is **NW** of yours	Zap a counter if it is **E** of yours	Zap a counter if it is **W** of yours	Zap a counter if it is **NE** of yours
Zap a counter if it is **SW** of yours	Zap a counter if it is **SE** of yours	Zap a counter if it is **N** of yours	Zap a counter if it is **SE** of yours
Zap a counter if it is **W** of yours	Zap a counter if it is **N** of yours	Zap a counter if it is **SW** of yours	Zap a counter if it is **NW** of yours

Teachers' note Use this sheet in conjunction with 'Zap 'em: 2'. The worksheet could be copied onto card and laminated to create a more permanent resource.

Zap 'em: 2

- **Play this game with a partner.**

N NW NE W E SW SE S

You need counters in two colours (eight of each colour)...

...and the cards cut from Zap 'em: 1.

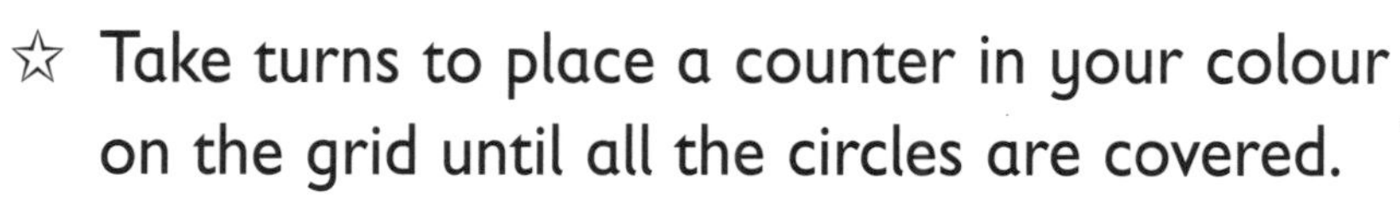

☆ Take turns to place a counter in your colour on the grid until all the circles are covered.

☆ Place the cards face down in a pile.

☆ Now take turns to pick a card. If one of your partner's counters can be reached from one of yours in the direction shown on the card, remove that counter. You can only zap one counter at a time.

☆ The winner is the first player to zap all their partner's counters.

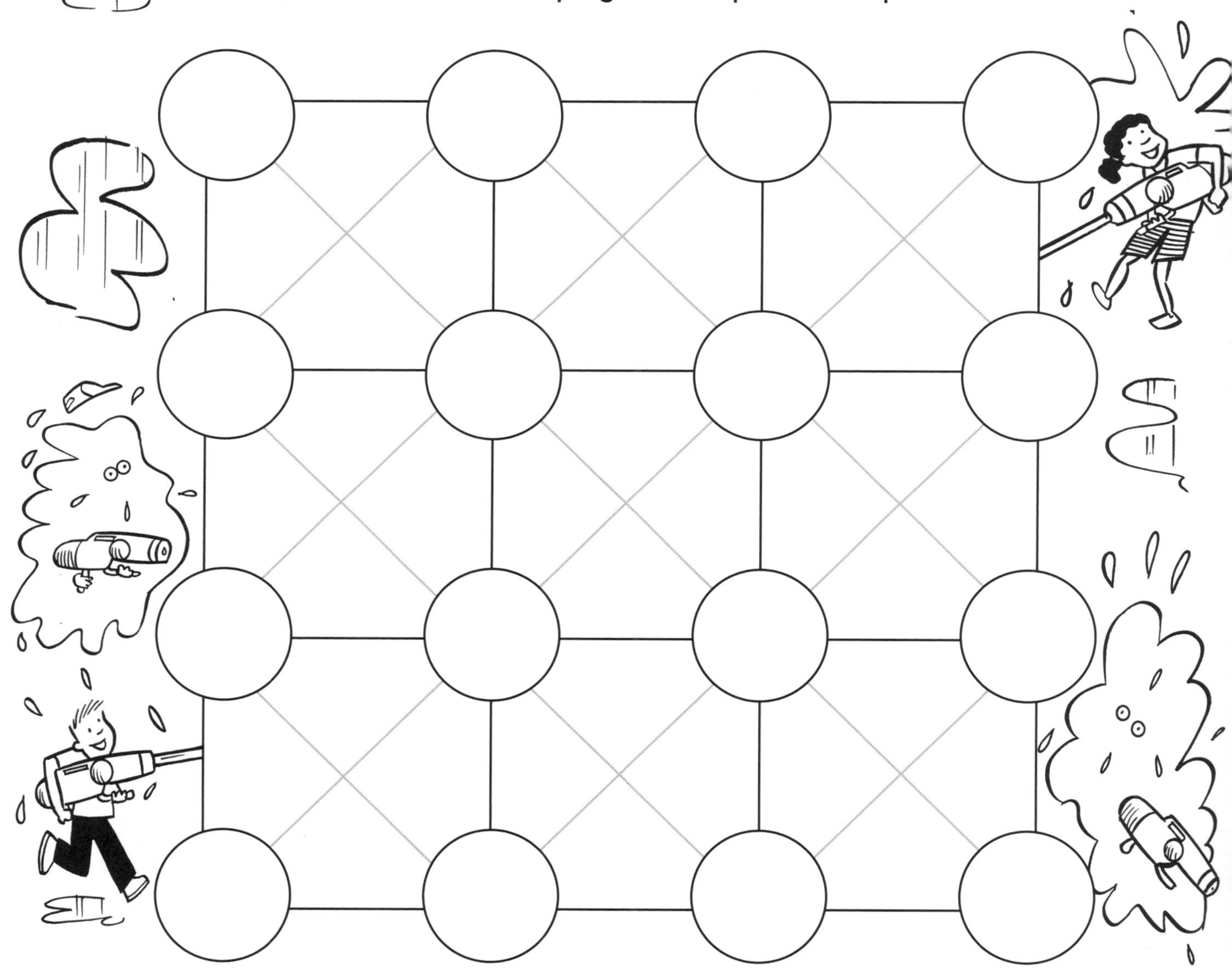

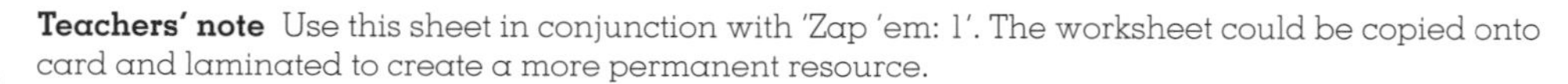

Teachers' note Use this sheet in conjunction with 'Zap 'em: 1'. The worksheet could be copied onto card and laminated to create a more permanent resource.

Loopy witches

☆ Cut out the cards.

☆ Answer the 'start' card. Find the answer on one of the other cards, then answer that question.

☆ Put the cards in a loop on the table.

Start **6 l** Griselda has 180 ml. If she pours it equally into six bottles, how much is in each bottle? B	**3 l** Three blue tins each hold 300 ml and a red tin holds 600 ml. How much do the tins hold altogether? C
575 ml A bowl and a jug together hold 500 ml. If the bowl holds 100 ml more than the jug, how much does the bowl hold? M	**30 ml** A bucket holds 500 ml. If 150 ml is already in the bucket, how much more could it hold? R
$1\frac{1}{2}$ l If a jug holds $1\frac{1}{2}$ l, how much do four jugs hold? K	**300 ml** Griselda drank 450 ml more than Zelda. If Griselda drank 550 ml, how much did Zelda drink? S
350 ml A bowl holds 28 l. If the bowl holds seven times more than the kettle, how much does the kettle hold? O	**13 l** A bucket holds 6 l more than a pan. If these containers hold 12 l altogether, how much does the pan hold? I
100 ml If a bucket holds $6\frac{1}{2}$ l, how much do two buckets hold? T	**4 l** Gertrude drank 350 ml more than Maud. If Gertrude drank 225 ml, how much did Maud drink? O

Teachers' note As a quick way of checking the children's answers, use the letters at the bottom right of each card. If the cards are in the correct order they will spell a word (answer on page 215). Remind the children that 'ml' stands for 'millilitres' and 'l' stands for 'litres'.

Crack the codes

- **Answer each question to find which code opens each safe.**

Safe letter	A	B	C	D	E	F	G	H
Code number								

A

  711
− 257

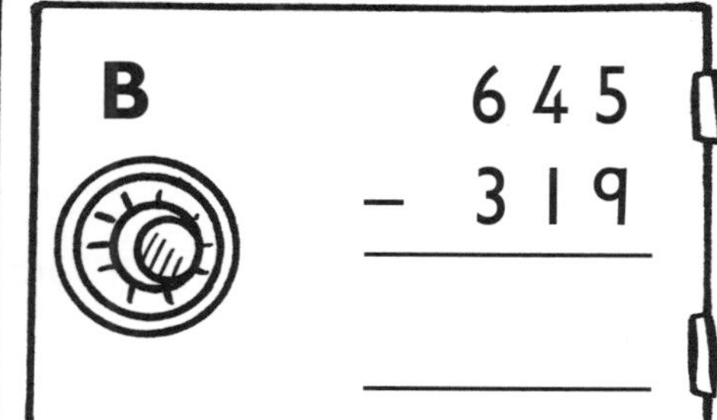
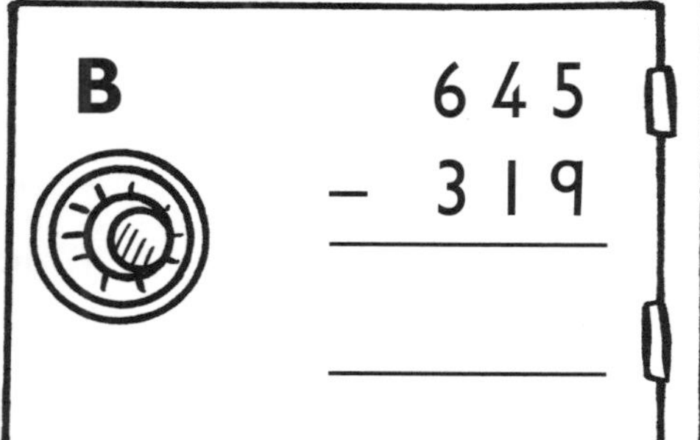

B

  645
− 319

C

  445
− 177

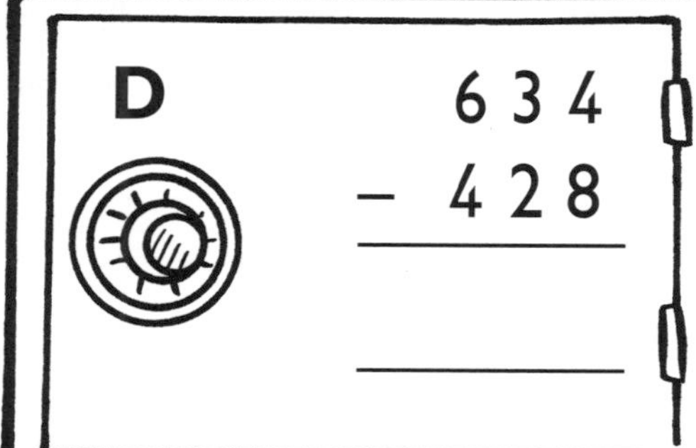

D

  634
− 428

E

  552
− 373

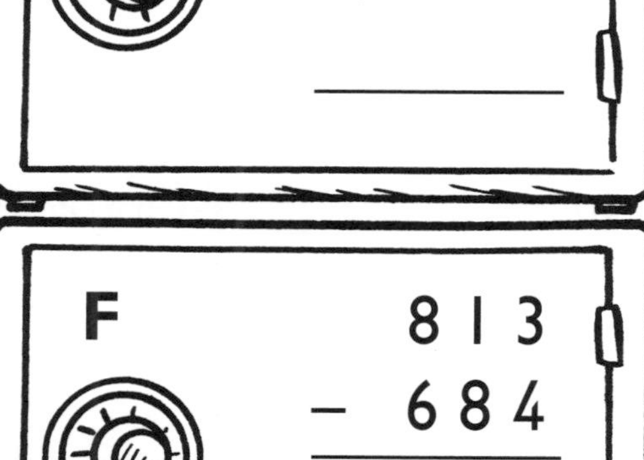

F

  813
− 684

G

  704
− 276

H

  921
− 672

CODES

1 **428**

2 **129**

3 **268**

4 **179**

5 **326**

6 **454**

7 **249**

8 **154**

9 **206**

Teachers' note Demonstrate suitable written methods of subtraction that the children could use to answer these questions. Encourage the children to estimate first and then check their answers using a written method of addition. As an extension, ask the children to make up their own 'safe' puzzle for a partner to solve.

A bucketful of fun

- **Choose one number from each bucket and cross it out. Write the numbers as an addition and find the total.**

NOW TRY THIS!

- **Partition these numbers.**

73·52 =

59·07 =

Teachers' note It can be very helpful to represent the values of each digit using a '100s' block of place value apparatus, such as Dienes blocks. Describe this as ONE bar of chocolate. The first two digits represent how many whole bars of chocolate there are. Explain that if one bar is broken into ten strips, these are tenths, and if broken into 100 small cubes, these are hundredths.

Marvel Mouse

- **How full is Marvel Mouse's power pack?**
- **Shade the power pack to match the decimal.**

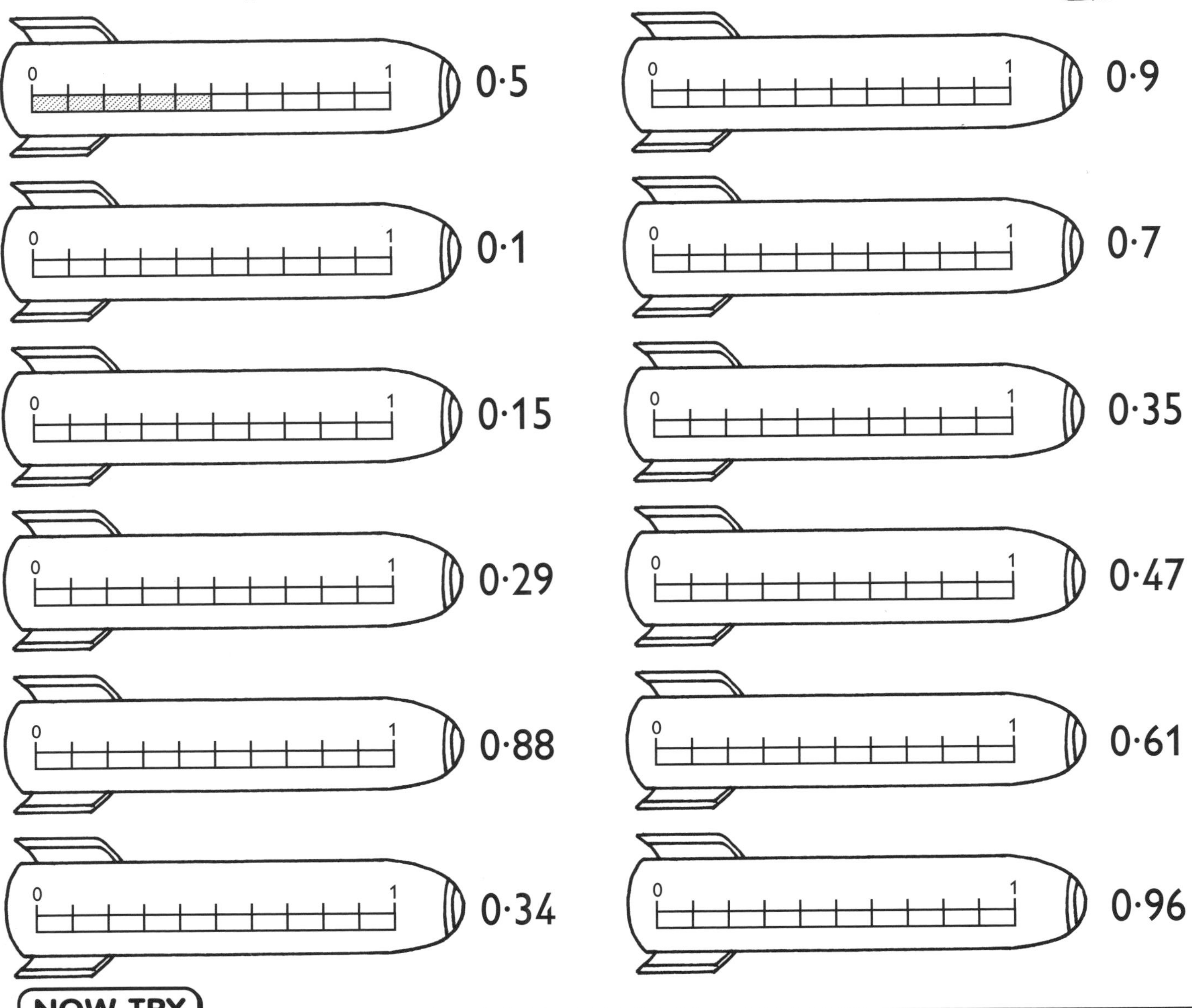

Some of these power packs are full.

- **Write one decimal to show how much power there is altogether.**

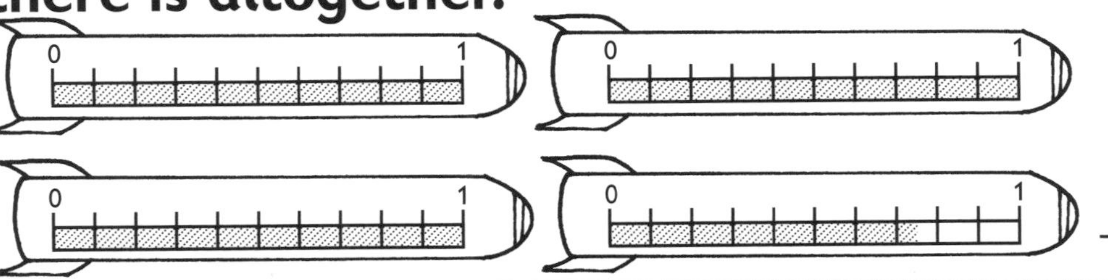

___

Teachers' note This sheet follows on from Super Squirrel. Encourage the children to estimate the hundredths as accurately as they can, for example by using the fact that five hundredths is halfway between two whole number of tenths. The extension activity encourages the children to consider decimals greater than one, for example 2·59.

Escape from Planet Zog!

- **Your mission is to fill in the missing decimals on the number line.**

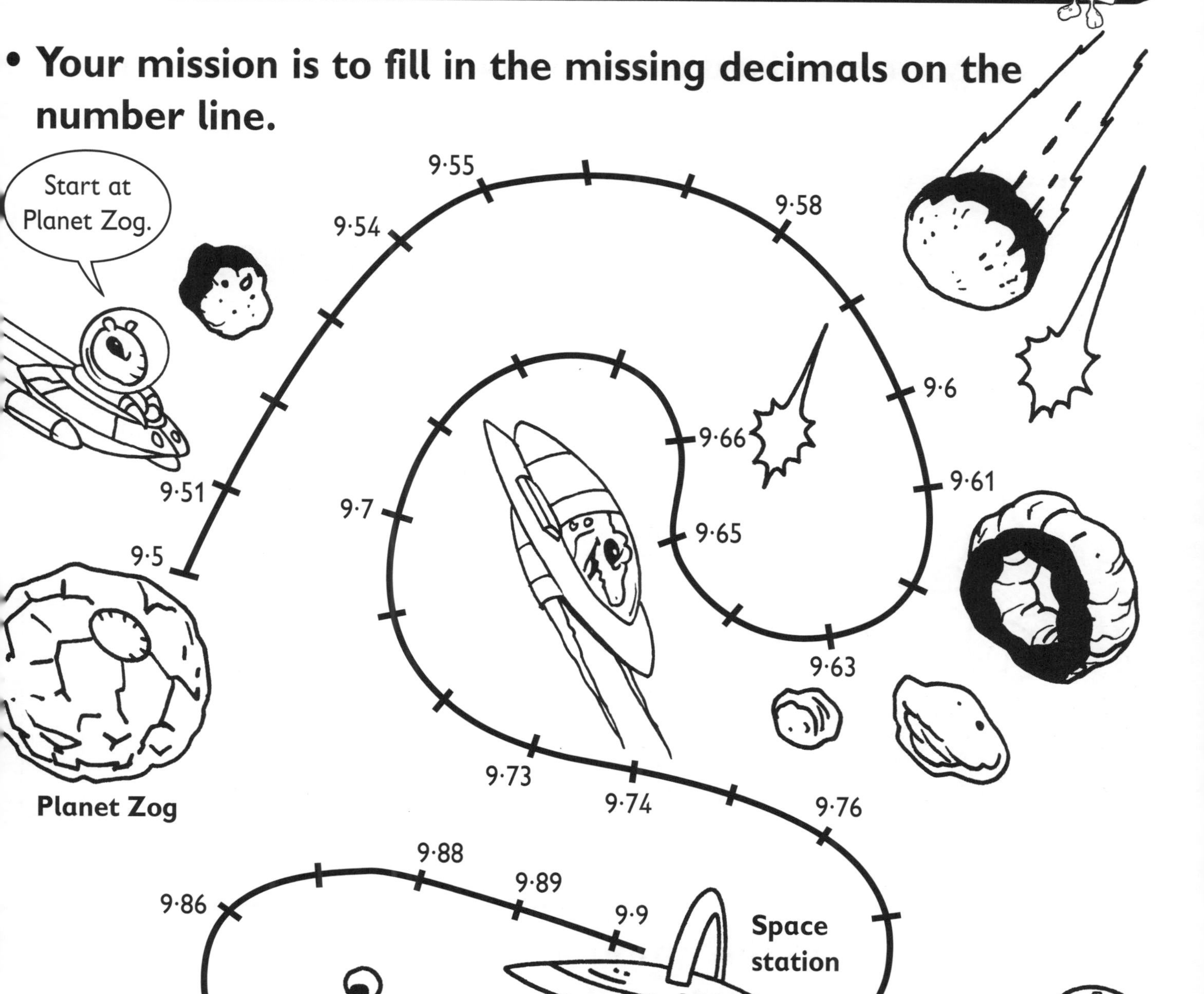

Play this game with a partner.

☆ Take turns to roll the dice and move forward that many hundredths.

☆ If you land on a decimal with no hundredths, move forward one tenth.

☆ If you land on a decimal with five hundredths, move back one tenth.

☆ The winner is the first player to reach the safety of the space station.

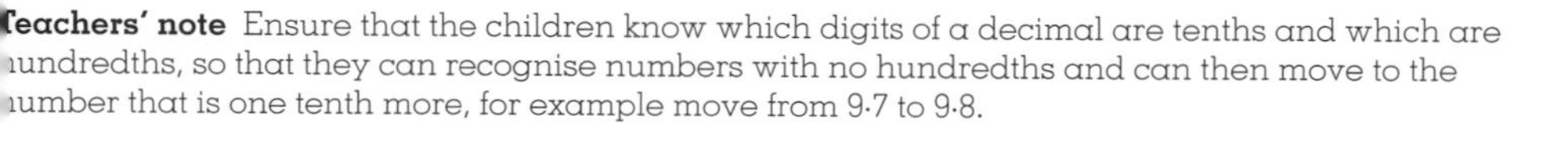
Teachers' note Ensure that the children know which digits of a decimal are tenths and which are hundredths, so that they can recognise numbers with no hundredths and can then move to the number that is one tenth more, for example move from 9·7 to 9·8.

Milking Milli

Milli the goat is milked every day.

- **Complete the chart to show how many millilitres of milk she gives each day.**

Milli is the Latin word for **thousand**.

Remember:
one litre is 1000 millilitres;
one-tenth of a litre is 100 ml.

Day	Amount of milk in **litres**	Amount of milk in **millilitres**
Monday	3 l	3000 ml
Tuesday	1·5 l	
Wednesday	2·4 l	
Thursday	1·7 l	
Friday	2·8 l	
Saturday	3·5 l	
Sunday	0·9 l	

NOW TRY THIS!

- **Fill in the amount of milk Milli gives in litres for the following week.**

Day	Litres	Millilitres
Monday	2·4 l	2400 ml
Tuesday		3300 ml
Wednesday		200 ml
Thursday		700 ml
Friday		1100 ml
Saturday		300 ml
Sunday		4400 ml

Teachers' note As the children become more familiar with the relationships between units they can begin to convert between them, including using decimals. Remind the children that the column after the decimal point tells you how many tenths of a litre (or how many lots of 100 ml) there are.

Fill it up!

- **Play this game with a partner.**

You need a dice and a blue colouring pencil.

☆ Take turns to roll the dice. Use the key to find out how much water to add to your container.

☆ Use a blue pencil to show each new amount of water.

☆ The winner is the first to **exactly** fill his/her container. (Miss a go if you roll an amount that is more than you need.)

100 ml

200 ml

300 ml

400 ml

500 ml

600 ml

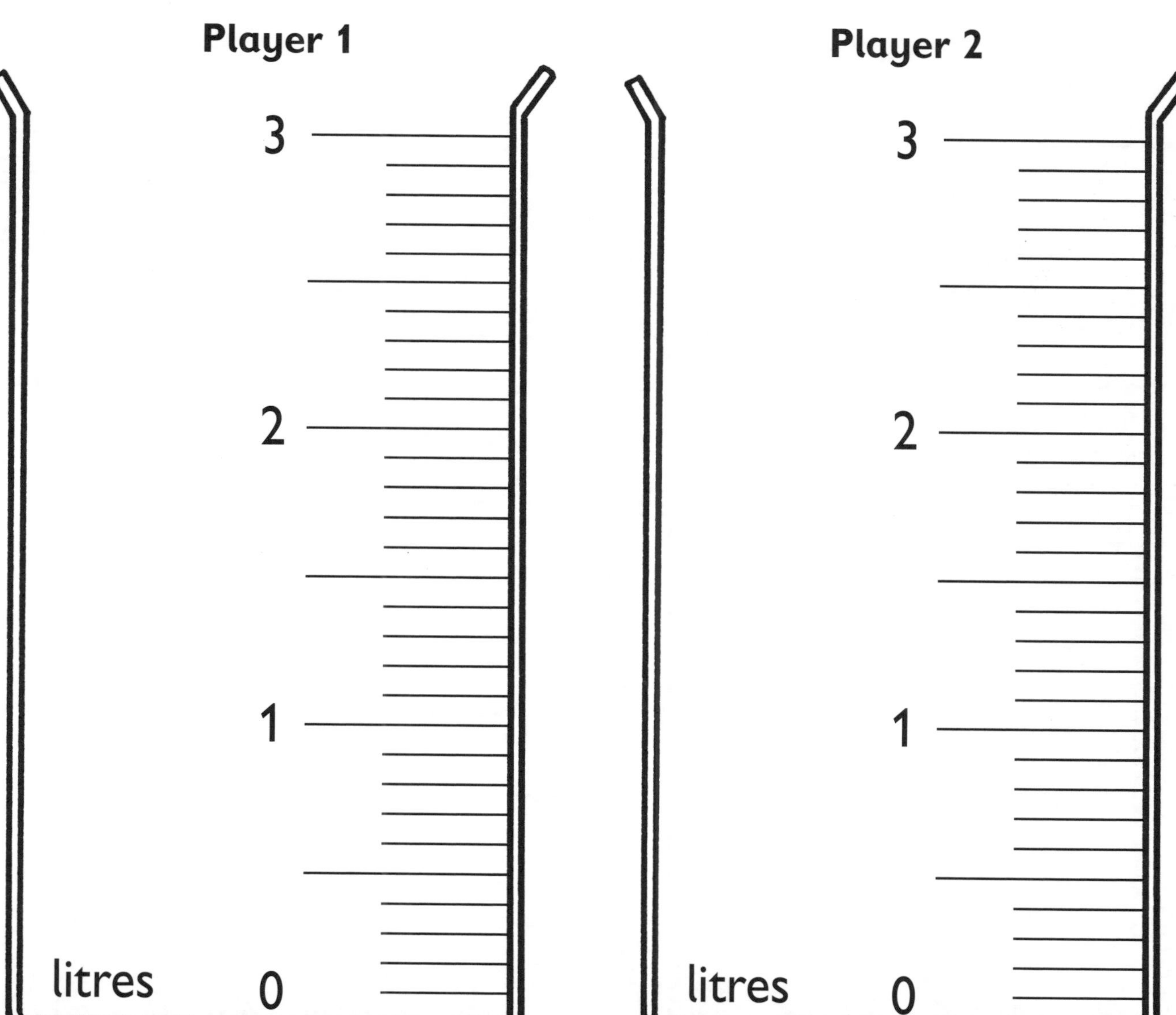

Potion pathways

☆ Read each scale. Tick the answer **yes** or **no** to each question.

☆ Go to **start**. Follow the yes/no routes to the correct pot. Colour it.

☆ Discuss your route with a partner.

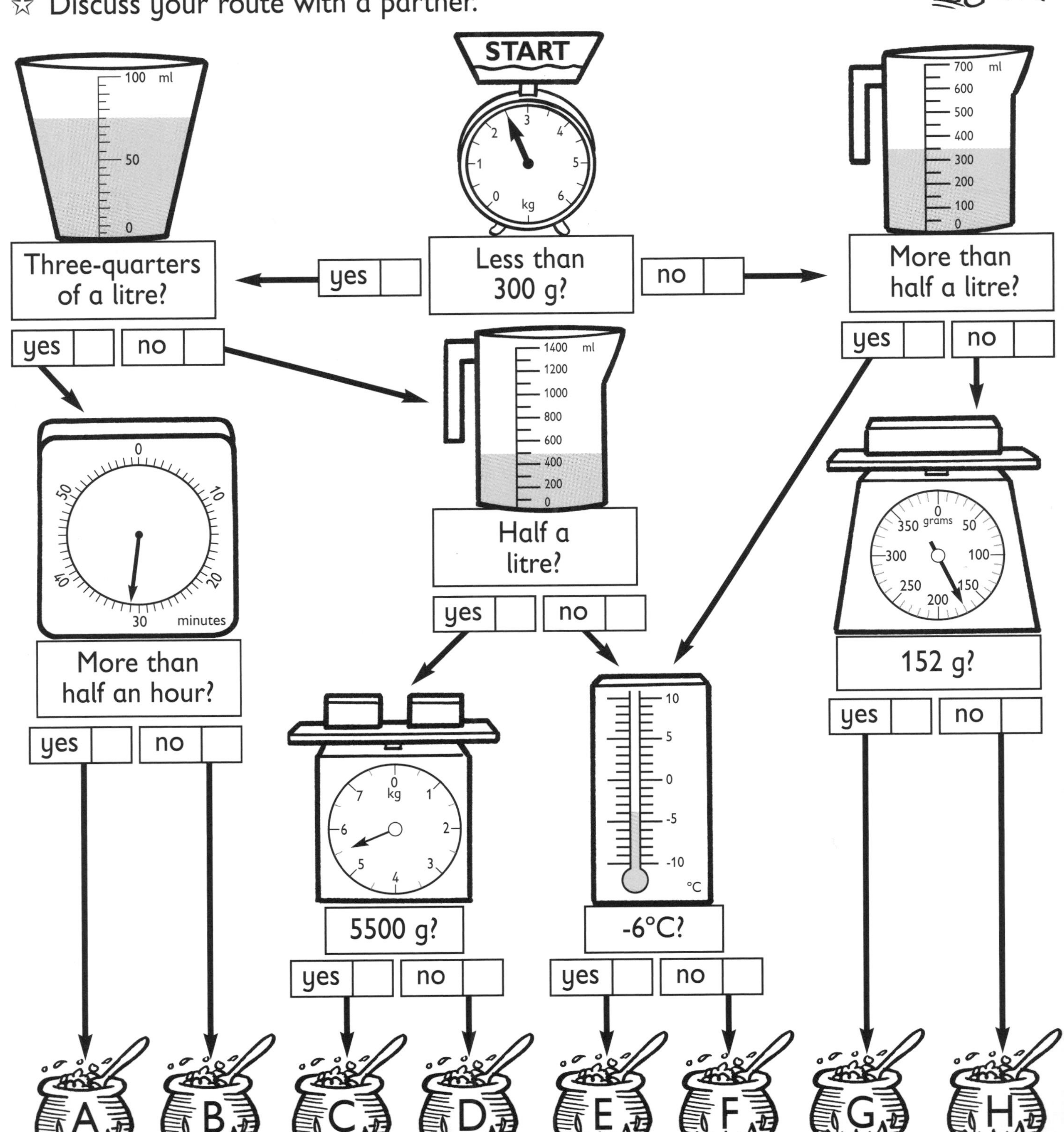

Teachers' note See the notes on page 20 that explain which errors children have made if they choose any of the incorrect pots. Remind the children of the relationships between grams and kilograms and millilitres and litres, and encourage them to say what a half and a quarter of a kilogram and a litre is in grams and millilitres respectively. Encourage discussion with partners.

Poorly pets

- **Draw the hands on the clock to show the time that each pet should take its next pill.**

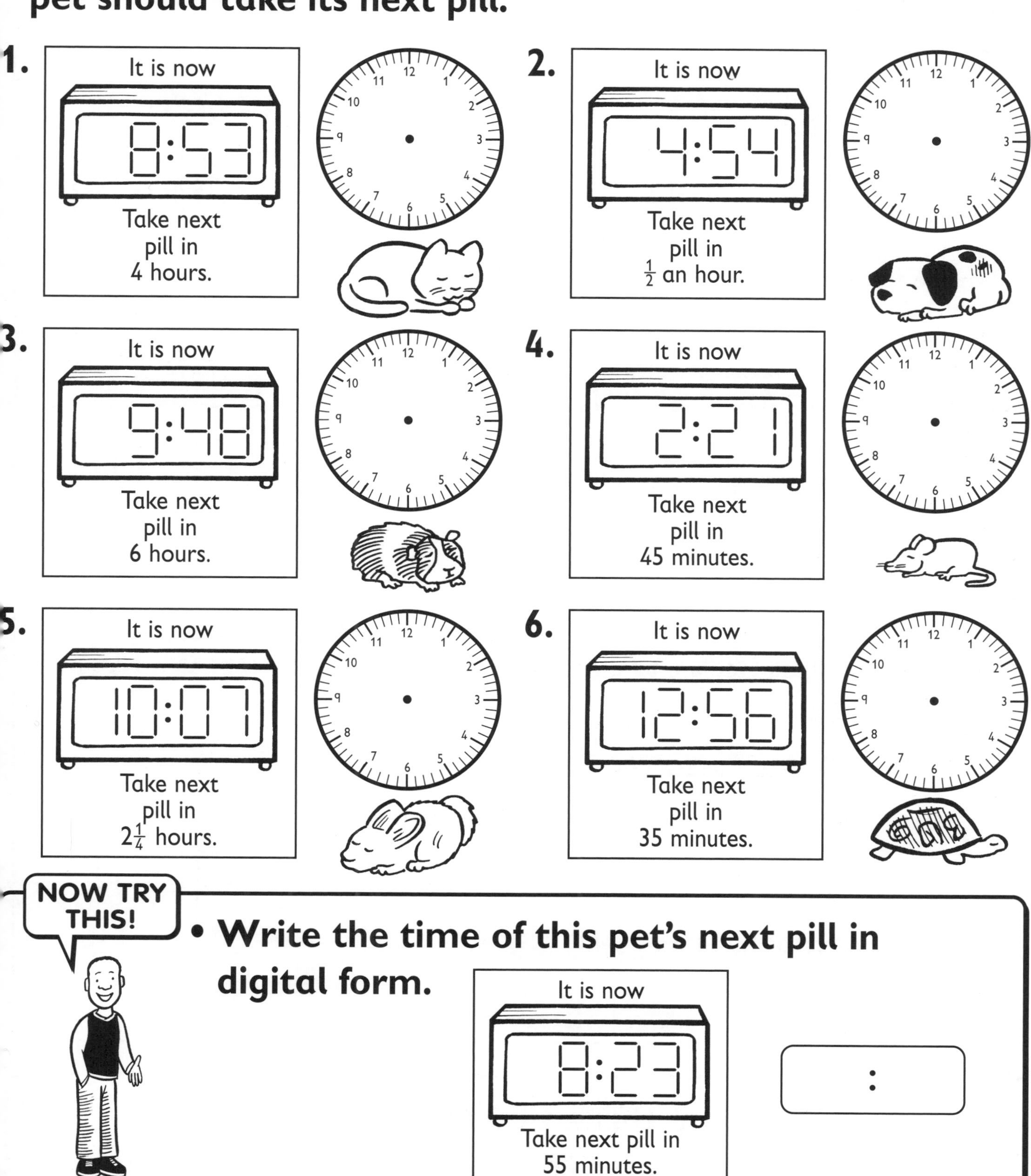

1. It is now 8:53
Take next pill in 4 hours.

2. It is now 4:54
Take next pill in $\frac{1}{2}$ an hour.

3. It is now 9:48
Take next pill in 6 hours.

4. It is now 2:21
Take next pill in 45 minutes.

5. It is now 10:07
Take next pill in $2\frac{1}{4}$ hours.

6. It is now 12:56
Take next pill in 35 minutes.

NOW TRY THIS!

- **Write the time of this pet's next pill in digital form.**

It is now 8:23
Take next pill in 55 minutes.

:

Teachers' note Provide the children with analogue clocks with moveable, geared hands to help them work out the new times.

The number 56 bus

- **This is part of a** timetable **for the number 56 bus from Mathschester to Addingham.**

Monday to Friday

Mathschester Bus Station	8:20	8:35	8:50	9:05	9:20	9:35
City Hospital	8:30	8:45	9:00	9:15	9:30	9:45
Football Stadium	8:40	8:55	9:10	9:25	9:40	9:55
Pyramid Shopping Centre	8:50	9:05	9:20	9:35	9:50	10:05
Oval Library	8:55	9:10	9:25	9:40	9:55	10:10
Oval Town Centre	8:59	9:14	9:29	9:44	9:59	10:14
Little Oval	9:09	9:24	9:39	9:54	10:09	10:24
Swimming Pool	9:19	9:34	9:49	10:04	10:19	10:34
Addingham Bus Station	9:32	9:47	10:02	10:17	10:32	10:47

1. How long does it take to get from:

(a) Mathschester Bus Station to City Hospital? _____ minutes

(b) Mathschester Bus Station to Pyramid Shopping Centre? _____ minutes

(c) the Football Stadium to Oval Library? _____ minutes

(d) Oval Town Centre to Little Oval? _____ minutes

(e) Little Oval to the Swimming Pool? _____ minutes

(f) the Swimming Pool to Addingham Bus Station? _____ minutes

2. Joe left Oval Library at 9:40. What time did he get to Little Oval? _____

3. Li left City Hospital at 9:30. What time did she get to Oval Town Centre? _____

NOW TRY THIS!

- **Make up three timetable questions for a partner to solve.**

Teachers' note Provide oral questions to give the children further practice of this kind of activity. Using this or other timetables, encourage the children to work out time intervals and to interpret the timetables.

Area llamas

- **Find the** area **of each llama.**

One has been done for you.

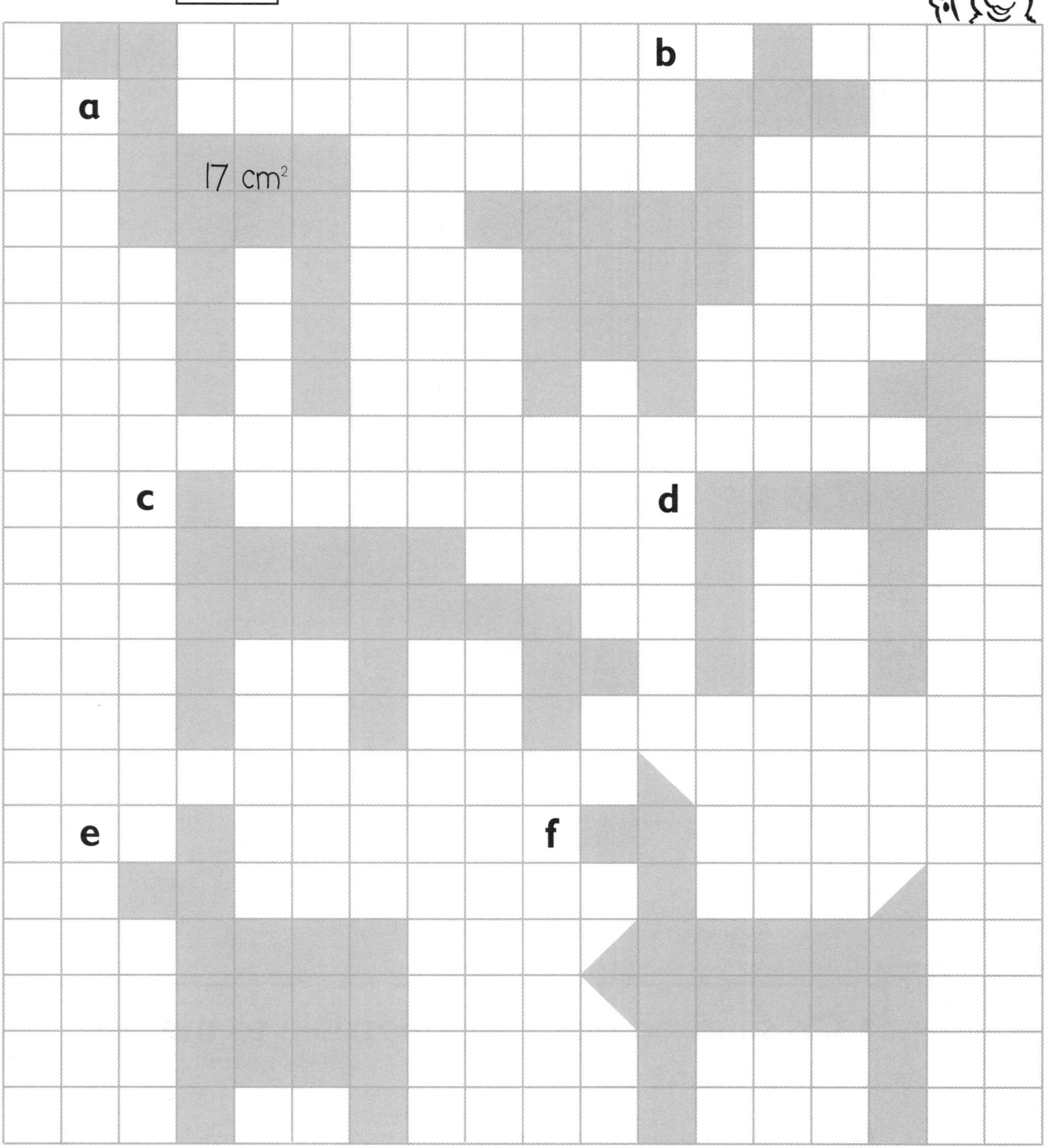

NOW TRY THIS!

- **On squared paper, draw llamas with areas of:**

15 cm^2 19 cm^2 22 cm^2

Teachers' note Introduce the children to the idea of area as the number of squares inside an outline and explain that centimetre squares, like the ones above, can be written as 'cm²'. For llama f, ensure the children realise that if a half-square is shaded this is counted as a half, not a whole.

Fair and square

1. What do you notice about the perimeter of each grey shape?

____

2. Now find the area of each grey shape. One has been done for you.

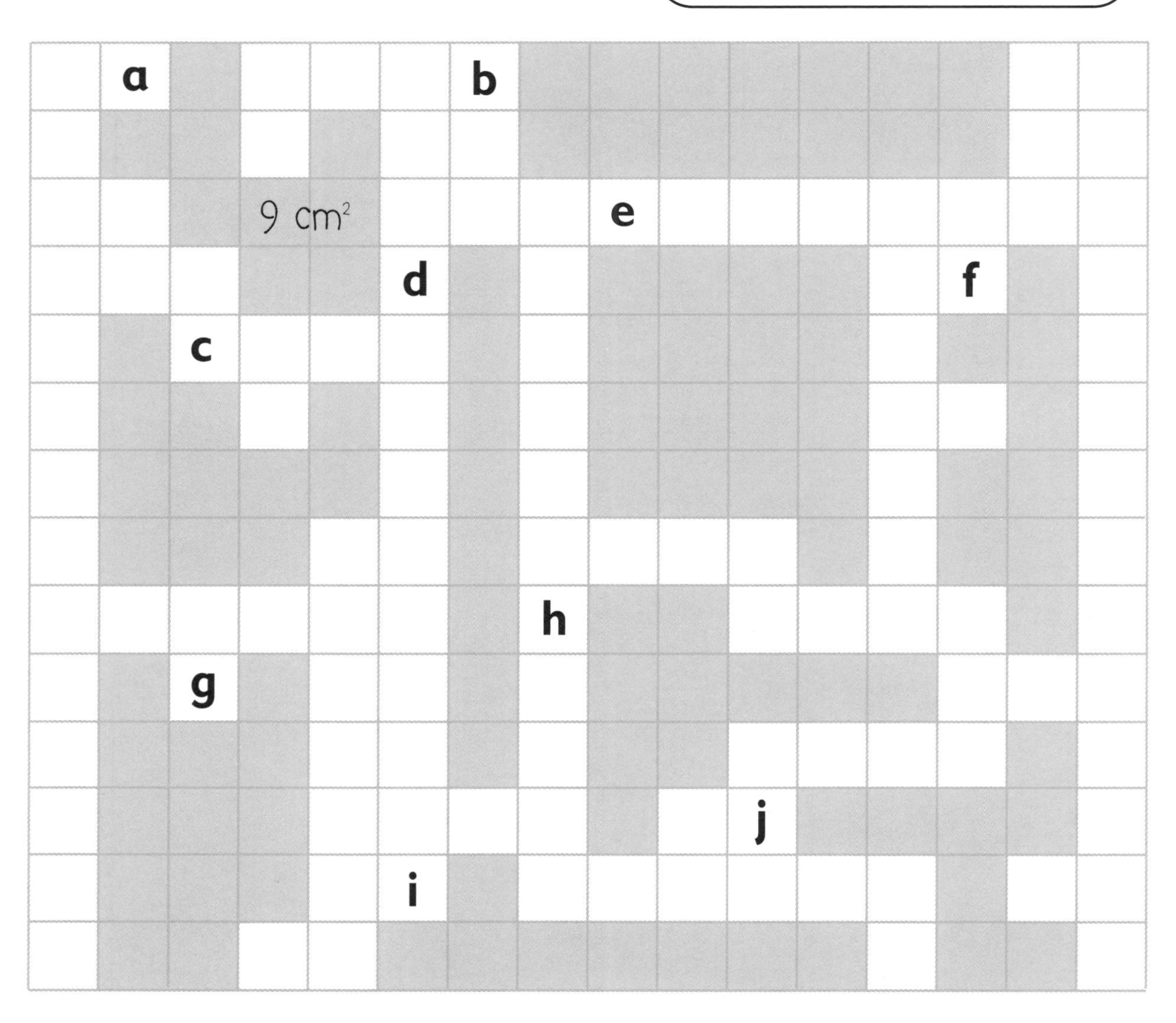

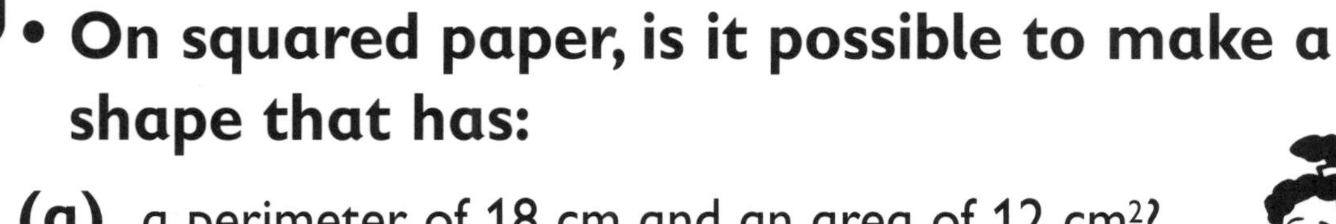

- **On squared paper, is it possible to make a shape that has:**

(a) a perimeter of 18 cm and an area of 12 cm^2?

(b) a perimeter of 18 cm and an area of 15 cm^2?

(c) a perimeter of 18 cm and an area of 16 cm^2?

Teachers' note Ensure the children understand that it may not be possible to make all the shapes in the extension activity. Explain also that the shapes must have edges that are horizontal and vertical, and not diagonal.

Angelina's angles

Angelina makes a hole in the centre of a circle of card. She knots a piece of wool, threads it through the hole and pulls it gently. She moves her hand to turn the wool through different angles.

- Estimate how many degrees she turns the wool through.

1.

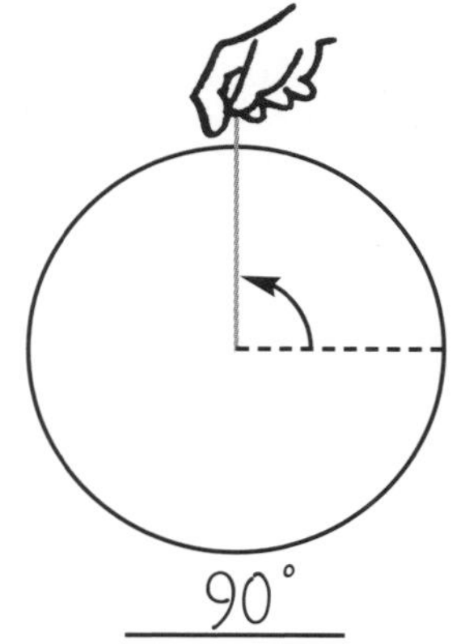

90°

2.

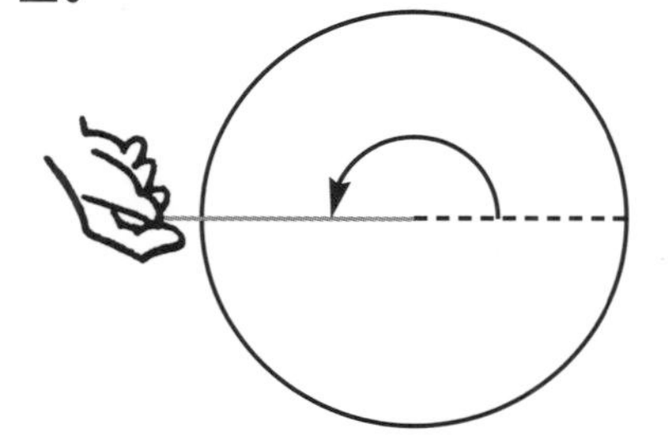

______

3.

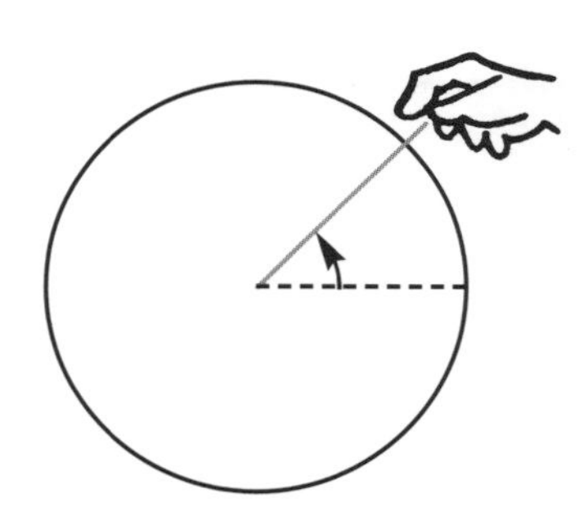

______

4.

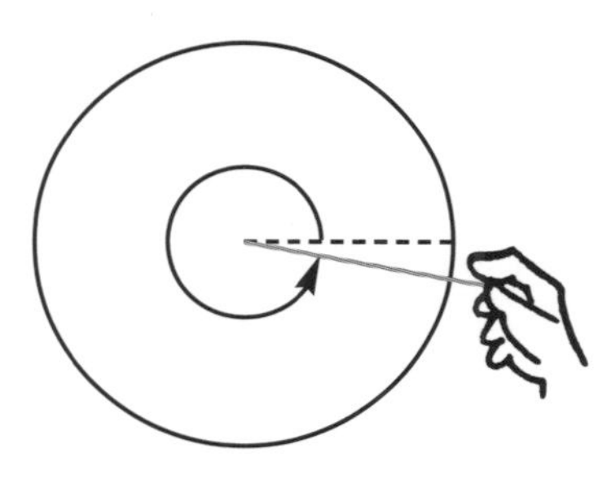

______

5.

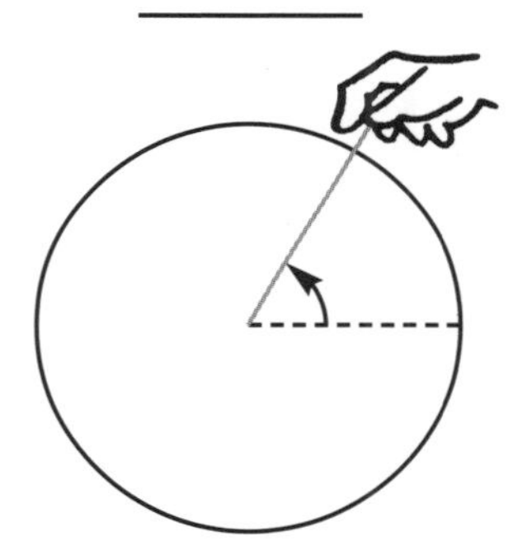

______

6.

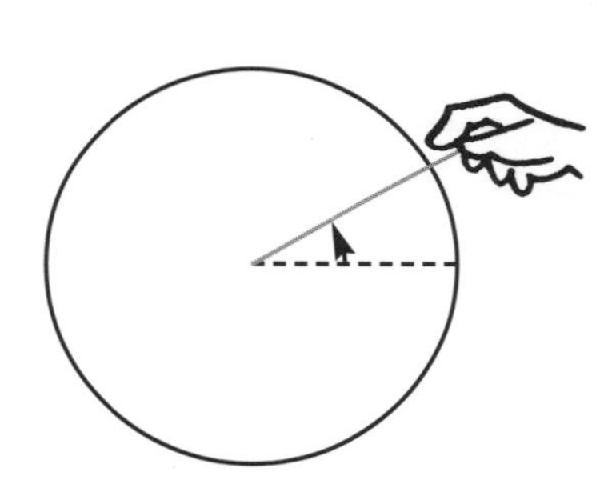

______

7.

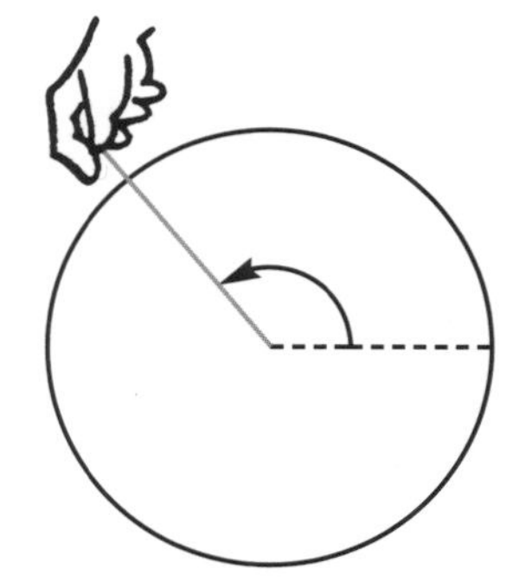

______

8.

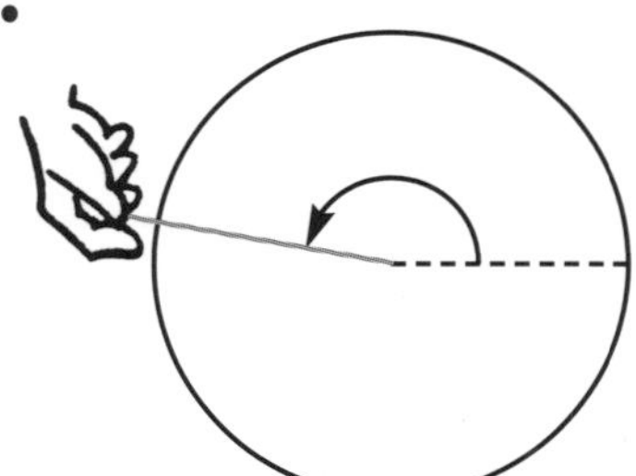

______

9.

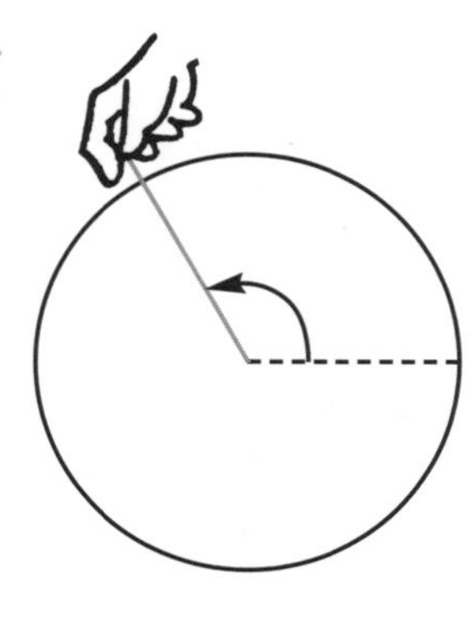

______

NOW TRY THIS!

- Write the angles in order of size, starting with the smallest. ______________________

Teachers' note Ensure the children know that angles are measured in degrees and that there are 90° in a right angle, 180° in a straight angle and 360° in a full turn. It is useful for children to make their own angle turner following Angelina's approach.

Quiz show

- **For each question, colour the correct calculation.**

1 A piece of string 108 cm long is cut into four equal pieces. How can you find the length of each piece?

A 108 + 4 **B** 108 × 4
C 108 – 4 **D** 108 ÷ 4

2 It takes Joe six minutes to wash a car. How can you find how many minutes it will take him to wash three cars?

A 6 + 3 **B** 6 × 3
C 6 – 3 **D** 6 ÷ 3

3 Kay has 560 ml of milkshake. She drinks 80 ml of it. How can you find how much she has left?

A 560 + 80 **B** 560 × 80
C 560 – 80 **D** 560 ÷ 80

4 Leo needs £42. He saves £3 each week. How can you find how many weeks it will take him to save the money?

A 42 + 3 **B** 42 × 3
C 42 – 3 **D** 42 ÷ 3

5 Thirty-two people live on a street. Four people live in each house. How can you find how many houses there are?

A 32 + 4 **B** 32 × 4
C 32 – 4 **D** 32 ÷ 4

6 It is 25 miles from Olby to Raw, and 17 miles from Weld to Raw. How can you find how far it is from Olby to Weld, via Raw?

A 25 + 17 **B** 25 × 17
C 25 – 17 **D** 25 ÷ 17

- **On the back of this sheet, write a question to match each of these calculations.**

A 35 + 27 **B** 26 × 5
C 56 – 35 **D** 126 ÷ 3

Teachers' note The numbers can be altered to provide differentiation. Encourage the children to write each question as a calculation and to describe their strategy for working out each answer, including showing this on a number line, using a written method, or on a 100-square.

Number sentences

- **Colour to show which number sentences could be used for each situation.**

1 James is nine years old. His father is 32 years old. How many years younger is James than his father?

A 9 + ☐ = 32	**B** 32 – ☐ = 9	**C** 32 – 9 = ☐

2 Sam's mum gives him 45 stickers to add to his collection and his dad gives him 38 stickers. If Sam now has 100 stickers, how many did he have to begin with?

A ☐ + 45 + 38 = 100	**B** 100 – 45 – 38 = ☐	**C** 45 + 38 – 100 = ☐

3 Chloe's photo album holds four photos per page. The album has eight pages. Chloe fills the album, but then takes out two photos. How many photos are in the album?

A ☐ + 4 × 8 = 2	**B** 4 × 8 – ☐ = 2	**C** 8 × 4 – 2 = ☐

4 After spending 78p and £1.36, Sara has 37p left. How much did she have to begin with?

A ☐ – 78 – 136 = 37	**B** 78 + 136 – 37 = ☐	**C** 78 + 136 + 37 = ☐

NOW TRY THIS!

- **On the back of this sheet, write number sentences to match this problem.**

Juggling balls come in bags of three. How many bags does Clive buy so that his six children can have four balls each?

Teachers' note Remind the children that the focus here is not on solving the problem, but on deciding which number sentences could represent the situation. Explain that several different number sentences could be used for each. Encourage the children to describe their reasoning and to make up problems like these of their own.

How?

- **Show how each child could have worked out the answer.**

1 Jen worked out the correct answer to 16×5.
Her answer was 80.

2 Alfie worked out the correct answer to $90 \div 5$.
His answer was 18.

3 Harry worked out the correct answer to $360 \div 3$.
His answer was 120.

4 Hannah worked out the correct answer to 24×8.
Her answer was 192.

- **Talk to a partner about which question you found the hardest.**

Teachers' note It is important that children are given the opportunity to consider different ways that answers to calculations could be found, including drawing, using practical material, number lines, 100-squares, place value cards, etc. Compare the children's completed worksheets and encourage them to say which methods they think are most useful or easy to work with.

Measuring methods

- **Show how each question could be answered.**

Use numbers or diagrams to help explain your working.

1 How many bottles, each holding a quarter of a litre, can be filled from a bucket holding $5\frac{1}{2}$ l?

2 I have three-quarters of a kilogram of flour. If I use 50 g each day, how many days will it take me to use all the flour?

3 Jo walks 125 m from her house to the bus stop and then back again each day. How many days will it take her to walk $3\frac{1}{2}$ km?

4 It takes a quarter of an hour for a train to travel 25 miles. At this speed, how far would it travel in two hours?

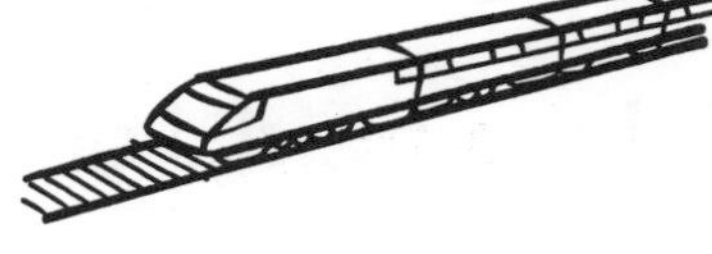

NOW TRY THIS!

- **How much less than 3 m is the total of these lengths? ____ cm**

$\frac{3}{4}$ m 75 cm 100 mm 0·6 m

Teachers' note Revise the equivalents of units of measurement, such as 10 mm = 1 cm, 100 cm = 1 m, 1000 m = 1 km, 1000 g = 1 kg and 1000 ml = 1 l. Discuss halves and quarters of whole large units, for example 1/ kg or 1/ l.

Field event

In a field, one-quarter **of the animals are horses.**

One-third **of the animals are cows.**

There are also 10 **sheep.**

- **How many:** **a** horses are there? ____ **b** cows are there? ____

  c animals are there altogether? ____

- **Write any multiple of 5 (except 10) into the empty box and solve the problem.**

In a field, one-quarter **of the animals are horses.**

One-third **of the animals are cows.**

There are also ____ **sheep.**

- **How many:** **a** horses are there? ____ **b** cows are there? ____

  c animals are there altogether? ____

Teachers' note Encourage the children to create a range of new questions of this type and to explain how each question could be solved. More confident children could explore solutions where one-eighth of the animals are horses and where the number of sheep is any multiple of 10.

Chocolate chunks

- **What amount of the whole bar is shaded? Write your answer as a decimal and as a fraction.**

1

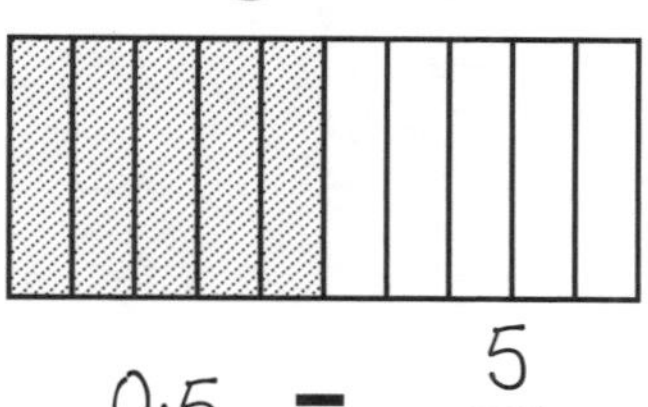

0·5 = $\frac{5}{10}$

2

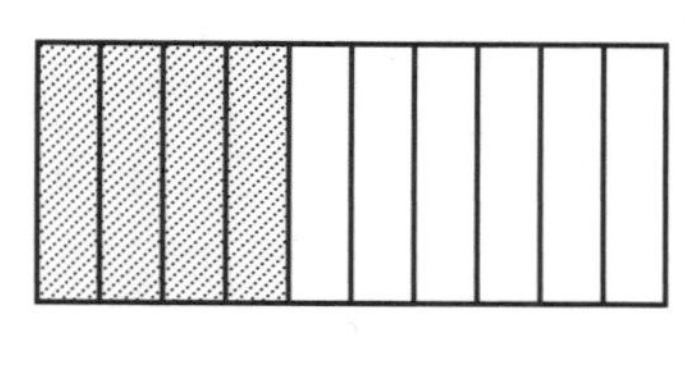

=

3

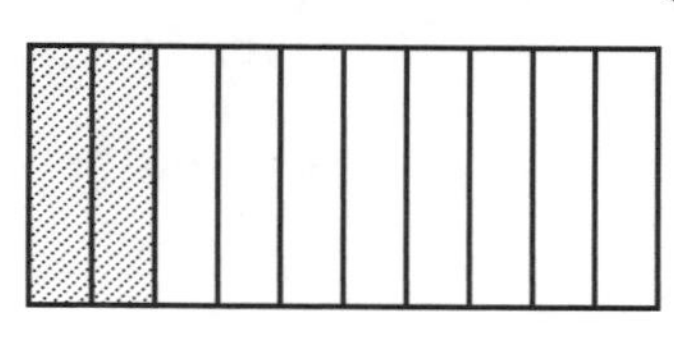

=

4

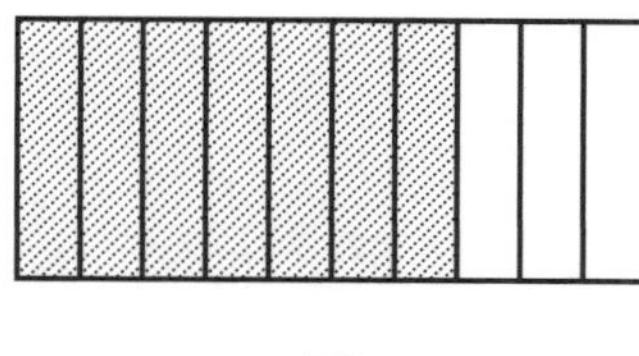

=

5

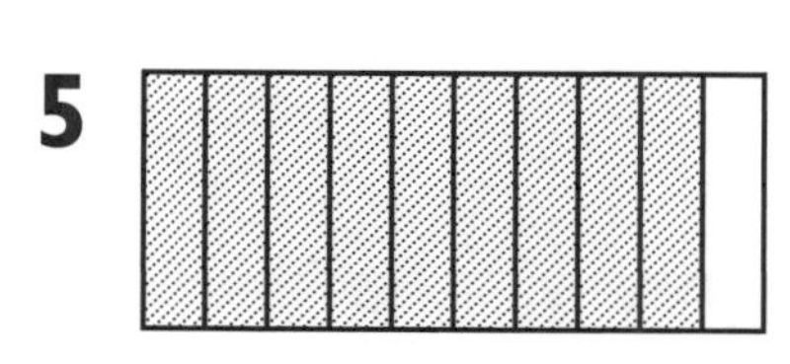

=

6

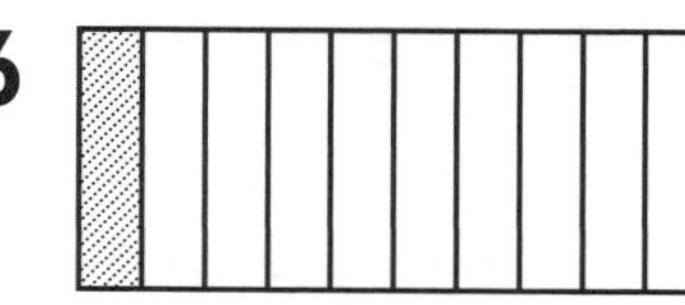

=

7

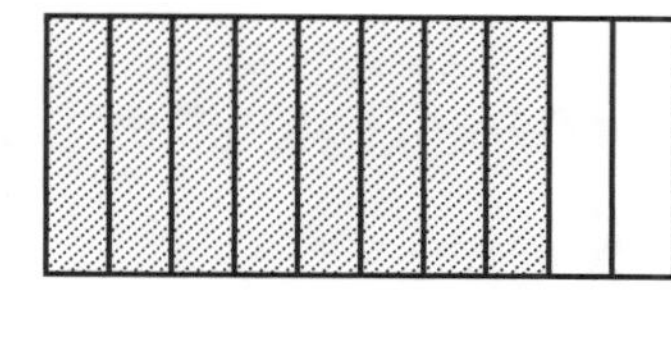

=

8

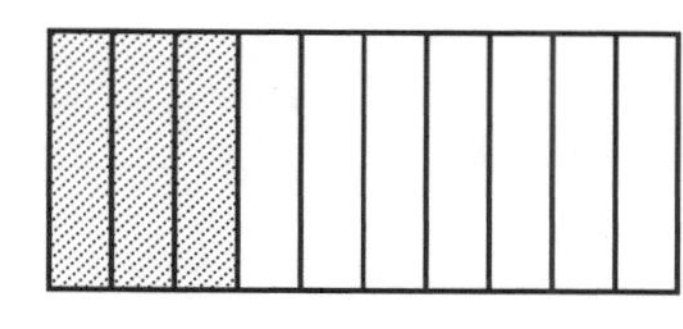

=

9

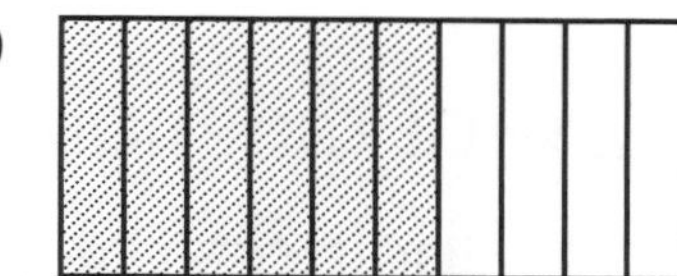

=

10

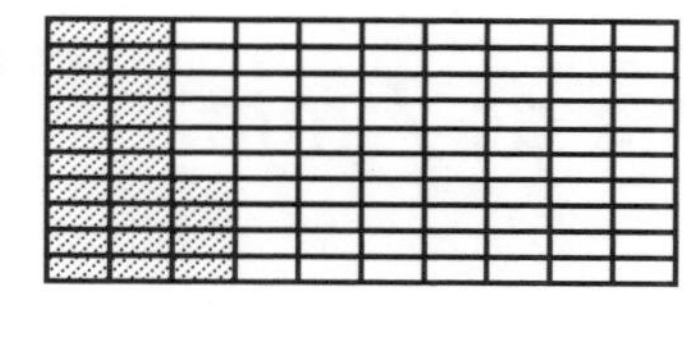

=

11

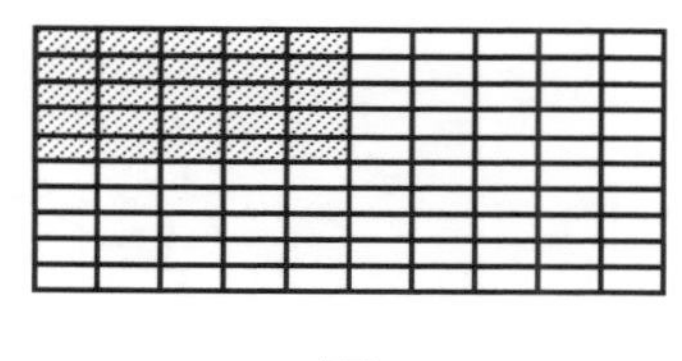

=

12

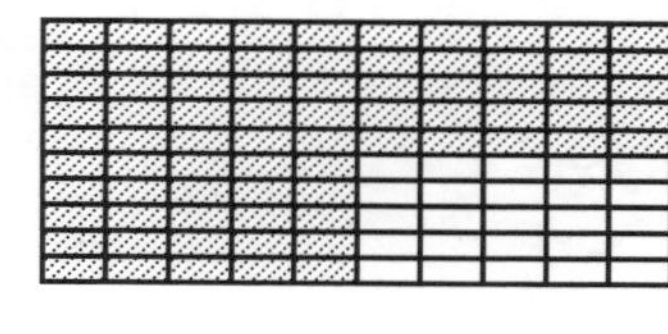

=

13

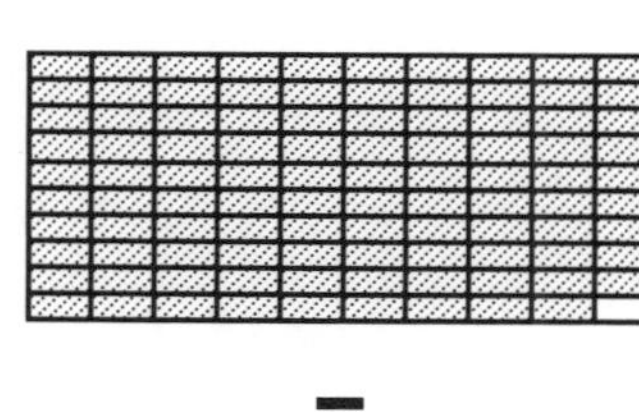

=

14

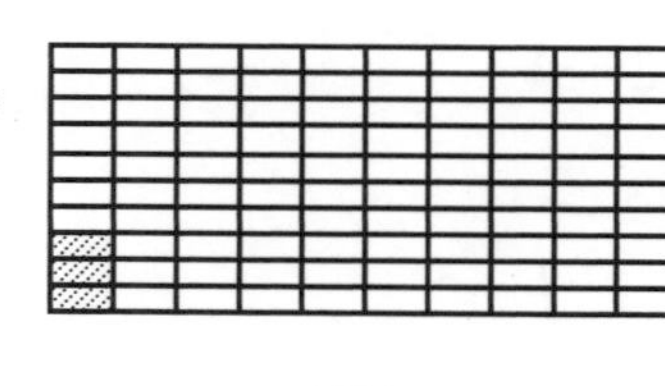

=

NOW TRY THIS!

- **Write two more equivalent fractions for each of the fractions you have written.**

Teachers' note When tackling the extension activity, encourage the children to give equivalent fractions using smaller numerators and denominators where possible. For example for '$\frac{25}{100}$' encourage the children to give the equivalent fraction '$\frac{1}{4}$' (in its simplest form).

Fraction Man

- **Fill in the zapped fractions.**

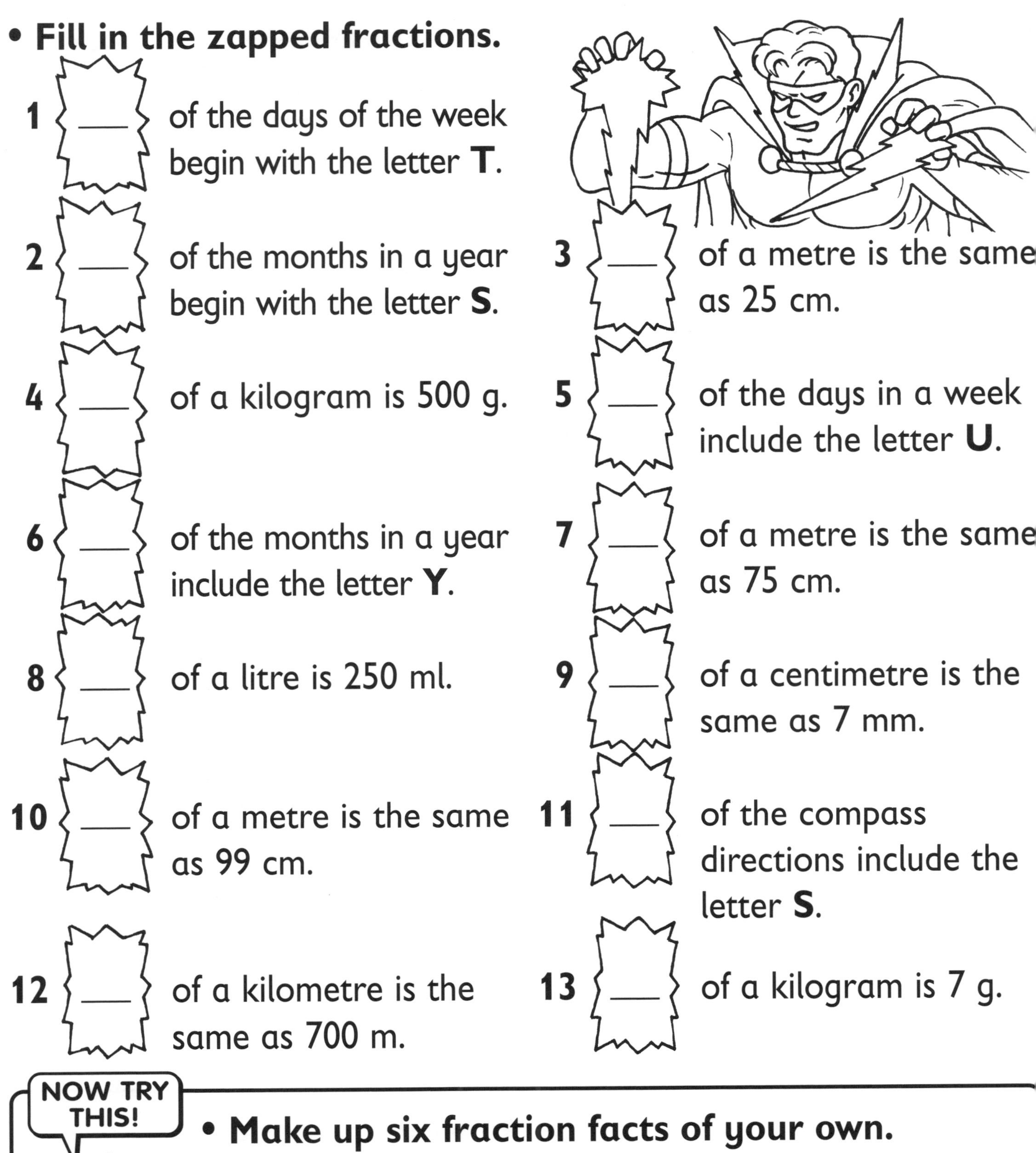

1 ___ of the days of the week begin with the letter **T**.

2 ___ of the months in a year begin with the letter **S**.

3 ___ of a metre is the same as 25 cm.

4 ___ of a kilogram is 500 g.

5 ___ of the days in a week include the letter **U**.

6 ___ of the months in a year include the letter **Y**.

7 ___ of a metre is the same as 75 cm.

8 ___ of a litre is 250 ml.

9 ___ of a centimetre is the same as 7 mm.

10 ___ of a metre is the same as 99 cm.

11 ___ of the compass directions include the letter **S**.

12 ___ of a kilometre is the same as 700 m.

13 ___ of a kilogram is 7 g.

NOW TRY THIS!

- **Make up six fraction facts of your own.**

Teachers' note This activity can lead to a range of areas of exploration. The children can be encouraged to appreciate equivalent fractions, for example understanding that $\frac{25}{100}$ is equivalent to $\frac{1}{4}$.

Twins

- **Write the two equivalent fractions in each pair.**

1

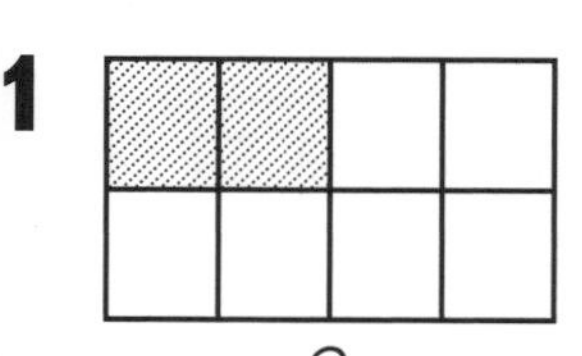 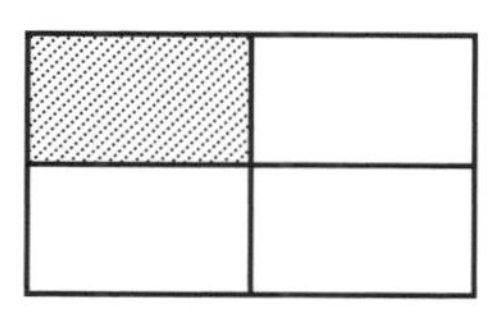

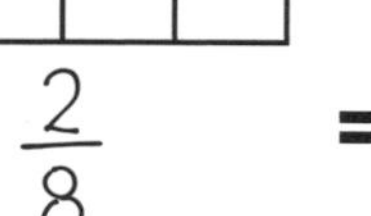

$\frac{2}{8}$ = ______

2

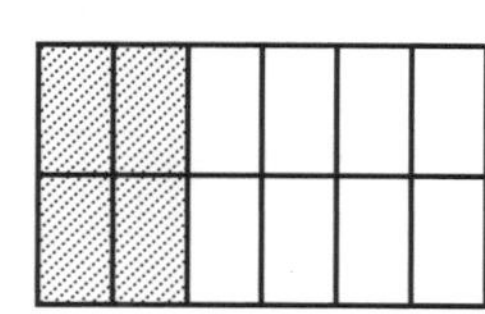

______ = ______

3

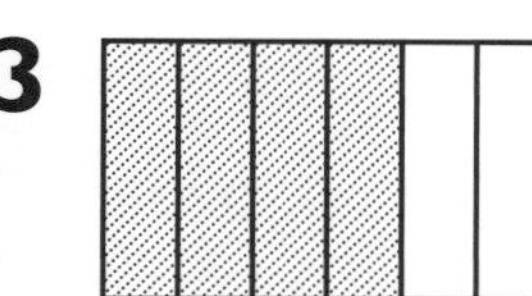 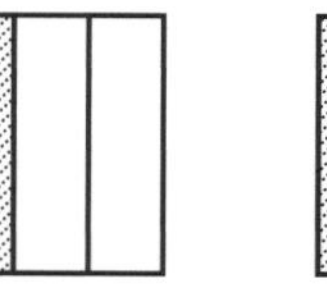 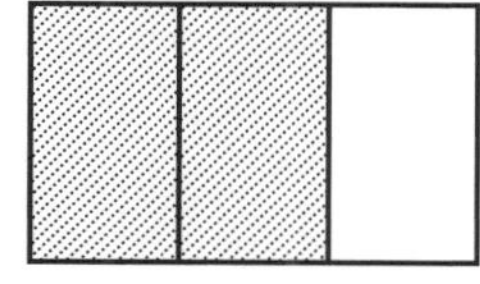

______ = ______

4

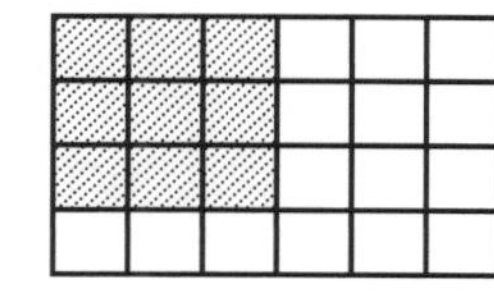 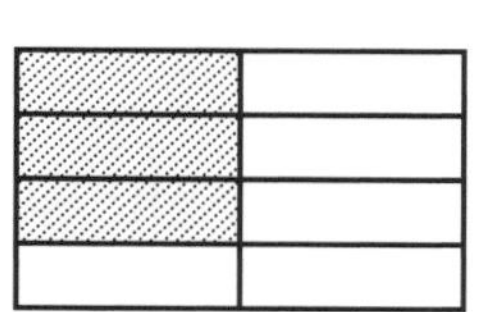

______ = ______

5

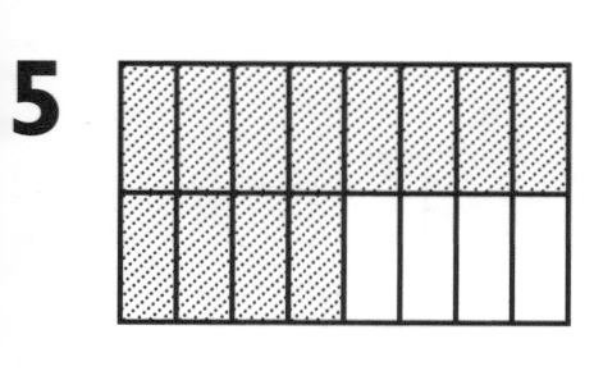 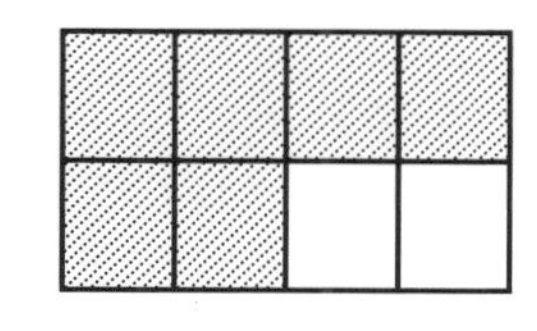

______ = ______

6

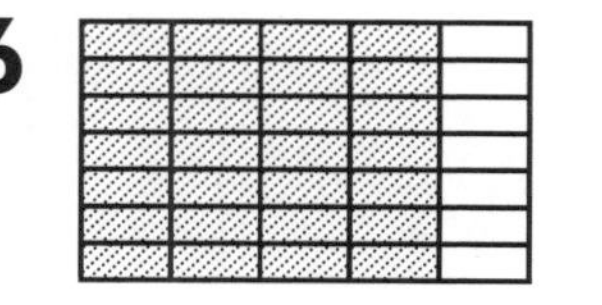

______ = ______

7

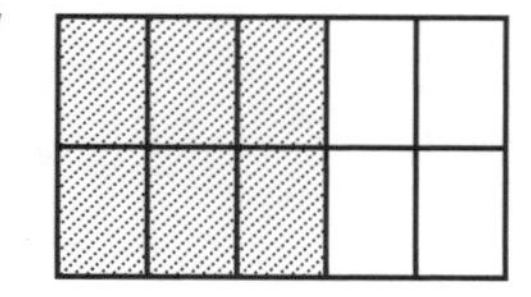

______ = ______

8

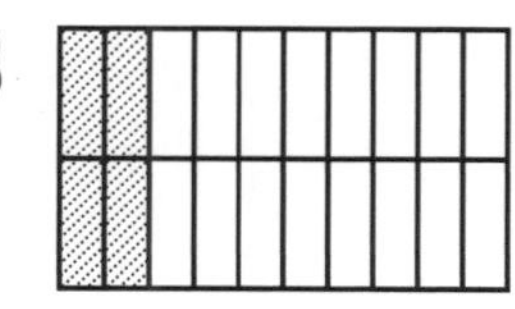 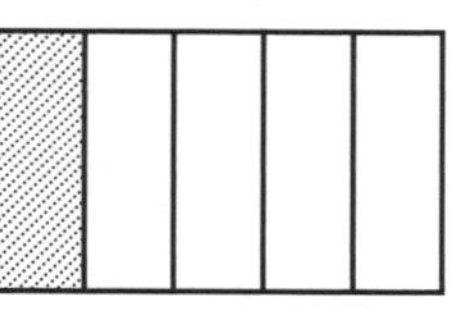

______ = ______

9

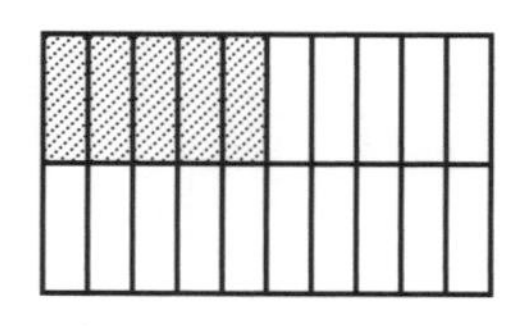

______ = ______

10

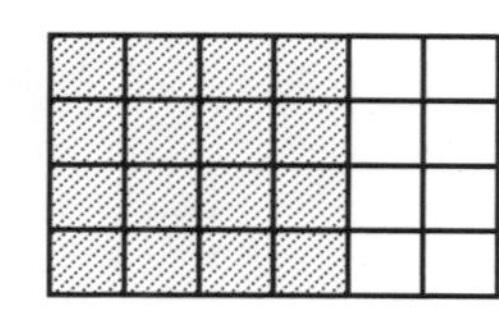 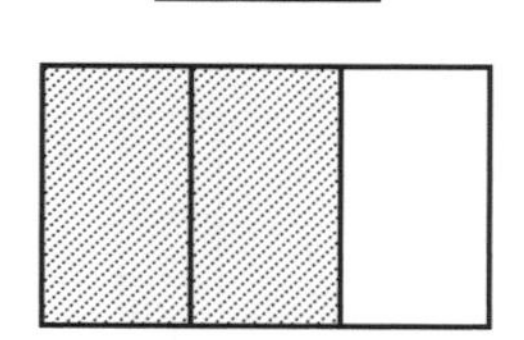

______ = ______

NOW TRY THIS!

- **Look at the numerators and denominators in each pair. What patterns do you notice?**

Talk to a partner.

Teachers' note Explain that in the same way that twins might be the same but have different names, fractions can stand for the same amount but be written with different numbers as their numerators and denominators.

Spelling fractions

- **Count the number of squares in each letter.**
- **Colour the fractions of each letter shown.**

You need different-coloured pencils.

1.

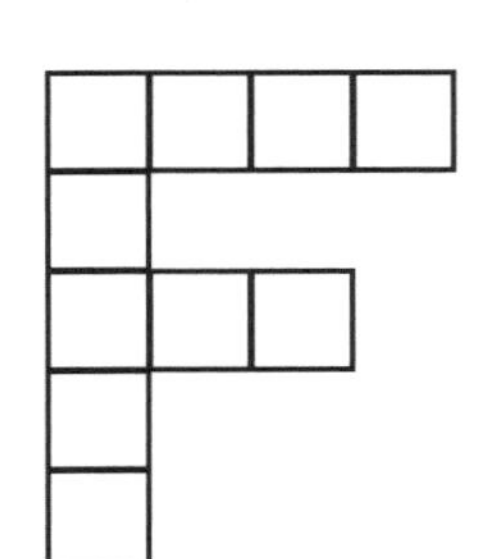

$\frac{2}{5}$ red $\frac{3}{10}$ yellow

2.

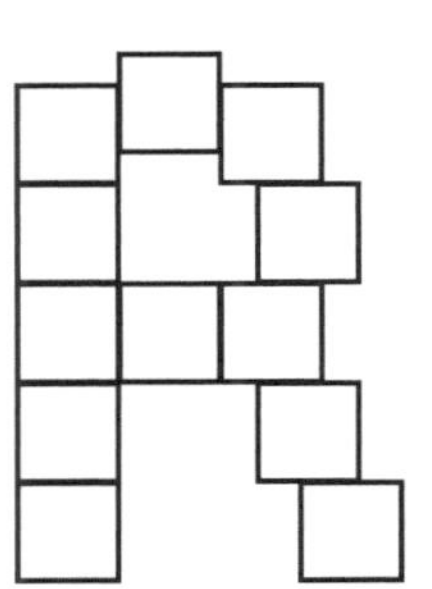

$\frac{1}{6}$ red $\frac{3}{4}$ blue

3.

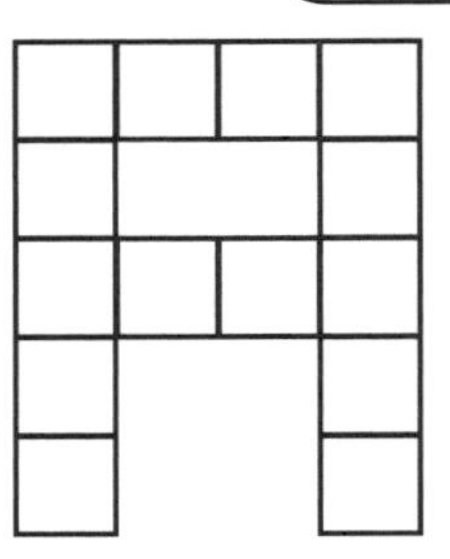

$\frac{1}{7}$ blue $\frac{1}{2}$ green

4.

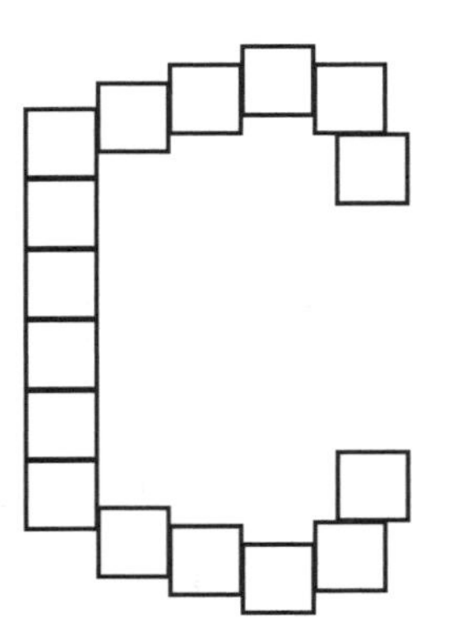

$\frac{3}{4}$ blue $\frac{1}{8}$ green

5.

$\frac{2}{3}$ red $\frac{1}{9}$ blue

6.

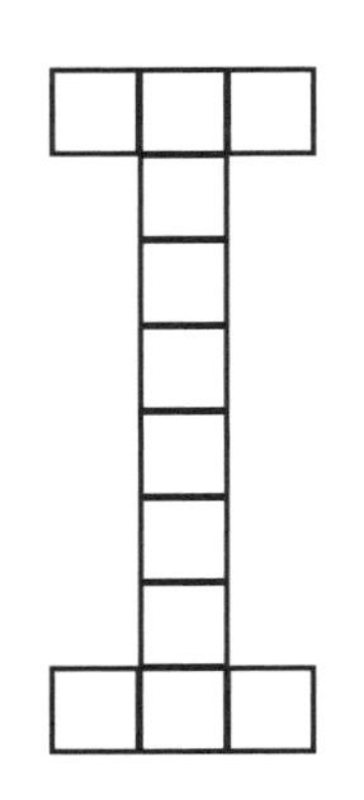

$\frac{1}{12}$ red $\frac{2}{3}$ yellow

7.

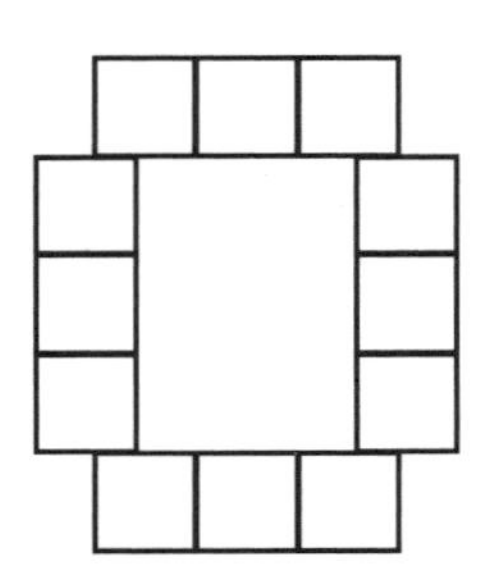

$\frac{1}{12}$ blue $\frac{5}{6}$ green

8.

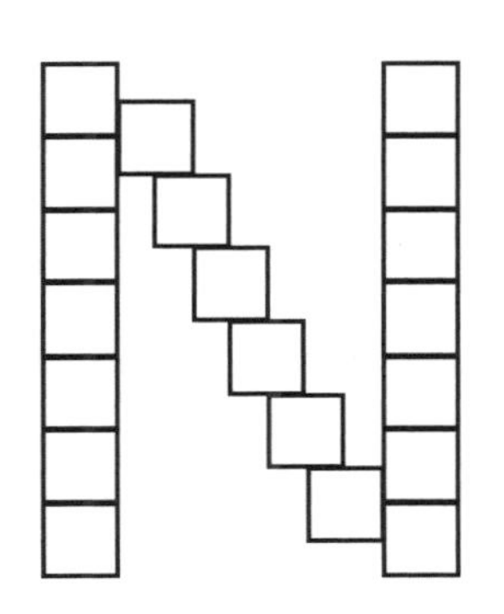

$\frac{3}{4}$ red $\frac{3}{20}$ blue

9.

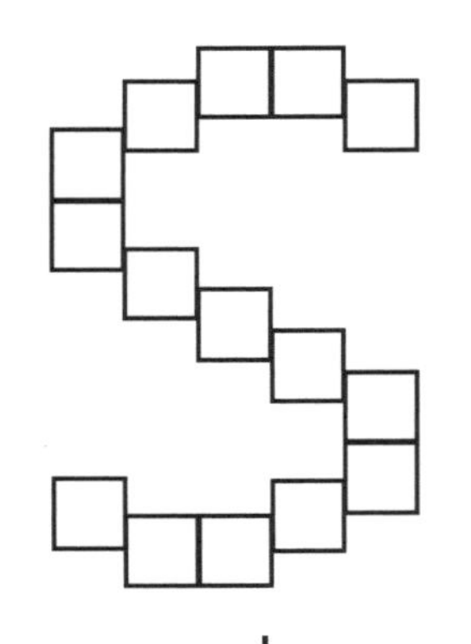

$\frac{3}{5}$ red $\frac{1}{3}$ yellow

NOW TRY THIS!

- **Alongside each letter, write what fraction is uncoloured.**

Teachers' note At the start of the lesson, demonstrate how to count the number of squares in each letter and then divide this number by the denominator (if this is a unit fraction). For the other fractions, multiply by the numerator, for example of 15 can be found by dividing 15 by 5 to find one-fifth (3), and then multiplying by 4 to find four-fifths, giving the answer 3 × 4 = 12.

Café life

• **Write number sentences to work out these problems.**

1 The café opens a box of 500 straws. If 20 are used each week, for how many weeks will the straws last?

500 ÷ 20 = 25

2 If a quarter of the 32 chairs in the café have arms, how many chairs do **not** have arms?

3 A cake costs £4.50 to make. It is cut into eight slices, and each slice sold for £1.25. How much profit is made?

4 A customer buys a £1.69 coffee, a 70p sausage roll and a £1.25 slice of cake. How much does he spend?

5 A milkshake is one-fifth of a litre. How many millilitres are needed to make three milkshakes?

6 A large coffee is 78p more than a small coffee. A large coffee costs £1.69. How much does a small coffee cost?

7 A customer has £5. How many 55p iced buns can she buy?

55p

• **Write a café question to match this number sentence:**

187 + 65 = ?

Teachers' note Note that different calculations could be written for each question. Ask the children to show how they might solve each question on a number line or 100-square. Encourage them to describe the strategies they used and to compare differences in the calculations suggested for each question, for example + 78 = 169 or 169 – 78 = .

Coin contest

Jo can use any <u>four</u> coins. **Sam can use any <u>six</u> coins.**

We must always use exactly this number of coins.

- **Tick to show who you think can make the most amounts between 20p and 50p.** ☐ Jo ☐ Sam
- **Which amounts between 20p and 50p can one of them make that the other cannot?**

Show your workings here.

NOW TRY THIS!

- **Design a leaflet or poster to show what you found out.**

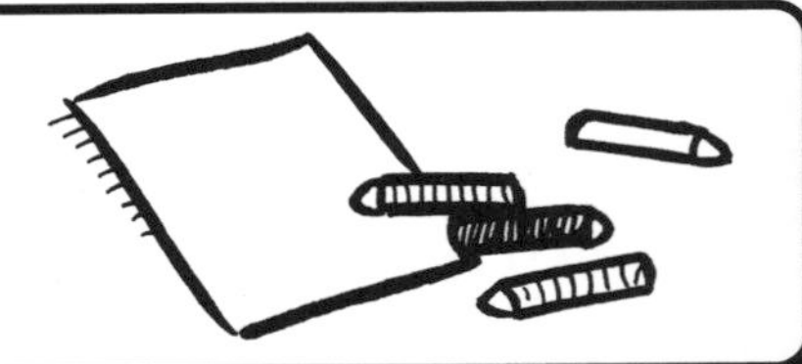

Teachers' note The numbers can be altered to provide differentiation, for example between 6p and 60p, or between 30p and 40p. Encourage the children to work systematically and to show their findings in a clear way so that others can understand them easily, for example using a table or diagrams.

Tent teaser

- **Use the clues to help you work out the total number of children at the camp.**

Work with a partner.

In tent D there are four children.

Three of the tents have the same number of children.

Tent C has the most children sleeping in it.
It has two more children than any other tent.

In Tent A there are two fewer children than in tent B.

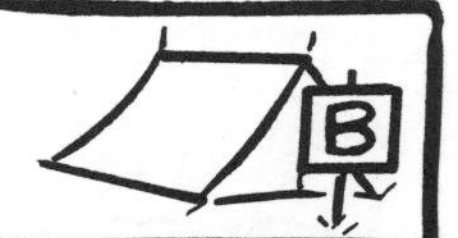

The total number of children in tent A and tent B is 10.

- **How many children are at the camp altogether?**

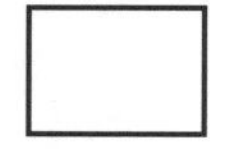

NOW TRY THIS!

- **Draw five tents of your own and decide how many children are in each tent.**
- **Make up clues for your partner to solve.**

Teachers' note If children are struggling with this activity, provide further clues. When completing the extension activity, encourage the children to check whether they have given a clue for each tent, without saying how many are in most of the tents. Display phrases like 'more than', 'fewer than', 'the most', the fewest' and 'the same number' to help the children make up their own clues.

Calculator cards

- **Cut out the cards and arrange them into sets with the same denominator.**
- **Use a calculator to convert each fraction to a decimal.**
- **Write the decimal on the back of the card.**

$\frac{4}{100}$ Divide 4 by 100	$\frac{6}{20}$ Divide 6 by 20	$\frac{1}{5}$ Divide 1 by 5	$\frac{6}{100}$ Divide 6 by 100	$\frac{7}{10}$ Divide 7 by 10
$\frac{2}{10}$ Divide 2 by 10	$\frac{10}{100}$ Divide 10 by 100	$\frac{2}{20}$ Divide 2 by 20	$\frac{1}{100}$ Divide 1 by 100	$\frac{7}{20}$ Divide 7 by 20
$\frac{5}{20}$ Divide 5 by 20	$\frac{3}{100}$ Divide 3 by 100	$\frac{3}{5}$ Divide 3 by 5	$\frac{1}{10}$ Divide 1 by 10	$\frac{9}{100}$ Divide 9 by 100
$\frac{7}{100}$ Divide 7 by 100	$\frac{6}{10}$ Divide 6 by 10	$\frac{1}{20}$ Divide 1 by 20	$\frac{12}{100}$ Divide 12 by 100	$\frac{4}{20}$ Divide 4 by 20
$\frac{4}{10}$ Divide 4 by 10	$\frac{3}{20}$ Divide 3 by 20	$\frac{11}{100}$ Divide 11 by 100	$\frac{10}{20}$ Divide 10 by 20	$\frac{3}{10}$ Divide 3 by 10
$\frac{8}{20}$ Divide 8 by 20	$\frac{8}{100}$ Divide 8 by 100	$\frac{5}{10}$ Divide 5 by 10	$\frac{4}{5}$ Divide 4 by 5	$\frac{2}{100}$ Divide 2 by 100
$\frac{2}{5}$ Divide 2 by 5	$\frac{9}{10}$ Divide 9 by 10	$\frac{5}{100}$ Divide 5 by 100	$\frac{9}{20}$ Divide 9 by 20	$\frac{8}{10}$ Divide 8 by 10

Teachers' note Encourage the children to notice patterns as they convert the fractions in each set to decimals. As an extension, the children could write about the patterns, for example in the 'fifths' set, the 'tenths' digit of the decimal is always even and is twice the numerator of the fraction. Equivalent fractions can also be explored.

'Wordsworth'

- **Use a fraction wall to help you fill in the missing words.**

1 **one whole** is worth the same as…

two halves four ______ ten ______ six ______

2 **one half** is worth the same as…

two ______ five ______ three ______ four ______

3 **one third** is worth the same as…

two ______ three ______ four ______ five ______

4 **one fifth** is worth the same as…

two ______ three ______ four ______ ten ______

NOW TRY THIS!

- **Fill in the missing words.**

three quarters is worth the same as…

six ______ nine ______ fifteen ______

Teachers' note The children will need a copy of the fraction wall on page 194 to help them complete this activity. Not all the solutions can be found on the fraction wall; encourage the children to look for patterns in the solutions. If possible, display some of the more difficult fraction names for the children to copy, for example: eighths, twelfths, fifteenths, twentieths, fiftieths.

Fraction wall

1 whole

$\frac{1}{2}$ $\frac{1}{2}$

$\frac{1}{3}$ $\frac{1}{3}$ $\frac{1}{3}$

$\frac{1}{4}$ $\frac{1}{4}$ $\frac{1}{4}$ $\frac{1}{4}$

$\frac{1}{5}$ $\frac{1}{5}$ $\frac{1}{5}$ $\frac{1}{5}$ $\frac{1}{5}$

$\frac{1}{6}$ $\frac{1}{6}$ $\frac{1}{6}$ $\frac{1}{6}$ $\frac{1}{6}$ $\frac{1}{6}$

$\frac{1}{7}$ $\frac{1}{7}$ $\frac{1}{7}$ $\frac{1}{7}$ $\frac{1}{7}$ $\frac{1}{7}$ $\frac{1}{7}$

$\frac{1}{8}$ $\frac{1}{8}$ $\frac{1}{8}$ $\frac{1}{8}$ $\frac{1}{8}$ $\frac{1}{8}$ $\frac{1}{8}$ $\frac{1}{8}$

$\frac{1}{10}$ $\frac{1}{10}$ $\frac{1}{10}$ $\frac{1}{10}$ $\frac{1}{10}$ $\frac{1}{10}$ $\frac{1}{10}$ $\frac{1}{10}$ $\frac{1}{10}$ $\frac{1}{10}$

$\frac{1}{12}$ $\frac{1}{12}$ $\frac{1}{12}$ $\frac{1}{12}$ $\frac{1}{12}$ $\frac{1}{12}$ $\frac{1}{12}$ $\frac{1}{12}$ $\frac{1}{12}$ $\frac{1}{12}$ $\frac{1}{12}$ $\frac{1}{12}$

$\frac{1}{16}$ $\frac{1}{16}$ $\frac{1}{16}$ $\frac{1}{16}$ $\frac{1}{16}$ $\frac{1}{16}$ $\frac{1}{16}$ $\frac{1}{16}$ $\frac{1}{16}$ $\frac{1}{16}$ $\frac{1}{16}$ $\frac{1}{16}$ $\frac{1}{16}$ $\frac{1}{16}$ $\frac{1}{16}$ $\frac{1}{16}$

$\frac{1}{20}$ $\frac{1}{20}$ $\frac{1}{20}$ $\frac{1}{20}$ $\frac{1}{20}$ $\frac{1}{20}$ $\frac{1}{20}$ $\frac{1}{20}$ $\frac{1}{20}$ $\frac{1}{20}$ $\frac{1}{20}$ $\frac{1}{20}$ $\frac{1}{20}$ $\frac{1}{20}$ $\frac{1}{20}$ $\frac{1}{20}$ $\frac{1}{20}$ $\frac{1}{20}$ $\frac{1}{20}$ $\frac{1}{20}$

Teachers' note This sheet should be used in conjunction with page 193. It can also be used for a variety of activities involving comparing and ordering fractions and identifying equivalent fractions.

Part and parcel

- **Join pairs of parcels whose fractions total 1.**
- **Write any missing fractions.**

NOW TRY THIS!

- **Tick which of these words have a total of 1.**

A	C	D	E	F	I	M	N	O	P	R	S	T	U	Y
$\frac{1}{10}$	$\frac{3}{5}$	$\frac{2}{5}$	$\frac{6}{10}$	$\frac{4}{10}$	$\frac{1}{2}$	$\frac{9}{10}$	$\frac{4}{5}$	$\frac{1}{5}$	$\frac{1}{4}$	$\frac{2}{10}$	$\frac{7}{10}$	$\frac{3}{10}$	$\frac{3}{4}$	$\frac{2}{4}$

ON AM PIP DO ODD TEA

UP IS IF CAT AID DAY

PAD TOY RAT FOOD DART FAST

Teachers' note For the extension activity, encourage the children to use the key to find the value of each letter and see whether the fractions add to make 1. Some rely on a simple understanding of equivalence, for example knowing that is equivalent to .

Loads-a-money!

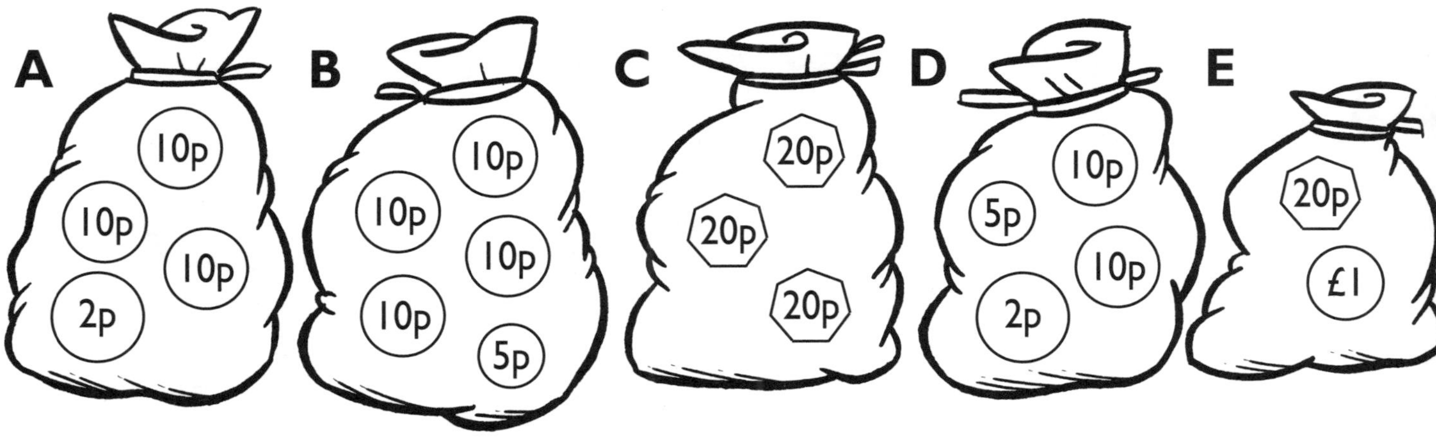

- **Find:**

1. $\frac{1}{4}$ of A = 8 p
2. $\frac{1}{6}$ of C = ______ p
3. $\frac{1}{5}$ of B = ______ p
4. $\frac{1}{3}$ of D = ______ p
5. $\frac{3}{4}$ of A = ______ p
6. $\frac{2}{5}$ of B = ______ p
7. $\frac{4}{5}$ of C = ______ p
8. $\frac{2}{3}$ of D = ______ p
9. $\frac{5}{6}$ of E = ______ p
10. $\frac{3}{8}$ of A = ______ p
11. $\frac{4}{9}$ of D = ______ p
12. $\frac{3}{10}$ of E = ______ p
13. $\frac{3}{20}$ of C = ______ p
14. $\frac{7}{15}$ of B = ______ p

- **Work out how much there is in bag F, if:** $\frac{5}{8}$ of F = 15

Teachers' note At the start of the lesson, demonstrate how a fraction of a quantity can be found by dividing by the denominator (to find the unit fraction) and then multiplying by the numerator, for example 4 fifths of 30 can be found by dividing 30 by 5 to find one-fifth (6), and then multiplying by 4 to find four-fifths, giving the answer 6 × 4 = 24.

Billy the Baker's cakes

- **Cut out the number cards and place them in the boxes.**
- **How many different questions and answers can you make?**

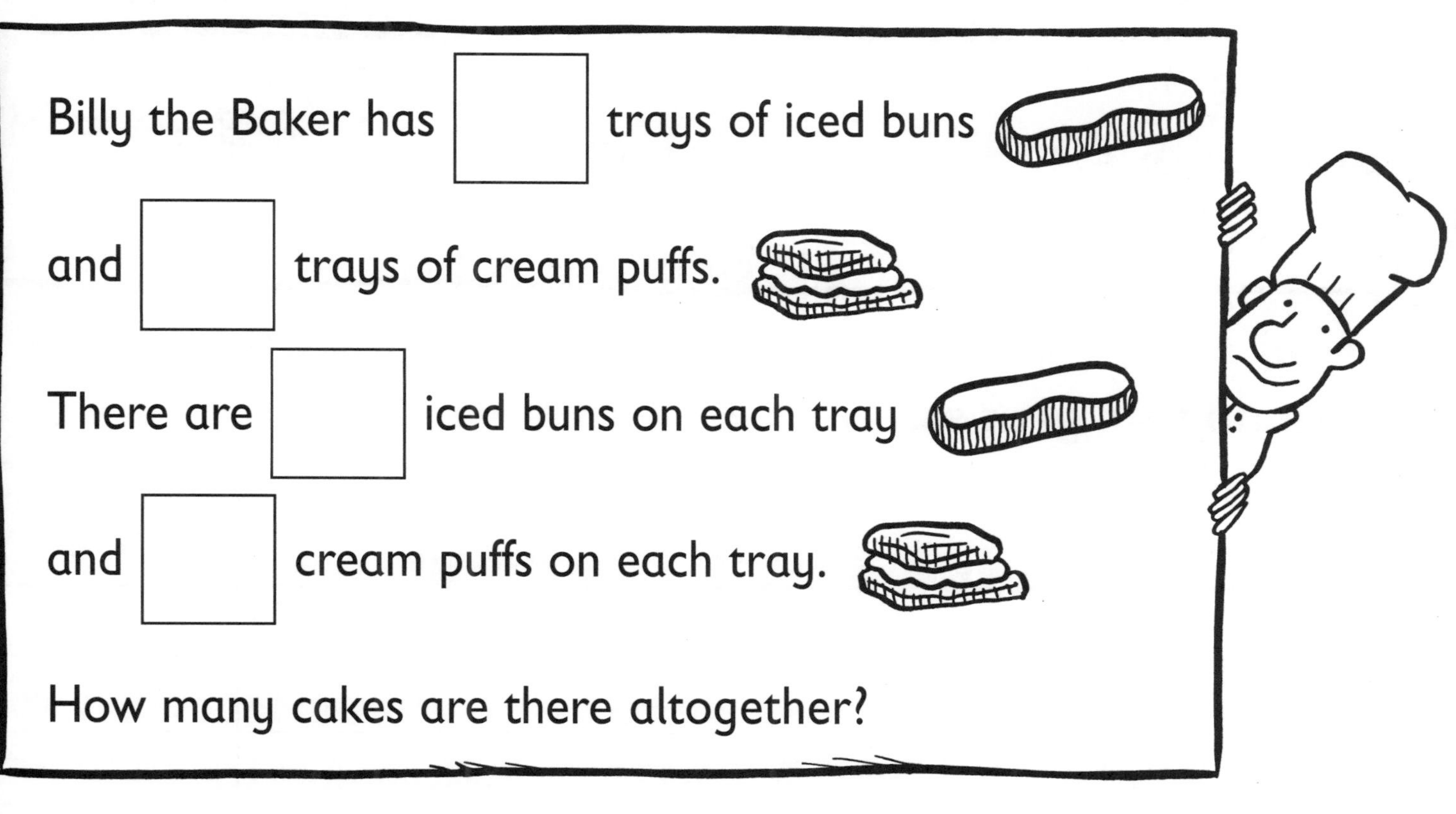

Billy the Baker has ☐ trays of iced buns

and ☐ trays of cream puffs.

There are ☐ iced buns on each tray

and ☐ cream puffs on each tray.

How many cakes are there altogether?

- **Write your questions and answers here.**

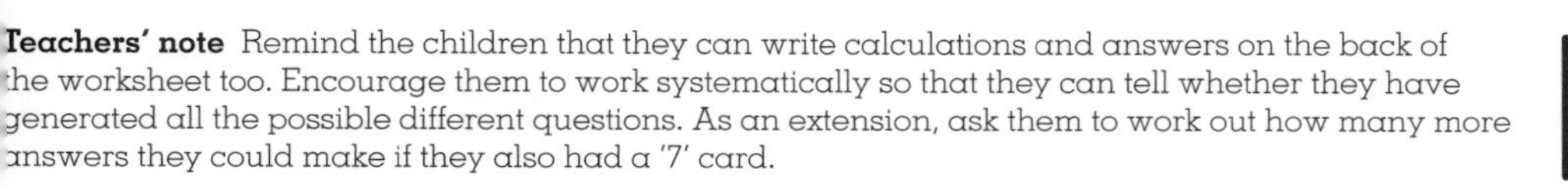

5	6	3	8	4

Teachers' note Remind the children that they can write calculations and answers on the back of the worksheet too. Encourage them to work systematically so that they can tell whether they have generated all the possible different questions. As an extension, ask them to work out how many more answers they could make if they also had a '7' card.

Sour grapes

There are many ways in which Jack can eat these six grapes. Here are just a few ways:

One grape at a time	Two grapes, then four grapes	Even six grapes at once!
1 + 1 + 1 + 1 + 1 + 1	2 + 4	6

- **Find all the different ways of eating one, two, three, four, five and six grapes.**

Number of grapes	Different ways	Total number of ways
1		
2		
3		
4		
5		
6		

Teachers' note Encourage the children to work systematically and to be convinced that there are no solutions that they have missed. If all the solutions are found, the children should be able to see patterns in the numbers. As an extension, ask the children to predict the number of ways for seven and eight grapes, and to explain their thinking to a partner.

Sheep and goats

• **Look at this fact:**

There are 10 sheep and 20 goats in a field.

• **Tick to show whether each statement is true or false.**

• **Use words or pictures to explain to a partner why.**

1 There is one sheep for every two goats.

true ☐ false ☐

2 Half of the animals in the field are sheep.

true ☐ false ☐

3 Three-quarters of the animals in the field are goats.

true ☐ false ☐

4 Ten out of the 30 animals are sheep.

true ☐ false ☐

5 One-third of the animals in the field are sheep.

true ☐ false ☐

6 Two-thirds of the animals in the field are goats.

true ☐ false ☐

• **Write some statements to match this fact:**

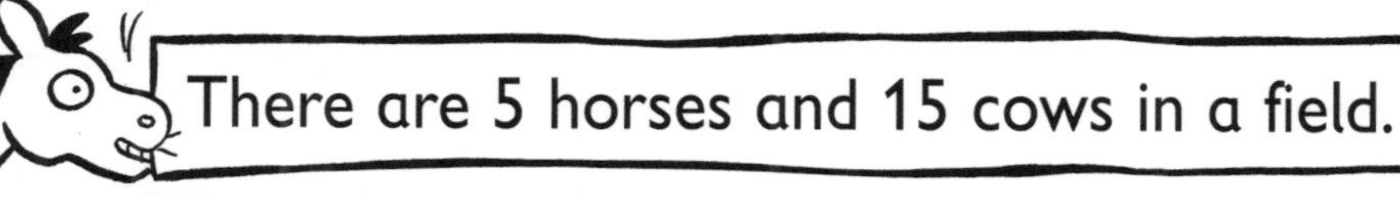

There are 5 horses and 15 cows in a field.

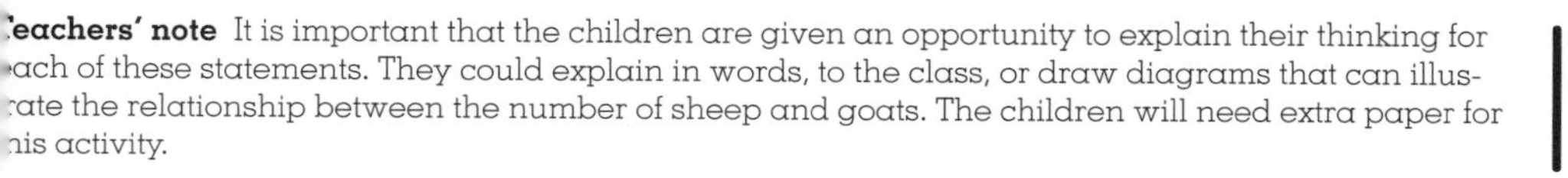

Teachers' note It is important that the children are given an opportunity to explain their thinking for each of these statements. They could explain in words, to the class, or draw diagrams that can illustrate the relationship between the number of sheep and goats. The children will need extra paper for this activity.

Connections

Each arrow means is a multiple of **.**
So 6 → 3 means 6 is a multiple of 3.

- **Notice that the arrow goes from the** larger **to the** smaller **number.**
- **Put the numbers shown in the box into the correct circles so that all the arrows are true.**

1.

3 5 10 30

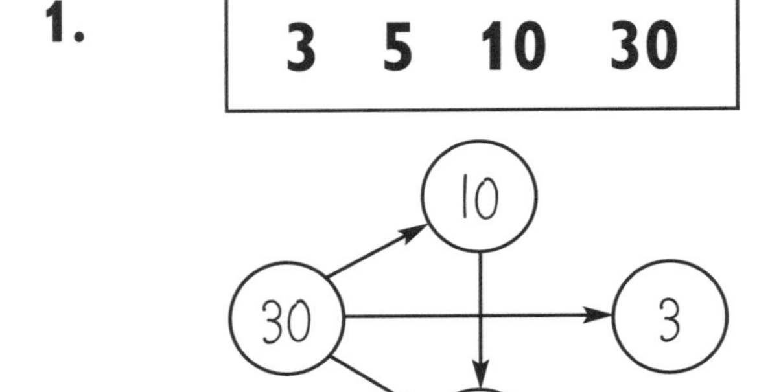

2.

3 4 8 24

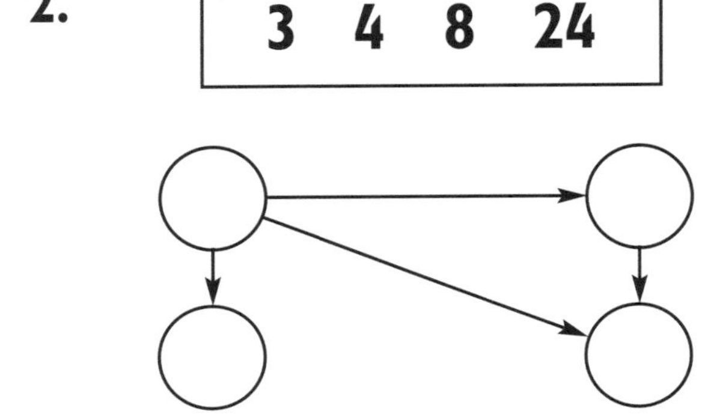

3.

3 4 6 9 36

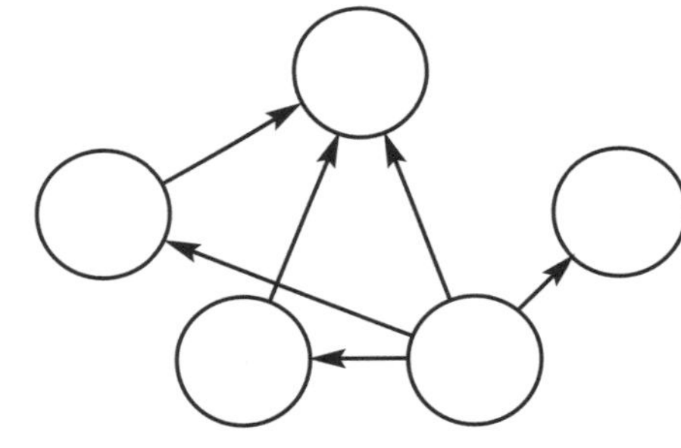

4.

3 6 7 21 42

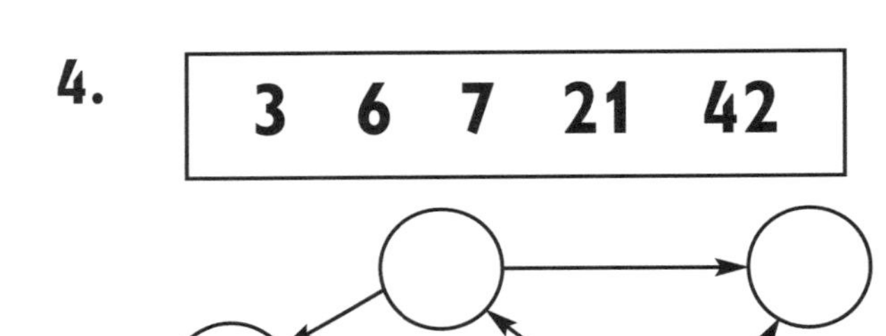

5.

6 7 8 14 48 56

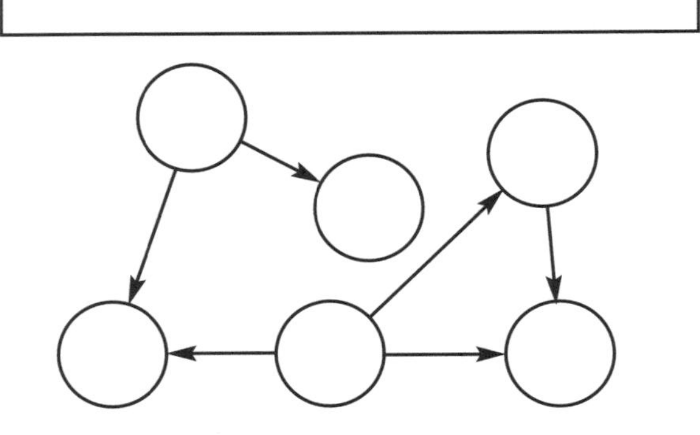

6.

2 4 8 16 32

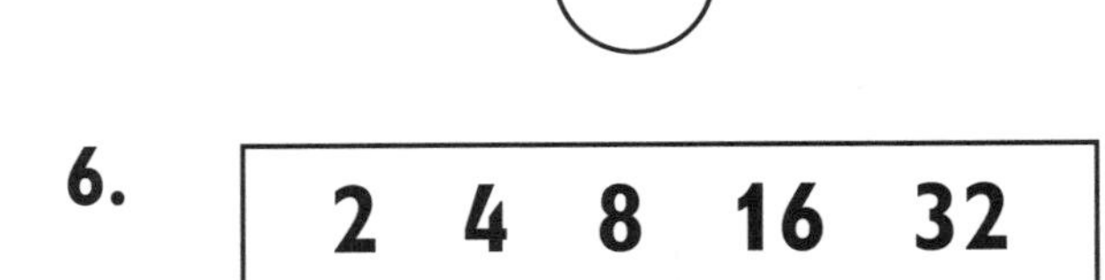

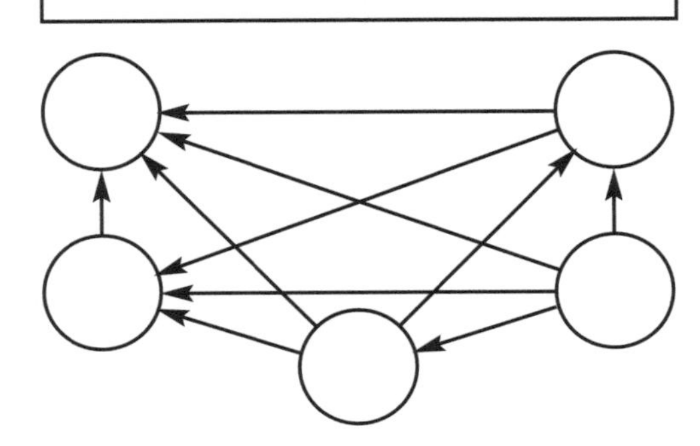

Teachers' note Once the children master what is expected here they can construct their own diagrams and identify which numbers are multiples of which. Similar diagrams can be drawn using the rule 'is a factor of' to encourage the children to identify which numbers are factors of others. As an extension activity, children could make diagrams of their own for a partner to solve.

World tour

Around the globe are multiples of numbers up to 10.

- **Play with a partner. You need one small counter and a dice.**

☆ Start in any position around the globe.

☆ Take turns to roll the dice and move the counter forward.

☆ The number you land on may be a multiple of more than one number but you can only cross off one of those numbers from your list.

☆ The winner is the first player to cross off all their numbers.

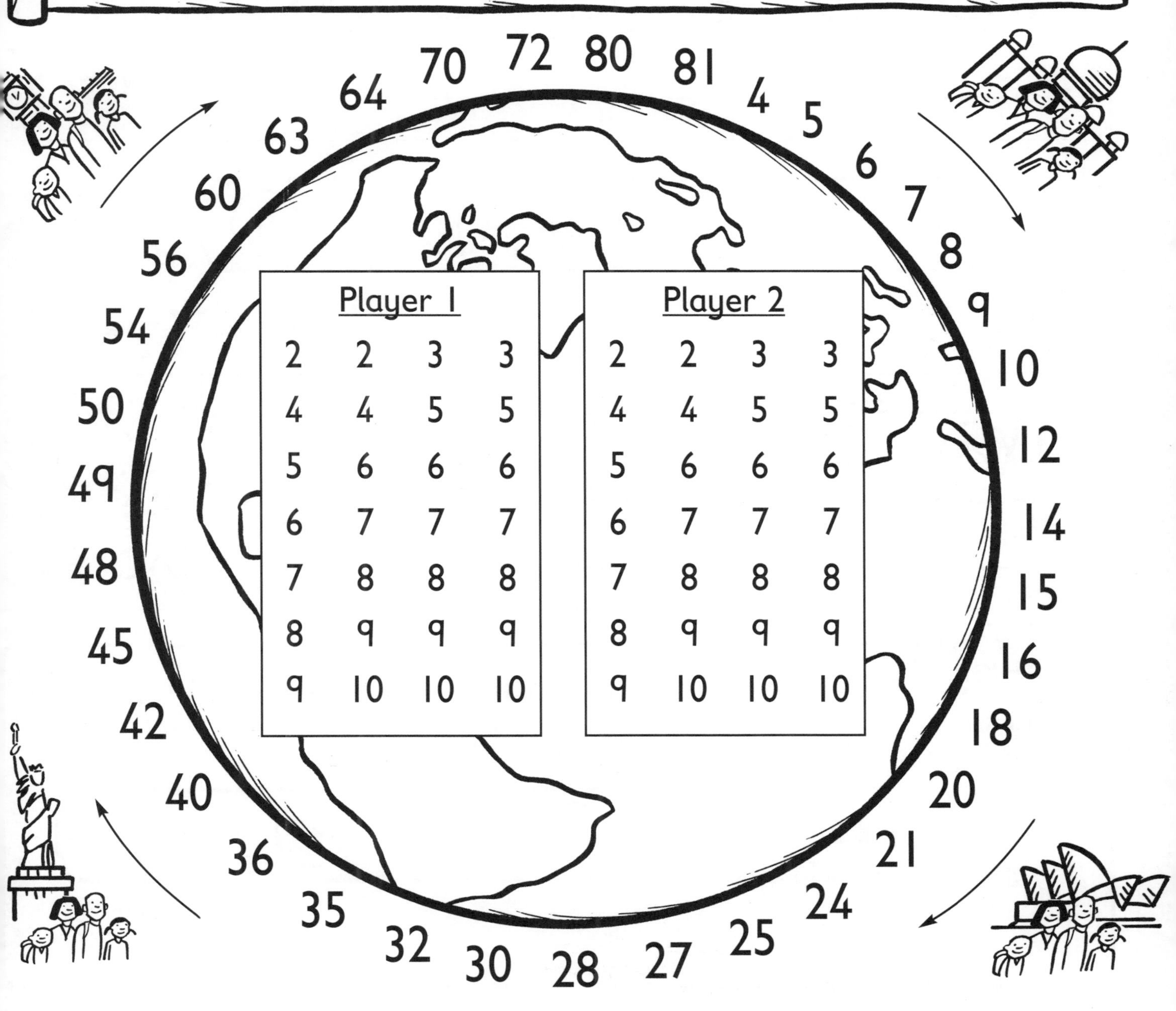

Teachers' note Children could be introduced to the term 'factor' if appropriate. Display the list of multiplication tables up to 10 × 10 for this activity and demonstrate how to use these to find a multiple of the number landed on. As an extension activity, ask the children which of the numbers around the globe is a multiple of 2, 3, 4, 5, 6 and 10.

Life's a lottery

- **Divide each of the winning balls by the bonus ball.**

1. 49 84 67 72 96 | 6 (bonus)

8 r1 ______ ______ ______ ______ ______

2. 56 74 37 80 47 | 7 (bonus)

______ ______ ______ ______ ______

3. 65 84 52 58 98 | 9 (bonus)

______ ______ ______ ______ ______

4. 85 42 54 64 95 | 8 (bonus)

______ ______ ______ ______ ______

- **Write what the bonus ball must be. Then divide by the bonus ball.**

14 r2 ______ ______ ______ ______

Teachers' note The children could be asked to give the remainder as a fraction, for example 8 and , rather than 8 r1.

Odd one out

- **Colour the odd one out in each row.**

0·5	$\frac{1}{2}$	$\frac{5}{10}$	$\frac{2}{4}$	0·1
$\frac{1}{5}$	$\frac{2}{10}$	0·2	$\frac{1}{10}$	$\frac{3}{15}$
0·4	$\frac{2}{5}$	$\frac{4}{10}$	0·8	$\frac{8}{20}$
$\frac{1}{4}$	$\frac{3}{12}$	0·3	$\frac{25}{100}$	0·25
$\frac{3}{4}$	0·75	$\frac{4}{5}$	$\frac{75}{100}$	$\frac{6}{8}$
$\frac{12}{20}$	$\frac{3}{5}$	0·6	$\frac{6}{10}$	$\frac{3}{10}$

NOW TRY THIS!

- **Play this 'pairs' game with a partner.**

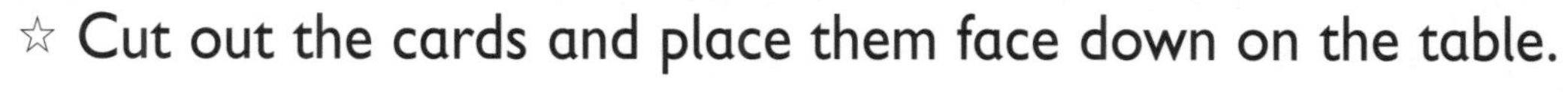

☆ Cut out the cards and place them face down on the table.

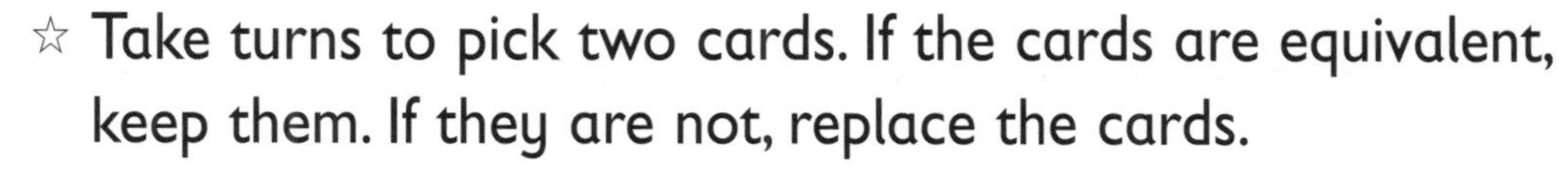

☆ Take turns to pick two cards. If the cards are equivalent, keep them. If they are not, replace the cards.

☆ The winner is the player with the most pairs at the end.

Teachers' note It is important that the children have a good understanding of equivalent fractions for this activity.

Cats' chorus

- **Fill in the numbers as you count on or back in steps of $\frac{1}{2}$, $\frac{1}{4}$ and $\frac{1}{3}$.**

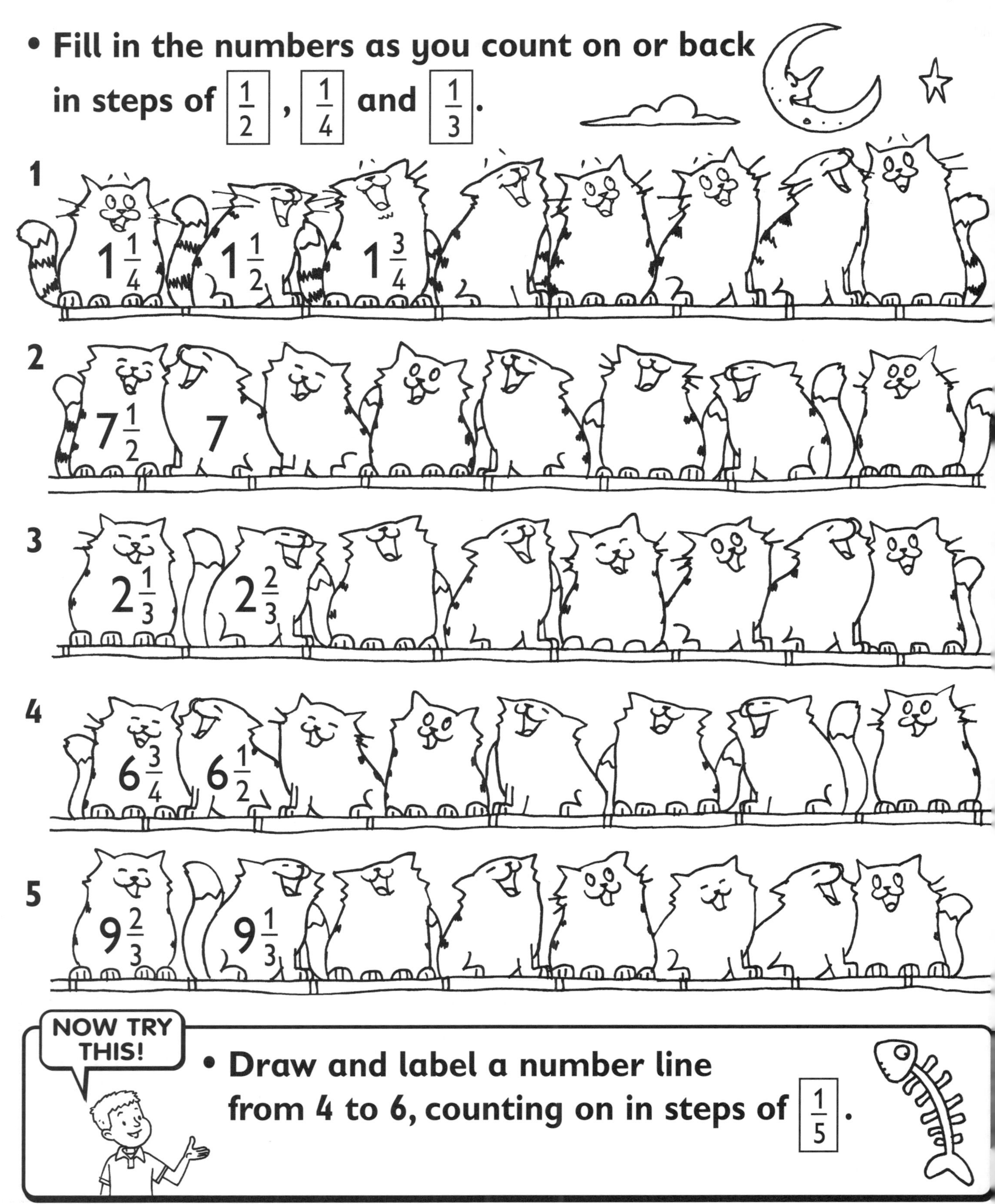

NOW TRY THIS!

- **Draw and label a number line from 4 to 6, counting on in steps of $\frac{1}{5}$.**

Teachers' note At the start of the lesson, practise counting in steps of one half, one quarter and one third. Watch out for children who say: 'six and one third, six and two thirds, six and three thirds…'. Point out that 'three thirds' is a whole and thus the next number should be 'seven'.

Mixed up

- **Join each mixed number to the correct place on the number line.**

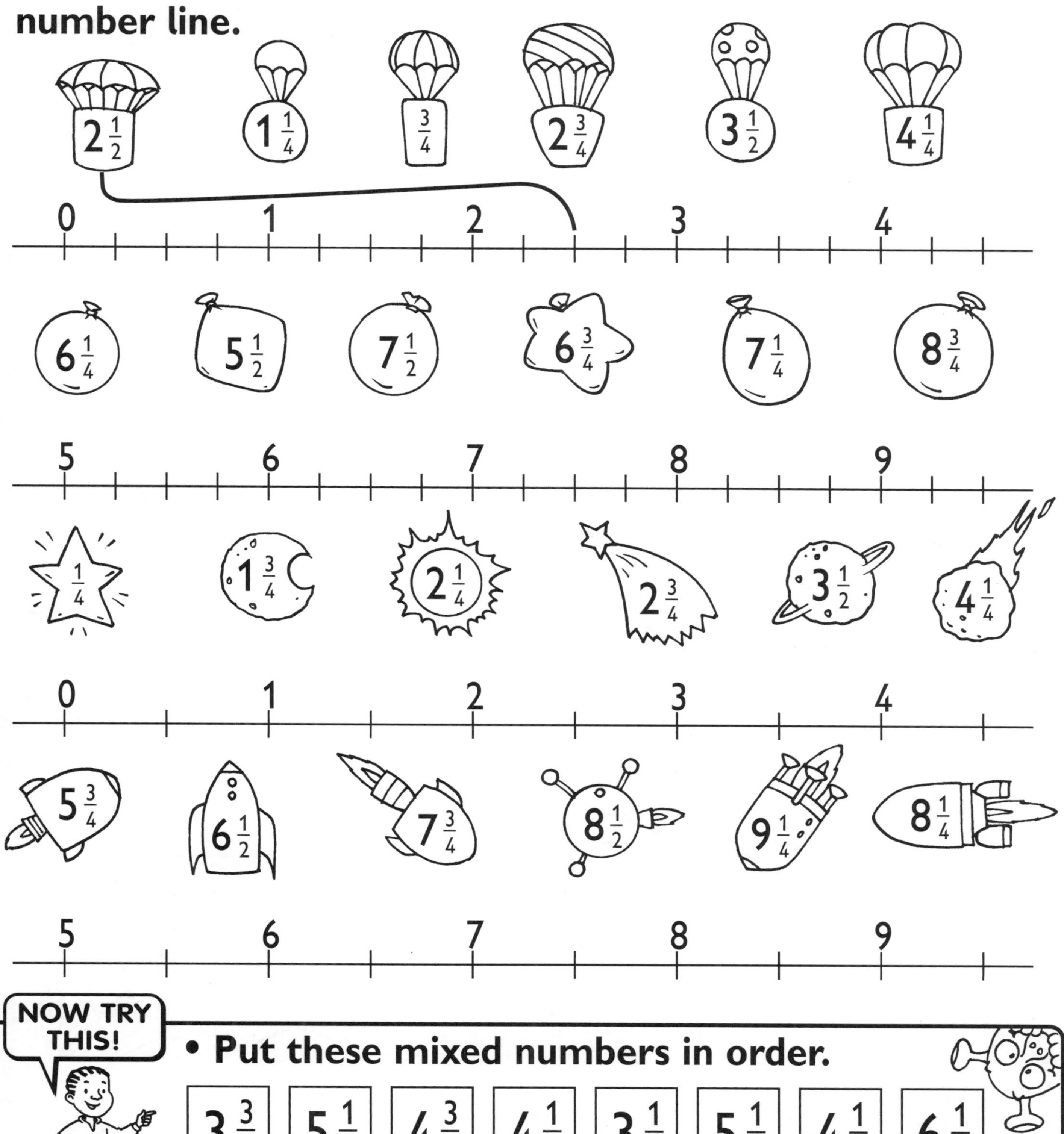

NOW TRY THIS!

- **Put these mixed numbers in order.**

$3\frac{3}{4}$	$5\frac{1}{2}$	$4\frac{3}{4}$	$4\frac{1}{2}$	$3\frac{1}{4}$	$5\frac{1}{4}$	$4\frac{1}{4}$	$6\frac{1}{4}$

$3\frac{1}{4}$, ______________________________

Teachers' note The third and fourth number lines do not contain marks for quarters. This will help the children to realise that quarters come halfway between whole numbers and halves on a number line, for example $1\frac{1}{4}$ comes halfway between 1 and $1\frac{1}{2}$.

A spoonful of medicine

A child's dose of medicine is a fraction of an adult's dose.

- **For each question work out a child's dose.**

1. $\frac{1}{4}$ of 20 ml = 5 ml
2. $\frac{1}{5}$ of 15 ml = ______ ml
3. $\frac{3}{4}$ of 24 ml = ______ ml
4. $\frac{2}{7}$ of 21 ml = ______ ml
5. $\frac{1}{3}$ of 24 ml = ______ ml
6. $\frac{3}{8}$ of 16 ml = ______ ml
7. $\frac{5}{9}$ of 18 ml = ______ ml
8. $\frac{5}{6}$ of 30 ml = ______ ml
9. $\frac{4}{5}$ of 25 ml = ______ ml
10. $\frac{5}{7}$ of 21 ml = ______ ml
11. $\frac{7}{10}$ of 30 ml = ______ ml
12. $\frac{7}{9}$ of 27 ml = ______ ml
13. $\frac{7}{8}$ of 32 ml = ______ ml

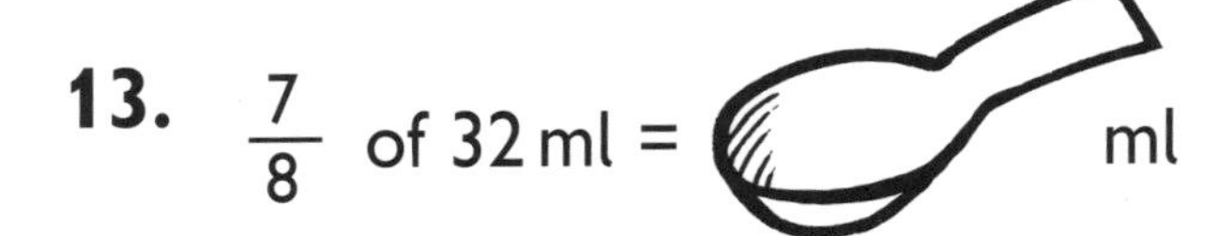

- **Fill in the adult's dose below.**

$\frac{6}{7}$ of ______ ml = 24 ml

Teachers' note The extension activity requires the children to realise that 24 ml is of the adult dose, and then they need to find one-sixth of 24 and multiply by 7 to give 28.

Drink up!

- **Answer the questions below about these drinks.**

Drink A	Drink B	Drink C	Drink D	Drink E
			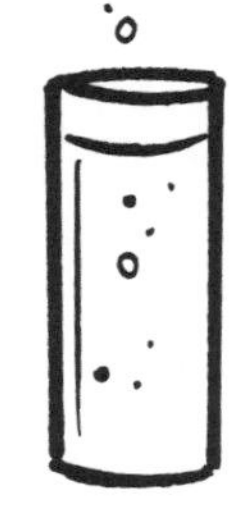	
400 ml	200 ml	450 ml	150 ml	50 ml

1. $\frac{1}{4}$ of A = ______ ml

2. $\frac{1}{5}$ of C = ______ ml

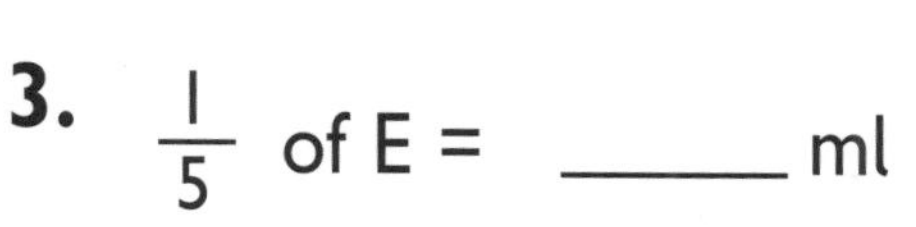

3. $\frac{1}{5}$ of E = ______ ml

4. $\frac{1}{3}$ of D = ______ ml

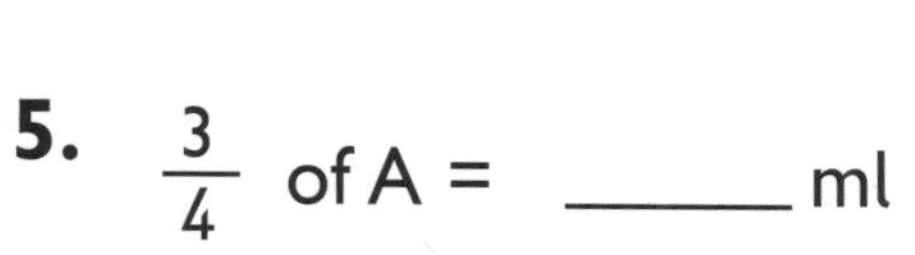

5. $\frac{3}{4}$ of A = ______ ml

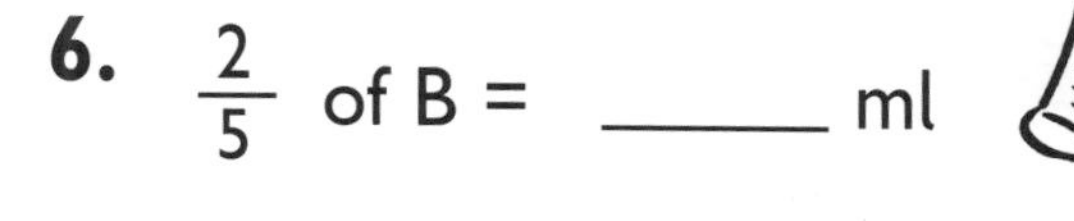

6. $\frac{2}{5}$ of B = ______ ml

7. $\frac{4}{5}$ of E = ______ ml

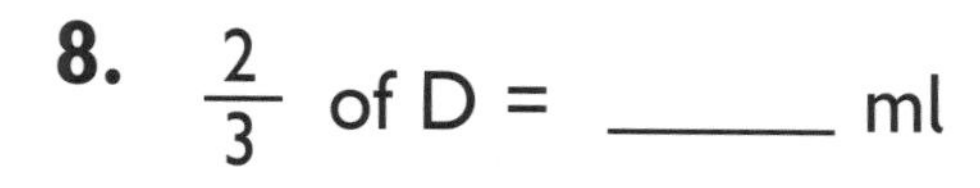

8. $\frac{2}{3}$ of D = ______ ml

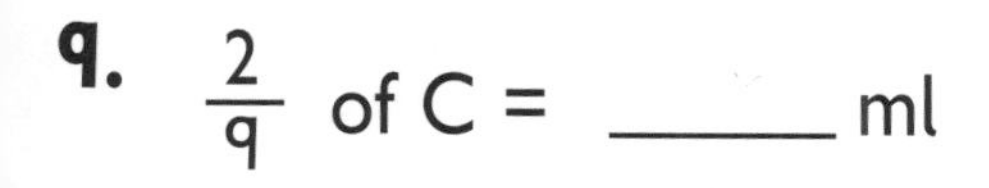

9. $\frac{2}{9}$ of C = ______ ml

10. $\frac{3}{8}$ of A = ______ ml

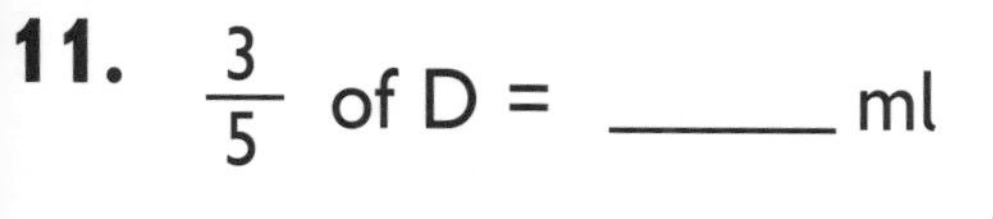

11. $\frac{3}{5}$ of D = ______ ml

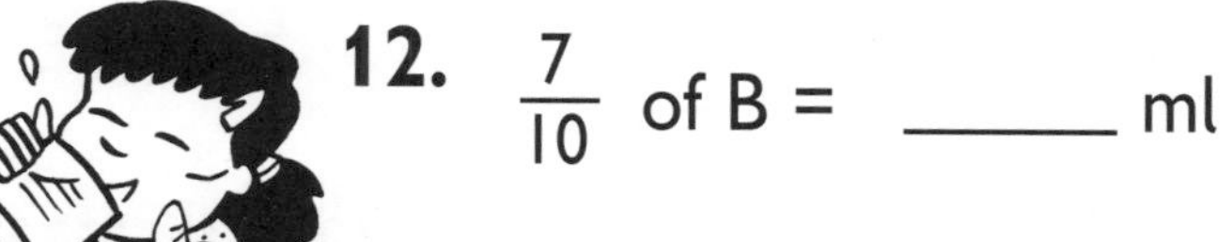

12. $\frac{7}{10}$ of B = ______ ml

13. $\frac{3}{25}$ of E = ______ ml

14. $\frac{9}{20}$ of A = ______ ml

- **Find $\frac{7}{25}$ of each drink.**

A	B	C	D	E
______ ml	______ ml	______ ml	______ ml	______ ml

Teachers' note At the start of the lesson, demonstrate how a fraction of a quantity can be found by dividing by the denominator (to find the unit fraction) and then multiplying by the numerator, for example of 30 can be found by dividing 30 by 5 to find one-fifth (6), and then multiplying by 4 to find four-fifths, giving the answer 6 × 4 = 24.

Nuts and raisins

• **Write the number of nuts and raisins in each bag.**

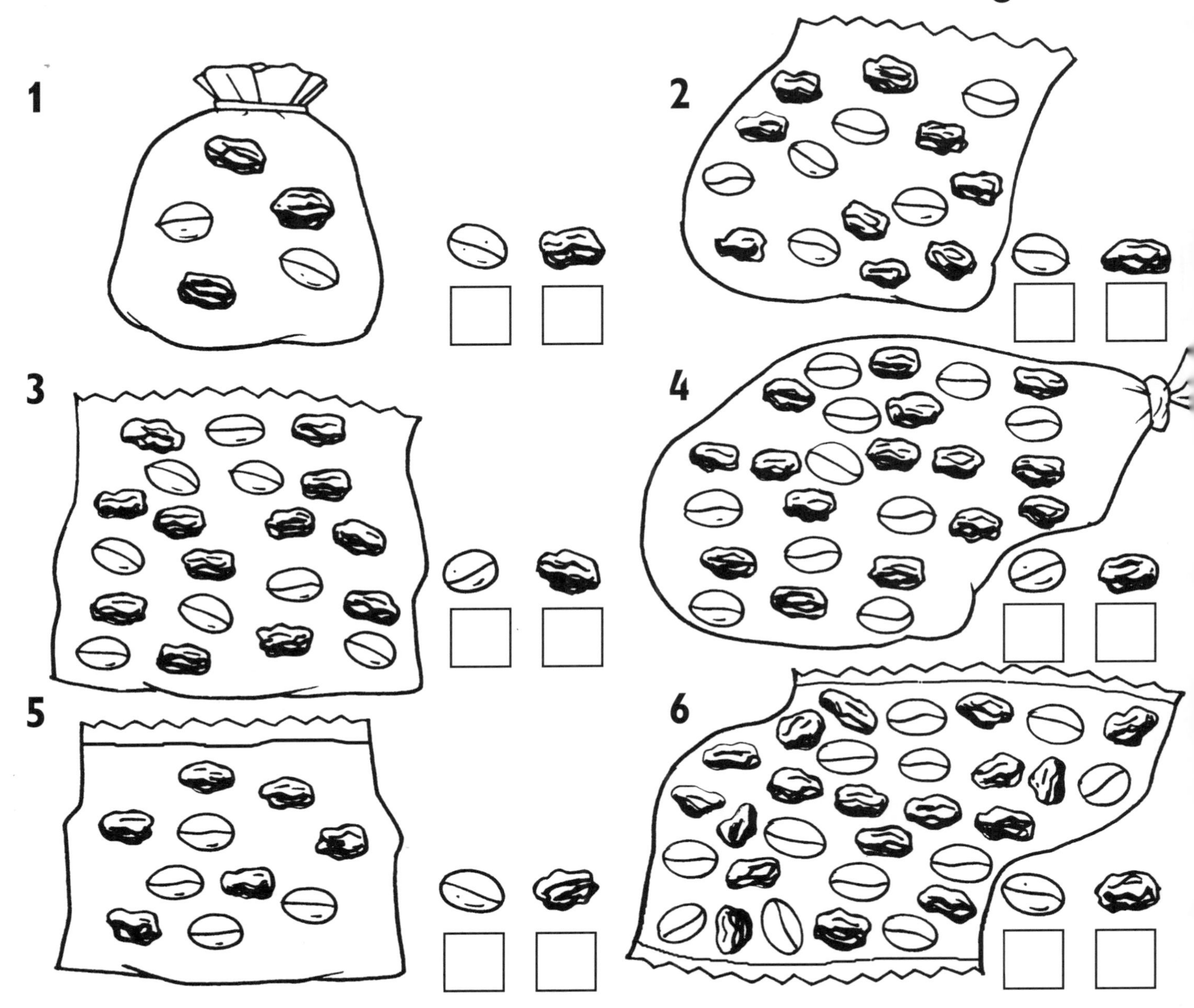

In each bag there are 3 raisins for every 2 nuts.

• **Circle groups of 2 nuts and 3 raisins to show this.**

• **Draw four different bags of nuts and raisins where there are 2 nuts for every 5 raisins.**

Teachers' note This introductory activity to ratio encourages the children to appreciate that, whilst there can be different numbers of items in each bag, the ratio of one item to another can be the same. This idea is emphasised by the children drawing rings around each group of 2 nuts and 3 raisins in each of the bags.

Pencil sharpeners

Each box contains some blue and some red sharpeners.

- **Colour the sharpeners to match the statement.**

1

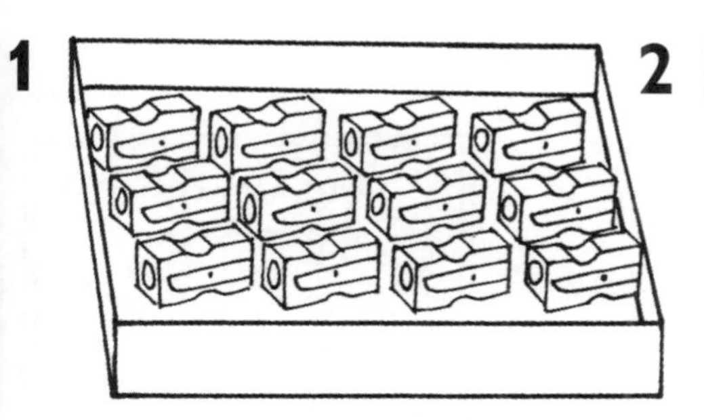

2 red for every 1 blue

2

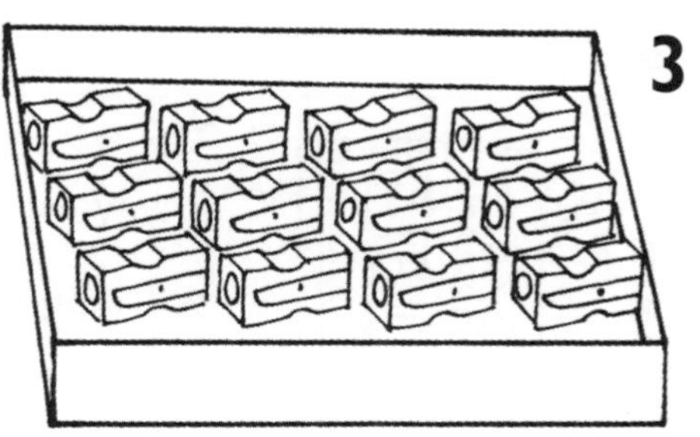

1 red for every 3 blue

3

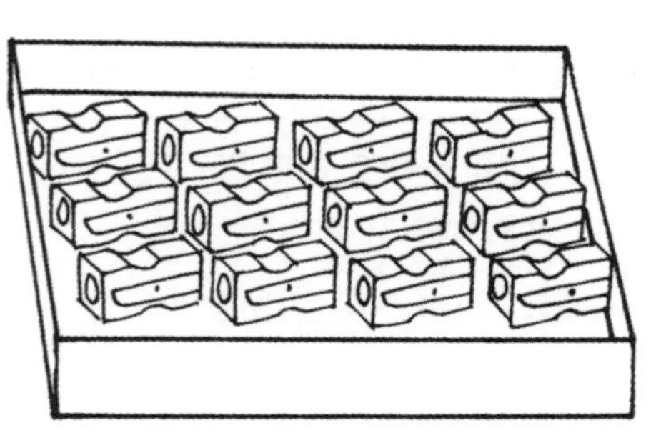

5 red for every 1 blue

4

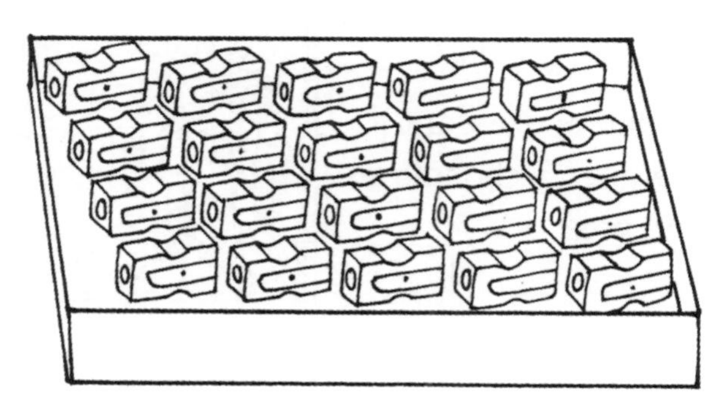

3 red for every 2 blue

5

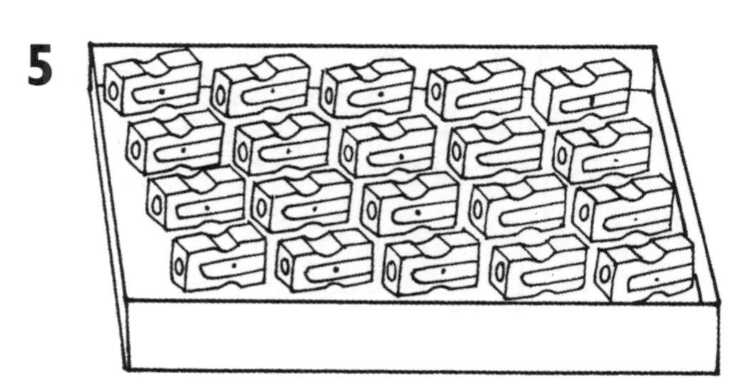

7 red for every 3 blue

6

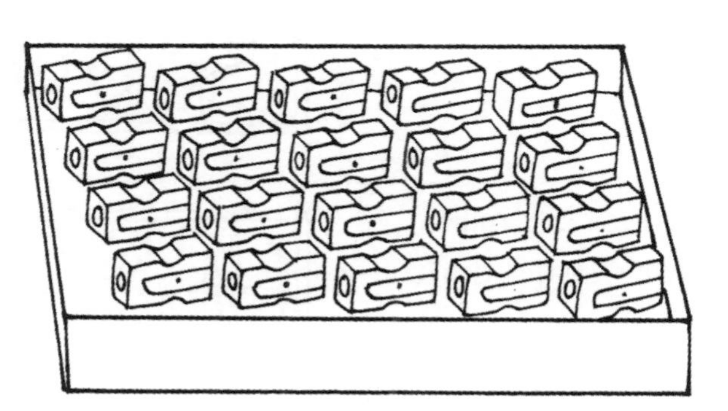

1 red for every 4 blue

7

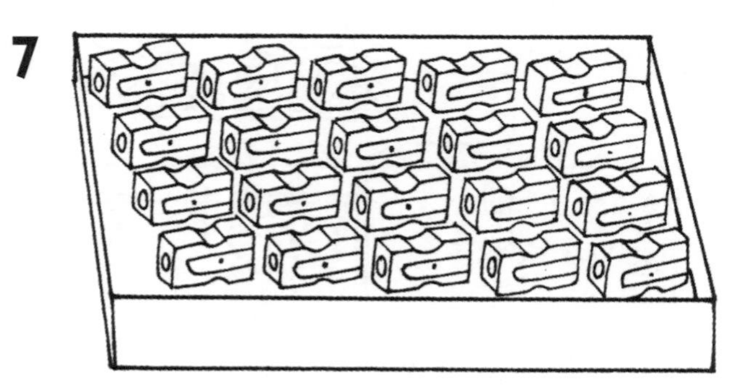

3 red for every 1 blue

NOW TRY THIS!

- **Under each statement, write how many sharpeners there are of each colour.**

red	blue
8	4

Teachers' note The children will need red and blue coloured pencils. When they have completed the sheet, encourage the children to notice the relationship between the statements and the total number of red and blue sharpeners in each box, for example '3 for every 2' gives the same result as '12 for every 8'.

Boxes of chocolates

In each box there are milk and dark chocolates.

- **Colour the chocolates brown (for milk) and black (for dark) to help you answer these questions.**

1 There are 3 milk for every 1 dark.

How many are milk if there are 20 chocolates in the box? ☐

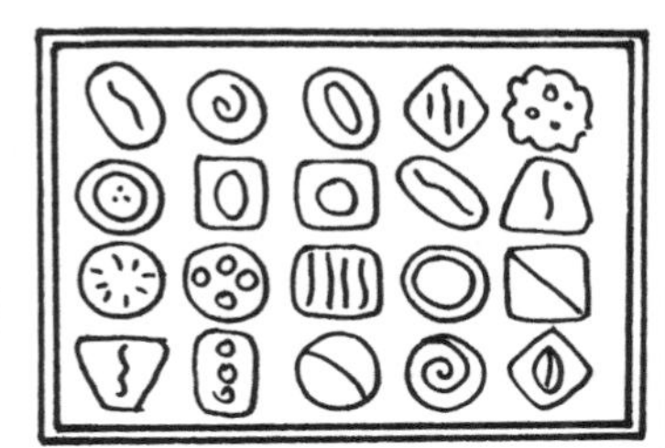

2 There are 3 milk for every 2 dark.

How many are dark if there are 20 chocolates in the box? ☐

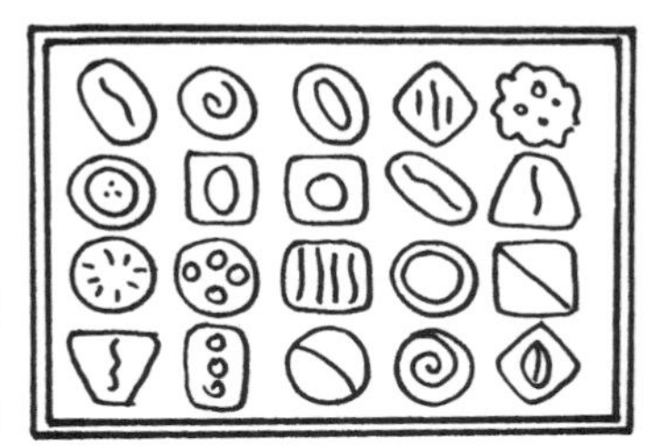

3 There are 2 milk for every 3 dark.

How many are milk if there are 25 chocolates in the box? ☐

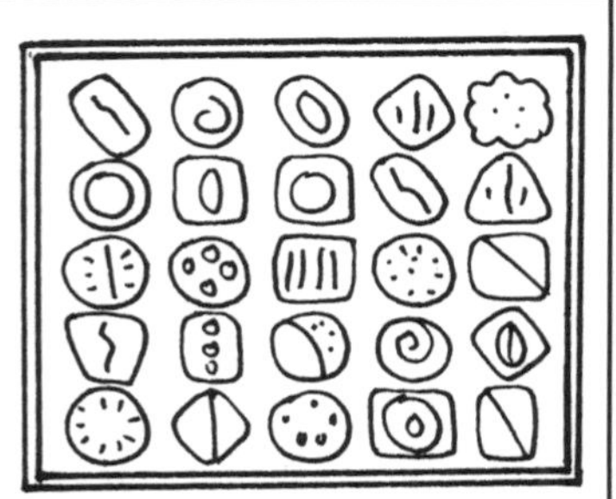

4 There are 4 milk for every 1 dark.

How many are dark if there are 25 chocolates in the box? ☐

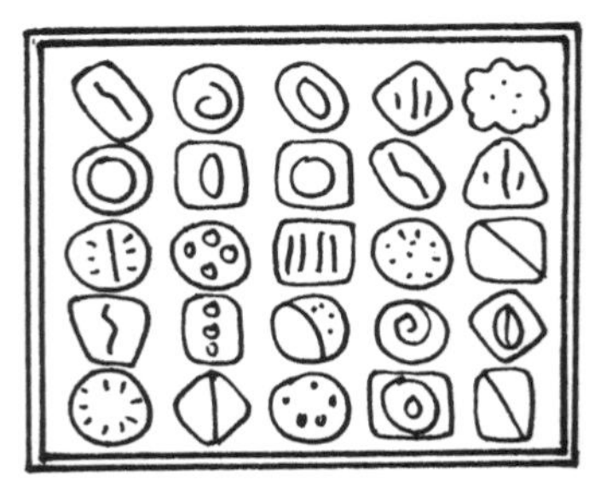

5 There is 1 milk for every 5 dark.

How many are milk if there are 24 chocolates in the box? ☐

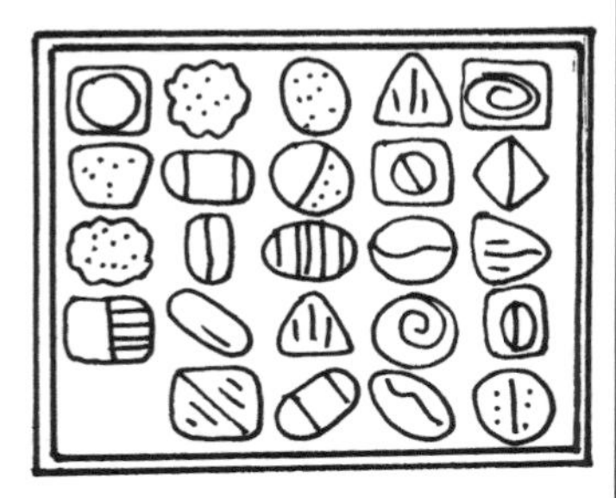

6 There are 5 milk for every 3 dark.

How many are dark if there are 24 chocolates in the box? ☐

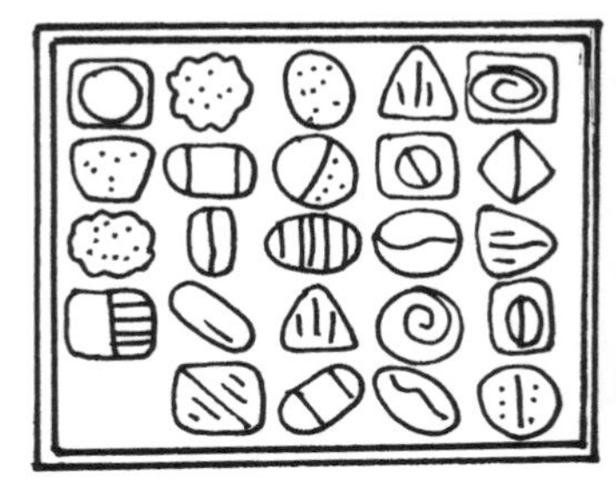

7 There are 2 milk for every 1 dark.

How many are milk if there are 24 chocolates in the box? ☐

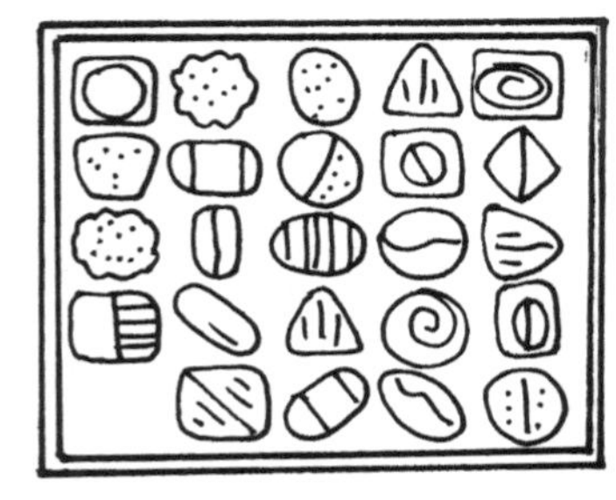

8 There is 1 milk for every 3 dark.

How many are dark if there are 24 chocolates in the box? ☐

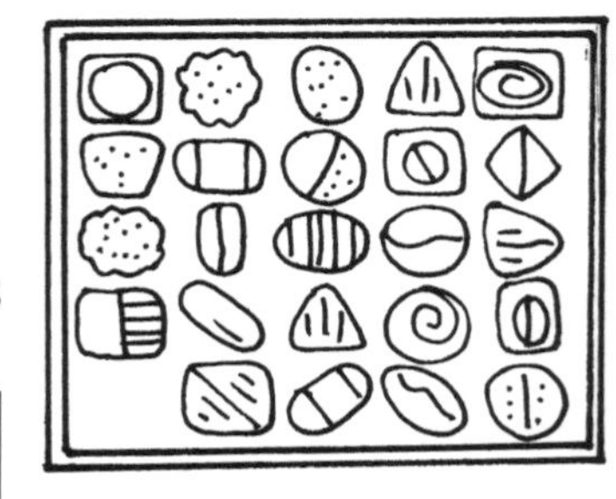

NOW TRY THIS!

- **Make up three more puzzles for a partner to solve.**

Teachers' note The children will need brown and black coloured pencils. For the extension activity ask the children to draw boxes containing 30 chocolates and to choose from the following: 2 for every 1, 1 for every 2, 4 for every 1, 1 for every 4, 2 for every 3, 3 for every 2, 5 for every 1, 1 for every 5, etc.

Puppy love

• **Complete the description of each litter of puppies.**

1

[1] black **for every** [3] golden.
[1] **out of** [4] puppies are black.

2

[ ] black **for every** [ ] golden.
[ ] **out of** [ ] puppies are black.

3

[ ] black **for every** [ ] golden.
[ ] **out of** [ ] puppies are black.

4

[ ] black **for every** [ ] golden.
[ ] **out of** [ ] puppies are black.

5

[ ] black **for every** [ ] golden.
[ ] **out of** [ ] puppies are black.

6

[ ] black **for every** [ ] golden.
[ ] **out of** [ ] puppies are black.

7

[ ] black **for every** [ ] golden.
[ ] **out of** [ ] puppies are black.

8

[ ] black **for every** [ ] golden.
[ ] **out of** [ ] puppies are black.

NOW TRY THIS!

• **Copy and complete this sentence for each litter.**

[ ] out of [ ] puppies are golden.

Teachers' note This activity encourages the children to appreciate the difference between ratio (for every) and proportion (out of every). Where 'ratio' describes part with part, 'proportion' describes part with the whole, for example the ratio '4 black for every 1 golden' is the same as the proportion '4 out of 5 puppies are black'.

Egghead

- **Complete the description of each nest of eggs.**

Nest A	Nest B
4 brown **for every** 4 white. 4 **out of** 8 eggs are brown.	☐ white **for every** ☐ brown. ☐ **out of** ☐ eggs are white.

Nest C	Nest D
☐ brown **for every** ☐ white. ☐ **out of** ☐ eggs are brown.	☐ brown **for every** ☐ white. ☐ **out of** ☐ eggs are brown.

Nest E	Nest F
☐ brown **for every** ☐ white. ☐ **out of** ☐ eggs are brown.	☐ brown **for every** ☐ white. ☐ **out of** ☐ eggs are brown.

NOW TRY THIS!

- **Match a nest to each statement.**

$\frac{1}{2}$ of the eggs are brown ☐

$\frac{1}{3}$ of the eggs are brown ☐

$\frac{3}{4}$ of the eggs are brown ☐

$\frac{9}{10}$ of the eggs are white ☐

$\frac{1}{4}$ of the eggs are brown ☐

$\frac{5}{8}$ of the eggs are white ☐

$\frac{1}{10}$ of the eggs are brown ☐

$\frac{3}{4}$ of the eggs are white ☐

$\frac{3}{8}$ of the eggs are brown ☐

$\frac{1}{2}$ of the eggs are white ☐

$\frac{2}{3}$ of the eggs are white ☐

$\frac{1}{4}$ of the eggs are white ☐

Teachers' note This activity encourages the children to appreciate that two statements can be made in each case, for example '$\frac{1}{3}$ of the eggs are white', so '$\frac{2}{3}$ of the eggs are brown'. The children will need to be aware that equivalent fractions are used, for example '9 out of 12' is given as '$\frac{3}{4}$'.

ungry Henry

• Estimate what proportion of the dog chew has not been eaten.

1 — $\frac{1}{6}$

2 — —

3 — —

4 — —

5 — —

6 — —

7 — —

8 — —

9 — —

10 — —

11 — —

• Shade about seven tenths of this line.

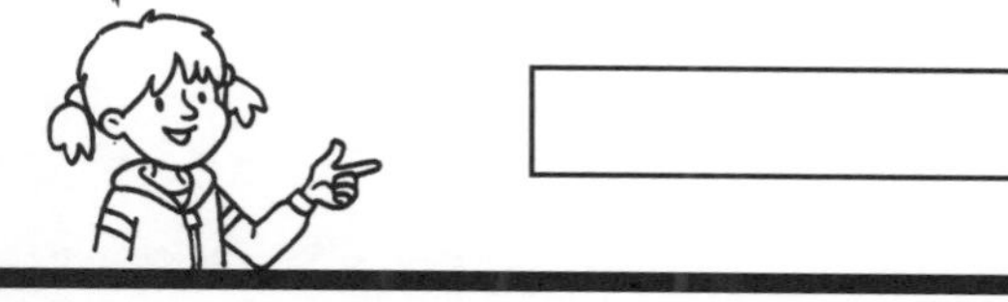

eachers' note At the start of the lesson, hold up some strips of paper. Fold them into equal parts nd ask the children to say what fraction of the whole strip each part is worth. Then hold up a strip hat has a quarter shaded but has no fold marks. Encourage the children to estimate the proportion haded and demonstrate by drawing lines to show where the fold marks would go.

Number puzzles – page 24
Solutions:
1 +10 **2** +9 **3** +11
4 +5 **5** +8 **6** +9

Metamorphosis – page 26
Solutions:
The end numbers are:
4803, 3759, 2633, 3766, 5483, 3098, 7592
Now try this!:
8882, 9212

Hotel lift – page 29
Solutions:
1 –5 **2** 3 **3** –3 **4** –5
5 –2 **6** 2 **7** –4

Caterpillar crawl – page 30
Solutions:
1 –2 **4** –5
2 a 3, –3 **b** –1, –5 **c** 2, –5 **d** –6, 4 **e** –4, 2
Now try this!
zero

Signs of a thaw – page 31
Solutions:
< > >
> < >
> > >
< < <
> < <

Difference walls – page 32
Solution:
CUBOID

Spot the dice – page 33
Solution:
1 80 **2** 40 **3** 24 **4** 64 **5** 80 **6** 32
7 48 **8** 64 **9** 56 **10** 88 **11** 72 **12** 96

Under the microscope – page 35
Solutions:
1 50mm **2** 70mm **3** 110mm **4** 140mm
5 190mm **6** 230mm **7** 270mm **8** 310mm

Calculator calamities: 1 and 2 – page 37–38
Solutions:
Calculator calamities: 1
1 + 300 **2** – 100 **3** + 20 **4** + 200
Calculator calamities: 2
1 + 12 **2** – 40 **3** – 378 **4** ÷ 2
Now try this!:
Calculator calamities: 1
+ 567
Calculator calamities: 2
x 2

3 for 2! – page 39
Solutions:
1 A saving 10p **2** A saving 50p
3 A saving 2p **4** A saving 9p
Now try this!:
They are both the same value.

Animal walkabout – page 40
Solutions:
1 3, 7, 11, 15, 19, 23
2 27, 24, 21, 18, 15, 12
3 21, 27, 33, 39, 45, 51
4 19, 28, 37, 46, 55, 64
5 79, 71, 63, 55, 47, 39
6 84, 91, 98, 105, 112, 119
Now try this!:
101, 97, 93, 89, 85, 81

Pocket money – page 42
Solutions:
1 £2.35 **2** £3.46 **3** £5.28 **4** £6.35 **5** £4.38

Exploding numbers – page 43
Solutions:
70 0.5 20 0.3
3 0.01 8 0.04
58.61
50 0.6 50 0.3
7 004 1 0.07
71.44
80 0.4 70 0.4
2 0.03 5 0.06
35.13
60 0.1 30 0
4 0.05 3 0.07

Curious cube – page 45
Solutions:
(a) 196 + 164 = 360 **(b)** 127 + 253 = 380
(c) 157 + 253 = 410 **(d)** 187 + 253 = 440
(e) 196 + 254 = 450 **(f)** 634 + 196 = 830
(g) 653 + 187 = 840 **(h)** 127 + 843 = 970
(i) 157 + 843 = 1000 **(j)** 843 + 187 = 1030
(k) 618 + 852 = 1470 **(l)** 958 + 852 = 1810

Supermarket stacks – page 46
Solutions:
1287
630 657
298 322 325

2197
1146 1051
607 539 512
313 294 245 267
Now try this!:
1459 should be ringed – the correct answer is 1469.

Animal antics – page 47
Solutions:
36 20 21 35 16 48 12 27 63
24 90 24 32 0 42 54 100 24
45 36 56 54 40 25 56 42 15
63 49 64 18 81 28 24 35 36

Tidying up – page 48
Solutions:

x 10	**x 100**
23→230	67→6700
11→110	2→200
70→700	58→5800
300→3000	34→3400
768→7680	84→8400
57→570	60→6000
÷ 10	**÷ 100**
840→84	4100→41
170→17	5000→50
400→40	600→6
9800→980	9700→97
500→50	

Codebreaker – page 50
Solution:
UNDERCOVER

Raffle tickets – page 52
Solutions:
1274 1589 3008 2784
2847 2918 3803 4268
3623 3428 4278 4383
4075 3826 5789 8367
5726 5310 6472 9573
4998 5099 5768 9245
6582 5108 6785 9254
6912 5743 7685 9425
7624 5831 8756 9452
7934 5924 8765 9542
Now try this!:
Four numbers from: 3799, 3800, 3801, 3802, 3803, 3804, 3805, 3806, 3807, 3808

Join the dots – page 53
Solution:
SOAP, PANE, GOAL, ZERO, CLAP, RAGS

Little Miss Moneybags! – page 55
Solutions:
1 £1.60, £2.60, £3.60, £4.60, £5.60, £6.60
2 £0.60, £0.70, £0.80, £0.90, £1.00, £1.10
3 £5.00, £4.50, £4.00, £3.50, £3.00, £2.50
4 £2.70, £2.90, £3.10, £3.30, £3.50, £3.70
5 £0.55, £0.45, £0.35, £0.25, £0.15, £0.05
6 £3.32, £5.32, £7.32, £9.32, £11.32, £13.32
Now try this!
£0.80, £0.85, £0.90, £0.95, £1.00, £1.05

Super Squirrel – page 59
Solutions:
1 0.2 **2** 0.5 **3** 0.6 **4** 0.1 **5** 0.9
6 0.3 **7** 0 **8** 0.4 **9** 0.7 **10** 0.8

Animal additions – page 60
Solutions:
(a) 1428 **(b)** 1108 **(c)** 1403
(d) 555 **(e)** 1046 **(f)** 971
(g) 428 **(h)** 1650 **(i)** 1490
(j) 451 **(k)** 1400 **(l)** 1505

Captain Dynamic – page 61
Solutions:
(a) 365 **(b)** 753
(c) 586 **(d)** 853
(e) 732 **(f)** 542

Movin' on – page 62
Solutions:
Only children beginning in position 4 escape to safety from the crocodiles.

Crazy calculations – page 63
Solutions:
64 x 6 = 384 76 x 7 = 532 47 x 3 = 141
58 x 4 = 232 55 x 8 = 440 39 x 9 = 351

Detective dog – page 64
Solutions:
1 48 **2** 37 **3** 67 **4** 75
5 79 **6** 69 **7** 86 **8** 89

Sponsored spell – page 65
Solutions:
1 £4.08 **2** £32.60 **3** £17.89 **4** £29.09
5 £20.71 **6** 67 **7** Jay **8** £8.06

Spend, spend, spend! – page 66
Solutions:
1 £66.57 **2** £110.80 **3** 6 **4** DVD **5** 7
6 £70.12 **7** £0.17 **8** a DVD and a CD

Splish! Splash! Splosh! – page 67
Solutions:
1 733 **2** 19
3 432 **4** 59
5 112 **6** 4
7 16 **8** 91
9 778 **10** 224
11 29 **12** 705

Confetti colours – page 68
Solutions:
1
blue red pink
green yellow pink
2
blue blue
orange blue
green red
3
red yellow green
pink red blue
4
yellow red
blue orange
red yellow

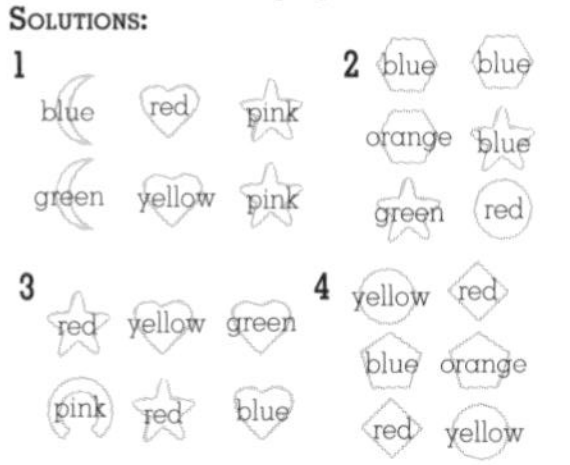

The rules of the rows – page 69
Solutions:
3 8 6 14
5 10 10 20
8 13 16 29
6 11 12 23
⬡ = □ + ○

Hard cards – page 70
Solutions:
1 even **2** odd **3** odd **4** odd **5** even
6 odd **7** even **8** even **9** even **10** even

Be a detective – page 71
Solutions:
1 47 **2** 60 **3** 70 **4** 45
5 81 **6** 49 **7** 85 **8** 45

Market stall – page 72
Solutions:
1 £2.96 **2** £1.95 **3** £5.80
4 £9.43 **5** £5.08 **6** £4.70

Sheila's shopping basket – page 73
Solutions:
1 £210 **2** £10 + £60, £20 + £50, £30 + £40
3 £360 **4** £10 + £20 + £30 + £60, £50 + £70, £40 + £80 or £10 + £50 + £60, £20 + £30 + £70
£40 + £80 or £20 + £40 + £60, £50 + £70, £10 + £30 + £80

In a flap – page 74
Solutions:
1 53 **2** 36 **3** 32 **4** 9 **5** 44 **6** 24 **7** 23
8 3 **9** 8 **10** 18 **11** 32 **12** 43 **13** 103 **14** 27

Cheese triangles – page 75
Solutions:
1 70° **2** 40° **3** 40° **4** 50° **5** 70° **6** 30° **7** 30°

Square dance – page 76
Solutions:
Possible answers include:
1200
600 500 100
400 800
200 700 300
1300
100 400 800
700 300
500 600 200
1400
800 500 100
200 600
400 300 700
1500
800 400 300
100 500
600 200 700

Party presents – page 80
Solutions:
Presents b, c, f, g and i should be coloured.
Now try this!
1 h **2** d **3** j **4** i **5** c **6** f

Cube challenge – page 81
Solutions:
a b c d e

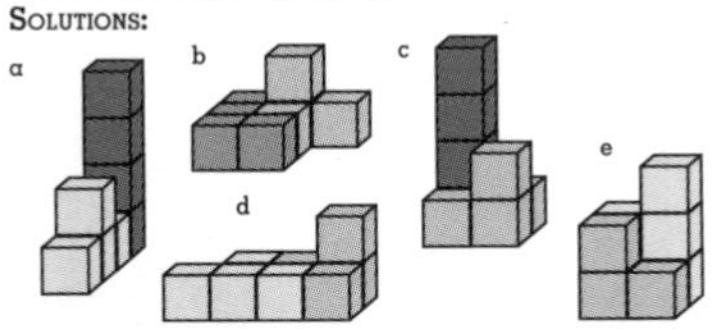

Now try this!:

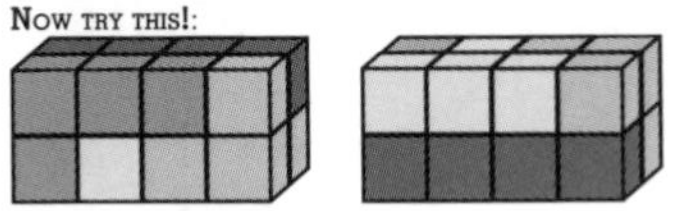

Necklace numbers – page 82
Solutions:
1 17, 20, 23, 26, 29, 32, 35, 38, 41
2 9, 13, 17, 21, 25, 29, 33, 37, 41
3 3, 8, 13, 18, 23, 28, 33, 38, 43
4 1, 7, 13, 19, 25, 31, 37, 43, 49
5 2, 7, 12, 17, 22, 27, 32, 37, 42
6 2, 5, 8, 11, 14, 17, 20, 23, 26
7 22, 26, 30, 34, 38, 42, 46, 50, 54
8 5, 11, 17, 23, 29, 35, 41, 47, 53

Sticks – page 83
Solutions:
The shaded shapes are Ali's and the unshaded shapes are Sally's.

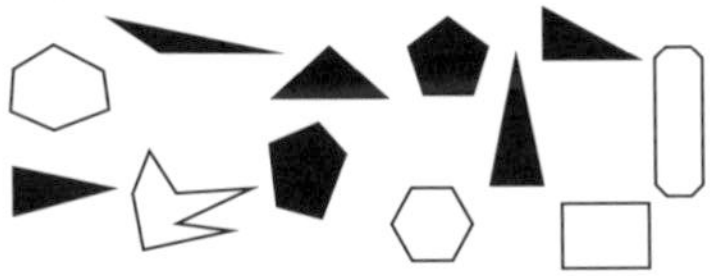

Dividing exactly – page 84
Solutions:
Hussain 50 Jane 21 Jermaine 28
Benny 27 Jenny 35 Penny 18
Now try this!
32: 1, 2, 4, 8, 16, 32

Andy, Sandy and Mandy – page 85
Solutions:
1 80 **2** 20 **3** 180 **4** 140 **5** 420 **6** 300
Now try this!
(a) 230 **(b)** 400 **(c)** 10

What a puzzle! – page 86
Solutions:
1 e.g. 357 + 62 = 419 **2** e.g. 935 – 71 = 864 **3** 359 x 2 = 718 **4** 834 x 9 = 7506

Double trouble – page 87
Solutions
1 55 miles **2** 72 miles
3 36 miles **4** 210 miles

At the sales – page 88
Solutions:
1 £62 **2** £74 **3** £79 **4** £67
5 £89 **6** £76 **7** £96 **8** £94

Solutions:

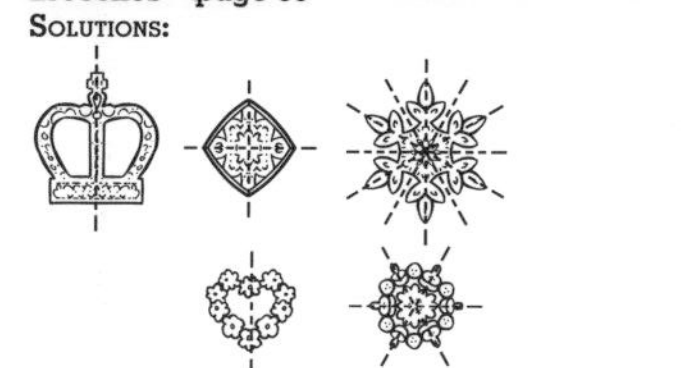

Decorations – page 90
Solutions:

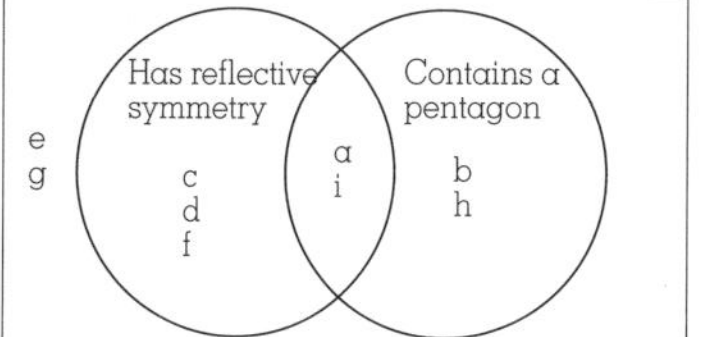

True statements – page 93
Solutions:
6 is a factor of 54
9 is a factor of 54
6 multiplied by 9 = 54
9 multiplied by 6 = 54
54 is the product of 6 and 9
54 is the product of 9 and 6
54 is a multiple of 6
54 is a multiple of 9
54 divided by 6 = 9
54 divided by 9 = 6

Halfway house – page 94
Solutions:
1 true **2** false **3** false **4** true

Badge sale – page 95
Solutions:
1 £1 2 £2.40 3 £3 4 60p
5 60p 6 £3.90 7 £1.75 8 £3.30
Now try this!
£5.47

Fair share: 1 and 2 – page 96–97
Solutions: Fair share: 1
1 £210 2 £10 + £60, £20 + £50, £30 + £40
3 £360 4 £10 + £20 + £30 + £60, £50 + £70, £40 + £80 or £10 + £50 + £60, £20 + £30 + £70 £40 + £80 or £20 + £40 + £60, £50 + £70, £10 + £30 + £80
Solutions: Fair share: 2
1 £360 2 £10 + £80, £20 + £70, £30 + £60, £50 + £40
3 £450
4 £10 + £90 + £50, £20 + £70+ £60, £30 + £40 + £80
or £10 + £60 + £80, £20 + £90 + £40, £30 + £50 + £70
or £10 + £20 + £30 + £90, £40 + £50+ £60, £70 + £80
or £10 + £20 + £30 + £40 + £50, £90 + £60, £70 + £80
or £20 + £30 + £40 + £60, £10 + £50+ £90, £70 + £80
or £10 + £30 + £40 + £70, £20 + £50+ £80, £60 + £90
or £10 + £30 + £50 + £60, £20 + £40+ £90, £70 + £80
or £10 + £20 + £50 + £70, £30 + £40+ £80, £60 + £90

Computer glitch – page 98
Solutions:
Wrong Wrong Correct Correct Wrong

Grid reasoning – page 99
Solutions:
Row 1, cover 5 and 5; Row 2, cover 4 and 2; Row 3, cover 1 and 1; Row 4, cover 9 and 5; Row 5, cover 3 and the second 3; Row 6, cover 7 and 3; Row 7, cover 3 and 1; Row 8, cover 7 and 5

Water slide – page 100
Solutions:
1300 16 000 700 70 200
150 500 2200 240 15 000
80 2600 1800 1700
Now try this!
(a) 2100 **(b)** 1900 **(c)** 220
(d) 13 000 **(e)** 7000 **(f)** 1700

Sitting ducks – page 101
Solutions:
3000 + 9000 + 6000 = 18 000
3000 + 8000 + 6000 = 17 000
4000 + 8000 + 6000 = 18 000
4000 + 8000 + 7000 = 19 000
4000 + 5000 + 7000 = 16 000
3000 + 8000 + 7000 = 18 000

Double bugs – page 102
Solutions:
Each bug should have a multiple of 1, 10 and 100 beginning with the following digits:
1 84 **2** 48 **3** 72 **4** 96
5 108 **6** 124 **7** 106 **8** 78
9 142 **10** 138 **11** 174 **12** 192

Half bugs – page 103
Solutions:
Each bug should have a multiple of 1, 10 and 100 beginning with the following digits:
1 12 **2** 18 **3** 21 **4** 33
5 42 **6** 24 **7** 36 **8** 28
9 37 **10** 43 **11** 46 **12** 49

Stick 'em up – page 104
Solutions:
1 9 **2** 7 **3** 8
4 7 **5** 8 **6** 8
7 7 **8** 9 **9** 9
Now try this!
(a) 9 **(b)** 7 **(c)** 56 **(d)** 9 × 9 **(e)** 6 **(f)** 8

Thinking thimbles – page 111
Solutions:
There are 27 solutions to this thimble problem:
Three starting 00: 000 001 002
Three starting 01: 010 011 012
Three starting 02: 020 021 022
Three starting 10: 100 101 102
Three starting 11: 110 111 112
Three starting 12: 120 121 122
Three starting 20: 200 201 202
Three starting 21: 210 211 212
Three starting 22: 220 221 222

Rain recorder – page 112
Solutions:
1 8cm **2** March and November **3** 4
4 a October **b** 4cm **5** Answers will vary.

No shoes allowed! – page 113
Solutions:
1 flip-flops 17 plimsolls 7 trainers 23 boots 1 wellies 4 school shoes 2
2 4 **3** 17 **4** plimsolls
5 a boots
b Because it was hot. Rationale: it was a summer fête. Lots of people were wearing flip-flops.
Now try this!
56 children went on the bouncy castle. This includes the two children who turned up wearing no shoes.

Rock, paper, scissors – page 114
Now try this!
33, 24, 43

Sorting symmetry – page 115
Solutions:

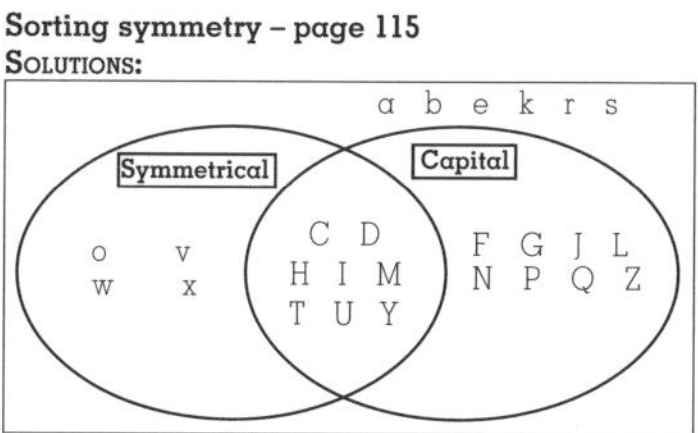

2 a 16
b 12
3 8
4 Responses might include knowledge of letters and use of the mirror/lines of symmetry.
5 Not symmetrical, not capital
Now try this!
Rectangle: Not symmetrical, not capital
Intersection: Symmetrical and capital

Monsters' tea party – page 116
Solutions:
1 16 **2** 7 **3** 7
4 Cornelius and Minnie **5** 11 **6** No

Odd one out: 1 and 2 – page 117–118
Solutions:
Set 1: the number of hamsters and rabbits needs correcting on the tally chart.
Set 2: toffee needs correcting on the pictogram.
Set 3: the number of ants needs correcting on the vertical bar chart.

Sweet success – page 123
Solutions:
Ways of sorting include: triangular sweets/stripy sweets; circular sweets/black sweets; rectangular sweets/white sweets; circular sweets/triangular sweets, etc.

Minibeasts – page 124
Solutions:
1 2 **2** 11 **3** 5
4 1 **5** worm **6** 30

Summer fête – page 125
Solutions:
1 30 **2** 45 **3** Tug-of-war
4 30 **5** 15

Mr Folly's lollies – page 126
Solution:
It is likely that the symbol will represent 5 or 10 lollies sold.

Game, set and match: 1 and 2 – page 127–128
Solutions: Game, set and match: 1
1 C **2** D **3** A **4** B

Mix and match: 1 and 2 – page 130–131
Solutions: Mix and match: 1
A and D B and G
C and F E and H

After-school sports – page 134
Solutions:
1 football
2 a It is likely that the children will say football.
b It is the most popular sport. Some might give the reason that it is their favourite sport.

c 15
d 17
3 There is not a correct answer here. The answer will depend on what children think. The important part is that they are able to give a reason for their decision.
Now try this!
Again, there is not a correct answer here.

Bounce 4 charity – page 137
Solutions:
1 £70
2 Class 2
3 a Class 1 and Class 4
b £80
4 It was quite a lot more than any other class. It could be explained by there being more children in that class, that they out-bounced the other classes, or that their donors were more generous. Encourage the children to think of likely explanations.
Now try this!
£360

Top of the mountain: 1 and 2 – page 138–139
Solutions:
Tally shows 17, 20 blue and white pencils altogether, Netball is the most popular sport, 11 people went sailing, Sparrows were seen most often, 25 more people have packed lunch than school dinners, Space Box was voted best film, Tim should be the school council member, A hamster should be the class pet, Polly and Molly laid 4 eggs altogether

Made to measure – page 140
Solutions:
1 140cm **2** 380cm
3 270cm **4** 50cm
5 90cm **6** 110cm
7 320cm **8** 460cm
9 230cm **10** 350cm

Time teaser – page 143
Solutions:
A 6:34pm **B** 7:00am **C** 2:49pm **D** 5:56am
E 7:07pm **F** 1:10am **G** 3:28am **H** 11:27am

Post office problems – page 144
Solutions:
1 800g **2** 1.8kg **3** 200g **4** 100g
5 A, B and D **6** 200g **7** 50g **8** 2.6kg

Fi's fruitcake – page 147
Solution:
25g ➛ 150g ➛ 250g ➛ 325g ➛ 475g ➛ 650g

Dan's day – page 150
Solutions:
These are the most likely answers:
Eating lunch
At school
In bed
Watching TV
In bed
Getting up
At school

Cinema seating – page 152
Now try this!
A3, B1, B2, B5, C1, C3, C5, C6, D1, D4, E3, E4, E5, F1

Counter attack – page 153
Solutions:
1 G1 **2** E1 **3** D6 **4** E5 **5** B5 **6** D3

Reading the signs – page 154
Solutions:
1 55miles **2** 72miles **3** 36miles **4** 21...

Tallest man ever – page 155
Solutions:
1 24cm **2** 74cm **3** 89cm
4 120cm **5** 123cm

Magic ingredients – page 156
Solutions:
192 warts 252 slugs 144 hairballs
512 maggots 684 eyeballs

Beautiful brooches – page 157
Solutions:
1 (a) D **(b)** C **(c)** A
2 (a) F **(b)** D **(c)** C
3 (a) D **(b)** C **(c)** B

Guinea pig food – page 159
Solutions:
1 2000g **2** 4500g **3** 1500g **4** 7300g
5 2800g **6** 5900g **7** 7000g **8** 100g

Scale shapes – page 160
Solutions:

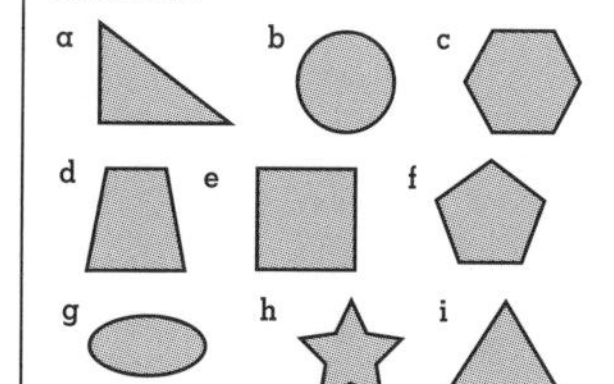

Hickory, dickory, dock – page 162
Solutions:

o'clock	1	2	3	4	5	6	7	8	9	10	11	12
angle	30°	60°	90°	120°	150°	180°	210°	240°	270°	300°	330°	360°

Magic spell – page 163
Solutions:
1 WAND **2** CARD **3** TRICK
4 RABBIT **5** CIRCLE

That's an order! – page 164
Solutions:
1 d, a, b, c **2** g, e, f, h
3 j, k, i, l **4** p, m, n, o

Loopy witches – page 167
Solutions:
The word is BROOMSTICK

Crack the codes – page 168
Solutions:

A	B	C	D	E	F	G	H
6	5	3	9	4	2	1	7

Milking Milli – page 172
Solutions:
3000ml 1500ml 2400ml 1700ml
2800ml 3500ml 900ml
Now try this!
2.41 3.31 0.21 0.71 1.11 0.31 4.41

Poorly pets – page 175
Solutions:
1 12:53 **2** 5:24 **3** 3:48
4 3:06 **5** 12:22 **6** 1:31

The number 56 bus – page 176
Solutions:
1 **(a)** 10 minutes **(b)** 30 minutes
(c) 15 minutes **(d)** 10 minutes
(e) 10 minutes **(f)** 13 minutes
2 9:54
3 9:59

Area llamas – page 177
Solutions:
a 17cm² **b** 19cm²
c 20cm² **d** 15cm²
e 17cm² **f** 19cm²

Fair and square – page 178
Solutions:
1 They all have a perimeter of 18 cm2.
2 **a** 9cm² **b** 14cm²
c 11cm² **d** 8cm²
e 17cm² **f** 9cm²
g 13cm² **h** 10cm²
i 8cm² **j** 8cm²
Now try this!
All are possible:
Perimeter 18 cm, area 12 cm²

Perimeter 18 cm, area 15 cm²

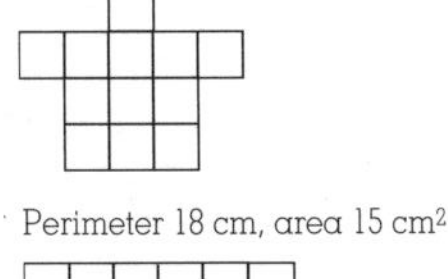

Perimeter 18 cm, area 16 cm²

Angelina's angles – page 179
Solutions:
Approximate answers:
1 90° **2** 180° **3** 45° **4** 350° **5** 60°
6 30° **7** 130° **8** 170° **9** 120°

Quiz show – page 180
Solutions:
1 D **2** B **3** C **4** D **5** D **6** A

Number sentences – page 181
Solutions:
1 A, B and C **2** A and B
3 B and C **4** A and C
Now try this!
8 bags

Measuring methods – page 183
Solutions:
1 22 bottles **2** 15 days
3 14 days **4** 200 miles

Field event – page 184
Solutions:
a 6 horses **b** 8 cows **c** 24 animals
Now try this!
The answer will depend on the multiple of 5 written into the box, but here are some possible solutions:
[5] sheep 3 horses, 4 cows, 12 animals altogether
[15] sheep 9 horses, 12 cows, 36 animals altogether
[20] sheep 12 horses, 16 cows, 48 animals altogether
[25] sheep 15 horses, 20 cows, 60 animals altogether

Chocolate chunks – page 185
Solutions:
1 0.5 $\frac{5}{10}$ **2** 0.4 $\frac{4}{10}$ **3** 0.2 $\frac{2}{10}$ **4** 0.7 $\frac{7}{10}$
5 0.9 $\frac{9}{10}$ **6** 0.1 $\frac{1}{10}$ **7** 8.0 $\frac{8}{10}$ **8** 0.3 $\frac{3}{10}$
9 0.6 $\frac{6}{10}$ **10** 0.24 $\frac{24}{100}$ **11** 0.25 $\frac{25}{100}$ **12** 0.75 $\frac{75}{100}$
13 0.99 $\frac{99}{100}$ **14** 0.04 $\frac{4}{100}$

Fraction Man – page 186
Solutions:
1 $\frac{2}{7}$ **2** $\frac{1}{12}$ **3** $\frac{1}{4}$ **4** $\frac{1}{2}$
5 $\frac{4}{7}$ **6** $\frac{4}{12}$ or $\frac{1}{3}$ **7** $\frac{3}{4}$ **8** $\frac{1}{4}$
9 $\frac{7}{10}$ **10** $\frac{99}{100}$ **11** $\frac{3}{4}$ or ($\frac{7}{8}$ if 8 points)
12 $\frac{7}{10}$ **13** $\frac{7}{1000}$

Twins – page 187
Solutions:
1 $\frac{2}{8} = \frac{1}{4}$ **2** $\frac{4}{12} = \frac{1}{3}$ **3** $\frac{4}{6} = \frac{2}{3}$ **4** $\frac{9}{24} = \frac{3}{8}$
5 $\frac{12}{16} = \frac{6}{8}$ **6** $\frac{28}{35} = \frac{4}{5}$ **7** $\frac{6}{10} = \frac{3}{5}$ **8** $\frac{4}{20} = \frac{1}{5}$
9 $\frac{5}{20} = \frac{1}{4}$ **10** $\frac{16}{24} = \frac{2}{3}$

Spelling fractions – page 188
Solutions:
1 4 red, 3 yellow **2** 2 red, 9 blue
3 2 blue, 7 green **4** 12 blue, 2 green
5 6 red, 1 blue **6** 1 red, 8 yellow
7 1 blue, 10 green **8** 15 red, 3 blue
9 9 red, 5 yellow
Now try this!
1 $\frac{3}{10}$ **2** $\frac{1}{12}$ **3** $\frac{5}{14}$ **4** $\frac{1}{8}$ or equivalent fraction
5 $\frac{2}{9}$ **6** $\frac{3}{4}$ or equivalent fraction **7** $\frac{1}{12}$
8 $\frac{1}{1}$ or equivalent fraction **9** $\frac{1}{16}$

Café life – page 189
Solutions:
Possible answers:
1 500 ÷ 20 = 25
2 32 ÷ 4 = 8, 32 – 8 = 24
3 8 x £1.25 = £10.00, £10.00 – £4.50 = £5.50
4 £1.69 + £0.70 + £1.25 = £3.64
5 1000 ml ÷ 5 = 200 ml, 200 ml x 3 = 600 ml
6 £1.69 – £0.78 = £0.91 7 55p x 9 = £4.95, so 9 can be bought.

Coin contest – page 190
Solutions:
Possible answers:
1 500 ÷ 20 = 25
2 32 ÷ 4 = 8, 32 – 8 = 24
3 8 x £1.25 = £10.00, £10.00 – £4.50 = £5.50
4 £1.69 + £0.70 + £1.25 = £3.64
5 1000 ml ÷ 5 = 200 ml, 200 ml x 3 = 600 ml
6 £1.69 – £0.78 = £0.91 7 55p x 9 = £4.95, so 9 can be bought.

Tent teaser – page 191
Solutions:
26 children 4 in tents A, D and E, 6 in tent B, and 8 in tent C.

Fraction wall – page 194
Solutions:
1 two halves four quarters
ten tenths six sixths
2 two quarters five tenths
three sixths four eighths
3 two sixths three ninths
four twelfths five fifteenths
4 two tenths three fifteenths
four twentieths ten fiftieths
Now try this!
six eighths, nine twelfths, fifteen twentieths

Part and parcel – page 195
Solutions:
Children should have joined the following fractions with a line:
$\frac{1}{9}$ and $\frac{8}{9}$ $\frac{5}{6}$ and $\frac{1}{6}$
$\frac{1}{5}$ and $\frac{4}{5}$ $\frac{2}{7}$ and $\frac{5}{7}$
$\frac{13}{20}$ and $\frac{7}{20}$ $\frac{9}{20}$ and $\frac{11}{20}$
$\frac{1}{4}$ and $\frac{3}{4}$ $\frac{4}{7}$ and $\frac{3}{7}$
$\frac{7}{10}$ and $\frac{3}{10}$ $\frac{5}{8}$ and $\frac{3}{8}$
$\frac{3}{5}$ and $\frac{2}{5}$ $\frac{4}{11}$ and $\frac{7}{11}$
Now try this!
The following words do not total 1:
DO IS IF PAD RAT FOOD FAST

Loads-a-money! – page 196
Solutions:
1 8 **2** 10 **3** 9 **4** 9 **5** 24
6 18 **7** 48 **8** 18 **9** 100 **10** 12
11 12 **12** 36 **13** 9 **14** 21
Now try this!
24p

Billy the baker's cakes – page 197
Solutions:
Answers plus equivalents:
3 × 4 + 5 × 6 = 42 3 × 4 + 5 × 8 = 52
3 × 4 + 6 × 8 = 60 3 × 5 + 4 × 6 = 39
3 × 5 + 4 × 8 = 47 3 × 5 + 6 × 8 = 63
3 × 6 + 4 × 5 = 38 3 × 6 + 4 × 8 = 50
3 × 6 + 5 × 8 = 58 3 × 8 + 4 × 5 = 44
3 × 8 + 4 × 6 = 48 3 × 8 + 5 × 6 = 54
4 × 5 + 3 × 6 = 38 4 × 5 + 3 × 8 = 44
4 × 5 + 6 × 8 = 68 4 × 6 + 3 × 5 = 39
4 × 6 + 3 × 8 = 48 4 × 6 + 5 × 8 = 64
4 × 8 + 3 × 5 = 47 4 × 8 + 3 × 6 = 50
4 × 8 + 5 × 6 = 62 5 × 6 + 3 × 4 = 42
5 × 6 + 3 × 8 = 54 5 × 6 + 4 × 8 = 62
5 × 8 + 3 × 4 = 52 5 × 8 + 3 × 6 = 58
5 × 8 + 4 × 6 = 64 6 × 8 + 4 × 5 = 68
6 × 8 + 4 × 3 = 60 6 × 8 + 5 × 3 = 63

Sour grapes – page 198
Solutions:

Number of grapes	Total number of ways
1	1
2	2
3	4
4	8
5	16
6	32

The doubling pattern can obviously be seen, thus seven grapes would have 64 solutions and eight grapes would have 128 solutions. The total set of solutions for five grapes and six grapes is given below. 16 solutions for five grapes:
1+1+1+1+1, 1+1+1+2, 1+1+2+1, 1+2+1+1, 2+1+1+1, 1+1+3, 1+3+1, 3+1+1, 1+4, 4+1, 1+2+2, 2+1+2, 2+2+1,
2+3, 3+2, 5
32 solutions for six grapes:
1+1+1+1+1+1, 1+1+1+1+2, 1+1+1+2+1, 1+1+2+1+1, 1+2+1+1+1, 2+1+1+1+1 1+1+1+3, 1+1+3+1, 1+3+1+1,
3+1+1+1, 1+1+4, 1+4+1, 4+1+1,
1+5, 5+1, 1+1+2+2, 1+2+1+2, 1+2+2+1, 2+2+1+1, 2+1+2+1, 2+1+1+2, 1+2+3, 1+3+2, 2+1+3, 3+1+2, 2+3+1,
3+2+1, 2+2+2, 3+3, 2+4, 4+2, 6

Sheep and goats – page 199
Solutions:
1 true **2** false **3** false
4 true **5** true **6** true

Connections – page 200
Solutions:

Life's a lottery – page 202
Solutions:
1 8 r1 14 11 r1 12 16
2 8 10 r4 5 r2 11 r3 6 r5
3 7 r2 9 r3 5 r7 6 r4 10 r8
4 10 r5 5 r2 6 r6 8 11 r7

Cats' chorus – page 204
Solutions:
1 $1\frac{1}{4}, 1\frac{1}{2}, 1\frac{3}{4}, 2, 2\frac{1}{4}, 2\frac{1}{2}, 2\frac{3}{4}, 3$ **2** $7\frac{1}{2}, 7, 6\frac{1}{2}, 6, 5\frac{1}{2}$, $5, 4\frac{1}{2}, 4$
3 $2\frac{1}{3}, 2\frac{2}{3}, 3, 3\frac{1}{3}, 3\frac{2}{3}, 4, 4\frac{1}{3}, 4\frac{2}{3}$ **4** $6\frac{3}{4}, 6\frac{1}{2}, 6\frac{1}{4}, 6, 5\frac{3}{4}$, $5\frac{1}{2}, 5\frac{1}{4}, 5$
5 $9\frac{2}{3}, 9\frac{1}{3}, 9, 8\frac{2}{3}, 8\frac{1}{3}, 8, 7\frac{2}{3}, 7\frac{1}{3}$

A spoonful of medicine – page 206
Solutions:
1 5ml **2** 3ml **3** 18ml **4** 6ml **5** 8ml
6 6ml **7** 10ml **8** 25ml **9** 20ml **10** 15ml
11 21ml **12** 21ml **13** 28ml

Nuts and raisins – page 208
Solutions:
1 2, 3 **2** 6, 9 **3** 8, 12
4 10, 15 **5** 4, 6 **6** 12, 18

Pencil sharpeners – page 209
Now try this!
1 8, 4 **2** 3, 9 **3** 10, 2 **4** 12, 8
5 14, 6 **6** 4, 16 **7** 15, 5

Boxes of chocolates – page 210
Solutions:
1 15 **2** 8 **3** 10 **4** 5
5 4 **6** 9 **7** 16 **8** 18

Puppy love – page 211
Solutions:
1 1, 3 / 1, 4 **2** 4, 1 / 4, 5 **3** 3, 2 / 3, 5 **4** 2, 5 / 2, 7
5 5, 2 / 5, 7 **6** 2, 3 / 2, 5 **7** 4, 3 / 4, 7 **8** 2, 5 / 2, 7
Now try this!
1 3, 4 **2** 1, 5 **3** 2, 5 **4** 5, 7
5 2, 7 **6** 3, 5 **7** 3, 7 **8** 5, 7

Egghead – page 212
Solutions:

Nest A	Nest B	Nest C	Nest D	Nest E	Nest F
4, 4	9, 3	3, 6	3, 5	1, 9	9, 3
4, 8	9, 12	3, 9	3, 8	1, 10	9, 12

(or equivalent ratios)
Now try this!
A E
C B
F D
E A
B C
D F

Hungry Henry – page 213
Solutions:
1 $\frac{1}{6}$ **2** $\frac{3}{5}$ **3** $\frac{4}{5}$ **4** $\frac{3}{4}$
5 $\frac{1}{4}$ **6** $\frac{2}{3}$ **7** $\frac{5}{6}$ **8** $\frac{1}{5}$
9 $\frac{7}{8}$ **10** $\frac{9}{10}$ **11** $\frac{1}{8}$